ADVANCES IN SOFTWARE SCIENCE AND TECHNOLOGY

VOLUME 5

ADVANCES IN SOFTWARE SCIENCE AND TECHNOLOGY
VOLUME 5

JAPAN SOCIETY FOR SOFTWARE SCIENCE AND TECHNOLOGY

ACADEMIC PRESS, INC.

Harcourt Brace & Company, Publishers

Boston San Diego New York
London Sydney Tokyo Toronto

Co-published for
Japan Society for Software Science and Technology
by Academic Press, Inc.
and
Iwanami Shoten, Publishers

This book is printed on acid-free paper. ♾

ACADEMIC PRESS. INC.
525 B Street, Suite 1900, San Diego CA 92101-4495

United Kingdom Edition published by
ACADEMIC PRESS LIMITED
24–28 Oval Road, London NW1 7DX

Library of Congress Catal Card Number: 90–660056

ISBN 0–12–037105–7
ISSN 1044–7997

AP Exclusive Sales Territory: United States, its territories and
dependencies, Canada, and Europe.
Iwanami Shoten Exclusive Sales Territory: Japan.
Nonexclusive sales rights throughout the rest of the world.

Printed in the United States of America

94 95 96 BC 9 8 7 6 5 4 3 2 1

Contributors

Numbers in parentheses refer to the pages on which the authors' contribution begin.

Kiyoshi Akama (45), Department of Computer Science, Hokkaido University, Kita–13 Nishi–8, Kita-ku, Sapporo, 060 Japan

Toru Aratani (145), Systems and Communications Lab., Fuji Xerox Co., Ltd., 134 Godocho, Hodogaya-ku, Yokohama-shi, Kanagawa, 240 Japan

Tsutomu Endo (183), Department of Computer and Intelligent Systems, Oita University, Oita, 870–11 Japan

Norio Fujimoto (217), The Sumitomo Marine and Fire Insurance Co. Ltd., 1–41–1 Koyasu-cho, Hachiouji, Tokyo, 192 Japan

Nobuhisa Fujinami (201), Sony Computer Science Laboratory Inc., Takanawa Muse Building, 3–14–13 Higashi-Gotanda, Shinagawa-ku, Tokyo, 141 Japan

Takeshi Imanaka (217), Central Research Laboratories, Matsushita Electric Industrial Co. Ltd., 3–1–1 Yagumo-nakamachi, Moriguchi, Osaka, 570 Japan

Masatomi Inagaki (145), Document Systems Development Center, Fuji Xerox Co. Ltd., 2–1 Sakado 3–chome, Takatsu-ku, Kawasaki-shi, Kanagawa, 213 Japan

Noriyuki Kamibayashi (145), Systems and Communications Lab., Fuji Xerox Co. Ltd., 134 Godocho, Hodogaya-ku, Yokohama-shi, Kanagawa, 240 Japan

Keiichi Kaneko (11), Department of Mathematical Engineering and Information Physics, Faculty of Engineering, University of Tokyo, 7–3–1 Hongo, Bunkyo-ku, Tokyo, 113 Japan

Kazuhiko Kato (119), Institute of Information Sciences and Electronics, University of Tsukuba, Tsukuba, Ibaraki, 305 Japan

Takashi Masuda (119), Department of Information Science, Faculty of Science, University of Tokyo, 7–3–1 Hongo, Bunkyo-ku, Tokyo, 113 Japan

Fumio Motoyoshi (91), Natural Language Section, Machie Understanding Division, Electrotechnical Laboratory, 1–1–4 Umezono, Tsukuba-shi, Ibaraki, 305 Japan

Takeo Murakami (119), Parallel Systems Laboratory, Fujitsu Laboratories Ltd., 1015 Kamikodanaka, Nakahara-ku, Kawasaki-shi, Kanagawa, 211 Japan

Ikuo Nakata (1), Institute of Information Sciences and Electronics, University of Tsukuba, Tsukuba, Ibaraki, 305 Japan

Hidehiro Ohki (183), Department of Computer and Intelligent Systems, Oita University, Oita, 870–11 Japan

Atushi Ohori (119), Kansai Laboratory, Oki Electric Industry, Cristal Tower, 1–2–27 Shiromi, Chuo-ku, Osaka, 540 Japan

Jun Rekimoto (239), Software Engineering Laboratory, NEC Corporation, 11–5, Shibaura 2–chome, Minato-ku, Tokyo, 108 Japan

Taisuke Sato (91), Machine Inference Section, Machine Understanding Division, Electrotechnical Laboratory, 1–1–4 Umezono, Tsukuba-shi, Ibaraki, 305 Japan

Hajime Sawamura (107), IIAS, Fujitsu Labs., 140 Miyamoto, Numazu, Shizuoka, 410–03 Japan

Kazuhiro Takaoka (183), Department of Computer and Intelligent Systems, Oita University, Oita, 870–11 Japan

Masato Takeichi (11), Department of Mathematical Engineering and Information Physics, Faculty of Engineering, Univerisity of Tokyo, 7–3–1 Hongo, Bunkyo-ku, Tokyo, 113 Japan

Yutaka Tomioka (25), Tokyo Information Systems Research Laboratory, AV & CC Systems Research and Development Center, Matsushita Electric Industrial Co. Ltd., 4–5–15 Higashi-shinagawa, Shinagawa-ku, Tokyo, 140 Japan

Jun'ichi Toyoda (217), The Institute of Scientfic and Industrial Research, Osaka University, 8–1 Mihogaoka, Ibaraki, Osaka, 567 Japan

Kuniaki Uehara (217), Department of Computer and Systems Engineering, Faculty of Engineering, Kobe University, 1–1 Rokkodai-cho, Nada, Kobe, 657 Japan

Toshinori Watanabe (65), Graduate School of Information Systems, University of Electro-Communications, 1–5–1 Chofugaoka, Chofu-shi, Tokyo, 182 Japan

Taichi Yasumoto (165), Department of Mathematical Sciences, Aichi University of Education, Kariya, 448 Japan

Yasuhiko Yokote (201), Sony Computer Science Laboratory Inc., Takanawa Muse Building, 3–14–13 Higashi-Gotanda, Shinagawa-ku, Tokyo, 141 Japan

Mineharu Yokoyama (145), Systems and Communications Lab. Fuji Xerox Co. Ltd., 2–1 Sakado 3–chome, Takatsu-ku, Kawasaki-shi, Kanagawa, 213 Japan

Taiichi Yuasa (165), Department of Information and Computer Science, Toyohashi University of Technology, Toyohashi, 441 Japan

Contents

Editor's Message

Masato Takeichi
Editor-in-Chief

This is the fifth issue of *Advances in Software Science and Technology*, an annual journal published by the Japan Society for Software Science and Technology (JSSST). The Society was founded in 1983 as a professional society dedicated to the advancement of the science and technology of computer software.

Unparalleled progress in hardware technology has been a driving force in modern computer technology. It has dramatically improved the performance and reliability, increased the level of complexity and sophistication, and created numerous new applications for computer systems. Progress in software technology, on the other hand, has been much more conservative. By and large, the volume and the quality of current software production depend on the skills and dedicated craftsmanship of programmers. With ever-increasing demands for software production, our ability to build and use computer systems is now limited mainly by our ability to produce software.

The advancement of software technology requires intense research efforts toward scientific understanding of software systems, organized efforts to improve the current practice of software production, and drastic improvement of software education and training programs. The JSSST was founded to provide leadership, to promote and exchange ideas and experience, and to develop and organize concerted efforts in this direction.

The society has published a domestic bimonthly journal, *Computer Software*, since 1984. This contains original technical contributions that are refereed in accordance with the normal scientific review process. In addition, it contains survey papers, tutorials, conference reports, and miscellaneous articles. The journal covers a broad range of computer software. Topics featured in recent issues include algorithms, theory of programs, programming languages and methodology, operating systems, computer architecture, software engineering, artificial intelligence, and natural language processing.

Advances in Software Science and Technology is a second journal published by the JSSST. It is an annual publication with the same scope as *Computer Software*, and is intended to give international exposure to the activities of JSSST and to promote the exchange of ideas and information among professionals and the public worldwide. Each issue of the journal contains original technical contributions as well as contributions that have appeared in previous issues of *Computer Software* in Japanese. The JSSST forms a special editorial committee for each issue of this journal, whose members are listed in the front page together with those of *Computer Software*.

As announced in the previous issue, the JSSST has decided to suspend the publication of this journal after the present issue. The society intends to explore other possibilities for increasing international activities, and has decided to sponsor international symposia on a periodical basis. The first was the *International Symposium on Object Technologies for Advanced Software* held in early November 1993. The proceedings are available as a book in the series "Lecture Notes in Computer Science" from Springer-Verlag. Other topical subjects will be addressed in future symposia.

CONTENTS OF PREVIOUS VOLUMES

VOLUME 1

Research Contributions

Tutorial

VOLUME 2

Research Contributions

Tutorial

Software Critique

VOLUME 3

Research Contributions

VOLUME 4

Surveys on Current Research in Japan

Research Contributions

Generation of Pattern-Matching Algorithms by Extended Regular Expressions

Ikuo Nakata

Summary. It is difficult to express the definition of the comments of C language in a regular expression. However, the definition can be expressed by a simple regular expression by introducing a special symbol, called the *any*-symbol, that represents *any single character*, or by introducing a kind of negation symbol into regular expressions. In general, the problem of string pattern matching can be expressed as such an extended regular expression, and the corresponding finite state automaton generated from the expression is equivalent to the Knuth-Morris-Pratt pattern–matching algorithm [4]. In particular, if we use the *any*-symbols, the pattern is not restricted to a string of characters. It can be any regular expression. Our method can also be applied to the problem of repeated pattern matching. The Aho-Corasick algorithm [3] can be derived mechanically from an extended regular expression that contains *any*-symbols.

1 Introduction

The definition of a comment of C language can be given as a string composed of three strings in the following order:

/* ,
a string that does not contain */ (may be an empty string),
*/ .

Expressing the above definition by a regular expression is complicated because it is difficult to express "a string that does not contain */." Here, */ means a string of length two composed of * followed by /.

Although we can use the negation symbols in *lex*, a well-known scanner generator, the expression for the comment is still complex—for example,

/*/*([^*/]|[^*]/|*[^/])****/ (1)

in [6], or

/*([^*]|***[^*/])****/ (2)

in [5]. Here, (,),|,*,[,],^ are meta symbols, * denotes the repetition of the immediate predecessor zero or more times, and [^*/] expresses one character that is neither * nor /.

This problem can be simply expressed if we can designate "a string that does not contain */" directly. If the expression of the above string is

ISBN 0-12-037105-7

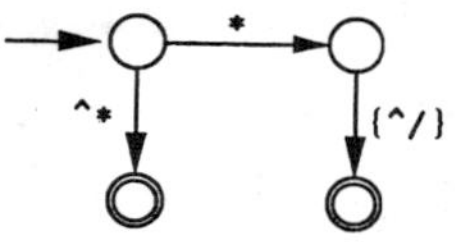

Fig. 1 The automaton to recognize ˆ(*/)

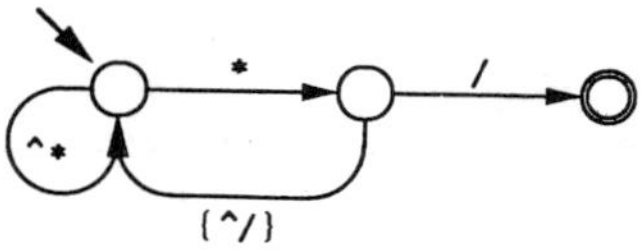

Fig. 2 DFA for (ˆ(*/))**/

ˆ(*/)

then the definition of the comment is

/*(ˆ(*/))**/.

This is the direct expression of the definition. Here, we define the meaning of ˆ(*/) to be "the head character of a string that does not contain */." In Figure 1, this definition is shown as an automaton that recognizes ˆ(*/).

In Figure 1, ˆ* denotes the transition by any character except *, and {ˆ/} indicates the look–ahead transition by ˆ/ (that is, the transition by looking at any character except / without reading the character). The automaton for the extended regular expression

(ˆ(*/))**/

is shown in Figure 2. It is obtained by applying the well–known algorithm that generates first an NFA (Nondeterministic Finite Automaton) from a regular expression and then transforms it into a DFA (Deterministic Finite Automaton) [1, 5]. This is the automaton that recognizes the string that follows the head string /* of a comment. It is also the pattern–matching automaton that recognizes "the first string */" in a given text.

Another regular expression for "the first string */" can be

•*<*/>

where • is defined, in the context of being followed by <*/>, as any character that is not the first character of */. Namely, • in this case is the indirect expression for ˆ(*/). • by itself means *any single character.* We can construct the DFA for •*<*/> as follows: construct the DFA for •*(*/) first, and then eliminate all the transitions from the state that reads */. The resultant automaton corresponds to the previous regular expression (2) (see page 59 of [5]). In this paper, we generalize the above method and describe a method that mechanically generates the pattern–matching algorithm for any regular expression α (in the following, we identify an automaton with the corresponding algorithm). If α represents a fixed character string, then the generated algorithm is equivalent to the pattern–matching algorithm of Knuth-Morris-Pratt (KMP) [4]. We further show a method for generating the algorithm of Aho-Corasick (A-C) [3], well known as an efficient algorithm that searches several patterns repeatedly.

2 The Knuth-Morris-Pratt Pattern–Matching Algorithm

2.1 Using *any*-symbols

Let Σ be an alphabet, α be a regular expression over Σ, and $[\alpha]$ be the language that α denotes. We add to Σ the special symbol $\bullet$. The meaning of $\bullet$ is defined as $[\bullet]=\Sigma$ when we ignore its context, and the context–dependent meaning is defined in the following. We introduce a form of regular expressions,

$$\bullet^{*} < \alpha >,$$

with the purpose of expressing the head string u of a given text x such that the tail of u is the first string that matches α. That is, $\bullet^{*} < \alpha >$ matches $u = vw$, where u is the shortest string such that u is the head of x, and $< \alpha >$ matches w. Here we take w as the first string if α matches both w and wz. We exclude the case $\varepsilon \in [\alpha]$, because in this case it matches every ε at any place in a given text. We define the above regular expression as follows:

Definition 1: *Let* $\varepsilon \notin [\alpha]$.*[*$\bullet^{*} < \alpha >$*]* $= \{ x \in \Sigma^{*} \mid$ *There exist* y *and* z *such that* $x=yz, z \in [\alpha]$, *and there exist no* x_i *such that* $x=x_1x_2x_3, x_2 \in [\alpha], x_3 \in \Sigma^{+}$ $\}$.

For example, if α=`ab*` and x=`cab`, then $\bullet^{*} < \alpha >$ matches `ca` because `b*` in α matches ε.

In the following, we consider the string pattern–matching problem. In a given text, the problem of searching the first string that is matched by α becomes the problem of recognizing the regular expression $\bullet^{*} < \alpha >$. We can construct the automaton for this expression with the following steps. First construct the NFA by appending the automaton for α to the one for $\bullet^{*}$. Next transform the NFA to the DFA by the well-known method. Then eliminate all the transitions from the states that contain the final states of the NFA for α. We will illustrate this by using the example expression `aa*bb`.

The automaton for $\bullet^{*}$ appended by the one for `aa*bb` is shown in Figure 3. In transforming this NFA to DFA, we follow the well-known method except for the $\bullet$-transitions. For the $\bullet$-transition from the state s to the state t in NFA, we add t to all the target states of other transitions from s in DFA, and we change the $\bullet$-transition to the transition by any character that is not contained in other transitions from s, as shown in Figure 4. For example, the target state of the `a`-transition in DFA of Figure 4 contains NFA States 1 and 2, because these are the target states of the `a`-transition and $\bullet$-transition in the NFA. Then, to make the first matched state into the final state, we eliminate all the transitions from the matched state—that is, the state that contains a final state in NFA. By applying these methods to Figure 3, we obtain Figure 5. Here, all the transitions from the state composed of NFA States 1 and 4 have been eliminated.

Figure 5 corresponds to the pattern–matching algorithm of Knuth-Morris-Pratt (KMP). However, KMP deals only with patterns of the form of $\alpha = a_1a_2\cdots a_n, a_i \in \Sigma$. Our method can deal with general regular expressions as patterns. For example, the above `aa*bb` is a regular expression that contains the repeating symbol *. The

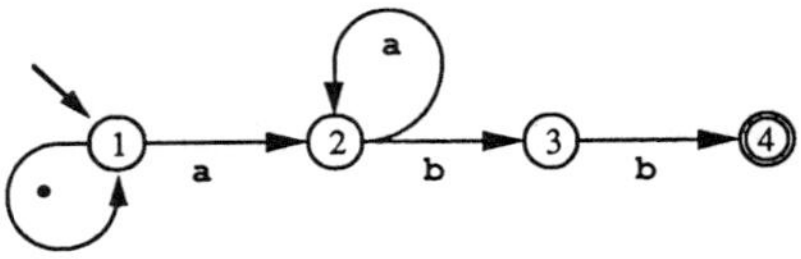

Fig. 3 NFA for •*aa*bb

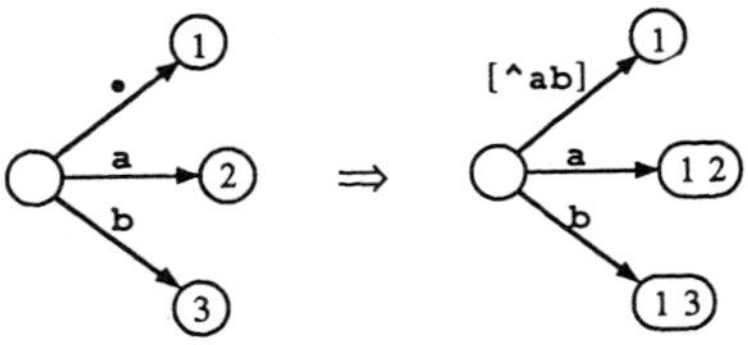

Fig. 4 Translation from NFA that contains • into DFA

corresponding automaton, the pattern–matching algorithm, can be generated by the usual method modified by the method shown in Figure 4.

2.2 Using negation symbols

• of $\bullet^*< \alpha >$ in the previous section can be interpreted as "the first character of strings that is different from α." To express this more directly, we introduce the notation $\hat{}\alpha$ and define it as follows. The meaning of $\hat{}\alpha$ is similar to the negation of α, but it depends on its context and is different from negation defined as $[\hat{}\alpha]=\Sigma^*-[\alpha]$ in [2].

Definition 2: *$[(\hat{}\alpha)\beta] = \{x \in \Sigma^* \mid$ There exist a and z such that $x=az, a \in \Sigma$, $z \in [\beta]$, and there exist no x_i such that $x=ax_1x_2, ax_1 \in [\alpha]\}$.*

By using this notation, the pattern–matching problem for α can be expressed as the problem of recognizing the regular expression

$$(\hat{}\alpha)^*\alpha.$$

Here, by Definition 2, $(\hat{}\alpha)$ is interpreted under its right-hand context. Therefore $(\hat{}\alpha)(\hat{}\alpha)\alpha$ is interpreted as $(\hat{}\alpha)((\hat{}\alpha)\alpha)$. Furthermore, we exclude the case $\varepsilon \in [\alpha]$, as in the previous section. Now, as an example, we present the pattern–matching

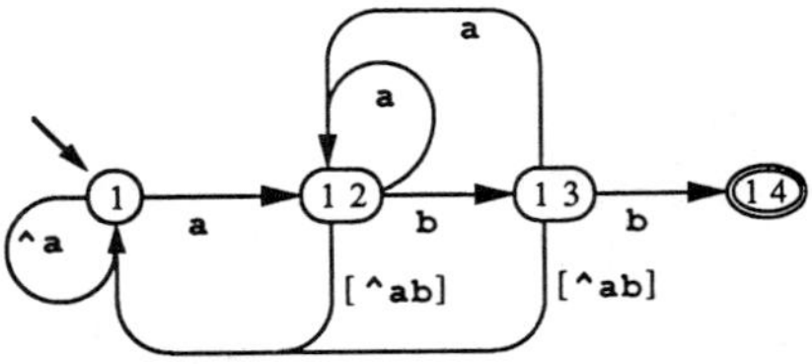

Fig. 5 DFA that recognize the first aa*bb

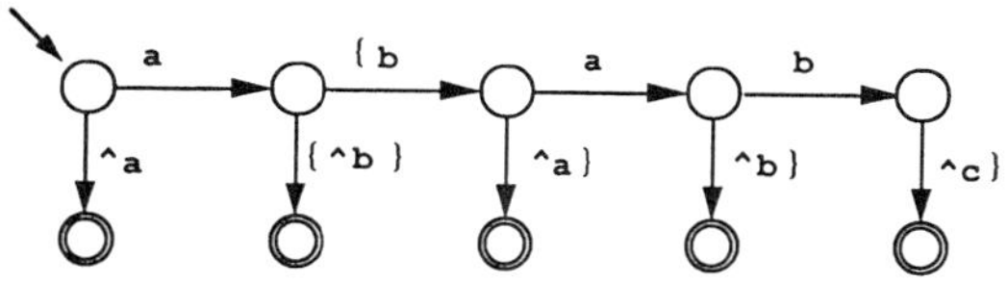

Fig. 6 DFA for ^(ababc)

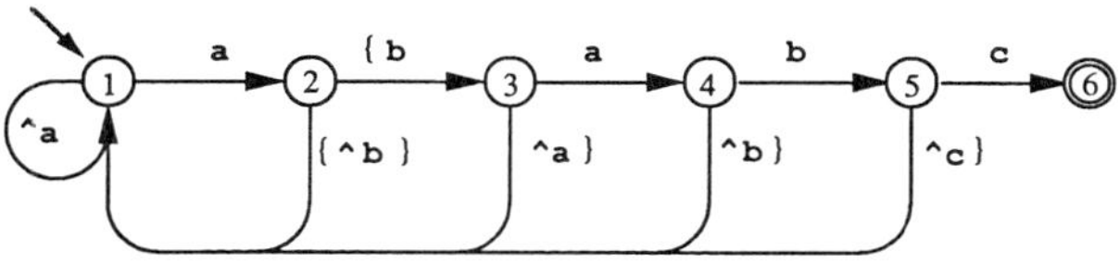

Fig. 7 DFA for (^(ababc))*ababc

problem for ababc; that is, we will construct DFA for

(^(ababc))*ababc.

DFA for ^(ababc) is shown in Figure 6.

In Figure 6, the strings composed of characters between { and } denote look-ahead strings; that is, state transitions occur by these characters as in a usual automaton, but, after recognizing $\hat{}(\alpha)$, these characters are treated as if they have not been read yet. In terms of an automaton, the input tape is marked at the beginning of $\{a$-transition, and the input tape is placed at the mark at the end of $a\}$-transition. DFA for (^(ababc))*ababc can be obtained by first applying the usual method for NFA construction to Figure 6 and ababc, then by applying the usual algorithm for translation from NFA to DFA. In this process, the characters accompanied by { or } are treated as ordinal characters. The result shown in Figure 7 is the naïve pattern matching algorithm.

For example, if the text

abcababd

is read by the automaton of Figure 7, the sequence of state transitions is

1a2b3c1{b1c1}a2b3a4b5d1{b1a2b3d1}{b1d1},

and the recognition fails. Here, the enclosing braces mean "reading again." In this algorithm, after ab^a (abc in this example) has been read, b^a is read again, as shown in a{b^a}. This is equivalent to reading two ^as at the initial state. The resultant state is the initial state as shown in 1{b1c1}. Therefore, in this case, it is equivalent to returning to the initial state without being read again. In other words, { and } can be eliminated from the automaton. By applying similar optimization to other transitions, DFA in Figure 8 is obtained. When ^c is read at State 5 of Figure 7, the transition proceeds strictly as 1{b1a2b3}, then the ^c that is last read should be read again to see whether it is a or not. This transition is shown in the transition from State 5 to State 3 in Figure 8. The algorithm of Figure 8 is equivalent to the pattern-matching algorithm of KMP (that is shown

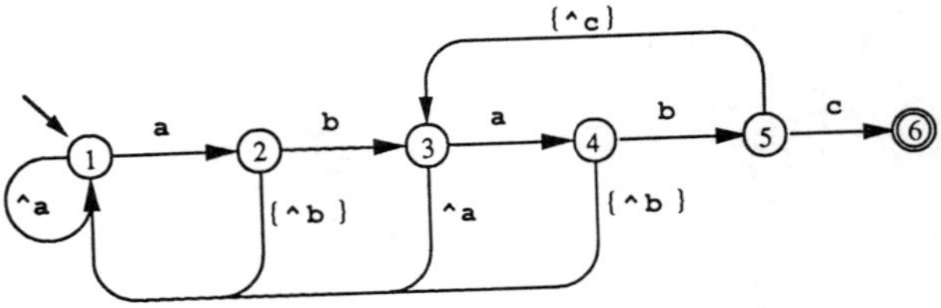

Fig. 8 DFA for (^(ababc))*ababc(after optimization)

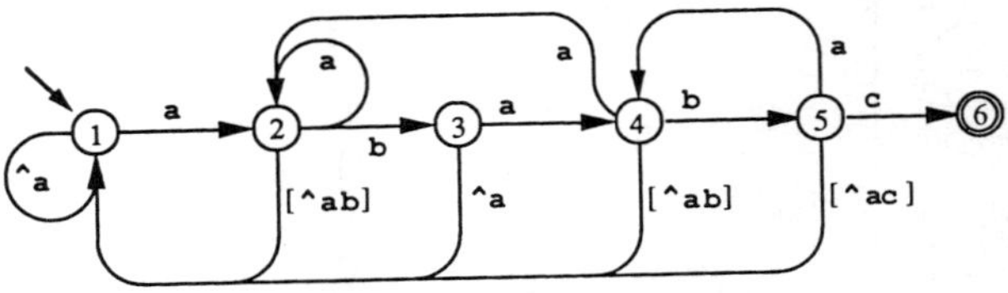

Fig. 9 DFA for •*< ababc >

in the first part of [4] and is referred in many text books of algorithms as KMP's pattern–matching algorithm).

Note that this optimization cannot be applied, in general, to the automaton that contains loops, because the string that should be read again cannot be determined uniquely. `aa*bb` in the previous section is such an example.

Figure 9 is obtained by applying the method in the previous section that uses *any*-symbols to the above example `ababc`. This is the optimized version of Figure 8, because this does not contain any read-again transitions. This is equivalent to the algorithm written in the last part of [4].

3 The Aho-Corasick Algorithm

The Aho-Corasick algorithm is well known as an efficient algorithm for searching several patterns simultaneously and repeatedly. This algorithm can be derived by a method similar to the one in the previous section.

3.1 Using *any*-symbols

In a given text x, in order to search all the strings that are matched by the patterns of α, it is sufficient to search for all the strings in the head part of x that are matched by α first, then to search for $\bullet\alpha$ in the head of x, and then to search for $\bullet\bullet\alpha$ in the head of x, and so on. Therefore this problem is equivalent to the problem of pattern matching with

$$\bullet^*\alpha.$$

The algorithm can be derived as DFA for $\bullet^*\alpha$ in which the state that contains the final states of α records the facts that it recognized α.

For example, let

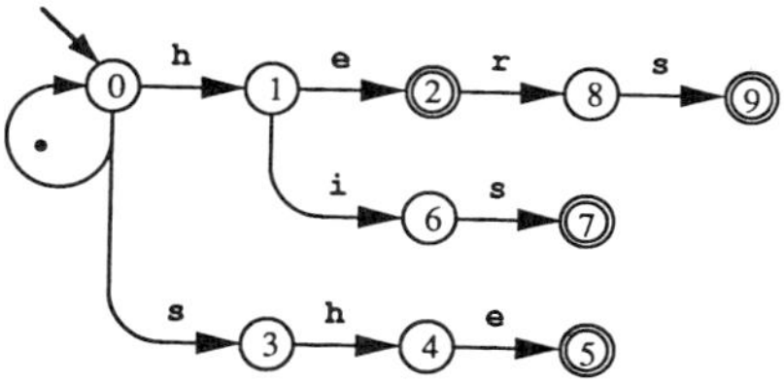

Fig. 10 NFA for •*(he|she|his|hers)

$\alpha =$ (he|she|his|hers).

This is the example in [3]. NFA for $\bullet{*}\alpha$ is shown in Figure 10.

DFA shown in Figure 11 can be obtained from this NFA by the well-known method modified by •-transitions, as shown in Figure 4. In Figure 11, every state contains one or more states in the original NFA, and numbers on the right side of a state are the numbers of the final states in NFA. The numbers 2, 5, 7, and 9 indicate that they are the states that record the recognition of **he**, **she**, **his**, and **hers**, respectively. An arrow to the number 0 in a triangle indicates the transition to the State 0 in the case of "other characters." For example, a state transition from State (0 1) to State 0 occurs in case of characters other than h, s, e, i. Although Figure 11 looks complex, it is not difficult to understand. For example, the transitions from State (0 2 5) are the same as the transitions from State (0 2) because there is no transition from State 5 in NFA. Similarly, the transitions from State (0 3 7) and from State (0 3 9) are the same as the ones from State (0 3). Every state of this DFA contains State 0 of NFA and the corresponding transitions. The rest of DFA that is shown in bold arrows in Figure 11 looks similar to Figure 10.

The algorithm in Figure 11 is the same as the final optimized algorithm in [3]. Here it is derived mechanically by slightly expanding the well-known method.

3.2 Using negation symbols

$\hat{}\alpha$ was introduced to indicate the head character of a string that is not matched by α. Here, we introduce one more symbol to indicate the head character of a string that is matched by α:

$$^{\circ}\alpha.$$

By using this symbol, the algorithm for searching all strings that are matched by α in a given text can be derived from the following regular expression:

$$(\hat{}\alpha|^{\circ}\alpha)*.$$

We need to add to the derived automaton the actions of recording the recognition of α that is found when $^{\circ}\alpha$ is recognized. By applying a similar method to the ones in Section 2.2 to this $(\hat{}\alpha|^{\circ}\alpha)*$, we can obtain an algorithm that is equivalent to

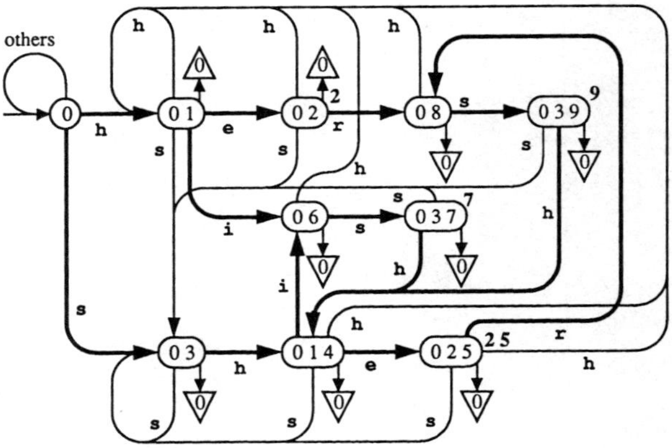

Fig. 11 DFA for repeated recognition of (he|she|his|hers)

the ones in [3]. However, we do not explain the method here, because it is not as simple as the previous method.

4 Conclusion

We introduced the symbol • for representing *any single character* in regular expressions, and by giving a context dependent interpretation to •* we showed that the definition of the comments in C language, which is difficult to define by a regular expression, can be expressed naturally by a simple expression. By applying this method to general regular expressions, the pattern–matching algorithm of Knuth-Morris-Pratt can be derived mechanically not only for the pattern of a character string but for the pattern expressed by a general regular expression. We also showed that a similar process is possible by introducing a symbol that indicates a kind of negation expressions.

Furthermore, we showed that the problem of repeated pattern matching for several patterns can be expressed in a simple regular expression by using •*, and the Aho-Corasick algorithm can be derived mechanically from the expression.

Although we did not invent any essentially new pattern–matching algorithm by these methods, we succeeded in generalizing the pattern expressions. Because the problems of pattern matching can be expressed in regular expressions, our methods can be implemented in lexical analyzer generators such as *lex*.

Acknowledgments. We would like to express our thanks to Prof. Masataka Sassa, Tokyo Institute of Technology, for his valuable comments.

References

[1] Aho, A. V., Sethi, R. and Ullman, J. D.: *Compilers: Principles, Techniques, and Tools*, Addison-Wesley, 1986.

[2] Aho, A. V., Sethi, R. and Ullman, J. D.: *Design and Analysis of Computer Algorithms*,

Addison-Wesley, 1974.

[3] Aho, A. V. and Corasick, M. J.: Efficient String Matching: An Aid to Bibliographic Search, *Comm. ACM*, Vol. 18, No. 6 (1975), pp. 333–340.

[4] Knuth, D. E., Morris, J. H. Jr. ,and Pratt, V. R.: Fast Pattern Matching in Strings, *SIAM J. Comput.*, Vol. 6, No. 2 (1977), pp. 323–350.

[5] Nakata, I.: *Compiler*, Sangyo-Tosho, Tokyo, 1981 (in Japanese).

[6] Schreiner, A. T. and Friedman, H. G. Jr.: *Introduction to Compiler Construction with UNIX*, Prentice-Hall, 1985.

Initially published in "Computer Software", Vol. 10, No. 1, in Japanese.

Ikuo Nakata
Institute of Information Sciences and Electronics
University of Tsukuba
Tsukuba, Ibaraki
305 Japan

Derivation of a Knuth-Morris-Pratt Algorithm by Fully Lazy Partial Computation

Keiichi Kaneko Masato Takeichi

Summary. A fully lazy evaluator always attains partial computation to some degree. However, a few optimization techniques in functional programming style seem to increase the extent of partial computation in fully lazy evaluation We demonstrate their availability by applying them to a naïve pattern-matching program to obtain a new program comparable to the Knuth-Morris-Pratt algorithm. In this process, we introduce a new evaluator that is an improved version of a conventional fully lazy evaluator for partial computation. Since this evaluator has the ability to translate function closures into source-level language, it is possible to visualize the residual programs.

1 Partial Computation and Fully Lazy Evaluation

The notion of partial computation goes back to the 1930's. A recent definition by *Futamura* [2] states that partial computation means specializing a generic program according to its operating environment to create a more efficient one.

In general, we may define a partial evaluator as a function Π that takes an $n(\geq 1)$-variable function f and a known datum k and returns a function that is obtained by specializing the first argument of f with respect to k. There are three ideal requirements for a partial evaluator Π:

1. **Soundness**. Π satisfies the equation $\Pi\ f\ k\ x_2\ \ldots\ x_n = f\ k\ x_2\ \ldots\ x_n$.
2. **Completeness**. Π performs all possible computations based on the known datum.
3. **Finiteness**. For all f, k, and $e_2, \ldots, e_n$, if $f\ k\ e_2\ \ldots\ e_n$ terminates, then $\Pi\ f\ k$ also terminates.

However, it is impossible for any partial evaluator to satisfy all of these requirements at the same time. An early partial evaluator satisfied the requirements of soundness and completeness but not finiteness. Recently a conventional evaluator has acquired finiteness based on abstract interpretation, in exchange for completeness.

To discuss fully lazy evaluation, we first need to define ordinary lazy evaluation. Lazy evaluation is a reduction strategy characterized as follows:

- When a function application is evaluated, its arguments are passed to the function body without being evaluated. Evaluations of arguments are caused by the first reference to the corresponding parameter, and the evaluation results are kept for successive references to the arguments.

ISBN 0-12-037105-7

When we have a language construct for introducing local variables,

```
let x = (1+2) in (x+x),
```

we may regard such an expression as a function application

```
(\x->x+x) (1+2)
```

and apply the evaluation mechanism described above. In the rest of this paper, we assume this with no explicit transformation. The programs shown are written in the functional language Haskell [4], but our system supports only a very restricted subset of the language's facilities.

Fully lazy evaluation is a variant of lazy evaluation, and is defined as follows:

- Every subexpression is evaluated at most once, after all the variables in it have been bound.

If an expression is evaluated in a fully lazy way, its subexpressions are evaluated only once—the first time their values are requested after the variables in them have been bound—and will not be evaluated again. Taking account of this feature, we may conclude that a fully lazy evaluator performs partial computation in a sense. We call such an evaluation process *fully lazy partial computation.*

To clarify how a fully lazy evaluator works as a partial evaluator, we give an interpretation of the process of partial computation in terms of lazy evaluation mechanisms. Several algorithms have been proposed for transforming programs into ones suitable for fully lazy evaluation [8,9]. These algorithms are based on binding-time analysis of the variables, and they transform programs into ones that are in the same language as the originals. The idea behind these algorithms is that we can make use of ordinary lazy evaluators for fully lazy evaluation. That is, evaluating the transformed program in an ordinary lazy way leads to fully lazy evaluation of the original program.

The lambda hoisting algorithm [9] transforms original programs into the fully lazy normal form by hoisting all the maximal free compound expressions to the outermost level, using local definitions, so that these expressions are bound as soon as the variables in them are bound. It is not necessary to hoist a maximal free expression that consists of a single variable, because its evaluation result must be stored in the outer binding mechanism. Figure 1 shows the formal specification of the fully lazy normal form. The context condition ensures that no free compound expression is left at the inner level. Once lambda hoisting has been done, lazy evaluation of the resultant program achieves fully lazy evaluation of the original program. It is very difficult to eliminate unnecessary parameter passing in fully lazy lambda lifting [8], because all the function definitions may be declared at the global level.

In implementing an interpreter for lazy evaluation, the use of an environment structure is convenient for maintaining the association of variables with their evaluation results. If we want to have evaluated results in the form of the source language, environments can be expressed directly in terms of local declarations.

To understand our fully lazy partial computation, consider an example in which a function `second` takes a list as its argument and returns the second element of the list. We may define the function `second` by partially parametrizing a dyadic function `nth` as

Syntax

```
e ::= e' | let x=e'; ...; x=e' in e'
e' ::= b | x | e' e' | \x->e
```

Context Condition

`e` contains no free occurrence of compound expressions.

Fig. 1 Formal specification of fully lazy normal form

```
second = nth 2

nth n xs = cond (n==1) (head xs) (nth (n-1) (tail xs)).
```

The function `nth` takes an integer `n` and a list `xs` and returns the `n`-th element of the list `xs`. A conditional function `cond` is introduced to illustrate the effect of fully lazy evaluation:

```
cond True = condTrue
cond False = condFalse

condTrue e e' = e
condFalse e e' = e'.
```

After lambda hoisting, the definition of the function `second` is transformed into

```
second = let nth = \n -> let a = cond (n==1); b = nth(n-1)
                         in \xs->a (head xs) (b (tail xs))
         in nth 2.
```

If we force evaluation of `second` by supplying a list of sufficient length, the subexpression `(nth 2)` is replaced by the evaluation result, and the definition of `second` changes to

```
second = let nth = \n -> let a = cond (n==1); b = nth(n-1)
                          in \xs->a (head xs) (b (tail xs))
         in let a = condFalse
                b = let a = condTrue; b = nth (1-1)
                    in \xs->a (head xs) (b (tail xs))
            in \xs->a (head xs) (b (tail xs)).
```

If we examine this expression carefully, we will see that the expressions `cond (n==1)` and `nth(n-1)` have already been computed. That is, the redices depending on `n` that are necessary to compute `second` have all been reduced. Hence the new definition is a better approach to

```
\xs->head (tail xs).
```

Actually the post-processor of our evaluator optimizes the residual program to obtain this expression.

This example shows an essential feature of fully lazy partial computation. Our fully lazy evaluator performs calculation of redices that depend only on the known datum `n`, and the evaluator leaves a residual program. In other words, the evaluator performs nothing but partial computation.

As mentioned above, a conventional partial evaluator needs abstract interpretation to satisfy the requirement of finiteness. There are cases in which it fails to perform computation. In contrast, our fully lazy partial evaluator performs partial computation lazily. Therefore it has the ability to replace every expression that does not include a free variable by the value of that expression. However, there are simple cases in which it fails to perform computation, although a conventional partial evaluator does well. To illustrate this, consider the expression

```
\x->condTrue (x+1) (x+2).
```

We may expect that computation by the partial evaluator will yield

```
\x->x+1,
```

but fully lazy evaluation performs computation of

```
condTrue (x+1) (x+2)
```

every time the variable `x` is bound.

In the next section, we describe in detail how our interpreter is improved to overcome these awkward cases.

2 A Fully Lazy Partial Evaluator

We introduce a transformation phase for post-processing residual programs obtained by fully lazy evaluation. This transformation reduces all the *simple* sets of redices in residual programs to obtain more efficient ones. We choose expressions to be reduced in this transformation so that the reduction process always terminates.

Definition *A set of outermost* `n` *redices* `((\x1->(\x2->...(\xn->e))) e1 e2 ... en)` *is called* simple *if the following conditions hold:*

1. *For all* `i`$(\mathtt{i} = 1, \ldots, \mathtt{n})$, `xi` *appears at most once in* `e`.
2. *There exists no local definition and no* λ*-expression in* `e`.
3. *The number of application nodes in* `e` *is less than* `n`.

The first condition requires linearity to avoid unnecessary recomputation of the argument `ei`; otherwise, the redex

```
(\x->x+x) (fact 10)
```

will be reduced to

```
(fact 10)+(fact 10),
```

which causes repeated calculation of `(fact 10)`. The second condition implies that the reduction should keep the result of lambda hoisting. Without this, the resultant programs might not be in the fully lazy normal form. For example, if we were allowed to take the redex

```
(\x->(...(\y->x)...))  (fact 10)
```

to obtain the following expression

```
(...(\y->fact 10)...),
```

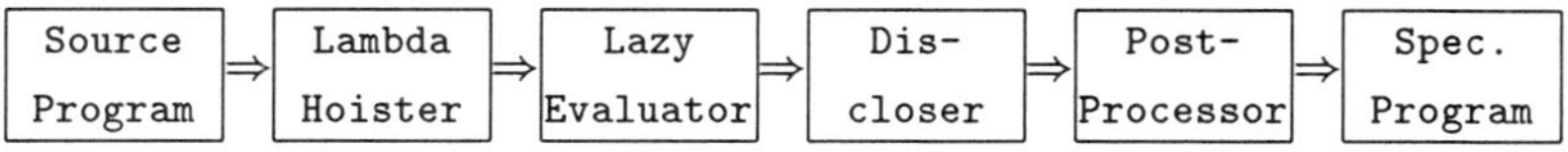

Fig. 2 A fully lazy partial evaluator

then the calculation of (fact 10) might be repeated every time y was bound. In addition, the third condition specifies that the number of application nodes after the reduction decreases by at least one, which ensures the halting property of reduction.

The post-processor identifies all the simple sets of redices in the residual program and reduces them to obtain a simpler expression. In addition, it performs the following optimizations after dependency analysis, which minimizes the number of constituents of each local definition:

- For an expression `let x=c in e`, where `c` is a constant value (such as a number or boolean), all free occurrences of the variable `x` in `e` are replaced by `c`, and the local definition is eliminated.
- For an expression `let x0=e0; ...; xn=en in e`, if all `xi` do not appear freely in `e`, the local definitions are eliminated.
- Primitive constant calculations, such as `1+2` and `1==2`, are replaced by their results.
- For an expression `let x=v in e`, where `v` is a variable, all free occurrences of `x` in `e` are replaced by `v`.
- The process of η-reduction is also performed.

Though these optimizations may have no influence on the reduction steps of resultant programs, they may produce new simple sets of redices. Hence the post–processor applies the reduction and optimization phases repeatedly until no transformation is detected.

Figure 2 shows the diagram of our fully lazy partial evaluator. Although there have been several systems that implement full laziness, none of them provides for *persistency*—that is, a mechanism in which all the computation results are stored at the global level [7]. Without persistency, it would be very difficult to use the result of partial computation. In our implementation, the residual program is kept in a global variable as a function closure.

A disclosing phase is placed between the lazy evaluator and the post-processor to transform the internal representation into our source language. A residual program is generally a function closure. It is a tuple that consists of a lambda variable `x`, an expression `e`, and an environment ρ. The discloser represents the environment by using local definitions and transforms the function closure into

`let` (representation of ρ) `in \x->e`.

An environment is a list of triplets of a variable, an expression or a value, and an environment. When the expression

```
let x1=e1; ...; xn=en in e
```

is evaluated in the environment ρ', the evaluator tries to evaluate the expression `e` in the following new environment ρ:

`ρ=[(x1,e1,ρ), ..., (xn,en,ρ)]++ρ'.`

Hence, when this kind of cyclic structure is found by the discloser, it is transformed into the previous `let`-expression. However, if the `ei` of the constituent `(xi,ei,ρ)` of the environment is the evaluation result, it must also be disclosed. This causes a dilemma, because the environment ρ may appear in the process disclosing `ei`. To resolve this problem, the discloser accumulates all the outer environments of the expression currently being processed and checks for duplication every time an environment appears. Data structures may be also cyclic and may cause infinite looping. Hence the discloser tries to find self-references with respect to all structures. If a self-reference is found, it is translated into

```
let p = ...p... in p.
```

3 Derivation of Knuth-Morris-Pratt Algorithms

In this section, we discuss several optimization techniques that have been proposed in contexts other than partial computation, and we show to what degree they are applicable for our purposes, giving experimental results. Finally, we present a technique for obtaining efficient residual programs by fully lazy partial computation.

3.1 Consel and Danvy's approach

Consel and Danvy [1] describe how a Knuth-Morris-Pratt algorithm [5] can be derived from a fairly naïve algorithm by applying a conventional partial evaluator whose source and residual programs are Scheme programs. We rewrite their original program `kmp` in Haskell, as shown in Figure 3. Consel and Danvy also present a function `kmp_0`, shown in Figure 4, which is a residual program of `kmp` specialized with respect to the pattern `[1,2,1,2,3]`.

We use both functions to estimate the attainment of our partial evaluator. In the following experiments, we count the β-reduction steps required to obtain the final results and compare them with those of `kmp` and `kmp_0`.

Experiment *Define a function* `kmpp` *as*

```
kmpp = kmp [1,2,1,2,3]
```

and

(a) *Evaluate the expression*

```
kmpp [1,2,1,3,1]
```

to force partial computation.

(b) *Evaluate the expression again to estimate the result of partial computation.*

(c) *After post-processing* `kmpp`*, evaluate the expression once more.*

(d) *Finally, evaluate the expression*

```
kmpp [2,1,2,1,3,1]
```

to estimate the effect of specialization.

```
kmp p d =
    let start p d = cond (null d) False (restart p d)
        restart p d = cond (head p == head d)
                        (cond (null(tail p)) True
                          (cond (null(tail d)) False
                            (loop (tail p) p (tail d))))
                        (start p (tail d))
        loop p p' d = cond (head p == head d)
                        (cond (null(tail p)) True
                          (cond (null(tail d)) False
                            (loop (tail p) p' (tail d))))
                        (let np=static_kmp p' (tail p')
                               (length(tail p')-(length p))
                         in (cond (np==p')
                              (cond (head p' == head p)
                                    (start p' (tail d))
                                    (restart p' d))
                              (loop np p' d)) )
        static_kmp p d n = static_loop p p d d n n
        static_loop p p' d d' n n' =
                cond (n==0)
                  (cond (n'==0) p
                    (cond (head p /= head d) p
                      (static_kmp p' (tail d') (n'-1))))
                  (cond (head p == head d)
                    (static_loop (tail p) p' (tail d) d' (n-1) n')
                    (static_kmp p' (tail d') (n'-1)))
    in cond (null p) True (start p d)
```

Fig. 3 A fairly naïve kmp function

Unless stated otherwise, all the experiments were done in the same manner.

The evaluation results of Consel and Danvy's functions are shown in Table 1. In this case, the function `kmp_0` is used instead of `kmpp` in the experimental procedure described above.

3.2 Simple evaluation

Table 2 shows the results of the first experiment with the function `kmp` in Figure 3. We follow the procedure given in the figure, using our fully lazy partial evaluator. According to the outcome for Stage (c), the residual program after post-processing

Table 1 Numbers of Reduction Steps in `kmp_0`

Stage	(a)	(b)	(c)	(d)
Steps	85	81	81	95

```
kmp_0 d =
    let start_1 d = cond (null d) False (restart_2 d)
        restart_2 d = cond ('1'==head d)
                      (cond (null(tail d)) False
                            (loop_3 (tail d)))
                      (start_1 (tail d))
        loop_3 d = cond ('2'==head d)
                      (cond (null(tail d)) False
                            (loop_4 (tail d)))
                      (restart_2 d)
        loop_4 d = cond ('1'==head d)
                      (cond (null(tail d)) False
                            (loop_5 (tail d)))
                      (start_1 (tail d))
        loop_5 d = cond ('2'==head d)
                      (cond (null(tail d)) False
                            (loop_6 (tail d)))
                      (restart_2 d)
        loop_6 d = cond ('3'==head d) True (loop_4 d)
    in start_1 d
```

Fig. 4 Consel and Danvy's residual function kmp_0

Table 2 Numbers of Reduction Steps in Simple Evaluation

Stage	(a)	(b)	(c)	(d)
Steps	400	90	81	396

achieves the same result as Consel and Danvy. However, Stage (d) requires almost the same number of reduction steps as Stage (a). This means that the resultant program does not have the power of the specialized pattern-matching algorithm. This is because the mismatch in the first element of the list `[2,1,2,1,3,1]` leads the computation into a new branch that has never been taken before. Since the result of the calculation of `static_kmp` is stored in another branch that is taken by evaluating with the list `[1,2,1,3,1]`, `static_kmp` is recomputed in the function `loop`, even when it is invoked with the same arguments.

In the rest of this section, we give several techniques for solving this problem in different ways.

3.3 Lazy memo-ization

We may apply the technique of lazy memo-ization proposed by *Hughes* [5] to solve the problem described above. When a memo-ized function is evaluated, a special function closure is returned in which argument-result pairs are stored. When the system encounters the closure with some argument, it evaluates the argument and searches for it among the stored pairs. If it finds the argument, it reuses the result.

Table 3 Numbers of Reduction Steps in Lazy Memo-ized Evaluation

Stage	(a)	(b)	(c)	(d)
Steps	397	90	81	313

Otherwise, it takes the same evaluation steps as for a normal closure. A hashing technique is used for the storage of argument-result pairs, so we may expect that the search is done in a constant time.

To accumulate the computation of `static_kmp`, we define it as

```
memo static_kmp p d n = static_loop p p d d n n.
```

Table 3 shows the experimental results of our lazy memo-ized evaluation.

The disclosing phase necessarily loses the power of special closures for memo-ized functions. Therefore Stage (c) is skipped when we count the reduction steps of Stage (d). That is, the procedure is followed twice: (a) → (b) → (c) and (a) → (b) → (d). Because of the effect of the memo-ization of the function `static_kmp`, the number of reduction steps in Stage (d) is 83 less than in Table 2, and a few steps are eliminated even in Stage (a). Now the reduction steps required for recomputation of the function `static_kmp` are completely eliminated. Let m and n be the length of the pattern and of the text, respectively. In the worst case, the function `loop` is called n times. It invokes the function `static_kmp` at most once every time it is called. Other computation in `loop` is performed in a constant time. Originally, $O(m)$ time is needed to calculate `static_kmp`. In this case, the pattern matching is done in $O(mn)$ time. We have specialized the function `static_kmp` so that it can be calculated in a constant time, and thus the matching is performed in $O(n)$ time. From this, we may conclude that we have obtained a new program comparable with the KMP algorithm.

3.4 Tabulation

Although lazy memo-ization succeeds in deriving a KMP algorithm, it is not wholly satisfactory. It breaks full laziness slightly because an argument for a special closure is always evaluated. Therefore we take another approach to accumulate the result of the function `static_kmp`. Looking carefully at the program in Figure 3, we find the following fact:

- If we apply the function `kmp` to a pattern `p'` when the function `static_kmp` is invoked in the function `loop`, its first and second arguments are always `p'` and `(tail p')`, respectively.

Hence we may rewrite the function `loop` in Figure 3 as in Figure 5, to let the system make use of this fact. The function `next` takes one argument `n` that represents the place of mismatch, and it returns a substring of the initial pattern taken by `kmp` to continue the pattern matching in the function `loop`. According to this transformation, when the function `next` is applied to some argument `n`, it is unfolded to store its result and refrain from recomputation caused by the same argument `n`.

```
next = static_kmp p (tail p)
loop p p' d = cond (head p == head d)
                (cond (null(tail p)) True
                  (cond (null(tail d)) False
                    (loop (tail p) p' (tail d))))
                (let np=next (length(tail p')-(length p))
                       -- refined
                 in (cond (np==p')
                      (cond (head p' == head p)
                           (start p' (tail d))
                           (restart p' d))
                      (loop np p' d)) )
```

Fig. 5 Introduction of a tabulation function

Table 4 Numbers of Reduction Steps in the Tabulated Program

Stage	(a)	(b)	(c)	(d)
Steps	400	90	81	349

Table 4 shows the result of the tabulated version. Because of the effect of notification, the number of reduction steps in Stage (d) is 47 less than in Table 1. Thus we have obtained another specialized KMP algorithm without any modifications of the laziness in the initial program.

3.5 Elimination of unnecessary parameter passings

We have derived KMP algorithms from a simple pattern-matching program by combining fully lazy evaluation with the techniques of lazy memo-ization and tabulation. However, the results of Stage (d) are poor in comparison with Consel and Danvy's. This is because their original program, written in Scheme, consists of a collection of global functions, and all the information must be passed as parameters. Hence it has a very unsuitable structure for fully lazy evaluation. Taking this into account, we may rewrite the program in Figure 3 to obtain a refined program suitable for lazy evaluation, as shown in Figure 6. If we apply the function `kmp` to the pattern `p'`, it is obvious that the first argument of the function `static_kmp` in the function `loop` is always `(tail p')`. The subexpression `(static_kmp (tail p'))` is automatically floated outside by lambda hoisting so that the evaluator does not compute it more than once. The experimental result is shown in Table 5. Because we have completely eliminated unnecessary parameter passing, the number of reduction steps in Stage (d) is identical with that in Table 1.

We have thus obtained an efficient KMP algorithm by simply applying our fully lazy partial evaluator to the refined program. The residual program consists of some hundred lines in Haskell representation. What we have to do is to eliminate redundant parameters that hinder fully lazy evaluation. It is an easy task to locate such parameters.

```
kmp p' d' =
    let start d = cond (null d) False (restart d)
              -- Depends solely on d
        restart d = cond (head p' == head d)
                        (cond (null(tail p')) True
                          (cond (null(tail d)) False
                            (loop (tail p') (tail d))))
                        (start (tail d))
        loop p d = cond (head p == head d)
                        (cond (null(tail p)) True
                          (cond (null(tail d)) False
                            (loop (tail p) (tail d))))
                        (let np=static_kmp (tail p')
                                (length(tail p')-(length p))
                         in (cond (np==p')
                              (cond (head p' == head p)
                                    (start (tail d))
                                    (restart d))
                              (loop np d)) )
        static_kmp d n = static_loop p' d d n n
        static_loop p d d' n n' =
                cond (n==0)
                  (cond (n'==0) p
                    (cond (head p /= head d) p
                      (static_kmp (tail d') (n'-1))))
                  (cond (head p == head d)
                    (static_loop (tail p) (tail d) d' (n-1) n')
                    (static_kmp (tail d') (n'-1)))
    in cond (null p') True (start d')
```

Fig. 6 The refined program

Redundant parameters are eliminated by using the following algorithm. For the original programs, we make two assumptions:

- User-defined identifiers are all renamed so that they are unique.
- Lambda expressions are eliminated by transforming them into local declarations.

We first consider a case in which there is no higher-order function. Let $G = (V, E)$ be the directed hyper-graph defined below.

- V: parameters used to define functions and locally defined variables;
- E: $e = (\{\mathtt{v1}, \ldots, \mathtt{vk}\}, \mathtt{vl}) \in E$, $(\mathtt{vi} \in V) \iff$ there exists an argument $\mathtt{e}$ corresponding to vl such that $FV(\mathtt{e}) = \{\mathtt{v1}, \ldots, \mathtt{vk}\}$.

For each vertex $\mathrm{v}(\in V)$, a value $val(\mathrm{v})$ is assigned. It is either an empty set ϕ, a singleton $\{\mathtt{e}\}$, or a top $\top$. A operator $\uplus$ is defined for these values:

Table 5 Numbers of Reduction Steps in the Refined Program

Stage	(a)	(b)	(c)	(d)
Steps	373	90	81	95

$$\phi \uplus X = X \uplus \phi = X,$$

$$\{\mathtt{e}\} \uplus \{\mathtt{e}'\} = \begin{cases} \{\mathtt{e}\}, & \text{if } \mathtt{e} = \mathtt{e}', \\ \top, & \text{otherwise}, \end{cases}$$

$$\top \uplus X = X \uplus \top = \top.$$

The equality of $\mathtt{e} = \mathtt{e}'$ means that they are literally equal. In addition, for each hyper-edge $e = (\{\mathtt{v1}, \ldots, \mathtt{vk}\}, \mathtt{vl})(\in E)$, we define an operation op_e.

- If there exists $\mathtt{vi}(1 \leq \mathtt{i} \leq k)$ such that $val(\mathtt{vi}) = \top$, assign $val(\mathtt{vl}) \leftarrow \top$. Otherwise, if there exists no $\mathtt{vi}(1 \leq \mathtt{i} \leq k)$ such that $val(\mathtt{vi}) = \phi$, assign $val(\mathtt{vl}) \leftarrow val(\mathtt{vl}) \uplus \{\mathtt{e}\,[val(\mathtt{v1})/\mathtt{v1}, \ldots, val(\mathtt{vk})/\mathtt{vk}]\}$, where $\mathtt{e}$ is the argument that corresponds to the hyper-edge e.

Then the following procedure eliminates unnecessary parameters:

Procedure

Step 1 *For all* $\mathtt{v}(\in V)$, $val(\mathtt{v}) \leftarrow \phi$.

Step 2 *For each* $\mathtt{v}(\in V)$, *update the values in the following way:*

Step 2.1 *If* $\mathtt{v}$ *is a parameter of the outermost function, then* $val(\mathtt{v}) \leftarrow \{\mathtt{v}\}$.

Step 2.2 *If there exist arguments* $\mathtt{e1}, \ldots, \mathtt{en}$ *corresponding to* $\mathtt{v}$ *such that* $FV(\mathtt{ei}) = \phi, (1 \leq \mathtt{i} \leq n)$, *then* $val(\mathtt{v}) \leftarrow val(\mathtt{v}) \uplus \{\mathtt{e1}\} \uplus \ldots \uplus \{\mathtt{en}\}$.

Step 3 *For all vertices* $\mathtt{v}(\in V)$ *whose assigned values have changed in previous update, update the values in the following way. If no such vertex exists, go to Step 4.*

Step 3.1 *For all* $e = (\{\mathtt{v1}, \ldots, \mathtt{vk}\}, \mathtt{vl})$ *such that* $\mathtt{v} \in \{\mathtt{v1}, \ldots, \mathtt{vk}\}$, *do the operation* op_e.

Step 3.2 *Go to Step 3.*

Step 4 *Transform the original program as follows. For each* $\mathtt{v}(\in V)$ *such that* $val(\mathtt{v}) = \{\mathtt{e}\}$, *if* $\mathtt{v}$ *is a parameter, eliminate the corresponding arguments and the occurrence of* $\mathtt{v}$ *in the left-hand side of the function definition, then replace all the occurrences of* $\mathtt{v}$ *with* $\mathtt{e}$.

As a result of Step 4, the same subexpression may appear in several places. Therefore we perform sharing analysis in lambda hoisting.

If there exist higher-order functions, the next operation is added at the end of Step 2.

Step 2.2 *If the function that is defined by using* v *is invoked and there exists no argument corresponding to* v, *assign* $val(\mathrm{v}) \leftarrow \top$.

We may apply the procedure recursively to the inner nest of local definitions. The free variables in the new input program are treated as constants.

4 Conclusions and Related Work

We have shown that a lazy evaluator can be used as a naïve partial evaluator with the help of source-to-source transformation processes before and after the ordinary evaluation of the program. These transformations are based only on the static structure of the program and require no semantic information for partial computation.

In deriving a Knuth-Morris-Pratt algorithm by using our fully lazy partial evaluator, we have examined several optimization techniques in functional programming. The lazy memo-ization mechanism improves the ability of the evaluator by annotating in function definitions the possibility of sharing results. If some function always takes the same argument after a known datum is supplied, it is possible to gather all the occurrences of the function with its argument into one local declaration in order to share its evaluated result. Hence the role of lazy memo-ization is replaced by tabulation in this case. When unnecessary parameters are eliminated, the possibility of detecting invariant subexpressions with respect to the known datum increases in the lambda hoisting algorithm, and the program may be transformed into a form in which tabulation is automatically achieved. We have given a practical algorithm for eliminating redundant parameters. In the algorithm, a directed hyper-graph is used to represent the dependency of parameters, and an abstract domain is used to express whether the set of possible arguments for each parameter is a singleton or not. The abstract value for each parameter is obtained by the iteration method.

It has been argued that partial evaluators based on evaluators of programs produce residual programs in a form of internal representation in a different way from that in which conventional ones produce source language programs. This is not the case for our partial evaluator. We have a disclosing phase that transforms programs in internal representation into equivalent programs in the source language. Admittedly, it may be claimed that this is possible because our lazy evaluator interprets the source program. However, it may be possible to include our post-processing phase in the compiled code if we sacrifice the possibility of obtaining expressions in the source language. This is a task we must work on.

We have also learned that persistency should be implemented in the system if we wish to enjoy the results of partial computation. It may be helpful to improve programs successively as computation proceeds.

Holst and Gomard have also succeeded in deriving KMP algorithms by using fully lazy evaluators and memo-ization [3]. The major difference between their method and ours is that they use strict memo-ization and require the function definition to be changed in order to restrict the domain of arguments, while we use lazy memo-ization and just put the annotation `memo` at the beginning of the function definition. However, we agree that methods such as memo-ization and tabulation are powerful tools when they are combined with a fully lazy evaluator.

We need to do more work to establish a method of partial computation based on full laziness.

References

[1] Consel, C. and Danvy, O.: Partial Evaluation of Pattern Matching in Strings, *Inf. Process. Lett.*, Vol. 30, No. 2 (1989), pp. 79–86.

[2] Futamura, Y.: Partial Computation of Programs. In Goto, E., Nakata, I., Furukawa, K., Nakajima, R. and Yonezawa, A. (eds.), *RIMS Symp. on Software Sci. and Eng.*, LNCS Vol. 147, Springer-Verlag, 1983, pp. 1–35.

[3] Holst, C. K. and Gomard, C. K.: Partial Evaluation Is Fuller Laziness, *Proc. Symp. on Partial Evaluation and Semantics-Based Program Manipulation, SIGPLAN Notices*, Vol. 26, No. 9 (1991), pp. 223–233.

[4] Hudak, P. et al.: *Report on the Programming Language Haskell*, Version 1.2, *ACM SIGPLAN Notices*, Vol. 27, No. 5 (1992), Section R.

[5] Hughes, R. J. M.: Lazy Memo-Functions. In Jouannaud, J.-P. (ed.), *Functional Programming Languages and Computer Architecture*, LNCS Vol. 201, Springer-Verlag, 1985, pp. 129–146.

[6] Knuth, D. E., Morris, J. H., and Pratt, V. R.: Fast Pattern Matching in Strings, *SIAM J. Comput.*, Vol. 6, No. 2 (1977), pp. 323–350.

[7] McNally, D. J. and Davie, A. J. T.: Two Models for Integrating Persistence and Lazy Functional Languages, *ACM SIGPLAN Notices*, Vol. 26, No. 5 (1991), pp. 43–52.

[8] Peyton Jones, S. L. and Lester, D.: A Modular, Fully Lazy Lambda Lifter in Haskell, *Software – Practice and Experience*, Vol. 21, No. 5 (1991), pp. 479–506.

[9] Takeichi, M.: Lambda-Hoisting: A Transformation Technique for Fully Lazy Evaluation of Functional Programs, *New Generation Computing*, Vol. 5 (1988), pp. 377–391.

Received August 1992

Keiichi Kaneko
Department of Mathematical Engineering and Information Physics
Faculty of Engineering
The University of Tokyo
Hongo, Bunkyo-ku, Tokyo
113 Japan

Masato Takeichi
Department of Mathematical Engineering and Information Physics
Faculty of Engineering
The University of Tokyo
Hongo, Bunkyo-ku, Tokyo
113 Japan

Computability of Modularization of Constraints

Yutaka Tomioka

Summary. We classify the computability of modularizing constraints by their syntactic properties. We show that for linear constraints, composing modularly defined predicates contributes to the computability of modularization and the possibility of termination of the Modularization Algorithm, while for non-linear constraints, it does not.

1 Introduction

In the last ten years, a new grammar formalism in which grammar is described as constraints among categories, with a primitive called *identicality*, has been developed and studied. As part of this research, declarative descriptions of language phenomena in Japanese and other languages based on Japanese Phrase Structure Grammar (JPSG)[5, 6, 12] have been carried out. At the same time, an attempt to implement identicality by unification and process-described constraints directly on computers has been made, leading to the development of a cu-Prolog interpreter [15, 16, 17, 18] whose primitive is an extended unification called *constraint unification*[7]. These two parallel research efforts, one that captures the grammars of natural languages as sets of constraints, and the other that attaches importance to the viewpoint of computation in language processing and understanding, have established a single method for describing grammar in computational linguistics.

JPSG, which was originally a linguistic framework for grammar, has grown into a computational linguistic framework for capturing language phenomena and describing them. We regard JPSG as a system for describing constraints that have the properties shown below [12]. Attempts have also been made to describe the constraints of several languages other than Japanese on the basis of JPSG.

1. JPSG describes relations among grammatical categories represented as sets of features.

   To describe the relations among grammatical categories, we assign to each category an internal structure represented as a set of features.

2. JPSG describes only those local constraints that are combined to capture an entire structure as a whole.

   By a local constraint, we mean a constraint on one branch of the binary tree structure[1] that we assume to represent a language structure whose nodes are grammatical categories. We call the constraint local if it refers to at most

[1] Although it is not essential to represent language structures by binary trees, we use them because of their merits from several viewpoints.

ISBN 0-12-037105-7

three categories that constitute one branch in the tree structure. In JPSG, all constraints are local; that is, each constraint refers to at most three categories in a branch.

3. All constraints described are processed directly on a computer.

   We describe constraints by means of Horn clauses, and process them directly on a computer, adding a computational meaning to support the description and modification of constraints.

We can characterize JPSG as a framework for describing grammars that have the above three properties.

In connection with the above three properties, a constraint processing system called cu-Prolog, whose processes describe constraints on a computer with a primitive operation called constraint unification, has been developed, in part because of the constraint processing of natural language grammars. One implementation of the above three properties captures the computational aspect of language phenomena by constraint transformation, which, as a consequence, requires that described constraints should be transformed automatically. However, computability of modularization, which is the main part of constraint unification, has not yet been adequately understood. Although it is known that there are constraints that cannot be modularized, constraint processing systems themselves are still not fully developed, and, even if a failure occurs in the modularization of constraints, we often cannot specify whether it results from the property of the constraint or from undetected problems in the systems.

In this paper, we clarify the possibility, the difficulty (or ease), and the computability of constraint modularization from the viewpoint of the syntactic properties of constraints. First we give a new meaning to constraint modularization. Then, referring to concepts used in the fields of functional programming and term rewriting systems, we classify constraints and discuss the possibility of their modularization.

In Section 2, we take a new viewpoint on the properties of modularizing constraints in relation to *terms* and their treelessness. In Section 3, referring to concepts in the field of term rewriting, we discuss factors that make modularization difficult or impossible, and we classify constraints according to their syntactic properties. As a consequence, we get a result that is negative in a certain respect. In Section 4, we give an example of describing constraints for Japanese grammar in order to consider the problems of application, and we suggest that, in spite of the problem shown in Section 3, this approach to describing constraints has enough power to support a computational mechanism for formalizing and describing grammar.

2 Properties of the Modularization of Constraints

In this section, we first present basic definitions of constraints and terms, then show a relationship between the treelessness of terms argued in [19] and the modularity of constraints. This gives a new meaning to the modularization of constraints.

2.1 Modular constraints

Definition 2.1 (Constraint) *A constraint is syntactically a Horn clause whose left-hand side is empty.*[2]

The informal semantics of the constraint

$@\ p_1(a_{11}, \ldots, a_{1m}), \ldots, p_k(a_{k1}, \ldots, a_{kn}).$

is as follows:

$\{< X_1, \ldots, X_l > \mid p_1(a_{11}, \ldots, a_{1m}), \ldots, p_k(a_{k1}, \ldots, a_{kn})\},$

where $X_1, \ldots, X_l$ are variables included in the above constraint,

where several assignments can be made for the variables. In other words, we regard the semantics of a constraint as a tuple of (possibly specified) variables that satisfies the constraint.

Definition 2.2 (Constraint definition) *A constraint definition is syntactically a Horn clause whose left-hand side is not empty.*

Definition 2.3 (Modularly defined predicate) *A predicate is modularly defined if each clause of its definitions satisfies either of the following conditions 1 and 2 individually:*

1. *The right-hand side of the clause is empty.*
2. *On the right-hand side of the clause,*

   every argument of atomic formulas is a variable,

   every variable occurs only once, and

   every predicate appearing is modularly defined.

Definition 2.4 (Modular constraint) *A constraint is modular if it satisfies the following condition:*

1. *On the right-hand side of the clause,*

   every argument of atomic formulas is a variable,

   every variable occurs only once, and

   every predicate appearing is modularly defined.

We call *modularization* the transformation of a constraint into the equivalent modular constraint (and new predicate definitions) and the transformation of a predicate definition into the equivalent modular definitions.

2.2 Treeless form [19]

Definition 2.5 (Term) *A term is defined as in Figure 1.* [3]

In a case term, **case** <term> **of** $\cdots$, <term> is called the *selector*, and <pattern>: <term>, which occurs in the part followed by **of**, is called one of the *branches*.

---

[2] To distinguish a constraint from a query in Prolog, we represent a constraint by a form such as "`@ append([a,b],Y,Z).`", as in cu-Prolog [18], rather than by the form of the corresponding query "`?-append([a,b],Y,Z).`".

[3] In a term rewriting system, a term is defined generally, although we use a limited definition that is sufficient for discussion of treeless forms.

```
<term>                  ::=  <variable> |
                             <constructor> { <term> }* |
                             <function> { <term> }* |
                             case <term> of
                                   <pattern>: <term> {, <pattern>: <term>}*
<pattern>               ::=  <constructor> { <variable> }*
<function definition>   ::=  <function> { <variable> }* = <term>
```

Fig. 1 Definition of terms

```
<treeless form>         ::=  <variable> |
                             <constructor> { <treeless form> }* |
                             <function> { <variable> }* |
                             case <variable> of
                                 <pattern>: <treeless form>
                                 {, <pattern>: <treeless form>}*
<pattern>               ::=  <constructor> { <variable> }*
<function definition>   ::=  <function> { <variable> }* = <term>
where the form is linear as a whole.
```

Fig. 2 Definition of treeless forms

Definition 2.6 (Linear) *A term is linear if each variable occurs at most once, where this definition is extended for case terms; a variable may appear in more than one branch of a case term.*

Definition 2.7 (Treeless form) *A treeless form is defined as in Figure 2.*

A treeless form is a term that has no intermediate structures that are not referred to afterwards. It is known that the transformation of a composition of functions with treeless definitions into a corresponding treeless form, if it is linear, has the good property shown in Theorem 2.1 [19].

Theorem 2.1 (Deforestation Theorem) *Every composition of functions with treeless definitions can be effectively transformed into a single function with a treeless definition, without loss of efficiency.*[4]

See *Wadler* [19] for the proof. The Deforestation Algorithm was created to realize the above transformations, whose main part is equivalent to that of unfolding in the Modularization Algorithm given in Section 2.4.

One point we should note here is that in this theorem, the inputs are limited to linear terms. The algorithm does not always terminate, especially when the input is not linear. All that can be claimed is that if the input is not linear, the output is linear only if the algorithm terminates successfully.

[4] By effectiveness we mean the complexity of instantiation on free variables included in the term.

Table 1 Notation

	Algorithm	Term	Constraint
Variable	v-initial string	small-initial string	capital-initial string
Constructor	c-initial	capital-initial	small-initial
Function	f-initial	small-initial	small-initial
Term	t-initial		
Pattern	p-initial		

2.3 Relationship between modular constraints and treeless forms

Although the concept of treeless forms originally comes from the fields of functional programming and term rewriting systems, there is a close relationship between treelessness of terms and modularity of constraints.

Theorem 2.2 *Every treeless form has a corresponding description of modular constraints.*

Proof. To prove the theorem, we show a correspondence between a term and constraints. We use the notation shown in Table 1. Let $C[\![t]\!]$ denote the result of transforming term t into constraints. We can transform a term into constraints by applying the rules shown in Figure 3. It is easily shown that the rules cover all possible terms. ■

Figure 4 shows an example of correspondence between term representation and constraint representation.

In connection with the case of treeless forms, we might expect that the proposition

> every constraint that is a composition of modularly defined predicates is modularizable

holds, although, in fact, this is not the case, as we show later.

2.4 Modularization algorithm

A simple algorithm for modularizing constraints, called the Modularization Algorithm, is presented in *Hasida and Sirai* [7]. We show a rough sketch of the algorithm in Figure 5.

When a constraint in the form

$$p_1(\cdots), p_2(\cdots), \ldots, p_k(\cdots) \qquad (\star)$$

is given, and the definitions of the predicates are given as

$$\begin{array}{ll} p_1(\cdots) \text{ :- xxx .,} & (1.1) \\ p_1(\cdots) \text{ :- xxx .,} & (1.2) \\ \cdots & \\ p_1(\cdots) \text{ :- xxx .,} & (1.n_1) \\ \vdots & \\ p_k(\cdots) \text{ :- xxx .,} & (k.1) \\ \cdots & \end{array}$$

(1) $C[\![v]\!] = v$.

(2) $C[\![c\ t_1\ \cdots\ t_k]\!] = c(C[\![t_1]\!],\ \ldots,\ C[\![t_k]\!])$.

(3) $C[\![f\ t_1\ \cdots\ t_k]\!]$:

(a) replace the occurrence with v, and

(b) add $f(C[\![t_1]\!],\ \ldots,\ C[\![t_k]\!],\ v)$ to the right-hand side of the clause.

(4) $C[\![$ **case** v **of** $p'_1\colon t'_1,\ \ldots,\ p'_n\colon t'_n]\!]$:

(a) make n copies of the clause in which the case term occurs,

(b) for the i-th copy (for $i = 1, \ldots, n$), replace every occurrence of v with $C[\![p'_i]\!]$, and

(c) replace the occurrence of this case term with $C[\![t'_i]\!]$.

(5) $C[\![$**case** $c\ t_1\ \cdots\ t_k$ **of** $p'_1\colon t'_1,\ \ldots,\ p'_n\colon t'_n]\!]$

$= C[\![t'_i\{t_1/v_1, \ldots, t_k/v_k\}]\!]$, where $p'_i = c\ v_1 \cdots v_k$.

(6) $C[\![$**case** $f\ t_1 \cdots t_k$ **of** $p'_1\colon t'_1,\ \ldots,\ p'_n\colon t'_n]\!]$:

(a) add $f(C[\![t_1]\!],\ \ldots,\ C[\![t_k]\!],\ v)$ to the right-hand side of the clause, and

(b) replace the occurrence of this case term with
$C[\![$**case** v **of** $p'_1\colon t'_1,\ \ldots,\ p'_n\colon t'_n]\!]$.

(7) $C[\![$**case** (**case** t_0 **of** $p_1\colon t_1,\ \ldots,\ p_m\colon t_m$) **of** $p'_1\colon t'_1,\ \ldots,\ p'_n\colon t'_n]\!]$
$= C[\![$**case** t_0 **of**

p_1: (**case** t_1 **of** $p'_1\colon t'_1,\ \ldots,\ p'_n\colon t'_n$),

...,

p_m: (**case** t_m **of** $p'_1\colon t'_1,\ \ldots,\ p'_n\colon t'_n$)$]\!]$.

(*) if the same form $C[\![\cdot]\!]$ appears as appeared before, define a new predicate and replace the occurrence with the new constraint.

Fig. 3 Rules for transformation of a term into constraints

$$p_k(\cdots) \text{ :- } \text{xxx .,} \qquad (k.n_k)$$

then the constraint is unfolded as follows:
for each unfolding,

1. choose one index, for example i, from 1 to k,
2. make $n - i$ copies of the constraint ($\star$),
3. for $j = 1 \ldots n_i$, try to unify $p_i(\cdots)$ in the target constraint with the left-hand side of the j-th definition clause of the predicate p_i.

   If it succeeds, then replace $p_i(\cdots)$ with the right-hand side of the definition clause;

   otherwise, delete the j-th copy.

Term Representation	Constraint Representation

append x_s y_s =
case x_s **of**
Nil: y_s,
Cons a x'_s:
Cons a (append x'_s y_s).
copy u_s =
case u_s **of**
Nil: Nil,
Cons b u'_s: Cons b (copy u'_s).
	`append([],W,W).`
	`append([A|X],Y,[A|Z])`
	`:-append(X,Y,Z).`
	
	`copy([],[]).`
	`copy([B|U],[B|V]):-copy(U,V).`

T⟦ append (copy x_s) Nil⟧.	`@ copy(X,Y), append(Y,[],Z).`
c0 $x_s \equiv$ T⟦ append (copy x_s) Nil⟧.	`c0(X,Y,Z) ⇔` `copy(X,Y), append(Y,[],Z).`

c0 x_s =
case x_s **of**
Nil: Nil,
Cons a x'_s: Cons a (c0 x'_s).
	`c0([],[],[]).`
	`c0([A|X],[A|Y],[A|Z])`
	`:- c0(X,Y,Z).`

Fig. 4 Correspondence between term representation and constraint representation

2.5 Processes of the Modularization Algorithm

To discuss the modularizability of constraints and the possibility of the Modularization Algorithm terminating, we argue the processes of the Modularization Algorithm. Since the main part of this argument involves unfolding constraints, we represent the processes by a directed graph, and pay attention to each unfolding process. In this graph, each node corresponds to a clause that appears in the way when a constraint is modularized, and each edge corresponds to one clause made by unfolding an atomic formula, which means that the number of edges going out from each node is equal to the number of clauses made by unfolding the atomic formula.

Note that modularization of constraints finishes when all leaves[5] become modular. Different graphs are made if the order of selection of atomic formulas to unfold is different, while the graphs' paths will meet afterwards if no failure of unfolding occurs on the paths.

Though we can choose arbitrarily which atomic formula is to be unfolded first, once we select one, we should unfold it for all definitions of the predicate of the atomic formula (except those that cannot be unified). Consequently, modularization succeeds as a whole if and only if every modularization succeeds for all edges.

Example 1 *When a predicate* `append` *is defined as*

```
append([],Y,Y).,
```

[5] They are not leaves because the structure is not strictly a tree.

Repeat the following until all constraints become modular:

(1) New Predicate Definition

Let the variables included in the target constraint be

$$V_1, V_2, \ldots V_n,$$

define a new predicate ck as in

$$ck(V_1, V_2, \ldots, V_n) \Leftrightarrow \text{the target constraint},$$

and replace the occurrence by

$$ck(V_1, V_2, \ldots, V_n).$$

(2) Unfolding

Choose one constraint from the new definitions or unmodular constraints, choose an appropriate atomic formula in the constraint, and replace it with its definition (i.e., unfold it).

(3) Folding

If a constraint that has already been modularized appears as a substructure of the target constraint, replace the substructure with the predicate that is the previously modularized result.

Fig. 5 The Modularization Algorithm

```
append([A|X],Y,[A|Z]) :- append(X,Y,Z).,
```

then the constraint

```
@ append(A,B,C), append(C,D,E).
```

can be modularized by two unfoldings (Figure 6). For further details, let c0 be defined as

```
c0(A,B,C,D,E) <==> append(A,B,C), append(C,D,E).,                   (*)
```

and we first get

```
1: c0(A,B,[],D,D) <-> append(A,B,[]).,                              (a)
2: c0(A,B,[C0|C],D,[C0|E])
       <-> append(A,B,[C0|C]), append(C,D,E).                       (b)
```

by unfolding the second atomic formula of `(*)`. *Next, by unfolding the formula* `append(A,B,[])` *in* `(a)`, *we transform* `(a)` *into*

```
1': c0([],[],[],D,D).                                               (a')
```

Then, let c1 be defined as

```
c1(A,B,C0,C,D,E)
  <==> append(A,B,[C0|C]), append(C,D,E).,                          (**)
```

and, by unfolding the first atomic formula of `(**)`, *we get*

```
3: c1([],[C0|C],C0,C,D,E) :- append(C,D,E).,                        (c)
4: c1([C0|A],B,C0,C,D,E)
       <-> append(A,B,C), append(C,D,E).
```

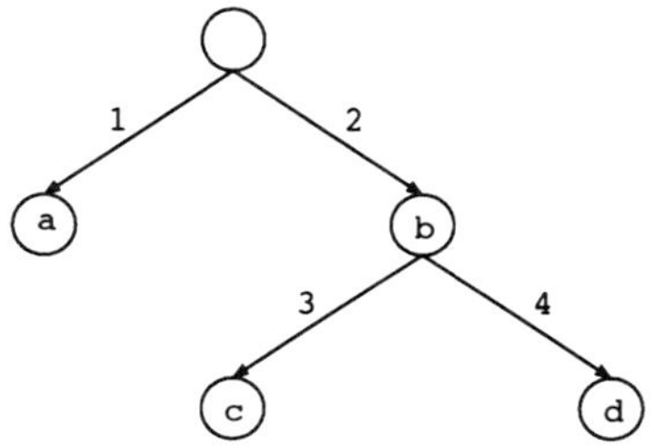

Fig. 6 Process of the modularization of **append**

```
      <-> c0(A,B,C,D,E).                                      (d)
```

Here (a') *and* (c) *are modularly defined as they are,* (b) *becomes modularly defined by defining a new predicate* c1, *and* (d) *becomes modularly defined by folding it. As a consequence, the result of the modularization is*

```
  @ c0(A,B,C,D,E).,
```

where each predicate is defined as follows:

```
  c0([],[],[],D,D).,
  c0(A,B,[C0|C],D,[C0|E]) :- c1(A,B,C0,C,D,E).,
  c1([],[C0|C],C0,C,D,E) :- append(C,D,E).,
  c1([C0|A],B,C0,C,D,E) :- c0(A,B,C,D,E).
```

Modularization processes are not necessarily terminated. We discuss this point in the next section.

3 Classification of Constraints

In this section, our purpose is to clarify the syntactic properties of constraints that are difficult to modularize. After we have defined basic terms, we list the key concepts for classifying constraints.

3.1 Definitions

Definition 3.1 (Linear) *A constraint is linear if each variable occurs at most once in the right-hand side of the Horn clause.*

To argue the recursiveness of a predicate, we consider a directed graph that represents the relations of reference for all clauses referred to. A node is assigned for each Horn clause that occurs, where several arcs come out from the node according to the following rule: if the clause has a right-hand side, make arcs from the node of the clause to the other nodes that correspond to the (unifiable) definition clauses for each predicate that occurs. The graph of reference for the predicate **append** in Example 1 is shown in Figure 7, where each clause is numbered as follows:

```
  (1) append([],Y,Y).,
  (2) append([A|X],Y,[A|Z]) :- append(X,Y,Z).,
  (3) @ append(A,B,C),append(C,D,E).
```

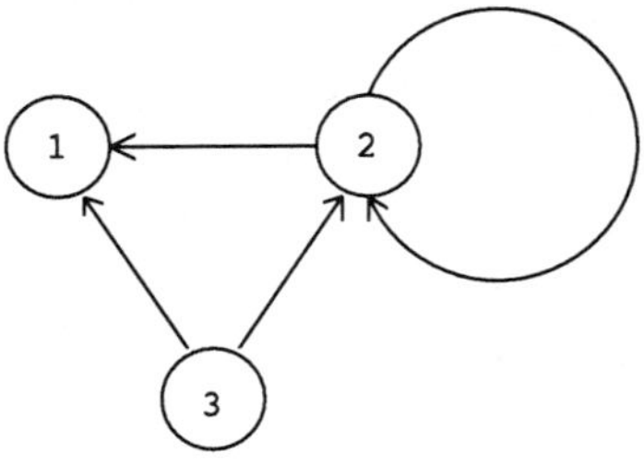

Fig. 7 Directed graph of reference for **append**

Definition 3.2 (Essentially recursive) *A clause is essentially recursive or has recursiveness in essence if, in the directed graph of reference, the node corresponding to the clause can reach a loop.*

We use the term recursive in the above sense, and we call definition clauses of a predicate recursive as a whole if they include recursive clauses. In the example shown in Figure 7, the definition clauses of **append** are recursive, and Constraint (3) is also recursive.

3.2 Key concepts for classification

We try to classify constraints according to the following four criteria:

- Recursiveness,
- Linearity,
- Existence of modular definitions,
- Data structure.

The following comments may be made:

1. Recursiveness

   If target constraints to be modularized are not recursive—that is, if the reference graph has no loop—then modularization obviously terminates.

   From now on, we consider only constraints with recursive predicates.

2. Linearity

   The concept of linearity is important when we consider the properties of term rewriting systems. The reasons for this are that linearity is a necessary condition for a system to be normal, and a normal system has the Church-Rosser property (or is confluent). In addition, linearity is important for the semantics of functions in functional programming.

   Nonetheless, many non-linear constraints are dealt with in Constraint Logic Programming. Here, we discuss the relation between linearity and the possibility of modularization.

3. Existence of modular definitions

For the Modularization Algorithm, if the propositions that

> if all predicates referred to have equivalent modular definitions, then the modularization terminates

and/or

> if all predicates referred to have equivalent modular definitions, then the constraints can be modularized

hold, it is easy to modularize constraints. From our experiences in describing constraints for Japanese grammar, we have a feeling that modularly defined recursive predicates play important roles in describing constraints. Unfortunately, the above propositions do not hold. We present two counter-examples.

Example 2 *Although the predicate* `append` *is modularly defined, the constraint*

```
@ append(X,X,Z).
```

is not modularizable.

Example 3 *Let the predicates* `p` *and* `q` *be defined as follows:*

```
p(c(X),c(c(Y))) :- p(X,Y).,
p(c(c(X)),c(Y)) :- p(X,Y).,
q(c(X),c(c(c(Y)))) :- q(X,Y).,
q(c(c(c(X))),c(Y)) :- q(X,Y).
```

For a constraint

```
@ p(X,Y), q(X,Y).
```

composed of the above modularly defined `p` *and* `q`*, the Modularization Algorithm never terminates, while there are corresponding modular constraints defined as follows:*[6]

$$\texttt{c0(X,Y)} \Leftrightarrow \texttt{p(X,Y),q(X,Y).},$$

where

$$\texttt{c0}(\texttt{c}^5\texttt{(X)},\ \texttt{c}^7\texttt{(Y)})\ \texttt{:-}\ \texttt{c0(X,Y).},$$
$$\texttt{c0}(\texttt{c}^7\texttt{(X)},\ \texttt{c}^5\texttt{(Y)})\ \texttt{:-}\ \texttt{c0(X,Y).},$$
$$\texttt{c0}(\texttt{c}^{16}\texttt{(X)},\ \texttt{c}^8\texttt{(Y)})\ \texttt{:-}\ \texttt{c0(X,Y).},$$
$$\texttt{c0}(\texttt{c}^8\texttt{(X)},\ \texttt{c}^{16}\texttt{(Y)})\ \texttt{:-}\ \texttt{c0(X,Y).}$$

Furthermore, adding the two clauses

---

6 By $\texttt{c}^5\texttt{(X)}$, for example, we mean `c(c(c(c(c(X)))))`.

```
p(0,0).,
q(0,0).
```

to the top of the definitions of `p` *and* `q`*, respectively, leads to almost the same result, which shows that the Modularization Algorithm does not necessarily terminate, even if the refutation can be finished in a finite number of resolutions and satisfiability can be proved for the corresponding Prolog query.*

4. Data structure

   Because of the properties of modularization, constraints that need to refer to global data structures cannot be modularized.

   Example 4 *A predicate for reversing lists,* `reverse`*, is defined as*

   ```
   reverse([],[]).,
   reverse([A|X],Z) :- reverse(X,Y),append(Y,[A],Z).,
   ```

   which does not have modular definitions.[7]

   Furthermore, as in Example 2, the problems of data structure combined with those of non-linearity often make it difficult to modularize the constraints, although we do not discuss the matter further here.

We define the following sets of constraints:

A: Modular constraints,

B: Constraints for which the Modularization Algorithm terminate,

C: Modularizable constraints,

D: Constraints composed of modularly defined predicates,

E: Constraints that can be made by modularly defined predicates.

Moreover, we consider three other factors that affect modularizability:

I: Non-recursive constraints,

II: Linear constraints,

III: Constraints that refer only to local structures.

For constraints included in I, it is easy to show that the Modularization Algorithm terminates, which means that $I \subset B$. We treat constraints other than I below.

[7] Here we assume the use of systems that support normal (one-way) lists.

3.3 Linearity and computability of modularization

Lemma 3.1 *If the target constraint to be modularized is linear, one unification of each atomic formula of the clause to the left-hand side of the corresponding definition clauses does not cause any dependency of variables between the atomic formula and the remaining formulas of the target constraint.*

Proof. The dependency arising as a result of one unification of an atomic formula to the left-hand side of the definition clauses is either

i) specification of a variable for a constructor application, or

ii) dependency (i.e., unification) of different variables

(or both). Since, from the assumption, a dependency that violates linearity is caused by this unification, and the (right-hand side of the) predicate definition is modular, the dependency of the left-hand side does not spread to the right-hand side. ■

Theorem 3.1 *If all predicates referred to are modularly defined, linear constraints are modularizable.*

Proof. To prove the theorem, we make the following two statements:

1. One unfolding does not cause the constraint to loose linearity.
2. Iteration of unfolding and new predicate definition terminates in a finite number of steps.

First we prove Statement 1. We argue the extent of dependency spreads when unification to the left-hand side of the definition clause succeeds. For a modular clause, all the arguments of the predicates in the right-hand side are variables and are different from each other, and the left-hand side of the clause loses linearity if there is more than one occurrence of one variable or of constructor application. Here, we classify specification caused by unification of the left-hand side of definitions into two cases:

(1) An argument of the left-hand side of the definition clause has complex structures.

(2) An argument of the target constraint has complex structures.

In the first case, the non-modularity is resumed here because the target constraint is linear. In the second case, some of the structures that violate the modularity spread to the right-hand side. However, since the definitions are modular, that does not violate the linearity.
Second, to prove Statement 2, it is sufficient to see that the complexity of the structure[8] of each argument is not increased by unfolding constraints. If the complexity decreases, it becomes 0 sooner or later, and, if the complexity does not change, the constraint can be folded. In both cases, the modularization terminates.
As a consequence, the modularization terminates in that condition. ■

[8] Here the structure means something like the depth of constructor applications.

For constraints of $\overline{I} \cap II$, that is, for linear constraints that use recursive predicates,

$$A \subset D \subset B \subset C \subset E$$

holds; this applies also to trivial relations on the definitions of the constraints.

3.4 Modularizability for non-linear constraints

For non-linear constraints, we cannot get any non-trivial relations. In other words, the composition of a modularly defined predicate does not contribute to making it easy or possible to modularize non-linear constraints.

We have already shown that $D - C \neq \phi$ in Example 2 and that $(C - B) \cap D \neq \phi$ in Example 3.

We give several other examples below.

Example 5 *When predicates* `p`, `q`, *and* `r` *are defined as*

```
p(c(X),c(c(Y))) :- p(X,Y).,
q(c(X),c(c(Y))) :- q(X,Y).,
r(c(X),c(c(Y))) :- r(X,Y).,
```

the Modularization Algorithm never terminates for a constraint

```
@ p(X,Y),q(X,Y),r(X,Y).
```

Furthermore, this constraint does not have any corresponding modular constraints, and is never satisfied.

Example 6 (Linear and unmodularizable constraint) *If a predicate* `p` *is defined as*

```
p(X) :- p([X]).,
```

`p` *does not have any modular definitions.*

Example 7 *If a predicate* `p` *is defined as*

```
p(X,Y,f(X,Y)).,
p(X,V,W) :- p(X,Y,U),p(Y,Z,V),p(U,Z,W).,
p(U,Z,W) :- p(X,Y,U),p(Y,Z,V),p(X,V,W).,
p(X,e,X).,
p(e,X,X).,
p(X,i(X),e).,
p(i(X),X,e).,
p(X,X,e).,
```

`p` *does not have any modular definitions.*

On the other hand, for the constraint

```
@ p(a,b,Z),p(b,a,Z).,
```

whereas the corresponding query

```
?- p(a,b,Z),p(b,a,Z).
```

can be refuted, the Modularization Algorithm never terminates, and it cannot be modularized, because the second and the third clauses of the definition of `p` *are essentially generators. However, since it is sufficient to show that the constraint to be modularized is satisfiable if it does not include any variables, a constraint* `@`

`p(b,a,f(a,b))` *can be modularized, although a storage problem may occur when breadth-first traverse is selected,*[9] *and the algorithm does not necessarily terminate when depth-first traverse is selected.*

4 Another Example

In this section, we demonstrate a way of formalizing and describing Japanese grammar based on JPSG, and in this connection, we present another example of constraint description and modularization. We also suggest that, by using *non-linear* or *recursive* constraints that are shown to make it difficult to modularize constraints, we can modularize these constraints and support the analysis of syntactic structures to the extent that this has concerned us.

We have described local constraints of Japanese based on JPSG, which include constraints for long-distance dependencies, such as nominal clauses and reflexive nouns. There we formalize language constraints as several Structural Principles, such as the Head Feature Principle, the Subcat Feature Principle, and the Binding Feature Principles, which constrain each branch of the tree structure. For example, when the Head Feature Principle is denoted as `hfp(D,H,M)` and the Subcat Feature Principle as `scp(D,H,M)`, in order to capture basic phrase structures, and when the Binding Feature Principles are denoted as `slp(D,H,M)` and `rfp(D,H,M)`, in order to capture phenomena of long-distance dependencies, the constraint on each branch `ltree(D,H,M)` is represented as

```
ltree(D,H,M)
:- hfp(D,H,M), scp(D,H,M), slp(D,H,M), rfp(D,H,M).,
```

where `D`, `H`, and `M` denote three categories that contribute to making a branch. Part of the description is shown in Figures 8 and 9. More specifically, the Head Feature Principle `hfp(D,H,M)` means that head features (that is, the core features and properties) of both the mother category and the right-hand one are identical for each branch, as shown in Figure 10. By means of these constraints, we capture basic phrase structures and the long-distance dependencies of both the gap of nominal clauses and the reflexive noun zibun "oneself," in Japanese. Japanese sentences such as

a. Ken-ga zibun-no kuruma-wo arau.
   Ken-SBJ self-GEN car-OBJ wash.
   Ken washes his car.

b. aisuru onna-ga zibun-no kuruma-wo arau otoko.
   love-REL woman-SBJ self-GEN car-OBJ wash-REL man.
   A man who loves the woman washing his car.
   (One interpretation of the ambiguous noun phrase.)

can be treated by these constraints.

After describing these constraints, we modularize them. An actual way of describing the constraints of grammar is as follows:

1. Describing structural principles individually. The goal here is to formalize language phenomena, describe them, and evaluate them on a computer.

[9] To *refute* the constraint, 14-depth traverse is required, and clauses with ten atomic formulas appear during the resolution.

```
%% constraints
ltree(D,H,M)
  :- hfp(D,H,M),scp(D,H,M), slp(D,H,M),rfp(D,H,M).

hfp(D,H,M) :- head(HH,H),head(HH,M).
scp(D,H,M)
  :- subcat(ScH,H),head(HD,D),subcat(ScM,M),
     del(ScH,HD,ScM),
     adjuncts(AdH,H),adjuncts(AdH,M).
scp(D,H,M)
  :- adjuncts(AdH,H),head(HD,D),adjuncts(AdM,M),
     del(AdH,HD,AdM),
     subcat(ScH,H),subcat(ScH,M).
scp(D,H,M)
  :- head(HH,H),dep(HH,D),
     subcat(ScH,H),subcat(ScH,M),
     adjuncts(AdH,H),adjuncts(AdH,M).
slp(D,H,M)
  :- pos(v,D),pos(v,H),
     adjuncts(AdD,D),subcat(ScD,D),
     dep(DH,H),
     slash(SlD,D),slash(SlH,H),slash(SlM,M),
     slb(AdD,ScD,DH,SlD,SlH,SlM).
slp(D,H,M) :- trans_sl(D,H,M).
rfp(D,H,M)
  :- refl(ReD,D),refl(ReH,H),refl(ReM,M),
     subcat(ScH,H),
     rfp(ReD,ReH,ReM,ScH).
```

Fig. 8 Example of describing principles in cu-Prolog

2. Making conjunctions of them. Here the constraints should be modularized automatically.
3. Making a parser and a generator for the language by using these constraints.
4. Evaluating the grammar description by referring to the above result. As well as evaluating constraints individually, we consider the relations among constraints.

Although we do not present other constraints here, these constraints, which include the recursive predicates shown in Figure 11, can be modularized, and the Modularization Algorithm could, at least theoretically, terminate.[10] However, the predicates shown in Figure 11 often cause trouble when we modularize them with cu-Prolog. Constraint transformation systems are still not fully developed, and they sometimes cause trouble as a result of modularization failure. They are expected to be improved in future.

[10] We can modularize these constraints manually.

```
%% features
head(Head, c(Head,Sc,Ad,Sl,R)).
pos(Pos, c(H,Sc,Ad,Sl,R)) :- pos_of_h(Pos,H).
gr(Gr, c(H,Sc,Ad,Sl,R)) :- gr_of_h(Gr,H).
dep(Dep, c(H,Sc,Ad,Sl,R)) :- dep_of_h(Dep,H).
subcat(Subcat, c(H,Subcat,Ad,Sl,R)).
adjuncts(Adj, c(H,Sc,Adj,Sl,R)).
slash(Slash, c(H,Sc,Ad,Slash,R)).
refl(Refl, c(H,Sc,Ad,Sl,Refl)).
pos_of_h(Pos, h(Pos,G,D,Se)).
gr_of_h(Gr, h(P,Gr,D,Se)).
dep_of_h(Dep, h(P,G,Dep,Se)).
sem_of_h(Sem, h(P,G,D,Sem)).
```

Fig. 9 Example of describing feature constraints in cu-Prolog

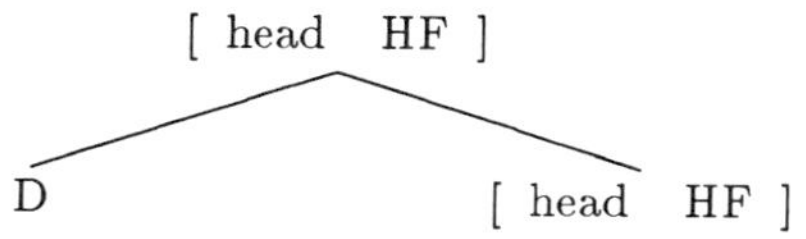

Fig. 10 Head feature principle

5 Conclusion

We have shown that modularization of constraints can be classified according to the syntactic properties of the constraints, as in Figure 12, in terms of the notations introduced in Section 3. In particular, we have shown that on a constraint composed of modularly defined predicates, the Modularization Algorithm terminates if the constraint is linear, and, by giving examples, we have pointed out some problems the algorithm faces when constraints are not linear.

On the other hand, despite the problems, in our experience of describing constraints for the Japanese language based on JPSG, it is possible to describe constraints without being troubled by un-modularizable ones. However, whether con-

```
append([],X,X).
append([A|X],Y,[A|Z]) :- append(X,Y,Z).

del([A|X],A,X).
del([B|X],A,[B|Y]) :- del(X,A,Y).

member(A,[A|X]).
member(A,[B|X]) :- member(A,X).
```

Fig. 11 Recursively defined predicates

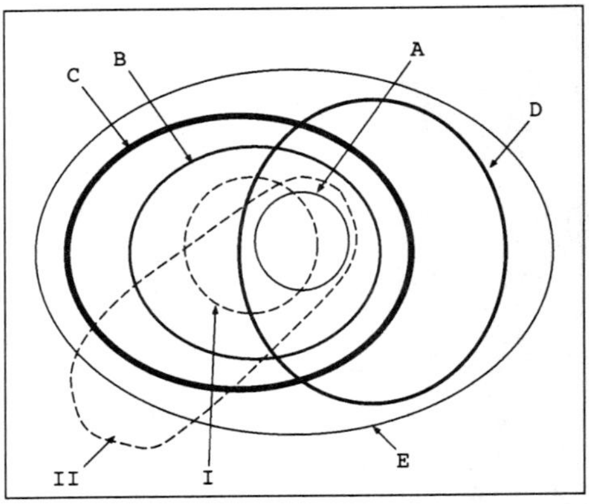

Fig. 12 Relations among sets

straints can be modularized automatically by a constraints transformation system is another question, on which we expect further research to be done.

Acknowledgements. I would like to thank members of working groups related to JPSG at ICOT for their useful discussions on grammar descriptions and the referees for their valuable comments.

References

[1] Chomsky, N.: *Lectures on Government and Binding*, Foris Publications, Dordrecht, 1981.

[2] Fuchi, K., Furukawa, K., and Mizoguchi, F. (eds.): *Program Transformation*, Kyouritu, Tokyo, 1989 (in Japanese).

[3] Fuchi, K., Mizoguchi, F., Furukawa, K., and Lassez, J.-L. (eds.): *Constraint Logic Programming*, Kyouritu, Tokyo, 1989 (in Japanese).

[4] Futatsugi, K. and Toyama, Y.: Term Rewriting Systems and Their Applications, *Journal of the Information Processing Society of Japan*, Vol. 24, No. 2 (1983), pp. 133–146 (in Japanese).

[5] Gunji, T.: *Japanese Phrase Structure Grammar: A Unification-Based Approach*, D. Reidel, 1987.

[6] Harada, Y., Gunji, T., Miyoshi, H., Sirai, H., and Hasida, K.: JPSG–A Phrase Structure Grammar for Japanese, *Advances in Software Science and Technology*, Vol. 1, No. 1(1989), pp. 1-15.

[7] Hasida, K. and Sirai, H.: Conditioned Unification, *Comput. Softw.*, Vol. 3, No. 4 (1986), pp. 28–38 (in Japanese).

[8] Ida, T.: *Fundamental Theories of Computational Models*, Iwanami, Tokyo, 1991 (in Japanese).

[9] Lloyd, J. W.: *Foundations of Logic Programming*, Second, Extended Edition, Springer-Verlag, 1987.

[10] Nakagawa, H.: Prolog Program Transformation of a Tree Manipulation Algorithm, *Transactions of the Information Processing Society of Japan*, Vol. 26, No. 5 (1985), pp. 870–876 (in Japanese).

[11] Pollard, C. and Sag, I.: *Information-Based Syntax and Semantics, Vol. 1: Fundamentals*, CSLI Lecture Notes No. 12, Center for the Study of Language and Information, Stanford University, 1988.

[12] Sirai, H., Gunji, T., Hasida, K., and Harada, Y.: Grammatical Description Based on Local Constraints, *IEICE Technical Report*, Vol. 87, No. 75 (1987), pp. 1–8 (in Japanese).

[13] Takano, A.: Generalized Partial Computation for a Lazy Functional Language, *Proc. Symposium on Partial Evaluation and Semantics-based Program Manipulation*, ACM SIGPLAN, 1991.

[14] Tomioka, Y.: Long-Distance Dependency from a Computational Point of View, *Metropolitan Linguistics*, Vol. 7 (1987), pp. 33–52.

[15] Tsuda, H.: cu-Prolog for Constraint-Based Grammar, *Proc. FGCS 1992*, 1992, pp. 347–356.

[16] Tsuda, H., Hasida, K., and Sirai, H.: JPSG Parser on Constraint Logic Programming, *Proc. 4th ACL European Chapter*, 1989, pp. 95–102.

[17] Tsuda, H., Hasida, K., and Sirai, H.: cu-Prolog and Its Application to a JPSG Parser. In Furukawa, K., Tanaka, H., and Fujisaki, T. (eds.): Logic Programming '89, Springer-Verlag, LNAI-485, 1989, pp. 134–143.

[18] Tsuda, H., Hasida, K., and Sirai, H.: cu-PrologIII system (cu-Prolog Version 3, System Documentation), Technical Report ICOT-TM1160, 1992 (in Japanese).

[19] Wadler, P.: Deforestation: Transforming Programs to Eliminate Trees, *Theor. Comput. Sci.*, Vol. 73 (1990), pp. 231–248.

Initially published in "Computer Software", Vol. 9, No. 6, in Japanese.

Yutaka Tomioka
Department of Mathematical Engineering and Information Physics
Faculty of Engineering, University of Tokyo
7–3–1 Hongo, Bunkyo-ku,
Tokyo 113 Japan
current affiliation: Tokyo Information Systems Research Laboratory
Matsushita Electric Industrial Co., Ltd.
4–5–15 Higashi-Shinagawa, Shinagawa-ku,
Tokyo 140 Japan

Declarative Semantics of Logic Programs on Parameterized Representation Systems

Kiyoshi Akama

Summary. Instead of starting with the usual concrete definitions of atoms and substitutions, we adopt abstract definitions of them and are constructing an axiomatic theory of logic programming, which we call the *GLP theory* (theory of *generalized logic programs*). This enables us to discuss logic programming at a new abstract level.

In this paper we introduce a new structure called *parameterized representation systems* (PRSs), which is an abstraction of the inter-relations between atoms, ground atoms, and substitutions in ordinary Prolog. We then introduce program clauses on a PRS and define generalized logic programs on it. We give a declarative semantics (minimal model semantics and least fixpoint semantics) and define the meaning of generalized logic programs.

The GLP theory greatly extends the concept of logic programs without sacrificing their important properties and major merits. It is applicable to many knowledge representation systems and programming languages, including context-free grammars, typed unification grammars, extensions of Prolog, and CLP languages.

1 Introduction

1.1 Axiomatization of the theory of logic programming

An atom is usually defined as an expression $p(t_1, t_2, \cdots, t_n)$, where p is a predicate and t_i is a term. A substitution is a finite set $\{x_1/t_1, x_2/t_2, \cdots, x_n/t_n\}$, where x_i is a variable and t_i is a term. The theory of logic programming is based on these definitions.

Instead of starting with such concrete definitions of atoms and substitutions, we have adopted abstract definitions of them and are constructing an axiomatic theory of logic programming. The logic programs formalized in this axiomatic theory are called *generalized logic programs*. We refer neither to predicates, variables, constants, nor functions, which are the basic components of ordinary atoms, nor to substitutions, which are defined on the concepts of variables and terms. The new axiomatic theory, called the *GLP theory* (theory of generalized logic programs), greatly extends the concepts of not only atoms and substitutions, but also logic programs, without losing the latters' important properties and major merits.

From the viewpoint of the GLP theory, traditional theories seem to include many overly specific definitions of concepts, which restrict the applicability of the

ISBN 0-12-037105-7

theorems and prevent us from understanding and utilizing the full power of logic programming.

1.2 Contents of the paper

This paper gives a declarative semantics of generalized logic programs [2], which is the most basic part of the GLP theory. Other parts of the GLP theory, including the theory of a procedural semantics of generalized logic programs, are discussed elsewhere [3, 4, 5, 6, 7, 8, 9, 10, 11, 12].

In this paper, we solve the following three problems :

- How can we axiomatize the theory of logic programs? The logic programs formalized in this axiomatic theory are called generalized logic programs.
- How can a declarative semantics of generalized logic programs be developed?
- What is the appropriate definition of the meaning of such a generalized logic program?

The solutions of these problems are closely related. We will introduce the structure called *parameterized representation systems* in terms of very simple axioms and define generalized logic programs on parameterized representation systems. This is the solution of the first problem. The solution will be justified by constructing a declarative semantics, which is the solution of the second problem. We will prove that the following three sets, which are separately determined by the given generalized logic program P, are identical; that is,

$$M_P = lfp(K_P) = K_P \uparrow \omega.$$

Using this, we will define the meaning of P as one of these three sets, which is the solution of the third problem.

This means that the main part of the declarative semantics in the existing theory of logic programs can be generally reconstructed on parameterized representation systems with a simple and clear structure.

The parameterized representation system is a very general (perhaps the most general) structure on which a declarative semantics (minimal model semantics and the least fixpoint semantics) can be properly discussed. By constructing parameterized representation systems that correspond to given knowledge representation systems, we can regard many such systems as generalized logic programs and can apply the declarative semantics in this paper to them all.

1.3 Definitions and notations

In this paper we use the following definitions and notations. The powerset of a set X is defined as the set of all subsets of X and is denoted by $powerset(X)$.

A partial mapping f from a set X to a set Y is defined as a triple $< X, Y, R >$ such that

1. R is a subset of $X \times Y$.
2. $(x, y_1), (x, y_2) \in R \rightarrow y_1 = y_2$.

A partial mapping f is a triple $< X, Y, R >$, but is often dealt with as if it were a subset R of $X \times Y$. Partial mapping $f =< X, Y, R >$ is said to be applicable to

$x \in X$ if $\exists y \in Y : (x, y) \in R$. We say that f is defined (respectively, undefined) at x if f is applicable (respectively, not applicable) to x. The domain of f, which is denoted by $Domain(f)$, is defined as the set of all elements in X to which f is applicable. We write $f(x) = y$ if $(x, y) \in R$. We also write $f(x) =$ undefined if f is not applicable to x. The set of all partial mappings from a set X to a set Y is denoted by $partial\_map(X, Y)$. $partial\_map(X)$ is defined as $partial\_map(X, X)$.

A mapping f from a set X to a set Y is defined as a partial mapping $< X, Y, R >$ such that $Domain(f) = X$. Mapping f is often called a total mapping in order to stress its applicability to all elements in X. The set of all mappings from a set X to a set Y is denoted by $map(X, Y)$. $map(X)$ is equivalent to $map(X, X)$.

2 Representation Systems and Parameterized Representation Systems

We now introduce the two most basic structures in the GLP theory: representation systems and parameterized representation systems.

2.1 Representation systems

An atom $p(g(X), X)$ determines a set $\{p(g(X), X) \mid X \text{ is a ground term }\}$, which is a subset of the set of all ground atoms. A logic program P consisting of a clause `mortal(X)` $\leftarrow$ `human(X)` and a clause `human(socrates)` $\leftarrow$ represents a set $\{$`mortal(socrates)`, `human(socrates)`$\}$, which is also a subset of the set of all ground atoms. As we can see in these examples, what is represented is very often a subset of a given set. This observation leads us to the following definition :

Definition 1 *A representation system is a triple* $< \mathcal{A}, \mathcal{G}, rep >$, *where* $\mathcal{A}$ *and* $\mathcal{G}$ *are arbitrary sets, and* rep *is a mapping from* $\mathcal{A}$ *to* $powerset(\mathcal{G})$. *For each element* a *in* $\mathcal{A}$, $rep(a)$ *is called a representation set of* a, *and* rep *is called a representation mapping.*

For example, let $\mathcal{A}$ be the set of all context-free grammars whose terminal symbols are elements of a set Σ. Let $\mathcal{G}$ be the set Σ^*— that is, the set of all strings on Σ. A subset of $\mathcal{G}$ is called a language on Σ. Each grammar a in $\mathcal{A}$ determines a language l on Σ, which defines the mapping $rep : \mathcal{A} \rightarrow powerset(\mathcal{G})$ such that $rep(a) = l$. Obviously $< \mathcal{A}, \mathcal{G}, rep >$ is a representation system. The representation set of a grammar is a language.

2.2 Parameterized representation systems

A parameterized representation system is a generalization of the interrelations between atoms (or terms), ground atoms (or terms), and substitutions.

Definition 2 *A parameterized representation system is defined as a four-tuple* $< \mathcal{A}, \mathcal{G}, \mathcal{S}, f >$, *where* $\mathcal{A}$, $\mathcal{G}$, *and* $\mathcal{S}$ *are arbitrary sets, and* f *is a mapping from* $\mathcal{S}$ *to* $partial\_map(\mathcal{A}, \mathcal{G})$. *Elements of* $\mathcal{A}$ *are called atoms.* $\mathcal{G}$ *is called the interpretation domain.*

In first-order logic, let $\mathcal{A}_1$ be the set of all atoms, $\mathcal{G}_1$ the set of all ground atoms, $\mathcal{S}_1$ the set of all substitutions, and f_1 the mapping that determines, for any substitution $s \in \mathcal{S}_1$, the partial mapping from $\mathcal{A}_1$ to $\mathcal{G}_1$ defined by the application of the substitution s to atoms in $\mathcal{A}_1$. Then it is clear that $\mathrm{PRS}_1 =< \mathcal{A}_1, \mathcal{G}_1, \mathcal{S}_1, f_1 >$ is a parameterized representation system.

Similarly, let $\mathcal{A}_2$ be the set of all terms, $\mathcal{G}_2$ the set of all ground terms, $\mathcal{S}_2$ the set of all substitutions, and f_2 the mapping that determines, for any substitution $s \in \mathcal{S}_2$, the partial mapping from $\mathcal{A}_2$ to $\mathcal{G}_2$ defined by the application of the substitution s to terms in $\mathcal{A}_2$. Then it is clear that $\mathrm{PRS}_2 =< \mathcal{A}_2, \mathcal{G}_2, \mathcal{S}_2, f_2 >$ is a parameterized representation system.

We can also consider more artificial examples. For example, let

$$\begin{aligned}
&\mathcal{A}_3 = \{x, y, z\},\\
&\mathcal{G}_3 = \{p, q, r, s, t\},\\
&\mathcal{S}_3 = \{a, b, c\},\\
&f_3 =< \mathcal{S}_3, partial_map(\mathcal{A}_3, \mathcal{G}_3),\\
&\qquad \{\ (a, < \mathcal{A}_3, \mathcal{G}_3, \{(x,p), (y,q), (z,r)\} >),\\
&\qquad\ \ (b, < \mathcal{A}_3, \mathcal{G}_3, \{(z,p)\} >),\\
&\qquad\ \ (c, < \mathcal{A}_3, \mathcal{G}_3, \{(x,q), (y,s)\} >)\ \} >.
\end{aligned}$$

Then the four-tuple $\mathrm{PRS}_3 = < \mathcal{A}_3, \mathcal{G}_3, \mathcal{S}_3, f_3 >$ is a parameterized representation system. Note that the definition of f_3 means that f_3 is a mapping from $\mathcal{S}_3$ to $partial\_map(\mathcal{A}_3, \mathcal{G}_3)$ such that $f_3(a)(x) = p$, $f_3(a)(y) = q$, $f_3(a)(z) = r$, $f_3(b)(x) =$ undefined, $f_3(b)(y) =$ undefined, $f_3(b)(z) = p$, $f_3(c)(x) = q$, $f_3(c)(y) = s$, and $f_3(c)(z) =$ undefined. Note also that b and c in $\mathcal{S}_3$ define partial mappings and that $\mathcal{A}_3$ and $\mathcal{G}_3$ are disjoint.

We give another example of a parameterized representation system, which will be used in a later explanation. Let $\mathcal{A}_4$ be the set of all atoms (in the usual form) consisting of predicates (`plus`,$\cdots$), numbers (0,1,2,3, $\cdots$), and variables (`X`,`Y`,`Z`, $\cdots$). $\mathcal{A}_4$ includes, for instance, `plus(X,3,Y)` and `positive(Z)`. Let $\mathcal{G}_4$ be the set of all atoms (in the usual form) consisting of predicates and numbers. $\mathcal{G}_4$ includes, for instance, `plus(1,3,4)` and `positive(34)`. Let $\mathcal{S}_4$ be the set of substitutions consisting of variables and numbers. For example, $\{\mathtt{X/2},\ \mathtt{Y/5}\}$ is in $\mathcal{S}_4$. Let f_4 be a mapping that gives, for any substitution $s \in \mathcal{S}_4$, a partial mapping from $\mathcal{A}_4$ to $\mathcal{G}_4$ that is determined by s. For example, $f_4(\{\mathtt{X/2}, \mathtt{Y/5}\})(\mathtt{plus}(\mathtt{X}, 3, \mathtt{Y}))$ $= \mathtt{plus}(2, 3, 5)$ and $f_4(\{\mathtt{X/2}\})(\mathtt{plus}(\mathtt{X}, 3, \mathtt{Y})) =$ undefined. From these, we define $PRS_4 =< \mathcal{A}_4, \mathcal{G}_4, \mathcal{S}_4, f_4 >$. Then PRS_4 is obviously a parameterized representation system.

2.3 Representation systems and parameterized representation systems

On the basis of the following proposition, we regard every parameterized representation system as a representation system.

Proposition 1 *If $< \mathcal{A}, \mathcal{G}, \mathcal{S}, f >$ is a parameterized representation system and $rep : \mathcal{A} \rightarrow powerset(\mathcal{G})$ is defined as*

$$rep(a) = \{g \mid \exists s \in \mathcal{S} : f(s)(a) = g \in \mathcal{G}\},$$

then triple $< \mathcal{A}, \mathcal{G}, rep >$ is a representation system.

Proof. Obvious from the definition. □

For example, in PRS_3, let $rep_3(x) = \{p, q\}$, $rep_3(y) = \{q, s\}$, and $rep_3(z) = \{r, p\}$; then $< \mathcal{A}_3, \mathcal{G}_3, rep_3 >$ is a representation system.

2.4 Notations

When we discuss one given parameterized representation system $< \mathcal{A}, \mathcal{G}, \mathcal{S}, f >$, each element s in $\mathcal{S}$ is utilized uniquely as a partial mapping $f(s)$ from $\mathcal{A}$ to $\mathcal{G}$ because f is fixed. Therefore, when there is no danger of confusion, we regard elements in $\mathcal{S}$ as partial mappings from $\mathcal{A}$ to $\mathcal{G}$, and we use the following notational convention. Each element in $\mathcal{S}$ that is identified as a partial mapping on $\mathcal{A}$ is denoted by a Greek letter such as θ, and application of such a partial mapping is represented in terms of postfix notation. For example, $s \in \mathcal{S}$ and $f(s)(a)$ are represented, respectively, as $\theta \in \mathcal{S}$ and $a\theta$.

In the rest of this paper, we assume that a parameterized representation system $< \mathcal{A}, \mathcal{G}, \mathcal{S}, f >$ is given.

3 Logic Programs on Parameterized Representation Systems

We introduce logical connectives and quantifiers and define formulae (p-formulae and c-formulae) on parameterized representation systems. Classifying c-formulae into subclasses, we introduce clauses, Horn clauses, and program clauses, and we define logic programs on parameterized representation systems.

The discussion here concerns only the syntax of the formulae. The semantics of the formulae is described in Section 4.

3.1 p-formulae on arbitrary sets

We introduce logical connectives and define p-formulae on an arbitrary set.

Definition 3 *$\neg$, $\wedge$ and $\vee$ are logical connectives.*

The intended meanings of the logical connectives are negation ($\neg$), conjunction ($\wedge$), and disjunction ($\vee$). We assume that the logical connectives are different from other symbols.

Definition 4 *For any set B, p-formulae on B are defined inductively as follows :*

1. *Each element of B is a p-formula on B, which is called an atom on B.*
2. *If b_1 and b_2 are p-formulae on B, then $(\neg b_1), (b_1 \wedge b_2)$, and $(b_1 \vee b_2)$ are p-formulae on B.*

We drop the parentheses from p-formulae when no confusion is possible. The set of all p-formulae on B is denoted by $PF(B)$.

We give some examples of p-formulae. Assume that B includes $p(X)$ and $q(X, Y, 2)$. Then they themselves and $\neg p(X)$, $\neg q(X, Y, 2)$, $p(X) \wedge q(X, Y, 2)$, and $\neg(p(X) \vee q(X, Y, 2))$ are p-formulae on B. When B includes 7 and $\{6, 4\}$, then $7 \vee \neg\{6, 4\}$ and $(\neg 7) \wedge (\neg(\neg\{6, 4\}))$ are p-formulae on B.

Most readers may feel it strange to regard such expressions as $7 \vee \neg\{6, 4\}$ as well-formed logical formulae. This is because, in conventional logic, 7 and $\{6, 4\}$ cannot be atoms. Note, however, that conventional logic has no mathematical evidence that could justify such a restriction on atoms. The GLP theory proves that such a restriction is unnecessary. The restriction often decreases the applicability of the theorems and prevents us from understanding and utilizing the full power of logic programming.

3.2 c-formulae on arbitrary sets

We introduce quantifiers and define c-formulae on an arbitrary set.

Definition 5 *$\forall$ and $\exists$ are quantifiers.*

$\forall$ and $\exists$ are called, respectively, a *universal quantifier* and an *existential quantifier*. We assume that quantifiers are different from other symbols.

Definition 6 *For any set B, c-formulae on B are defined inductively as follows :*

1. *If b is a p-formula on B, then $(\forall b)$ and $(\exists b)$ are c-formulae on B. $(\forall b)$ is called a universal closure, and $(\exists b)$ is called an existential closure.*
2. *If b_1 and b_2 are c-formulae on B, then $(\neg b_1)$, $(b_1 \wedge b_2)$, and $(b_1 \vee b_2)$ are c-formulae on B.*

We drop the parentheses from c-formulae when no confusion is possible. The set of all c-formulae on B is denoted by $CF(B)$.

We give some examples of c-formulae. When B includes $f(X, Y, 1)$, then $(\forall \neg f(X, Y, 1))$ and $(\exists f(X, Y, 1)) \wedge (\forall f(X, Y, 1))$ are c-formulae on B. When B includes 7 and $\{8, 2\}$, then $\forall(7 \vee \neg\{8, 2\})$ and $\exists((\neg 7) \wedge (\neg(\neg 7)))$ are c-formulae on B.

In conventional logic, expressions that have no bound variables between quantifiers and formulae are called universal closures or existential closures. $(\forall p(X, Y, 1))$ is a universal closure, and $(\exists p(X, Y, 1))$ is an existential closure. They are equal to, respectively, $(\forall X, \forall Y : p(X, Y, 1))$ and $(\exists X, \exists Y : p(X, Y, 1))$. Since c-formulae of the form $(\forall b)$ and $(\exists b)$ correspond to universal closures or existential closures, they have only one quantifier in front of a p-formula and have no bound variables. Other forms of universally or existentially quantified expressions, such as $(\forall X, \exists Y : p(X, Y, 1))$, are not necessary, at least for the theory in this paper. The meanings of c-formulae are defined in terms of the interpretations in Section 4.

3.3 Logic programs on parameterized representation systems

We now introduce clauses, Horn clauses, and program clauses as subclasses of c–formulae, and we define logic programs on parameterized representation systems.

Definition 7 *A positive literal on $\mathcal{A}$ is an element of $\mathcal{A}$, and a negative literal on $\mathcal{A}$ is the negation of an element of $\mathcal{A}$— that is, $(\neg a)$, where $a \in \mathcal{A}$. A literal on $\mathcal{A}$ is a positive literal on $\mathcal{A}$ or a negative literal on $\mathcal{A}$.*

Definition 8 *A clause on $\mathcal{A}$ is a c-formula of the form*

$$\forall(L_1 \vee L_2 \vee \cdots \vee L_m),$$

where L_i $(i = 1, 2, \cdots, m)$ is a literal on $\mathcal{A}$.

We will denote the clause with positive literals $A_1, A_2, \cdots, A_k$ and negative literals $\neg B_1, \neg B_2, \cdots, \neg B_n$ by

$$A_1, A_2, \cdots, A_k \leftarrow B_1, B_2, \cdots, B_n.$$

Definition 9 *A Horn clause on $\mathcal{A}$ is a clause on $\mathcal{A}$ with at most one positive literal.*

Definition 10 *A program clause on $\mathcal{A}$ is a clause with precisely one positive literal,*

$$H \leftarrow B_1, \cdots, B_n.$$

H is called the head and $B_1, \cdots, B_n$ is called the body of the program clause

Definition 11 *A logic program on $\mathcal{A}$ is a (possibly infinite) set of program clauses on $\mathcal{A}$.*

A logic program on $\mathcal{A}$ is also called a logic program on a parameterized representation system $< \mathcal{A}, \mathcal{G}, \mathcal{S}, f >$ or, simply, a logic program. This convention is also applied to other concepts such as literals, clauses, Horn clauses, and program clauses.

For example, $P = \{y \leftarrow x \quad ; \quad x \leftarrow\}$ is a logic program on PRS_3, where ";" separates program clauses.

We often call logic programs on parameterized representation systems *generalized logic programs* (GLPs) to stress the distinction from conventional logic programs.

3.4 Programs with infinite clauses

Conventional logic programs are restricted to a set with a finite number of clauses. This is partly because, when we represent clauses in the usual enumerative manner, infinite clauses can neither be stored in finite memory, nor be searched enumeratively in finite time.

Infinite clauses are, however, very useful from the theoretical viewpoint. For example, consider a parameterized representation system $PRS_4 =< \mathcal{A}_4, \mathcal{G}_4, \mathcal{S}_4, f_4 >$. Assume that `plus` is a predicate. A program P_1 that defines the `plus` relation for all non-negative integers can be written as follows :

$$P_1 = \{\texttt{plus}(x, y, z) \leftarrow \mid x + y = z, x \in N, y \in N, z \in N\},$$

where N is the set of all non-negative integers. P_1 consists of infinite clauses. On the other hand, there is no program that has finite clauses and defines the same `plus` relation.

However, in $\mathrm{PRS}_1 = < \mathcal{A}_1, \mathcal{G}_1, \mathcal{S}_1, f_1 >$, if we represent non-negative integers $0,1,2,3,\cdots$ by $0, s(0), s(s(0)), s(s(s(0))), \cdots$, then the `plus` relation for non-negative integers can be represented by the following finite program P_2:

$$P_2 = \{ \texttt{plus(s(X),Y,s(Z))} \leftarrow \texttt{plus(X,Y,Z)} \quad ; \quad \texttt{plus(0,Y,Y)} \leftarrow \}.$$

If we do not exclude the infinite program P_1, we can discuss the equivalent transformation of the infinite program P_1 into the finite program P_2 theoretically. It is the role of theoretical analysis to transform infinite programs into finite programs in order to increase the possibility of running programs on real machines.

Conventional theory does not deal with such infinite cases. But it has not been clarified whether there is any theoretical reason why we cannot consider infinite clauses. The GLP theory shows that such a restriction is not necessary, at least as long as we are discussing the declarative semantics of generalized logic programs.

4 Interpretations and Models

4.1 Interpretations

In order to discuss the meanings of c–formulae on a parameterized representation system, we define interpretations, which determine the truth or falsity of all c-formulae.

Definition 12 *An interpretation I on $\mathcal{G}$ is defined as a subset of the interpretation domain $\mathcal{G}$. An interpretation I is often regarded as a mapping from $\mathcal{G}$ to $V = \{true, false\}$, which is determined by $I(g) = true \Leftrightarrow g \in I$.*

If $\mathcal{G}$ is regarded as the Herbrand base in conventional theory, the meaning of the definition is more easily understood.

4.2 Associated mappings of logical connectives

Logical connectives are naturally associated with the following mappings :

Definition 13 *Let V be $\{true, false\}$. Negation $\neg$ is associated with the mapping $\neg : V \rightarrow V$. Conjunction $\wedge$ and disjunction $\vee$ are associated with the mappings $\wedge : V \times V \rightarrow V$ and $\vee : V \times V \rightarrow V$, respectively. We use $\neg$, $\wedge$, and $\vee$ not only as logical connectives, but also as the associated mappings. The three associated mappings are defined in the usual way [19].*

The two associated mappings $\wedge$ and $\vee$ are extended to the operation of any number (possibly infinite) of inputs that are given by a partial mapping to V.

Definition 14 *Let S be any set and v be any partial mapping from S to $V =$ $\{$ true, false $\}$. We define $[\wedge v(s) \mid s \in S]$ as true if $v(s)$ is true for all $s \in S$ such that $v(s)$ is defined and $[\vee v(s) \mid s \in S]$ as true if $v(s)$ is true for some $s \in S$ such that $v(s)$ is defined.*

4.3 Truth or falsity of p-formulae on $\mathcal{G}$

We define a mapping that determines the truth or falsity of p-formulae on the interpretation domain $\mathcal{G}$.

Definition 15 *An interpretation I on $\mathcal{G}$ determines the mapping val_I from $PF(\mathcal{G})$ to $V = \{true, false\}$ by the following formulae, where $g \in \mathcal{G}$ and $x, y \in PF(\mathcal{G})$:*

1. $val_I(g) = I(g)$.
2. $val_I(\neg x) = \neg val_I(x)$.
3. $val_I(x \wedge y) = val_I(x) \wedge val_I(y)$.
4. $val_I(x \vee y) = val_I(x) \vee val_I(y)$.

In $PRS_3 = \langle \mathcal{A}_3, \mathcal{G}_3, \mathcal{S}_3, f_3 \rangle$, when $I = \{p, q\}$, $val_I(q \vee (\neg p)) = true$ because $val_I(q) = true$, $val_I(p) = true$, and $val_I(\neg p) = false$. Similarly, $val_I(s \vee (\neg q)) = false$, because $val_I(s) = false$, $val_I(q) = true$, and $val_I(\neg q) = false$.

4.4 p-formulae on $\mathcal{A}$ and on $\mathcal{G}$

We extend the partial mapping $f(s) : \mathcal{A} \rightarrow \mathcal{G}$ to get a partial mapping $inst_s$ from $PF(\mathcal{A})$ to $PF(\mathcal{G})$.

Definition 16 *For any element s in $\mathcal{S}$, a partial mapping $inst_s$ from $PF(\mathcal{A})$ to $PF(\mathcal{G})$ is defined as follows, where $a \in \mathcal{A}$ and $x, y \in PF(\mathcal{A})$:*

1. $inst_s(a) = f(s)(a) \cdots if\ f(s)(a)$ *is defined.*
2. $inst_s(a) =$ *undefined* $\cdots if\ f(s)(a)$ *is undefined.*
3. $inst_s(\neg x) = \neg inst_s(x)$.
4. $inst_s(x \wedge y) = inst_s(x) \wedge inst_s(y)$.
5. $inst_s(x \vee y) = inst_s(x) \vee inst_s(y)$.

$inst_s(x)$ is defined if $f(s)(a)$ is defined for any atom a that appears in $x \in PF(\mathcal{A})$.

In $PRS_3 = < \mathcal{A}_3, \mathcal{G}_3, \mathcal{S}_3, f_3 >$, let u be a p-formula $y \vee (\neg x)$ on $\mathcal{A}_3$. Then,

1. $inst_a(u) = (q \vee (\neg p)) \quad \in PF(\mathcal{G}_3)$.
2. $inst_b(u) =$ undefined $\quad \cdots \quad f_3(b)(x)$ and $f_3(b)(y)$ are undefined.
3. $inst_c(u) = (s \vee (\neg q)) \quad \in PF(\mathcal{G}_3)$.

4.5 Truth or falsity of c-formulae on $\mathcal{A}$

We now give the semantics of c-formulae on $\mathcal{A}$. Universal and existential closures in the GLP theory are included in c-formulae. In conventional theory, universal and existential quantifiers bind all variables in universal and existential closures. On the other hand, in the definition of c-formulae in the GLP theory, we do not use the concept of variables. How can we give well-defined semantics to universal or existential closures in the GLP theory without referring to the concept of variables? We can solve this problem by defining the truth or falsity of c-formulae on $\mathcal{A}$ in the following way :

Definition 17 *An interpretation I on $\mathcal{G}$ determines the mapping $value_I$ from $CF(\mathcal{A})$ to $V = \{true, false\}$ as follows, where $z \in PF(\mathcal{A})$ and $x, y \in CF(\mathcal{A})$:*

1. $value_I(\forall z) = [\wedge val_I(inst_s(z)) \mid s \in \mathcal{S}]$.
2. $value_I(\exists z) = [\vee val_I(inst_s(z)) \mid s \in \mathcal{S}]$.
3. $value_I(\neg x) = \neg value_I(x)$.
4. $value_I(x \wedge y) = value_I(x) \wedge value_I(y)$.
5. $value_I(x \vee y) = value_I(x) \vee value_I(y)$.

This definition is based on the observation that universal (respectively, existential) closures are equivalent in conventional theory to the conjunction (respectively, disjunction) of all ground instances of them, and that ground instances of them can be generated by $inst_s$ in the GLP theory. Note that only the elements $s \in \mathcal{S}$ such that $inst_s(z)$ are defined are related to the values of $value_I(\forall z)$ and $value_I(\exists z)$.

In $PRS_3 = < \mathcal{A}_3, \mathcal{G}_3, \mathcal{S}_3, f_3 >$, let u be a p-formula $y \vee (\neg x)$ on $\mathcal{A}_3$. Then, $\forall u$ is a c-formula on $\mathcal{A}_3$. Let us find $value_I(\forall u)$ for an interpretation $I = \{p, q\}$. As has already been shown, $inst_a(u) = (q \vee (\neg p))$, $inst_b(u) =$ undefined, and $inst_c(u) = (s \vee (\neg q))$. Therefore,

$$value_I(\forall u) = val_I(q \vee (\neg p)) \wedge val_I(s \vee (\neg q)).$$

We already know that $val_I(q \vee (\neg p)) = true$ and $val_I(s \vee (\neg q)) = false$. Therefore, $value_I(\forall u) = false$.

4.6 Models

The concept of models is defined by using the mapping $value_I$ in the same way as in conventional theory of logic programs.

Definition 18 *An interpretation I on $\mathcal{G}$ is a model of a subset E of $CF(\mathcal{A})$ if $value_I(e) = true$ for every element e in E. The set of all models of E is denoted by $Model(E)$. An interpretation I on $\mathcal{G}$ is a model of an element e of $CF(\mathcal{A})$ if I is a model of $\{e\}$. The set of all models of e is denoted by $Model(e)$.*

Again we use $u = y \vee (\neg x)$ in $PRS_3 = < \mathcal{A}_3, \mathcal{G}_3, \mathcal{S}_3, f_3 >$ and show that an interpretation $I = \{p, q, r, s\}$ is a model of $\{\forall u\}$. We already know that

$$value_I(\forall u) = val_I(q \vee (\neg p)) \wedge val_I(s \vee (\neg q)).$$

When $I = \{p, q, r, s\}$, we have $val_I(q) = true$, $val_I(p) = true$, and $val_I(\neg p) = false$. Then, $val_I(q \vee (\neg p)) = true$. Similarly, $val_I(s) = true$, $val_I(q) = true$, and $val_I(\neg q) = false$. Then, $val_I(s \vee (\neg q)) = true$. Therefore, $value_I(\forall u) = true$; that is, $I = \{p, q, r, s\}$ is a model of $\{\forall u\}$.

4.7 Logical consequences

Logical consequences are defined in terms of models in the usual way.

Definition 19 *Let E_1 and E_2 be subsets of $CF(\mathcal{A})$. E_2 is a logical consequence of E_1 ($E_1 \models E_2$) if it is true that, for any interpretation I on $\mathcal{G}$, if I is a model of E_1, then I is a model of E_2. A c-formula $e \in CF(\mathcal{A})$ is a logical consequence of E_1 ($E_1 \models e$) if $E_1 \models \{e\}$. E_2 is a logical consequence of a c-formula $e \in CF(\mathcal{A})$ ($e \models E_2$) if $\{e\} \models E_2$.*

In $PRS_3 = < \mathcal{A}_3, \mathcal{G}_3, \mathcal{S}_3, f_3 >$, let $E_1 = \{\forall(y \vee (\neg x)), \forall x\}$ and $E_2 = \{\forall y\}$. Then, for any interpretation I,

$value_I(\forall(y \vee (\neg x))) = val_I(q \vee (\neg p)) \wedge val_I(s \vee (\neg q))$,
$value_I(\forall x) = val_I(p) \wedge val_I(q)$.

The models of E_1 are $I_1 = \{p, q, s\}$, $I_2 = \{p, q, r, s\}$, $I_3 = \{p, q, s, t\}$, and $I_4 = \{p, q, r, s, t\}$. On the other hand, for any interpretation I,

$value_I(\forall y) = val_I(q) \wedge val_I(s)$.

Therefore, each model (I_1, I_2, I_3, and I_4) of E_1 is also a model of E_2. This means that $E_1 \models E_2$.

5 Minimal Model Semantics

We prove that there is a minimal model of any logic program on a parameterized representation system. We will show in Section 7.2 that the meaning of a logic program on a parameterized representation system should be the minimal model of such a logic program.

Proposition 2 (Model Intersection Property) *If $\{M_j \mid j \in J\}$ is a non-empty set of models of a Horn clause h, then the interpretation $[\bigcap M_j \mid j \in J]$ is also a model of h.*

Proof. See the appendix. □

Proposition 3 *If there is a model of a set of Horn clauses P, then there is a minimal model M_P, and*

$$M_P = [\bigcap M \mid M \in Model(P)].$$

Proof. Let $\{M_j \mid j \in J\}$ be the set of all models of P. From the assumption, this set is not empty. Let h be any element of P; then M_j is a model of h. Since h is a Horn clause and $\{M_j \mid j \in J\}$ is a non-empty set of the models of h, then, from Proposition 2, the interpretation $M_P = [\bigcap M_j \mid j \in J]$ is also a model of h. Since h is any element of P, M_P is a model of P. Since M_P is a subset of any element of $\{M_j \mid j \in J\}$, and $\{M_j \mid j \in J\}$ is the set of all models of P, M_P is the minimal model of P and $M_P = [\bigcap M \mid M \in Model(P)]$. □

Theorem 1 *Every logic program P has a minimal model M_P, and*

$$M_P = [\bigcap M \mid M \in Model(P)]$$

Proof. Let c be any program clause of a logic program P. We can assume that $c = \forall(H \vee B)$, where H is the head of c, and B is $\neg B_1 \vee \neg B_2 \vee \cdots \vee \neg B_n$ for $n \geq 0$. Let an interpretation M on $\mathcal{G}$ be defined by $\mathcal{G}$. Then,

$$\begin{aligned} value_M(c) &= value_M(\forall(H \vee B)) \\ &= [\wedge val_M(inst_s(H \vee B)) \mid s \in \mathcal{S}] \\ &= [\wedge(val_M(inst_s(H)) \vee val_M(inst_s(H \vee B))) \mid s \in \mathcal{S}] \\ &= [\wedge(true \vee val_M(inst_s(H \vee B))) \mid s \in \mathcal{S}] \\ &= true. \end{aligned}$$

Thus M is a model of c. Since c is any element of P, M is a model of P. Consequently, P is a set of Horn clauses that has a model. Using Proposition 3, we can conclude that there is a minimal model M_P of P and that $M_P = [\bigcap M \mid M \in Model(P)]$. □

Let $P = \{y \leftarrow x \quad ; \quad x \leftarrow\}$ be a program on $PRS_3 = < \mathcal{A}_3, \mathcal{G}_3, \mathcal{S}_3, f_3 >$. Since P is identical to $E_1 = \{\forall(y \vee (\neg x)), \forall x\}$ in Section 4.7, the models of P are $I_1 = \{p, q, s\}$, $I_2 = \{p, q, r, s\}$, $I_3 = \{p, q, s, t\}$, and $I_4 = \{p, q, r, s, t\}$. It is obvious that M_P, the minimal model of P, is equal to $I_1 = I_1 \cap I_2 \cap I_3 \cap I_4$.

6 Least Fixpoint Semantics

6.1 Least fixpoint theory on a complete lattice

We review the least fixpoint theory on a complete lattice [19, 22].

A set S is a *partially ordered set* if S is associated with a partial order on S For every subset X of a partially ordered set S, the *least upper bound* of X, denoted by $lub(X)$, is unique, if it exists. Similarly, the *greatest lower bound* of X, denoted by $glb(X)$, is unique, if it exists. A partially ordered set L is a *complete lattice* if $lub(X)$ and $glb(X)$ exist for any subset X of L.

In the following, we assume that L is a complete lattice, that $\leq$ is a partial order on L, that $\perp$ is the minimal element in L, and that $F : L \rightarrow L$ is a mapping on L.

F is *monotonic* if $x \leq y$ implies that $F(x) \leq F(y)$ for any element x, y in L. A subset X of L is *directed* if every finite subset of X has an upper bound in X. F is *continuous* if $F(lub(X)) = lub(F(X))$ for any directed subset $X \subset L$.

$a \in L$ is a *fixpoint* of F if $F(a) = a$. $a \in L$ is a *least fixpoint* of F if a is a fixpoint of F and if $a \leq b$ for any fixpoint b of F. The least fixpoint of F is uniquely determined if it exists. The least fixpoint of F is denoted by $lfp(F)$ if it exists. $F \uparrow \omega$ is defined as $lub\{F^n(\bot) \mid n \geq 0\}$, where $F^0(x) = x$ and $F^n(x) = F(F^{n-1}(x))$ for $n \geq 1$.

Assume that F is continuous; then,

1. F is monotonic.
2. F is increasing; that is, $F^{n+1}(\bot) \geq F^n(\bot)$ for any $n \geq 0$.
3. $\{F^n(\bot)\}$ $(n \geq 0)$ is directed.

From these definitions and observations, we have the following theorem [19]:

Theorem 2 *If $F : L \rightarrow L$ is continuous, then $lfp(F) = F \uparrow \omega$.* □

6.2 Least fixpoints of T and K

In this section we assume that $T : L \rightarrow L$ is continuous.

For every element x, y in L, we define $x + y = lub\{x, y\}$. Let T_1 and T_2 be mappings on L. The mapping $T_1 + T_2$ on L is defined by

$$\forall x \in L : [T_1 + T_2](x) = T_1(x) + T_2(x).$$

Let $K : L \rightarrow L$ be defined by $K = T + I$, where I is the identity mapping on L.

Proposition 4 *K is continuous.*
Proof. Let X be a directed subset of L. ¿From the continuity of T, $K(lub(X))$ $= T(lub(X)) + lub(X) = lub(T(X)) + lub(X) = lub(T(X) + X) = lub(K(X))$. □

We prove that $K^n(\bot) = T^n(\bot)$ for all $n \geq 0$ and that $K \uparrow \omega = T \uparrow \omega$.

Proposition 5 *For all $n \geq 0$, $K^n(\bot) = T^n(\bot)$.*
Proof. We prove that $K^n(\bot) = T^n(\bot)$ for all $n \geq 0$ by induction. When $n = 0$, $K^0(\bot) = T^0(\bot)$ is obvious, since it is equivalent to $\bot = \bot$. Next we assume that $K^k(\bot) = T^k(\bot)$, and we prove $K^{k+1}(\bot) = T^{k+1}(\bot)$. Since $T^{n+1}(\bot) \geq T^n(\bot)$ for any $n \geq 0$, we have $K^{k+1}(\bot) = K(K^k(\bot)) = K(T^k(\bot)) = T(T^k(\bot)) + T^k(\bot) = T^{k+1}(\bot) + T^k(\bot) = T^{k+1}(\bot)$. □

Proposition 6 *$K \uparrow \omega = T \uparrow \omega$.*
Proof. Using Proposition 5, $K \uparrow \omega = lub\{K^n(\bot) \mid n \geq 0\} = lub\{T^n(\bot) \mid n \geq 0\}$ $= T \uparrow \omega$. □

We thus obtain the following theorem :

Theorem 3 *$lfp(K) = K \uparrow \omega = T \uparrow \omega = lfp(T)$.*
Proof. Obvious from the continuity of T and K, Theorem 2, and Proposition 6. □

6.3 Least fixpoint semantics

In this section we give the least fixpoint semantics of logic programs on parameterized representation systems. Let P be a logic program on a parameterized representation system. First we define an *immediate-consequence transformation* T_P that gives the result of one-step inference by the rules in a program P, and we prove that T_P is continuous. Next we define a *knowledge-increasing transformation* $K_P = T_P + I$ that represents the increase of knowledge by one-step inference by the rules in a program P. From Theorem 3, we conclude that K_P has the least fixpoint $lfp(K_P)$ and that it is equal to $K_P \uparrow \omega$.

Let Δ be a parameterized representation system $< \mathcal{A}, \mathcal{G}, \mathcal{S}, f >$. Let L be $powerset(\mathcal{G})$. Then L is a complete lattice with the inclusion relation as a partial order whose minimal element $\perp$ is the empty set $\emptyset$.

We define mappings T_P and K_P for a logic program P on Δ.

Definition 20 *Let P be a logic program on Δ. For each program P we define a transformation T_P on the power set L of $\mathcal{G}$ as follows. For any x in $L = powerset(\mathcal{G})$, we define*

$T_P(x) = \{g \mid \exists H, \exists B_1, \cdots, \exists B_m, \exists\theta : Cond(g, P, H, B_1, \cdots, B_m, \mathcal{S}, \theta, x)\}$,

where $Cond(g, P, H, B_1, \cdots, B_m, \mathcal{S}, \theta, x)$ is the conjunction of

1. *$H \leftarrow B_1, \cdots, B_m$ is a program clause in P.*
2. *$\theta \in \mathcal{S}$.*
3. *θ is applicable to H and $B_1, \cdots, B_m$.*
4. *$B_1\theta, \cdots, B_m\theta$ are elements in x.*
5. *$g = H\theta$.*

T_P is called the immediate-consequence transformation of P.

In the following, we use $Cond(g, x)$ as an abbreviation of the above-defined condition, $Cond(g, P, H, B_1, \cdots, B_m, \mathcal{S}, \theta, x)$.

Let $P = \{y \leftarrow x \;\; ; \;\; x \leftarrow\}$ be a program on $PRS_3 = < \mathcal{A}_3, \mathcal{G}_3, \mathcal{S}_3, f_3 >$. Then, $T_P(\emptyset) = \{p, q\}$, $T_P(\{r\}) = \{p, q\}$, $T_P(\{p, s\}) = \{p, q\}$, $T_P(\{p, q\}) = \{p, q, s\}$, $T_P(\{p, q, s\}) = \{p, q, s\}$, $T_P(\{p, q, r, t\}) = \{p, q, s\}$, $T_P(\{q, r, s, t\}) = \{p, q, s\}$ and $T_P(\{p, q, r, s, t\}) = \{p, q, s\}$. More generally, $T_P(S) = \{p, q\}$ if $q \notin S$, and $T_P(S) = \{p, q, s\}$ if $q \in S$.

Proposition 7 *Let X be a directed subset of L. Then $\{g_1, g_2, \cdots, g_n\} \subset lub(X)$ if $\{g_1, g_2, \cdots, g_n\} \subset x$ for some $x \in X$.*

Proof.

1. **[if]** Assume that $\{g_1, g_2, \cdots, g_n\} \subset x$ for some $x \in X$. Since $x \subset lub(X)$, we have $\{g_1, g_2, \cdots, g_n\} \subset lub(X)$.
2. **[only if]** Assume that $\{g_1, g_2, \cdots, g_n\} \subset lub(X)$. Since $lub(X)$ is the union of all the sets in X, there are n elements $x_1, x_2, \cdots, x_n$ in X such that $g_i \in x_i (i = 1, 2, \cdots, n)$. Since X is directed, there is an element $x \in X$ such that $x_i \subset x (i = 1, 2, \cdots, n)$. Therefore $\{g_1, g_2, \cdots, g_n\} \subset x$ and $x \in X$. □

Proposition 8 *$T_P : L \rightarrow L$ is continuous.*

Proof. Let X be a directed subset of L. From Proposition 7, $Cond(g, lub(X))$ if $\exists x \in X : Cond(g, x)$. Therefore we have

$g \in T_P(lub(X))$
$\Leftrightarrow \exists H, \exists B_1, \cdots, \exists B_m, \exists \theta : Cond(g, lub(X))$.
$\Leftrightarrow \exists H, \exists B_1, \cdots, \exists B_m, \exists \theta, \exists x \in X : Cond(g, x)$.
$\Leftrightarrow \exists x \in X : g \in T_P(x)$.
$\Leftrightarrow g \in lub(T_P(X))$.
Therefore $T_P(lub(X)) = lub(T_P(X))$. □

Definition 21 *For any logic program P, a transformation K_P on the powerset L of $\mathcal{G}$ is defined by $K_P = T_P + I$, where I is the identity mapping on L. K_P is called the knowledge-increasing transformation of P.*

Let $P = \{y \leftarrow x \quad ; \quad x \leftarrow\}$ be a program on $PRS_3 = < \mathcal{A}_3, \mathcal{G}_3, \mathcal{S}_3, f_3 >$. Then, $K_P(\emptyset) = \{p, q\}$, $K_P(\{r\}) = \{p, q, r\}$, $K_P(\{p, s\}) = \{p, q, s\}$, $K_P(\{p, q\}) = \{p, q, s\}$, $K_P(\{p, q, s\}) = \{p, q, s\}$, $K_P(\{p, q, r, t\}) = \{p, q, r, s, t\}$, $K_P(\{q, r, s, t\}) = \{p, q, r, s, t\}$, and $K_P(\{p, q, r, s, t\}) = \{p, q, r, s, t\}$.

Theorem 4 $lfp(K_P) = K_P \uparrow \omega = T_P \uparrow \omega = lfp(T_P)$.
Proof. Obvious from Theorem 3, Proposition 8, and Definition 21. □

In spite of Theorem 4, I believe that it is better to use the fixpoints of K_P, rather than the fixpoints of T_P, in order to define the semantics of P. This is because the fixpoints of T_P do not seem to have any natural and intuitive interpretation for explaining the semantics of P. On the other hand, the fixpoints of K_P are meaningful, because x is a fixpoint of K_P if we cannot increase x by using the rules in P.

Let $P = \{y \leftarrow x \quad ; \quad x \leftarrow\}$ be a program on $PRS_3 = < \mathcal{A}_3, \mathcal{G}_3, \mathcal{S}_3, f_3 >$. Then, the fixpoints of K_P are

1. $K_P(\{p, q, s\}) = \{p, q, s\}$.
2. $K_P(\{p, q, r, s\}) = \{p, q, r, s\}$.
3. $K_P(\{p, q, s, t\}) = \{p, q, s, t\}$.
4. $K_P(\{p, q, r, s, t\}) = \{p, q, r, s, t\}$.

Obviously the least fixpoint of K_P is $\{p, q, s\}$. On the other hand, since
$K_P(\emptyset) = \{p, q\}$,
$K_P^2(\emptyset) = K_P(\{p, q\}) = \{p, q, s\}$,
$K_P^3(\emptyset) = K_P(\{p, q, s\}) = \{p, q, s\}$,
we can conclude that $K_P \uparrow \omega = \{p, q, s\}$. Hence,

$$lfp(K_P) = K_P \uparrow \omega = \{p, q, s\}.$$

7 Semantics of Generalized Logic Programs

7.1 Minimal model = least fixpoint

In this section we prove that an interpretation I is a model of P if I is a fixpoint of K_P; that is,

$$I \in Model(P) \Leftrightarrow K_P(I) = I.$$

Using this relation, we also prove that the minimal model M_P of a logic program P and the least fixpoint $lfp(K_P)$ of K_P are identical.

Theorem 5 *Let P be a logic program, I an interpretation on $\mathcal{G}$, and K_P the knowledge-increasing transformation of P; then*

$$I \in Model(P) \Leftrightarrow K_P(I) = I.$$

Proof.

$$
\begin{array}{ll}
 & I \in Model(P) \\
\Leftrightarrow & \forall c \in P : value_I(c) = true. \\
\Leftrightarrow & \text{For any clause } (H \leftarrow B_1, \cdots, B_m) \text{ in } P, \\
 & \quad value_I(\forall(H \vee \neg B_1 \vee \cdots \vee \neg B_m)) = true. \\
\Leftrightarrow & \text{For any clause } c = (H \leftarrow B_1, \cdots, B_m) \text{ in } P \text{ and} \\
 & \text{for any element } \theta \in \mathcal{S} \text{ applicable to } c, \\
 & \quad val_I(H\theta \vee \neg B_1\theta \vee \cdots \vee \neg B_m\theta) = true.
\end{array}
$$

Here we can transform the subformula in the above expression as follows :

$$
\begin{array}{ll}
 & val_I(H\theta \vee \neg B_1\theta \vee \cdots \vee \neg B_m\theta) = true \\
\Leftrightarrow & val_I(H\theta) \vee \neg val_I(B_1\theta) \vee \cdots \vee \neg val_I(B_m\theta) = true. \\
\Leftrightarrow & \text{If } val_I(B_1\theta) \wedge \cdots \wedge val_I(B_m\theta) = true, \text{ then } val_I(H\theta) = true. \\
\Leftrightarrow & \text{If } (B_1\theta \in I), \cdots, (B_m\theta \in I), \text{ then } H\theta \in I.
\end{array}
$$

Therefore the whole formula can be transformed as follows :

$$
\begin{array}{ll}
\Leftrightarrow & \text{For any clause } c = (H \leftarrow B_1, \cdots, B_m) \text{ in } P \text{ and} \\
 & \text{for any element } \theta \in \mathcal{S} \text{ applicable to } c, \\
 & \quad \text{if } (B_1\theta \in I), \cdots, (B_m\theta \in I), \text{ then } H\theta \in I. \\
\Leftrightarrow & \text{For any clause } c = (H \leftarrow B_1, \cdots, B_m) \text{ in } P \text{ and} \\
 & \text{for any element } \theta \in \mathcal{S} \text{ applicable to } c, \\
 & \quad \text{if } g = H\theta, (B_1\theta \in I), \cdots, (B_m\theta \in I), \text{ then } g \in I. \\
\Leftrightarrow & \forall g \forall H, \forall B_1, \cdots, \forall B_m, \forall \theta : [\, Cond(g, I) \rightarrow g \in I \,]. \\
\Leftrightarrow & \forall g : [\,[\, \exists H, \exists B_1, \cdots, \exists B_m, \exists \theta : Cond(g, I)\,] \rightarrow g \in I\,]. \\
\Leftrightarrow & \text{If } g \in T_P(I), \text{ then } g \in I. \\
\Leftrightarrow & T_P(I) \leq I. \\
\Leftrightarrow & T_P(I) + I = I. \\
\Leftrightarrow & K_P(I) = I.
\end{array}
$$

□

Let $P = \{y \leftarrow x \quad ; \quad x \leftarrow\}$ be a program on $PRS_3 = < \mathcal{A}_3, \mathcal{G}_3, \mathcal{S}_3, f_3 >$. Then the models of P are (as shown in Section 5) $I_1 = \{p, q, s\}$, $I_2 = \{p, q, r, s\}$, $I_3 = \{p, q, s, t\}$, and $I_4 = \{p, q, r, s, t\}$. The fixpoints of K_P are (as shown in Section 6.3) $\{p, q, s\}$, $\{p, q, r, s\}$, $\{p, q, s, t\}$, and $\{p, q, r, s, t\}$. These models and fixpoints correspond to each other.

Theorem 6 $M_P = lfp(K_P)$.

Proof.

$$
\begin{array}{lll}
M_P & = min\ \{\ I \mid I \in Model(P)\} & \\
 & = min\ \{I \mid K_P(I) = I\ \} & \text{from Theorem 5} \\
 & = lfp(K_P). &
\end{array}
$$

□

7.2 Semantics of generalized logic programs

From Theorems 6 and 4, we conclude that $M_P = lfp(K_P) = K_P \uparrow \omega$. On the basis of this result, we define the representation set $REP(P)$ of a logic program P on a parameterized representation system as follows :

Definition 22 *Let PROG be the set of all the logic programs P on a parameterized representation system* $< \mathcal{A}, \mathcal{G}, \mathcal{S}, f >$. $REP : PROG \rightarrow powerset(\mathcal{G})$ *is the mapping that gives* M_P *(which is equal to* $lfp(K_P)$ *and* $K_P \uparrow \omega$*) for each element P in PROG.*

Proposition 9 $< PROG, \mathcal{G}, REP >$ *is a representation system.*
Proof. Obvious from the definition. □

Assume that $P = \{y \leftarrow x, z \leftarrow\}$ is a program on the parameterized representation system $< \mathcal{A}_3, \mathcal{G}_3, \mathcal{S}_3, f_3 >$. Then all models of P are $\{p, q, r, s\}$ and $\{p, q, r, s, t\}$. Obviously the minimal model of P is $\{p, q, r, s\}$. Since $K_P(\emptyset) = \{p, r\}$, $K_P(\{p, r\}) = \{p, q, r\}$, $K_P(\{p, q, r\}) = \{p, q, r, s\}$, and $K_P(\{p, q, r, s\}) = \{p, q, r, s\}$, we have $K_P \uparrow \omega = \{p, q, r, s\}$. Since the fixpoints of K_P are $\{p, q, r, s\}$ and $\{p, q, r, s, t\}$, the least fixpoint of K_P is $\{p, q, r, s\}$. Hence the meaning of P is

$$REP(P) = M_P = lfp(K_P) = K_P \uparrow \omega = \{p, q, r, s\}.$$

8 Concluding Remarks

In the first part of this paper, we introduced a structure called parameterized representation systems (PRSs), which forms the basis of generalized logic programs. A parameterized representation system is an abstraction of the interrelations between atomic formulae (or terms), ground atomic formulae (or terms), and substitutions.

We then defined formulae on a PRS, and introduced subclasses of the formulae, such as clauses, Horn clauses, and program clauses on a PRS. We defined logic programs, interpretations, models, and logical consequences based only on a PRS.

We proved that any logic program on a PRS has a minimal model. We also discussed the least fixpoint semantics for logic programs on a PRS, where the immediate-consequence transformation T_P and the knowledge-increasing transformation $K_P = T_P + I$ play an important role. We proved that K_P has the least fixpoint $lfp(K_P)$ and that it is equal to $K_P \uparrow \omega$. Finally, we proved that the minimal model M_P and the least fixpoint $lfp(K_P)$ are equal. We can summarize these results as

$$M_P = lfp(K_P) = K_P \uparrow \omega,$$

which defines the representation set (meaning) of a generalized logic program P.

This paper has concentrated on the declarative semantics of generalized logic programs based on parameterized representation systems. For further discussions about unification, inference, unfolding, program transformation, resolution, and other procedural aspects of generalized logic programs, we previously introduced another structure, called *specialization systems* [3]. Specialization systems are considered to be a subclass of parameterized representation systems, and all the results in this paper can be applied to them. Moreover, using logic programs on specialization systems, we previously discussed unification [3], inference [4, 7], unfolding [9, 10], program transformation [9], SLD resolution [3], types [12], and other aspects of declarative programs [5, 8, 11] at a new abstract level.

Many knowledge representation systems and programming languages, including context-free grammars, extension of Prolog, CLP languages [6, 18], and typed unification grammars [12, 16], can be regarded as generalized logic programs, because appropriate parameterized representation systems or specialization systems can be constructed for them. I believe that the GLP theory will provide a unified theoretical foundation for declarative knowledge representation systems and declarative programming languages.

Acknowledgements. The author is grateful to Professor Eiichi Miyamoto of Hokkaido University for his helpful advice. The author would also like to thank the members of PTP (icot working group) and WOL (workshop on learning) and the anonymous referees for their comments and suggestions.

References

[1] Ait-Kaci, H. and Nasr, R.: LOGIN: A Logic Programming Language with Built-in Inheritance, *J. of Logic Programming*, Vol. 3, No. 3 1986, pp. 185–215 .

[2] Akama, K.: Declarative Semantics of Logic Programs on Parameterized Representation Systems, *Hokkaido University Information Engineering Technical Report*, HIER-LI-9001, 1990.

[3] Akama, K.: Generalized Logic Programs on Specialization Systems and SLDA Resolution, *Hokkaido University Information Engineering Technical Report*, HIER-LI-9002, 1990.

[4] Akama, K.: Inference Rules for Generalized Logic Programs, *Hokkaido University Information Engineering Technical Report*, HIER-LI-9005, 1990.

[5] Akama, K.: Constructing Specialization Systems, *Hokkaido University Information Engineering Technical Report*, HIER-LI-9006, 1990.

[6] Akama, K.: CLP ⊂ GLP, *Hokkaido University Information Engineering Technical Report*, HIER-LI-9009, 1990.

[7] Akama, K.: Sufficient Conditions of Two Inference Rules for Generalized Logic Programs, *Proc. of the Logic Programming Conference '91* 1991, pp. 161–170.

[8] Akama, K.: Foundations of Predicate Invention, *Proc. of the Logic Programming Conference '91* 1991, pp. 171–180.

[9] Akama, K.: Unfolding of Generalized Logic Programs, *Preprints Work. Gr. for Artificial Intelligence, IPSJ* 83-3-AI 1992, pp. 43–52.

[10] Akama, K.: Sound and Complete Unifier Set and mgu, *Hokkaido University Information Engineering Technical Report*, HIER-LI-9212, 1992.

[11] Akama, K.: Homomorphism Theorem of Generalized Logic Programs, *Preprints Work. Gr. for Programming, IPSJ* PRG-9-6 (1992), pp. 41–48.

[12] Akama, K.: Typed Unification Grammars as Generalized Logic Programs, *Hokkaido University Information Engineering Technical Report*, HIER-LI-9216, 1992.

[13] Apt, K.R. and van Emden, M,H.: Contribution to the Theory of Logic Programming, *J. ACM*, Vol. 29, No. 3 1982, pp. 841–862.

[14] Chang, C.L. and Lee, R.C.: *Symbolic Logic and Mechanical Theorem Proving*, Academic Press, New York, 1973.

[15] Clark, K.L.: Logic Programming Schemes, *Proc. of the international conference on fifth generation computer systems* 1988, pp.120–139.

[16] Emele, M. and Zajac, R.: Typed Unification Grammars, *Proc. of COLING '90* 1990, pp. 293–298.

[17] Jaffar, J., Lassez, J.L., and Maher, M.J : Logic Programming Language Scheme, *Logic programming, functions, relations, and equations*, Prentice Hall 1986, pp. 441–467.

[18] Jaffar, J. and Lassez, J.L.: Constraint Logic Programming, *Technical Report, Department of Computer Science*, Monash University, June 1986.

[19] Lloyd, J.W.: *Foundations of Logic Programming*, Second edition, Springer-Verlag, 1987.

[20] Nakashima, H.: Term Description: A Simple Powerful Extension to Prolog Data Structures, *Proc. of IJCAI-IX* 1985, pp.708–710.

[21] Robinson, J.A.: A Machine-Oriented Logic Based on the Resolution Principle, *J. ACM*, Vol. 12, No. 1 1965, pp. 23–41.

[22] Tarski, A.: A Lattice-Theoretical Fixpoint Theorem and Its Applications, *Pacific J. Math.*, Vol. 5 1955, pp. 285–309.

[23] Van Emden, M.H. and Kowalski, R.A.: The Semantics of Predicate Logic as a Programming Language, *J. ACM*, Vol. 23, No. 4 1976, pp. 733–742.

Appendix

Proof for Model Intersection Property

Assume that $\{M_j \mid j \in J\}$ is a non-empty set of models of a Horn clause h. Let $h = (\forall L)$, $L = L_1 \vee L_2 \vee \cdots \vee L_n$ and $M = [\bigcap M_j \mid j \in J]$. From the definition of models,

$$\forall j \in J : value_{M_j}(h) = true.$$

We transform this formula :

$$\Leftrightarrow \forall j \in J : value_{M_j}(\forall L) = true.$$
$$\Leftrightarrow \forall j \in J : [\, \wedge val_{M_j}(inst_s(L)) \mid s \in \mathcal{S}\,] = true.$$

Let s be any element of $\mathcal{S}$ such that $inst_s(L)$ is defined. Then

$$\forall j \in J : val_{M_j}(inst_s(L)) = true.$$

Since $L = L_1 \vee L_2 \vee \cdots \vee L_n$, this is equivalent to

$$\Leftrightarrow \forall j \in J, \exists k : val_{M_j}(inst_s(L_k)) = true.$$

For any j, let L_{k_j} be one of the literals L_k that satisfy $val_{M_j}(inst_s(L_k)) = true$; then

$$\text{(f)} \quad \forall j \in J : val_{M_j}(inst_s(L_{k_j})) = true.$$

Here the following two cases are possible :

(1) For all j, L_{k_j} is a positive literal.

(2) For some j, L_{k_j} is a negative literal.

- Case (1): Assume that L_{k_j} is a positive literal for all j. Since a Horn clause has at most one positive literal, there is an atom L_i such that $L_{k_j} = L_i$ for any j. Letting $g = inst_s(L_i)$, (f) is transformed as follows :

$$
\begin{aligned}
& \forall j \in J : [\, val_{M_j}(inst_s(L_{k_j})) = true \,] \\
\Leftrightarrow\ & \forall j \in J : [\, val_{M_j}(inst_s(L_i)) = true \,]. \\
\Leftrightarrow\ & \forall j \in J : [\, val_{M_j}(g) = true \,]. \\
\Leftrightarrow\ & \forall j \in J : [\, g \in M_j \,]. \\
\Leftrightarrow\ & g \in M. \\
\Leftrightarrow\ & val_M(g) = true. \\
\Leftrightarrow\ & val_M(inst_s(L_i)) = true. \\
\rightarrow\ & val_M(inst_s(L)) = true.
\end{aligned}
$$

- Case (2): Assume that L_{k_j} is a negative literal $\neg a$ for $j = i$, and let $inst_s(\neg a) = \neg g$. Then, from (f),

  $$val_{M_i}(inst_s(L_{k_i})) = true.$$

  This is transformed as follows :

  $\Leftrightarrow val_{M_i}(inst_s(\neg a)) = true.$
  $\Leftrightarrow val_{M_i}(\neg g) = true.$
  $\Leftrightarrow val_{M_i}(g) = false.$
  $\Leftrightarrow g \notin M_i.$
  $\rightarrow g \notin M.$
  $\Leftrightarrow val_M(g) = false.$
  $\Leftrightarrow val_M(\neg g) = true.$
  $\Leftrightarrow val_M(inst_s(\neg a)) = true.$
  $\Leftrightarrow val_M(inst_s(L_{k_i})) = true.$
  $\rightarrow val_M(inst_s(L)) = true.$

In both Cases (1) and (2), we have $val_M(inst_s(L)) = true$. This is proved for any $s \in \mathcal{S}$ such that $inst_s(L)$ is defined, and therefore

$$[\wedge val_M(inst_s(L)) \mid s \in \mathcal{S}] = true.$$

This is transformed as follows :

$\Leftrightarrow value_M(\forall L) = true.$
$\Leftrightarrow value_M(h) = true.$
$\Leftrightarrow M \in Model(h).$
$\Leftrightarrow [\bigcap M_j \mid j \in J] \in Model(h).$

Initially published in "Computer Software", Vol. 10, No. 1, in Japanese.

Kiyoshi Akama
Department of Information Engineering
Faculty of Engineering
Hokkaido University
Kita-ku, Sapporo
060 Japan

TAMPOPO: An Evolutionary Learning Machine Based on the Principle of Realtime Minimum Skyline Detection

Toshinori Watanabe

Summary. A class of learning problems is formulated as a minimum skyline detection problem for an unknown, time-varying nonlinear function. As a solution to this problem, a constructive proof of the existence of a realtime minimum skyline detector called **TAMPOPO** is given, along with its formal specification in *Concurrent Prolog*. Its behavioral semantics, including its adaptability to both stable and unstable environments, are analyzed along the lines of fixed point theory. TAMPOPO is an open system with a memory of experience and a memory rewriting mechanism. It is assumed to have *a priori* knowledge—the Lipsitz constant—of a nonlinear function's topology. Each experience not resident on the minimum skyline is rewritten by a superior one nearer to the minimum-skyline. Residents on the minimum skyline constitute the fixed point of the rewriting mechanism. Moreover, the rewriting mechanism can catch up with fixed point changes by employing a form of *primitive consciousness* that detects and deletes specious experience through topological knowledge of the environment. These features make TAMPOPO more adaptable to time-varying unknown environments than traditional learning machines.

1 Introduction

Realization of a system that is able to choose an appropriate behavior C for any environmental condition K based on its experience has been a common goal in the design of learning systems. Usually it is assumed that an evaluation mechanism notifies the system of an outcome J of the action C chosen under K. In this case, *experience* denotes a set of the triple (K, C, J) accumulated by the system.

Various adaptive systems, both natural and artificial, can be understood and/or designed by using this rather simple learning system concept. For example, by taking K, C, and J as a stimulus, an action, and a reward, respectively, we obtain a primitive model of animal behavior formation. Taking them as an environmental condition, a species, and the fertility of the species, we obtain a model of niche formation by living creatures. Taking them as features of a handwritten character, a recalled character code, and an evaluation of the recall, we obtain an adaptive handwritten character recognizer.

The mathematical abstraction of the learning problem is the autonomous formation of a function $F_s : K \rightarrow C$ under an evaluation scheme giving J. Depending

ISBN 0-12-037105-7

on the variations of the representation scheme F_s and the domain structures of K, C, and J, various learning machines have been proposed.

Neural nets (NNs) and siblings use indirect schemes to represent F_s by a nonlinear network with modifiable weights W [2,7,9,17]. Generally, small finite sets are assumed for C and J. Learning consists of weight modifications, and experience is memorized in the form of weight distribution. Because of its structural resemblance to a real brain, the distributed memory of NN has great scientific attractiveness. However, owing to the difficulty of distributed memory management, it is not necessarily attractive in real engineering applications.

In this sense, a genetic algorithm (GA) is more pragmatic than an NN [8]. In contrast to an NN, a GA adopts a direct scheme to represent F_s. Experience is pooled in the form (K, C, W) to form a memory, where W denotes the importance weight of the experience. For a new situation, an experience is recalled from the memory by using a selection function and applied to the real world. Learning is made possible by feeding back the outcome of the application to the W of the recalled experience. Although a GA can offer a learning machine that is elegant and powerful, both the selection and weight modification functions should be designed appropriately. Moreover, owing to the purely feedback-based slow learning speed, a GA is weak for time-varying systems. Obsolete experience that gained a high W in the old environment will live long in the new environment, although it has low utility.

Instance-based learning (IBL) and siblings also use a direct representation scheme for F_s [1]. Experience is memorized in the form (K, C). Generally, a small discrete set is assumed for C and *good* or *bad* for J. Learning is performed by accumulating experiences that the memory failed to distinguish correctly.

Although the memory mechanism is very simple, a large memory is required even for small K and C. Moreover, owing to its failure-dependent learning mechanism, IBL is less immune to noisy environments than NN.

TAMPOPO originated in the author's design for a nonlinear programming algorithm selection system [24] and was applied to the experimental realization of a self-organizing computer operating system [26]. In these applications, the central role of TAMPOPO was the automatic or semi-automatic formation of the mapping $F_s : K \to C$ in changing environment. K and C were vectors composed mainly of real numbers. A real value could be given as J by a human evaluation or by a built-in evaluation function $F_e : (K, C) \to J$. Because of these requirements, TAMPOPO could not be designed as a sibling of NNs. Rather, it was designed on the evolution principle. Experience in the form (K, C, J) was gathered to form a memory of limited size. Learning was realized by a memory manager that not only recalls, for a given K, an appropriate experience, but also stores a new experience by deleting an inferior one. An informal presentation of these ideas appeared in an earlier paper [25]. The direct use of experience and the use of an innovative memory rewriting technique are the main features that TAMPOPO has in common with one or both of GAs and IBL. Its distinguishing feature is the use of topological knowledge of F_e, the constant *Lipsitz*. Although *Lipsitz* should be given by some means such as F_e sampling, the overall behavior can be enhanced because of the avoidance of the inefficient feedback learning common to GAs. Not only the ability to recall an appropriate experience, but also the ability to detect inferior experience, could be realized by the use of topological knowledge. Further, a certain *primitive consciousness* can also be realized by which specious experience can be detected in the face of environmental change. Owing to these new features, TAMPOPO is more robust in changing environments than are conventional learning machines.

In the latter half of the 1980s, a new trend emerged in which diverse topics such as evolution, games, and learning were unified as categories of adaptation phenomena in nonlinear systems. Various adaptive systems ranging from biological immune systems to artificial learning machines were shown to be governed by a similar nonlinear kinetic equation [4,8,10,11,12]. The leader in this field, Fermer, pointed out several open problems:

(P1) How can evolution be characterized in dynamic terms?
(P2) Can we utilize the automatic design capability of evolution?
(P3) What are the simplest models that show nontrivial adaptation?
(P4) How do we measure (define) adaptability?
(P5) Can life be generated in a purely artificial environment?

These indicate that the definition of adaptive systems, including learning machines, is still open. What are the appropriate definitions of environment, learning system, evaluation, and environmental change? How should their interrelations be specified? How should the adaptation process be described? All these questions are topics of current research.

On the basis of these observations, this paper proposes a new logical formulation of learning problems in a changing environment. After a formal description of TAMPOPO, its behavioral semantics will be given in terms of the fixed point theory. In Section 2, a learning problem is formulated as a theorem-proving problem in a system composed of concurrent processes—an environment, a learning system, and a learning progress evaluator—connected by a message stream. In Section 3, the definition of TAMPOPO is given in clausal form. In Section 4, the definition of TAMPOPO in Section 3 is shown to have a fixed-point semantics in its memory-rewriting operation and can be a solution to the problem posed in Section 2.

2 Learning Problem Formulation

2.1 Informal preview of the learning problem

(1) System Construction A system that can choose an appropriate response to a condition imposed by the environment might be considered to be intelligent. The word *appropriate* presumes the existence of some measure for evaluating the response adopted in the situation. Let us denote the environment as E, the intelligent system as S, the set of imposed environmental conditions as K, the set of responses as C, the set of effectiveness as J, and the set of time as T. In this arrangement, S can be seen as a mapping $F_s : K \rightarrow C$, and E can be seen as a combination of a K-generator and a mapping $F_e : (K, C, T) \rightarrow J$. E is said to be *time-varying* when F_e depends on T.

Example 1 *Let K be the state vector, C the control signal at K, and J the control effectiveness evaluation (the smaller the better) of a control system S. Let K and*

C be real values. If we choose the evaluation function of E as $J = |K + C|$, S learns the control law: $C = -K$, and in any state K, a control signal $C = -K$ is generated by S to maintain the original state K.

Example 2 *The automatic handwritten character recognizer S associates K with a set of feature vectors of handwritten characters, and C with a set of machine character codes, respectively. E might be the human user who gives the effectiveness score J to each recognition action of S. E is time-independent when the user is consistent in evaluating the score J; otherwise, it is time-varying.*

Example 3 *Let K be the environmental conditions on the Earth, C the set of species living on the Earth, and J a measure of the fitness of a species for its local environment. F_s becomes the niche profile of living creatures on the Earth.*

(2) Real-time Learning Let $Messages = [(K_t, C_t, J_t, \_)|TailMessages]$ be a list representation of messages shared by E and S, where $TailMessages$ denotes the tail part of the $Messages$. $K_t \in K$ is an environmental condition at time t, $C_t \in C$ is a response at time t, and $J_t \in J$ is the evaluation of the pair (K_t, C_t) at time t. The underline character "_" denotes a spare field used later. S is said to perform real-time learning if the generated $Messages$ form an improving series; that is, if any of its elements is outperformed by some younger element.

Example 4 *In the case of $K \in R^1$, $C \in R^1$, and $J \in R^1$, the following time series might be an improving series. (1.0,0.7,0.6,_) is clearly an improvement on (1.0,1.0,1.0,_), since $K_1 = K_3 = 1.0$. Further, (0.78,0.4,0.5,_) seems to be an improvement on (0.8,0.5,0.6,_), although $K_2 = 0.8 \neq K_4 = 0.78$.*

$$Messages = [(1.0, 1.0, 1.0, \_), (0.8, 0.5, 0.6, \_), (1.0, 0.7, 0.6, \_), (0.78, 0.4, 0.5, \_)].$$

(3) Recalling a Similar Experience The probability that we have $K_{t_1} = K_{t_2}$ for $t_1 \neq t_2$ in the $Messages$ might not be high. To cope with this problem, S should recall a similar experience in response to a new situation. It should also learn by using similar, but non-identical, experiences.

Example 5 *Suppose that a set of experiences is gained by S as below and that $K_t = 0.95$ is given by E. Of the two candidates, (1.0,1.0,1.0,_) and (1.0,0.7,0.6,_), both having K close to 0.95, $C \simeq 0.7$ would be the best response of S.*

$$[(1.0, 1.0, 1.0, \_), (0.8, 0.5, 0.6, \_), (1.0, 0.7, 0.6, \_), (0.78, 0.4, 0.5, \_)].$$

(4) Adaptability to Environmental Change If two experiences $(K_{t_1}, C_{t_1}, J_{t_1}, \_)$ and $(K_{t_2}, C_{t_2}, J_{t_2}, \_)$ satisfying $(K_{t_1}, C_{t_1}) \simeq (K_{t_2}, C_{t_2})$ and $J_{t_1} \neq J_{t_2}$ are given, we think that the environment E has been changed between t_1 and t_2. In other words, we represent environmental changes by the time change of Fe. S should detect this environmental change and renew the $Memory$ appropriately.

(5) Timing of Action Evaluation In this paper, an immediate outcome of J for an action is assumed. If an outcome will be given for a chain of actions, C should be defined as a vector composed of these actions. If an outcome will be given after some delay, as in time series forecasting, the outcome for the action at t can be defined as a weighted sum of Js around $t + L$, where L is a predefined mean delay time. See *Sutton* [22] for further discussions on action evaluation methods.

2.2 Formulation of the learning problem

Concurrent Prolog (CP), which is based on predicate logic, is used as a specification language to give a formulation that is both logical and clear (see *Shapiro* [21]). The predicate $p(T1, \ldots, Tn)$ with functor p and arity n will be abbreviated as p/n.

Definition 2.2.1 *The world W is composed of an environment E and a learning system S. E and S are concurrent, perpetual, and recursive processes connected by a message stream, Messages (see Figure 1). Let W, E, and S be represented by predicates world/6, environment/4, and system/5, respectively. Their connection is defined as follows (S and E communicate by Messages):*

$world(Messages, Clock, KDom, CDom, Topology, MaxPopulation) :-$
$environment(Messages, KDom, Clock, Topology),$
$system(Messages, Memory, CDom, Topology, MaxPopulation).$

where

$Messages ::= [(K, C, J, M)|Messages].$
$Clock ::= Time\ counter.$
$KDom ::= The\ domain\ of\ the\ signal\ K.$
$CDom ::= The\ domain\ of\ the\ response\ C.$
$Topology ::= Parameter(s)\ representing\ the\ topology\ of\ Fe.$
$MaxPopulation ::= Population\ limit\ of\ the\ memory\ Memory.$
$M ::= A\ memo\ stating\ whether\ the\ experience\ data\ have\ been\ memorized.$

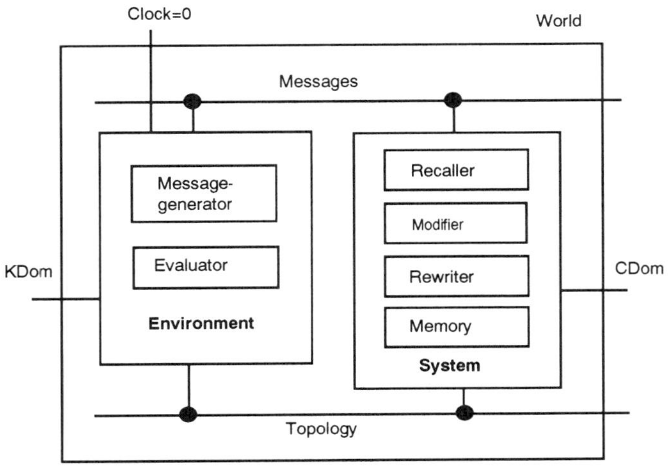

Fig. 1 Overview of the world.

Definition 2.2.2 *The predicate environment/4 is a combination of two predicates, message_generator/2 and evaluator/3. The former generates unit messages* $(K, \_, \_, \_)$ *in the Messages stream, one by one. The latter, upon receiving* $(K, C, \_, \_)$, *adds the evaluation J to generate (K, C, J, _). The response C is returned from S by a backward communication [21]. eval(T) denotes the value of the term T.*

$environment(Messages, KDom, Clock, Topology) :-$
$message\_generator(Messages, KDom),$
$evaluator(Messages, Clock, Topology).$
$message\_generator([Kh|Others], KDom) :-$
$a\_message(Kh, KDom),$
$message\_generator(Others, KDom).$
$a\_message(Kh, KDom) :-$
$\%Generate\ a\ message\ Kh \in KDom.$
$evaluator([(K, C, J)|Others], Clock, Topology) :-$
$evaluate\_one(K, C, Clock, Topology, J),$
$evaluator(Others, eval(Clock + 1), Topology).$
$evaluate\_one(K, C, Clock, Topology, J) :-$
$\%Calculate\ the\ score\ J\ of\ the\ combination\ (K, C, Clock)$

Definition 2.2.3 *system(Messages, Memory, CDom, Topology, MaxPopulation) gets messages via Messages from E. Each message is in the form (K, _, _, _). It then decides an appropriate response C that is sent back to E after instantiation of the undefined value "_" to C. In this instance, (K, _, _, _) is changed to (K, C, _, _). The response C is generated by using the contents of the Memory, CDom, and Topology. After receiving the back message (K, C, J, _) from E, the Memory is rewritten. The upper limit of the memory, MaxPopulation, is taken into consideration in this rewriting operation. The realization of these functions will be explained in Section 3.*

Definition 2.2.4 *The predicate improved/2 verifies that Messages is an improving series. The predicate dominated_by_someone/3 asserts that the experience (K, C, J, Memo) is dominated by some member of Mtail. (Note that all the members of Mtail are younger than (K, C, J, Memo).) The semicolon indicates a logical OR.*

$improved([(K, C, J, Memo)|Mtail], Topology) :-$
$dominated\_by\_someone((K, C, J, Memo), Mtail?, Topology),$
$improved(Mtail?, Topology).$
$dominated\_by\_someone(Mh, [(K, C, J, Memo)|Mtt], Topology) :-$
$Memo = out|$
$dominated\_by\_someone(Mh, Mtt?, Topology).$
$dominated\_by\_someone((Kh, Ch, Jh,), [(K, C, J, Memo)|Mtt], Topology) :-$
$Memo = in|$
$dominate((K, C, J), (Kh, Ch, Jh), Topology);$
$dominated\_by\_someone((Kh, Ch, Jh), Mtt?, Topology).$
$dominate(A, B, Topology) :-$
$superior(A, B, Topology); abnormally\_superior(B, A, Topology).$
$\%The\ experience\ A\ dominates\ B.\ See\ Definitions$ 3.2.11 *and* 3.2.12.

Problem 2.2.1 *The problem in this paper is how to construct a system/5 that makes the following world/5 true.*

$world(Messages, Clock, KDom, CDom, Topology) :-$
$environment(Messages, KDom, Clock, Topology),$
$system(Messages, [\ ], CDom, Topology, MaxPopulation),$
$improved(Messages, Topology).$

In other words, *system*/5 should be designed so as to generate an improving *Messages* series that makes *improved*/2 always *true*. One role of *environment*/4 is the initial message generation of $Messages ::= [(K, \_, \_, \_)|RestMessages]$, and the other is the generation of the evaluated series $Messages ::= [(K, C, J, \_)| RestMessages]$. *system*/5 generates an intermediate series $Messages ::= [(K, C, \_, \_)|RestMessages]$. As it is very difficult to obtain a general solution to this problem, the following restrictions are imposed.

Supposition 2.2.1 *All the domains KDom, CDom, and J are Euclidean. In other words,* $KDom \in R^{|KDom|}$, $CDom \in R^{|CDom|}$, *and* $J \in R^1$. *The adaptive controller in Example 1 meets these conditions.*

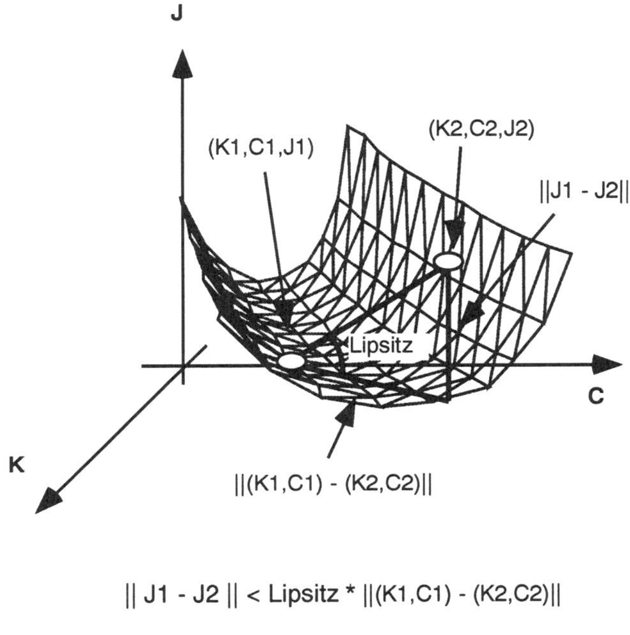

Fig. 2 Lipsitz condition for Fe.

Supposition 2.2.2 *The function* $Fe : (K, C, Clock) \rightarrow J$ *is assumed to meet the Lipsitz condition:* $\forall Clock \exists Lipsitz.lipsitz(KDom, CDom, Clock, Lipsitz)$. *This* *proposition asserts that in given domains KDom and CDom there exists a constant Lipsitz that makes lipsitz(KDom, CDom, Clock, Lipsitz) true for all Clock. The definition of lipsitz/4 is shown below. The Lipsitz constant is a global topology of Fe, so we use Lipsitz instead of Topology.* $\|X\|$ *denotes the norm of X (see Figure 2). In Example 1, we can choose Lipsitz = 2, since J meets the condition* $max(dJ/d(K,C)) = 1$.

$lipsitz(KDom, CDom, Clock, Lipsitz) :-$
$\quad member(K1, KDom), member(K2, KDom),$
$\quad member(C1, CDom), member(C2, CDom),$
$\quad evaluate\_one(K1, C1, Clock, Lipsitz, J1),$
$\quad evaluate\_one(K2, C2, Clock, Lipsitz, J2),$
$\quad \|J1 - J2\| < Lipsitz * \|(K1, C1) - (K2, C2)\|.$

Supposition 2.2.3 *The environmental changes occur not continuously, but discretely. In our model, this can be represented as follows (assume that* $Fe_1 \rightarrow Fe_2$ *at* $Clock = t_1$*):*

$evaluate\_one(K, C, Clock, Lipsitz, J) :-$
$\quad Clock \leq t_1 | J = Fe_1(K, C, Lipsitz).$
$evaluate\_one(K, C, Clock, Lipsitz, J) :-$
$\quad Clock > t_1 | J = Fe_2(K, C, Lipsitz).$

Definition 2.2.5 *If the environment is time-independent,* $Fe : (K, C, Clock) \rightarrow J$ *becomes time-independent; that is,* $Fe : (K, C) \rightarrow J$*. During such an interval, we can define MSLFeK, the minimum skyline of Fe seen from K, as follows (Figure 3):*

$MSLFeK =$
$\quad [(K, Cm, Fe(K, Cm)) | Fe(K, Cm) < Fe(K, C), C \neq Cm, K \in KDom, C \in CDom].$

MSLFeK is the set of lowest points (we assume that lower ones are better) of Fe for each K.
Discussions 2.2.1 *From this definition, it is clear that for a given K, the member* $(K, Cm, Fe(K, Cm)) \in MSLFeK$ *dominates other points* $[(K, Cother, Fe(K, Cother)) | Cother \in CDom]$*, establishing the relation*

$dominate((K, Cmin, Fe(K, Cmin)), (K, Cother, Fe(K, Cother)), Lipsitz).$

Suppose that for any K, S can generate a chain of C converging to $MSLFeK$; then it is intuitively clear that in time some younger experience $(Ky, Cy, Fe(Ky, Cy))$ will dominate some older one $(Ko, Co, Fe(Ko, Co))$. In other words, $Messages$ becomes an improving series, whose definition we have already given, and Problem 2.2.1 can be solved. Stated informally, we can solve the problem by constructing a real-time minimum skyline detector S for an unknown nonlinear function Fe. As the memory size is limited by $Maxpopulation$, only an approximation of $MSLFeK$ can be made. The approximation can be enhanced by enlarging $Maxpopulation$. Learning in a time-varying environment will be realized if S can catch up with the time change of $MSLFeK$.

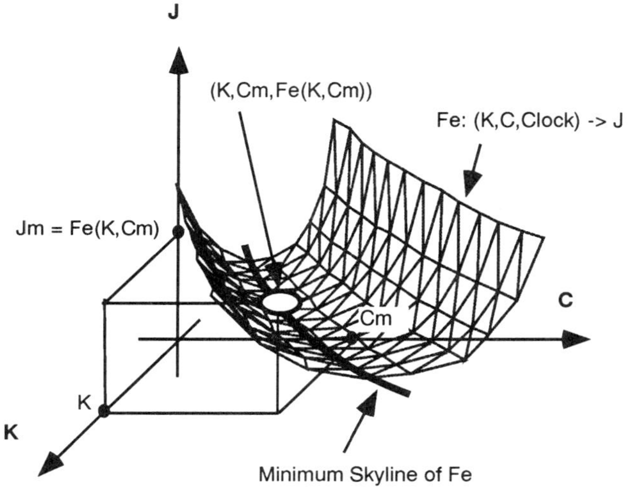

Fig. 3 Minimum skyline of Fe seen from K.

Supposition 2.2.4 *To simplify later discussions by avoiding pathological cases, we assume that MSLFeK has a unique minimum for each K; that is,* $(K, Cm_1, Jm_1), (K, Cm_2, Jm_2) \in MSLFeK \Rightarrow Cm_1 = Cm_2, Jm_1 = Jm_2$. *In Example 1, this assumption is valid, since the optimal* $C_m (= -K)$ *is unique for any* K.

2.3 Brief sketch of the solution

An informal sketch of the solution to Problem 2.2.1 is given here as a guide to the formal descriptions in subsequent chapters (see Figure 1).

(1) Message_generator (Definition 2.2.2) This generates environmental conditions—that is, a series of Ks—and sends them to $system/5$ via $Messages$.

(2) Recaller (Definition 3.2.2) This module chooses an appropriate (Kr, Cr, Jr) from $Memory$ in $system/5$. The appropriate experience is the safest one for the given environmental condition K (Figure 5). The safest experience is the one having a Cr whose estimated worst contribution at K has the highest value. The worst contribution of each experience at K can be estimated by using the *Lipsitz* of Fe (Figure 2).

(3) Modifier (Definition 3.2.6) Cr on the recalled experience (Kr, Cr, Jr) is mutated to Cm by some statistical method such as random vector addition. Many variations of Steps 2 and 3 above are possible. In subsequent sections, the best two elements are recalled in Step 2, and their Crs are crossed over to give a Cm in step 3. This is to allow self-adaptation of the mutation rate—that is, the gradual decrease in the rate as experience converges to $MSLFeK$.

(4) Evaluator (Definition 2.2.2) The function value $Jm = Fe(K, Cm, Clock)$ is given for the proposed pair (K, Cm). An experience (K, Cm, Jm) is newly created at this point.

(5) Rewriter (Definition 3.2.9) This module deletes any experiences that are inferior to or abnormally superior (i.e., specious) to the new experience (K, Cm, Jm). The concepts of inferiority and abnormal superiority are defined as follows (Figure 4):

(5.1) (Kd, Cd, Jd) is inferior to the new experience (K, Cm, Jm) If the score Jd of (Kd, Cd, Jd) is outperformed by the estimated worst contribution of Cm at Kd—that is, if $Jd > Jm + Lipsitz * \|(Kd, Cm) - (K, Cm)\| = Jm + Lipsitz * \|Kd - K\|$—then (Kd, Cd, Jd) is said to be inferior to (K, Cm, Jm). Note the use of Supposition 2.2.2 to derive the estimation. Since inferior experiences will never be recalled, they can be deleted from $Memory$.

(5.2) (Kd, Cd, Jd) is superior to the new experience (K, Cm, Jm) If the score Jd of (Kd, Cd, Jd) is better than the estimated best contribution of Cm at Kd—that is, if $Jd < Jm - Lipsitz * \|Kd - K\|$—then (Kd, Cd, Jd) is said to be superior to (K, Cm, Jm). However, we say that (Kd, Cd, Jd) is abnormally superior to (K, Cm, Jm) if $Jd < Jm - Lipsitz * \|(Kd, Cd) - (K, Cm)\|$. From Supposition 2.2.2, this will never happen in a stable environment. A possible cause would be an environmental change that caused an upward shift (along the J axis) of Fe near (K, Cm). In this case, an obsolete (Kd, Cd, Jd) can be deleted from $Memory$. Any superior experience except an abnormally superior one is defined as normally superior.

(5.3) (Kd, Cd, Jd) is equivalent to (K, Cm, Jm) In other cases, the two are defined to be equivalent (non-comparable).

(6) Adaptability of TAMPOPO In Section 4, it will be proved that $MSLFeK$ is composed of fixed points of the memory rewriter given in (5). In time, any point outside $MSLFeK$ is replaced by a point nearer to $MSLFeK$. Whereas the deletion mechanism of (5.1) performs a crucial role in a stable environment, the abnormally superior deletion mechanism of (5.2) accelerates the adaptation to environmental changes.

3 Formal Specification of TAMPOPO

3.1 Goal and related terms

Definition 3.1.1 The Goal *TAMPOPO is the system S that is envoked by the following topmost goal that appeared in Definiton 2.2.1 of the world W.*

$$:-system(Message, Memory, CDom, Lipsitz, MaxPopulation).$$

Definition 3.1.2 Related Terms *The definitions of arguments appearing in the goal are as follows:*

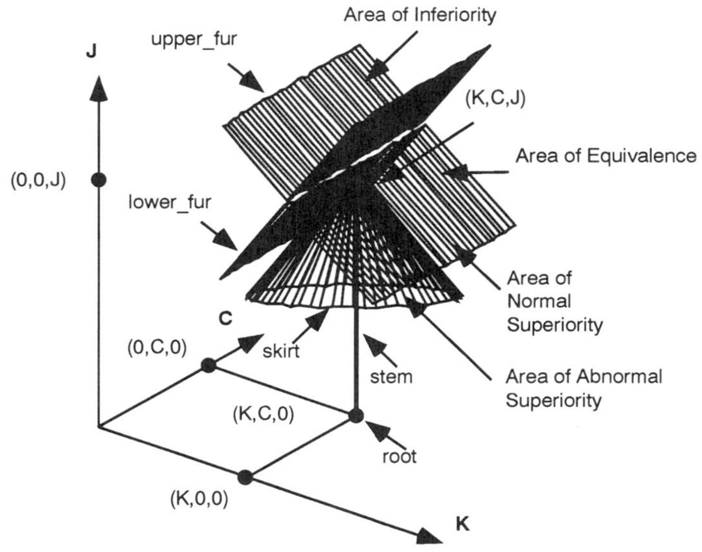

Fig. 4 Multi-dimensional representation of an experience by TAMPOPO.

$Messages ::= [(K, C, J, M)|RestMessages].$
$Memory ::= [(K, C, J)|RestMemory],\ initially\ Memory ::= [\ ].$
$CDom ::= [C_1, C_2, ..., C_n],\ (C_i \in [0, 1]\ for\ i = 1, \ldots, n).$
$Lipsitz ::= Problem - specific\ Lipsitz\ constant\ of\ Fe\ given\ a\ priori.$
$MaxPopulation ::= Maximum\ number\ of\ data\ storable\ in\ the\ memory.$

3.2 Behavior specification as a perpetually recursive process

Definition 3.2.1 system (Message, Memory, CDom, Lipsitz, MaxPopulation) *This clause can be invoked only when Cm and Jm are not instantiated. This condition is checked by two guards, $var(Cm)$ and $var(Jm)$. $recall/5$ recalls an experience Recalled out of $Memory$ in the given K. $modify/5$ modifies Recalled into $(K, Cm, \_, \_)$. $rewrite/5$ rewrites the current $Memory$ of $system/5$ as a new $Memory1$ by using the new experience $(K, Cm, Jm, Memo)$. The term $X?$ annotated with "?" is the read-only term of CP. The goal with a read-only term $X?$ is forced to suspend execution until X is instantiated (see Appendix). Consequently, the last recursive call of $system/5$ using $Memory1?$ can start only after $rewrite/5$ has finished. The read-only mark changes only the behavior of the clause; the logical meaning remains unchanged. Therefore, "?" will be omitted in ordinary discussions.*

$system([(K, Cm, Jm, Memo)|Mt], Memory, CDom, Lipsitz, MaxPopulation) :-$
$\quad var(Cm), var(Jm)|recall(K?, Memory?, CDom, Lipsitz, Recalled),$

$modify(K?, Recalled?, CDom, Lipsitz, (K, Cm, \_, \_)),$
$rewrite((K?, Cm?, Jm?, Memo), Memory?, Memory1, Lipsitz, MaxPopulation),$
$system(Mt?, Memory1?, CDom, Lipsitz, MaxPopulation).$

Definition 3.2.2 recall(K,Memory,CDom,Lipsitz,Recalled) *An experience appropriate to a given condition K is recalled from the Memory as Recalled. When the current memory is vacant, the first clause returns a random vector in CDom. When the memory contains only one element, One, the second clause returns it directly. In other cases, when more two or more elements are contained, the best two elements are returned by the third clause. Two solutions with bad scores,* $J = 99, 100$*, are artificially set as initial seeds. The reason for the best-two search will be explained in Definition 3.2.8.*

$recall(K, [\,], CDom, \_, [(K, Cr, \_)]) :-$
$random\_vector(CDom, Cr).$
$recall(K, [One], \_, \_, [One]).$
$recall(K, Memory, CDom, Lipsitz, Recalled) :-$
$random\_vector(CDom, C1), random\_vector(CDom, C2)|$
$recall\_auf(K?, Memory?, [(K, C1?, 99), (K, C2?, 100)], Lipsitz, Recalled).$
$random\_vector(CDom, Cr) :-$
$\%Generate\ a\ random\ Cr\ in\ CDom.$

Definition 3.2.3 recall_auf(K,Memory,[CRb,CRs],Lipsitz,Recalled) *The best two elements of Memory for a given K are searched for and returned as Recalled. [CRb, CRs] denotes the two current bests during the search.*

$recall\_auf(\_, [\,], Recalled, \_, Recalled).$
$recall\_auf(K, [Mh|Mt], [CRb, CRs], Lipsitz, Recalled) :-$
$safe(K, Mh, CRb, Lipsitz)|$
$recall\_auf(K, Mt?, [Mh, CRb], Lipsitz, Recalled).$
$recall\_auf(K, [Mh|Mt], [CRb, CRs], Lipsitz, Recalled) :-$
$safe(K, CRb, Mh, Lipsitz), safe(K, Mh, CRs, Lipsitz)|$
$recall\_auf(K, Mt?, [CRb, Mh], Lipsitz, Recalled).$
$recall\_auf(K, [Mh|Mt], [CRb, CRs], Lipsitz, Recalled) :-$
$otherwise|$
$recall\_auf(K, Mt?, [CRb, CRs], Lipsitz, Recalled).$

Definition 3.2.4 safe(K,(Ka,Ca,Ja),(Kb,Cb,Jb),Lipsitz) *This clause checks whether the experience* (Ka, Ca, Ja) *is safer than* (Kb, Cb, Jb) *at* K*. Two upper_fur/3 calculate the estimations* Va *and* Vb*. If* $Va < Vb$*, this predicate becomes true (see Figures 4 and 5).*

$safe(K, (Ka, Ca, Ja), (Kb, Cb, Jb), Lipsitz) :-$
$upper\_fur((K, Ca, Va), (Ka, Ca, Ja), Lipsitz),$
$upper\_fur((K, Cb, Vb), (Kb, Cb, Jb), Lipsitz),$
$Va < Vb.$

Definition 3.2.5 upper_fur((K,C,V),(Kr,Cr,Jr),Lipsitz) *From Supposition 2.2.2, the estimated value* V *of* Fe *at* (K, C)*, based on the experience* (Kr, Cr, Jr)*, can be estimated to fall within the following interval:*

$$[Jr - Lipsitz * \|(K, C) - (Kr, Cr)\|, Jr + Lipsitz * \|(K, C) - (Kr, Cr)\|].$$

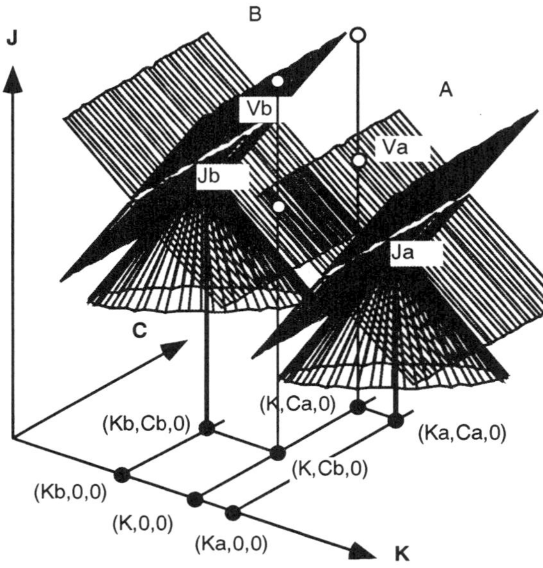

Fig. 5 Recalling a safe experience A at K.

upper_fur/3 estimates the worst (largest) value, and lower_fur/3 estimates the best (smallest) value. The set of (K, C, V) *satisfying upper_fur/3 forms a cone surface, named Upper Cone Surface, opening upward with a vertex at* (Kr, Cr, Jr). *Assuming that we adopt the recalled* Cr *without modification—that is,* $C = Cr$ *—for a given* K, *we get the estimated value*

$$V = Jr + Lipsitz * \|(K, Cr) - (Kr, Cr)\| = Jr + Lipsitz * \|K - Kr\|$$

This forms a valley-shaped (degenerated) cone surface in $KDom \times CDom \times J$ *that is independent of* C. *We name it the Upper Valley of* (Kr, Cr, Jr). *For lower_fur/3, a similar argument can be used to define Lower Cone (but we avoid this). We name the surface of the lower cone a Skirt of* (Kr, Cr, Jr). *Figure 4 gives the multi-dimensional geometrical representation of an experience in TAMPOPO.*

$upper\_fur((K, C, V), (Kr, Cr, Jr), Lipsitz) :-$
$\quad V := Jr + Lipsitz * \|(K, C) - (Kr, Cr)\|.$
$lower\_fur((K, C, V), (Kr, Cr, Jr), Lipsitz) :-$
$\quad V := Jr - Lipsitz * \|(K, C) - (Kr, Cr)\|.$

Discussion 3.2.1 TAMPOPO=DANDELION=Small Wild Plant *Figure 4 clarifies the above discussion. To give a clear view, the infinitely extended cone was trimmed in the figure. The shape resembles that of a dandelion having a root at* $(K, C, 0)$, *a stem connecting* $(K, C, 0)$ *and* (K, C, J), *and a set of furry seeds* *extending from* (K, C, J)*. As well as these resemblances in their shapes, the behavior of the memory rewriting process resembles the life of a dandelion. At various places (K's) in the field (KDom), new generations (Cs in CDom) are implanted. Each samples has an adaptability score* $J = Fe(K, C)$*. Those having high adaptability (small J) can transmit their genes (C's) to their descendants. Through yearly successions of generations (perpetual rewriting of the Memory), dandelions find their appropriate niches (MSLFeK) in the field. This similarity is the reason that we choose the metaphoric name TAMPOPO, which is the Japanese word for dandelion.*

Discussion 3.2.2 TAMPOPO=DANDELION=Knowledge *But there remains another story: adaption to environmental changes. The above, blind evolutionary process responds weakly to environmental changes, since it sticks to past glory. Superiors in the old environment, which are now inferiors in the new environment, are recalled repeatedly in vain, causing gradual extinction of the dandelion species. The avoidance of extreme specialization and the adoption of consciousness are two promising strategies. Although the former has been extensively studied in Neo-Darwinian schools, little attention has been paid to the latter, which in the author's opinion might have been the driving force behind the development of the brain. TAMPOPO would be blind without the built-in abnormally_superior/3. To detect changes, it uses a set of environmental knowledge, Lipsitz. Here, we find a strong tie between knowledge and consciousness. In French, the meaning of dandelion includes the idea of knowledge, providing added support for the name TAMPOPO.*

Definition 3.2.6 modify(K,Recalled,CDom,Lipsitz,(K,Cm,_,_)) *The recalled experience in the list, Recalled, is modified to generate an intermediate* $(K, Cm, \_, \_)$*. The underline character denotes a free data field. If* $Recalled = [(Kr, Cr, \_)]$*, then the first clause replaces Kr with K and adds a perturbation to Cr, thus generating Cm. If Recalled contains two elements near to each other, the second clause applies. The Cb and Cs are crossed over by cross_over/3 to generate Cm. In other cases, the third clause adds a perturbation Pv to Cr, thus generating Cm.*

```
modify(K, [(Kr, Cr, _)], CDom, _, (K, Cm, _, _)) :-
  perturbed_vector(CDom, Pv)|
  Cm := (Cr + Pv).
modify(K, [(Kb, Cb, Jb), (Ks, Cs, Js)], CDom, Lipsitz, (K, Cm, _, _)) :-
  near((Kb, Cb, Jb), (Ks, Cs, Js), Lipsitz)|
  cross_over(Cb, Cs, Cm).
modify(K, [(Kb, Cb, Jb), (Ks, Cs, Js)], CDom, Lipsitz, (K, Cm, _, _)) :-
  otherwise|
  perturbed_vector(CDom, Pv)
  Cm := (Cb + Pv).
perturbed_vector(CDom, Pv) :-
  %Generate a perturbation vector Pv in CDom.
```

Definition 3.2.7 near((Kb,Cb,Jb),(Ks,Cs,Js),Lipsitz) *This clause judges whether the point* (Ks, Cs, Js) *is near to* (Kb, Cb, Jb) *by verifying whether the former lies in the Skirt of the latter (see Definition 3.2.5).*

$near((Kb, Cb, Jb), (Ks, Cs, Js), Lipsitz) :-$
$lower\_fur((Ks, Cs, Vs), (Kb, Cb, Jb), Lipsitz)|$
$Vs >= 0.$

Definition 3.2.8 cross_over(X,Y,Z) *Two vectors, X and Y, are crossed over to generate a new vector Z.*

$cross\_over(X, Y, [X1|Y2]) :-$
$length(X, L), length(Y, L),$
$random\_integer(P, [0, L])|$
$cut(X, P, X1, X2),$
$cut(Y, P, Y1, Y2).$
$length(X, L) : -\%L$ *is the dimension of* X.
$random\_integer(P, [0, L]) : -\%P$ *is a random integer in* $[0, L]$.
$cut(X, P, X1, X2) : -\%X$ *is partitioned at* P *into* $X1$ *and* $X2$.

Definition 3.2.9 rewrite((K,C,J,Memo),Memory,Memory1,Lipsitz,Max-Population) *By using a new experience* $(K, C, J, Memo)$, *the* $Memory$ *is rewritten into* $Memory1$. $partition/7$ *uses* (K, C, J) *to partition* $Memory$ *into four groups:* $Inferior$, $Equiv$, $NSuperior$, *and* $ASuperior$. *Then* $renew\_memory/7$ *constructs* $Memory1$ *by using the result.*

$rewrite((K, C, J, Memo), Memory, Memory1, Lipsitz, MaxPopulation) :-$
$partition(Memory, (K, C, J), Inferior, Equiv, NSuperior,$
$ASuperior, Lipsitz),$
$renew\_memory((K, C, J, Memo), Inferior, Equiv, NSuperior, ASuperior,$
$MaxPopulation, Memory1).$

Definition 3.2.10 partition(Memory,(K,C,J),Inferior,Equiv,NSuperior, ASuperior,Lipsitz) *The* $Memory$ *is partitioned into three groups in accordance with the new data* (K, C, J). $Inferior$ *is the group dominated by the new data.* $Equiv$ *is the non-comparable group.* $NSuperior$ *is the group that dominates the new data.* $ASuperior$ *is the group that dominates the new data but violates the Lipsitz condition of Definition 2.2.2. The first clause is for vacant memory. The second detects an inferior experience* $(K1, C1, J1)$ *by checking whether the new experience is a superior of it, then adds it to* $Inferior$. *The third detects an abnormally superior* $(K1, C1, J1)$ *and adds it to* $ASuperior$. *The fourth and the last are for equivalent and normally superior elements, respectively (see Figure 6).*

$partition([\,], \_, [\,], [\,], [\,], [\,], \_).$
$partition([(K1, C1, J1)|Mt], (K, C, J), [(K1, C1, J1)|Inferior],$
$Equiv, NSuperior, ASuperior, Lipsitz) :-$
$superior((K, C, J), (K1, C1, J1), Lipsitz)|$
$partition(Mt?, (K, C, J), Inferior, Equiv, NSuperior, ASuperior, Lipsitz).$
$partition([(K1, C1, J1)|Mt], (K, C, J), Inferior, Equiv,$
$NSuperior, [(K1, C1, J1)|ASuperior], Lipsitz) :-$
$abnormally\_superior((K1, C1, J1), (K, C, J), Lipsitz)|$
$partition(Mt?, (K, C, J), Inferior, Equiv, NSuperior, ASuperior, Lipsitz).$
$partition([(K1, C1, J1)|Mt], (K, C, J), Inferior,$
$[(K1, C1, J1)|Equiv], NSuperior, ASuperior, Lipsitz) :-$

$equivalent((K1, C1, J1), (K, C, J), Lipsitz)|$
$partition(M?, (K, C, J), Inferior, Equiv, NSuperior, ASuperior, Lipsitz).$
$partition([(K1, C1, J1)|Mt], (K, C, J), Inferior, Equiv,$
$[(K1, C1, J1)|NSuperior], ASuperior, Lipsitz) :-$
$otherwise|$
$partition(Mt?, (K, C, J), Inferior, Equiv, NSuperior, ASuperior, Lipsitz).$

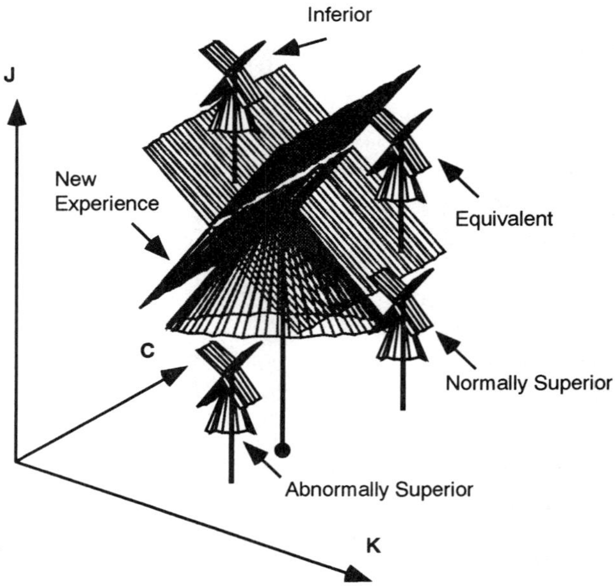

Fig. 6 Classification of old experiences by a new TAMPOPO.

Definition 3.2.11 superior((K1,C1,J1),(K2,C2,J2),Lipsitz) *This clause checks whether $(K1, C1, J1)$ is a superior of $(K2, C2, J2)$ by examining whether the latter is contained in the upper cone of the former. If this condition is true in a stable Fe, the former is certainly a superior. But in a time-varying environment where Fe shifts upward, there is a chance that an old, obsolete experience might seem to dominate a younger one. To avoid this anomaly, $(K1, C1, J1)$ should always be younger than $(K2, C2, J2)$. This requirement is always met because of the second clause of partition/7, in which superior/3 is used (see Definition 3.2.10).*

$superior((K1, C1, J1), (K2, C2, J2), Lipsitz) :-$
$upper\_fur((K2, C1, V2), (K1, C1, J1), Lipsitz)|$
$J2 > V2.$

Definition 3.2.12 abnormally_superior((K1,C1,J1),(K2,C2,J2),Lipsitz) *This clause checks whether $(K1, C1, J1)$ is abnormally superior to $(K2, C2, J2)$ by* *examining whether the former is under the Skirt of the vertex (K2, C2, J2). For time-independent Fe, this is never the case, owing to Supposition 2.2.2. For time-varying Fe, the vertex (K2, C2, J2) should be younger than (K1, C1, J1) in order for the condition to be met. But the condition is met by partition/7, in which this clause is used (see Definition 3.2.10).*

$abnormally\_superior((K1, C1, J1), (K2, C2, J2), Lipsitz) :-$
$\quad lower\_fur((K1, C1, V), (K2, C2, J2), Lipsitz)|$
$\quad J1 =< V.$

Definition 3.2.13 equivalent((K1,C1,J1),(K2,C2,J2),Lipsitz) *This clause checks the equivalence of (K1, C1, J1) and (K2, C2, J2) by examining whether the former is in the equivalence (indifference) area of the latter.*

$equivalent((K1, C1, J1), (K2, C2, J2), Lipsitz) :-$
$\quad upper\_fur((K1, C2, Vu), (K2, C2, J2), Lipsitz),$
$\quad lower\_fur((K1, C2, Vl), (K2, C2, J2), Lipsitz),$
$\quad Vl < J1 < Vu.$

Definition 3.2.14 renew_memory((K,C,J,Memo),Inferior,Equiv, NSuperior,ASuperior,MaxPopulation,Memory) *The new Memory is constructed by gathering usable fractions of old memory. Since Inferior is useless and ASuperior is inadmissible, only Equiv and NSuperior are usable. The new data (K, C, J) should be added if possible. The first clause is for non-full memory without NSuperior. In this case, the new data (K, C, J) and the Equiv are appended to form the new Memory. The marking Memo = in indicates that the new data is memorized in Memory. (Memo is a log-data for behavior analysis of the program. It has no practical role in learning.) The second clause is for full memory without NSuperior. In this case, only Equiv can enter Memory. Since the new data cannot enter, owing to the population limit, it is thrown away with the marking Memo = out. The third clause is for the case of NSuperior. In this case, Equiv and NSuperior are added to form the new Memory. The new data is thrown away, since it is dominated. Of these cases, only the first allows the new data to enter a new Memory.*

$renew\_memory((K, C, J, Memo), Inferior, Equiv, [\,], ASuperior,$
$\qquad MaxPopulation, Memory) :-$
$\quad not\_full(Equiv, MaxPopulation)|$
$\quad Memory = [(K, C, J)|Equiv], Memo = in.$
$renew\_memory((K, C, J, Memo), Inferior, Equiv, [\,], ASuperior,$
$\qquad MaxPopulation, Memory) :-$
$\quad full(Equiv, MaxPopulation)|$
$\quad Memory = Equiv, Memo = out.$
$renew\_memory((K, C, J, Memo), Inferior, Equiv, NSuperior, ASuperior,$
$\qquad MaxPopulation, Memory) :-$
$\quad NSuperior \neq [\,]|$
$\quad Memory = [Equiv|NSuperior], Memo = out.$
$full(Set, MaxPopulation) :-$
$\quad length(Set, Maxpopulation)|true.$

$not\_full(Set, MaxPopulation) :-$
$length(Set, L), L < MaxPopulation | true.$

4 Behavior Analysis of TAMPOPO

4.1 Recalling an experience similar to a new situation

Definition 4.1.1 *Suppose condition K, responses Ca and Cb to be adopted under the condition, and their score estimations $[Ja_{min}, Ja_{max}]$ and $[Jb_{min}, Jb_{max}]$ are given. Then Ca is said to be $safer$ than Cb at K if $Ja_{max} < Jb_{max}$. Here, a lower score is assumed to be better than a higher score.*

Proposition 4.1.1 *The predicate $upper\_fur((K, Cr, V), (Kr, Cr, Jr), Lipsitz)$ estimates the maximum (worst) score V of the response Cr at K.*

Proof.
(1) $\|V - Jr\| \leq Lipsitz * \|(K, Cr) - (Kr, Cr)\|$ (Supposition 2.2.2).
(2) $V \leq Jr + Lipsitz * \|(K, Cr) - (Kr, Cr)\|$ ((1)).
(3) $Jr + Lipsitz * \|(K, Cr) - (Kr, Cr)\|$ is the worst value brought by Cr at K ((2)).
(4) $upper\_fur/3$ calculates the right side of (2) (Premise, Definition 3.2.5). ■

Proposition 4.1.2 *$safe(K, (Ka, Ca, Ja), (Kb, Cb, Jb), Lipsitz)$ verifies that Ca is safer than Cb at K (see Figure 5).*

Proof.
(1) $safe/4$ estimates worst scores Va and Vb, obtained by Ca and Cb at K, and checks whether $Va < Vb$ (Premise, Definition 3.2.4, Proposition 4.1.1).
(2) Ca is safer than Cb (Definition 4.1.1, (1)). ■

Proposition 4.1.3 *Assume that two initial candidates $[CRb, CRs]$ are given and that $safe(K, CRb, CRs, Lipsitz)$ is true; then the predicate $recall\_auf/5$ recalls the best two of CRb, CRs, and $Memory$.*

Proof. By induction on the size of the $Memory$. (Basis) If $Memory = [\,]$ then $Recalled = [CRb, CRs]$, from the first clause of Definition 3.2.3.
(Hypothesis) Next assume that the proposition is true for $Memory = Mt$.
(Induction) Then the proposition becomes true for $Memory = [Mh|Mt]$. We have three cases concerning the safety of Mh in comparison with CRb and CRs:
(1) $safe(K, Mh, CRb, Lipsitz)$,
(2) $safe(K, CRb, Mh, Lipsitz) \wedge safe(K, Mh, CRs, Lipsitz)$,
(3) otherwise.
For these cases, the current two bests can be changed to $[Mh, CRb]$, $[CRb, Mh]$, and $[CRb, CRs]$, respectively (the last case is no change). Clauses in Definition 3.2.3 reduce any of these states to a new state having two new bests and a reduced memory. From the hypothesis, each of these new cases returns the solution. ■

Proposition 4.1.4 *The predicate $recall(K, Memory, CSuperior, Lipsitz, Recalled)$ recalls at most two safe candidate responses for any K.*

Proof. From the above cases, using Definition 3.2.2.
(1) If $Memory = [\,]$, then $Recalled = [(K, Cr, \_)]$, from the first clause.
(2) If $Memory = [One]$, then $Recalled = [One]$, from the second clause.

(3) If $Memory = [Mh|Mt]$, then $recall\_auf(K, Memory, [CRb, CRs], Lipsitz, Recalled)$ is used. From Proposition 4.1.3, $reall\_auf/5$ returns two safe sclutions in $Recalled$. ∎

Proposition 4.1.5 *$modify(K, Recalled, CDom, Lipsitz, (K, Cm, \_, \_))$ generates a new $(K, Cm, \_, \_)$ using K and $Recalled$.*

Proof. From Definition 3.2.6.
(1) If $Recalled = [(Kr, Cr, \_)]$, then $Cm = Cr + Pv$, where Pv is a random vector.
(2) If $Recalled = [(Kb, Cb, Jb), (Ks, Cs, Js)]$, then Cm is a cross-over of Cb and Cs. ∎

Theorem 4.1.1 *For any condition K, TAMPOPO can recall a safe response Cm.*

Proof.
(1) For $Messages = [(K, Cm, Jm, Memo)|Mt]$ generated by $environment/4$, $system/5$ invokes predicates $recall/5$ and $modify/5$ (Definition 3.2.1).
(2) $recall/5$ generates at most two safe experiences in $Recalled$ (Proposition 4.1.4).
(3) $modify/5$ generates a $(K, Cm, \_, \_)$ by using $Rcalled$ (Proposition 4.1.5). ∎

4.2 Learning in a stable environment

Definition 4.2.1 *When the predicate $evaluate\_one(K, C, Clock, Lipsitz, J)$ used to define the environment E in Definition 2.2.2 is independent of $Clock$, E is said to be time-independent or stable. $evaluate\_one(K, C, \_, Lipsitz, J)$ is the time-independent version of it that has a don't care (DC) variable "_" in place of $Clock$.*

Definition 4.2.2 *In a stable environment E, the minimum skyline of Fe seen from K is defined as follows. We abbreviate the skyline as $MSLFeK$. This formula is introduced only for the definition, not for calculation.*

$set\_of((Kms, Cms, Jms),$
$\forall C \neq Cms.better((Kms, Cms, Jms), (Kms, C, J), Lipsitz, Clock)),$
$MSLFeK).$
$set\_of(A, B, C) :- \%C\ is\ the\ set\ of\ A\ satisfying\ the\ condition\ B.$
$better((Kms, Cms, Jms), (Kms, C, J), Lipsitz, Clock) :-$
$evaluate\_one(Kms, C, Clock, Lipsitz, J),$
$evaluate\_one(Kms, Cms, Clock, Lipsitz, Jms),$
$Jms < J.$

Proposition 4.2.1 *$superior((Kms, Cms, Jms), (Kms, C, J), Lipsitz)$ is true for $(Kms, Cms, Jms) \in MSLFeK$ and $(Kms, C, J) \notin MSLFeK$.*

Proof.
(1) $better((Kms, Cms, Jms), (Kms, C, J), Lipsitz, Clock)$ (Premise, Definition 4.2.2).
(2) $Jms < J$ ((1), Definition 4.2.2).
(3) $V2 = Jms + Lipsitz * \|(Kms, Cms) - (Kms, Cms)\| = Jms \wedge (J > V2)$ ((2)).
(4) $upper\_fur((Kms, Cms, V2), (Kms, Cms, Jms), Lipsitz) \wedge (J > V2)$ ((3), Definition 3.2.5).
(5) $superior((Kms, Cms, Jms), (Kms, C, J), Lipsitz)$ ((4), Definition 3.2.11). ∎

Proposition 4.2.2 *$superior((K,C,J),(Kms,Cms,Jms),Lipsitz)$ is false for $(Kms,Cms,Jms) \in MSLFeK$ and $(K,C,J) \notin MSLFeK$.*

Proof. By Reductio ad Absurdum
(1) $superior((K,C,J),(Kms,Cms,Jms),Lipsitz)$ (Null Hypothesis).
(2) $upper\_fur((Kms,C,V2),(K,C,J),Lipsitz) \wedge Jms > V2$ ((1), Definition 3.2.11).
(3) $V2 = J + Lipsitz * \|(Kms,C) - (K,C)\| \wedge Jms > V2$ ((2), Definition 3.2.5).
(4) $Jms - J > Lipsits * \|(Kms,C) - (K,C)\|$ ((3)).
(5) Contradiction ((4), Supposition 2.2.2). ■

Proposition 4.2.3 *$abnormally\_superior((K,C,J),(Kms,Cms,Jms),Lipsitz)$ is false for $(Kms,Cms,Jms) \in MSLFeK$ and $(K,C,J) \notin MSLFeK$ in a stable E.*

Proof. By Reductio ad Absurdum
(1) $abnormally\_superior((K,C,J),(Kms,Cms,Jms),Lipsitz)$ (Null Hypothesis).
(2) $lower\_fur((K,C,V),(Kms,Cms,Jms),Lipsitz) \wedge J < V$ ((1), Definition 3.2.12).
(3) $V = Jms - Lipsitz * \|(Kms,Cms) - (K,C)\| \wedge J < V$ ((2), Definition 3.2.5).
(4) $Jms - J > Lipsits * \|(Kms,Cms) - (K,C)\|$ ((3)).
(5) Contradiction ((4), Supposition 2.2.2). ■

Theorem 4.2.1 *The minimum skyline of Fe, $MSLFeK$, is the fixed point of TAMPOPO.*

Proof. By Reductio ad Absurdum
(1) $rewrite((K,C,J,Memo),Memory,Memory1,Lipsitz,MaxPopulation)$ rewrites $(Kms,Cms,Jms) \in MSLFeK$ by some $(K,C,J) \notin MSLFeK$ (Null Hypothesis).
(2) (Kms,Cms,Jms) is grouped into either $Inferior$ or $ASuperior$ by $partition(Memory,(K,C,J),Inferior,Equiv,NSuperior,ASuperior,Lipsitz)$ (Definition 3.2.9, 3.2.14).
(3) Case1: $superior((K,C,J),(Kms,Cms,Jms),Lipsitz)$ (Definition 3.2.10).
(4) Contradiction ((3), Proposition 4.2.2).
(5) Case2: $abnormally\_superior((K,C,J),(Kms,Cms,Jms),Lipsitz)$ (Def. 3.2.10).
(6) Contradiction ((5), Proposition 4.2.3). ■

Definition 4.2.3 *The superior set $SuperiorSet$ of the point $(Kn,Cn,Jn) \notin MSLFeK$ is defined by the following formula. This formula is introduced only for the definition, not for the calculation.*

$$
\begin{aligned}
&set\_of((K,C,J),\\
&\quad evaluate\_one(K,C,Clock,Lipsitz,J) \wedge\\
&\qquad (J < Jn - Lipsitz * \|(K,Cn) - (Kn,Cn)\|),\\
&\quad SuperiorSet).
\end{aligned}
$$

Proposition 4.2.4 *The superior set of (Kn,Cn,Jn) does not contain the point itself.*

Proof.
(1) $(Kn,Cn,Jn) \in SuperiorSet$ (Null Hypothesis).
(2) $Jn < Jn - Lipsitz * \|(Kn,Cn) - (Kn,Cn)\| = Jn$ (Definition 4.2.3).
(3) Contradiction ((2)). ■

Proposition 4.2.5 *$(Kn, Cn, Jn) \notin MSLFeK$ is deleted by any element of its $SuperiorSet$.*

Proof.
(1) $(Kd, Cd, Jd) \in SuperiorSet$ (Assumption).
(2) $Jd < Jn - Lipsitz * \|(Kd, Cn) - (Kn, Cn)\|$ ((1), Definition 4.2.4).
(3) $Jn > V2 \wedge V2 = Jd + Lipsitz * \|(Kd, Cn) - (Kn, Cn)\|$ ((2)).
(4) $upper\_fur((Kn, Cd, V2), (Kd, Cd, Jd), Lipsitz) \wedge Jn > V2$ ((3), Definition 3.2.5).
(5) $superior((Kd, Cd, Jd), (Kn, Cn, Jn), Lipsitz)$ ((4), Definition 3.2.11).
(6) (Kn, Cn, Jn) is grouped into $Inferior$ ((5), Definition 3.2.10).
(7) (Kn, Cn, Jn) is deleted from $Memory$ ((6), Definition 3.2.14). ■

Proposition 4.2.6 *Let the superior set of $(Kn, Cn, Jn) \notin MSLFeK$ be Sn. Then $Sn \cap MSLFeK \neq \phi$.*

Proof.
(1) $(Kn, Cmn, Jmn) \in MLSFeK$ (Assumption).
(2) $Cn \neq Cmn$ ((1), Premise).
(3) $\forall C \neq Cmn.better((Kn, Cmn, Jmn), (Kn, C, J), Lipsitz, Clock)$ ((1), Definition 4.2.2).
(4) $evaluate\_one(Kn, Cn, Clock, Lipsitz, Jn) \wedge$
$evaluate\_one(Kn, Cmn, Clock, Lipsitz, Jmn) \wedge$
$Jmn < Jn$ ((2), (3), Definition 4.2.2).
(5) $Jn = Jn - 0 = Jn - Lipsitz * \|(Kn, Cn) - (Kn, Cn)\|$ (Obvious).
(6) $evaluate\_one(Kn, Cmn, Clock, Lipsitz, Jmn) \wedge Jmn < Jn - Lipsitz*$
$\|(Kn, Cn) - (Kn, Cn)\|$ ((3), (5)).
(7) $(Kn, Cmn, Jmn) \in Sn$ ((6), Definition 4.2.3). ■

Definition 4.2.4 *Let the superior set of (K_i, C_i, J_i) be S_i and $(K_{i+1}, C_{i+1}, J_{i+1}) \in S_i$, $(i = 0, \ldots, \infty)$. The series S_i $(i = 0, \ldots, \infty)$ is called a superior set series, or SSS, corresponding to the experience series $(K_0, C_0, J_0), (K_1, C_1, J_1), \ldots$.*

Proposition 4.2.7 *Let the series S_i $(i = 0, \ldots, \infty)$ be SSS of $(K_0, C_0, J_0), (K_1, C_1, J_1)$, ... Then $S_{i+1} \subset S_i$ $(i = 0, \ldots, \infty)$.*

Proof.
(1) $(K_{i+1}, C_{i+1}, J_{i+1}) \in S_i, (i = 1, \ldots, \infty)$ (Assumption).
(2) $(K_{i+1}, C_{i+1}, J_{i+1})$ and (K_i, C_i, J_i) satisfy the formula
$J_{i+1} < J_i - Lipsitz * \|(K_{i+1}, C_i) - (K_i, C_i)\|$ (Definition 4.2.3).
(3) $(K_{i+2}, C_{i+2}, J_{i+2})$ and $(K_{i+1}, C_{i+1}, J_{i+1})$ satisfy the formula
$J_{i+2} < J_{i+1} - Lipsitz * \|(K_{i+2}, C_{i+1}) - (K_{i+1}, C_{i+1})\|$ ((2), $i \rightarrow i+1$).
(4) $(K_{i+2}, C_{i+2}, J_{i+2})$ and (K_i, C_i, J_i) satisfy the formula
$J_{i+2} < J_i - Lipsitz * \|(K_{i+2}, C_i) - (K_i, C_i)\|$ ((2), (3), (4+)).
(5) $(K_{i+2}, C_{i+2}, J_{i+2})$ $(\in S_{i+1}) \in S_i$ of (K_i, C_i, J_i) ((4), Definition 4.2.3).
(6) $S_{i+1} \subseteq S_i$ ((5)).
(7) $(K_{i+1}, C_{i+1}, J_{i+1})$ $(\in S_i) \notin S_i$ (Proposition 4.2.4).
(8) $S_{i+1} \subset S_i$ ((6), (7)).
(4+)

$$J_{i+2} < J_{i+1} - \mathit{Lipsitz} * \|(K_{i+2}, C_{i+1}) - (K_{i+1}, C_{i+1})\|,$$
$$< J_i - \mathit{Lipsitz} * \|(K_{i+1}, C_i) - (K_i, C_i)\| - \mathit{Lipsits} * \|(K_{i+2}, C_{i+1}) - (K_{i+1}, C_{i+1})\|,$$
$$= J_i - \mathit{Lipsitz} * \|(K_{i+1}, C_i) - (K_i, C_i)\| - \mathit{Lipsits} * \|(K_{i+2}, C_i) - (K_{i+1}, C_i)\|,$$
$$< J_i - \mathit{Lipsitz} * \|(K_{i+2}, C_i) - (K_i, C_i)\|.$$ ■

Proposition 4.2.8 *Let the series S_i $(i = 0, \ldots, \infty)$ be SSS of $(K_0, C_0, J_0) \notin MSLFeK$. Then SSS converges to $MSLFeK$.*

Proof.
(1) SSS is a convergent series (Proposition 4.2.7).
(2) $S_i \cap MSLFeK \neq \phi$ (Definition 4.2.6).
(3) SSS converges to $MSLFeK$ ((1),(2)). ■

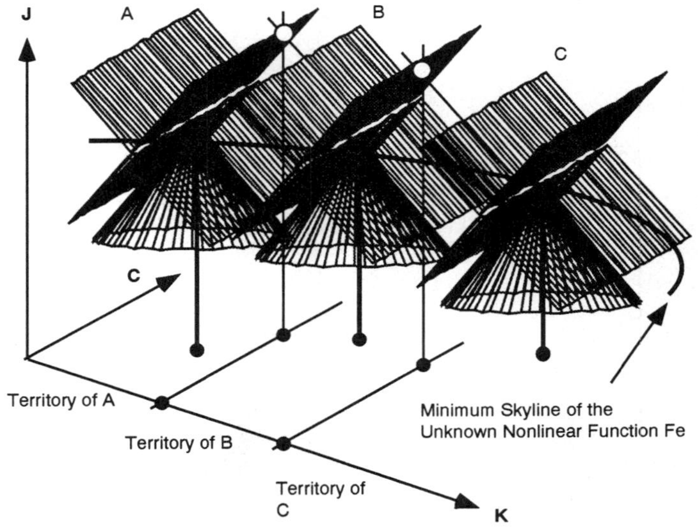

Fig. 7 Convergence of TAMPOPO to a minimum skyline.

Theorem 4.2.2 *In stable environments, TAMPOPO detects the $MSLFeK$ of the unknown nonlinear function $Fe : (K, C, Clock) \to J$ (Figure 7).*

Proof.
(1) $MSLFeK$ is the set of fixed points of Fe (Theorem 4.2.1).
(2) Any $(K, C, J) \notin MSLFeK$ is rewritten (Proposition 4.2.5).
(3) The rewriting converges to $MSLFeK$ (Proposition 4.2.8). ■

4.3 Learning in a time-varying environment

Definition 4.3.1 *The environment is said to be time-varying when the score J calculated by the predicate evaluate_one$(K, C, Clock, Lipsitz, J)$ depends on $Clock$.*

Definition 4.3.2 *We say that an old experience* (K, C, Jo) *exists above or below a new environment if* (K, C, Jo) *is above* (K, C, Jn) *or below it—that is, if* $Jo > Jn$ *or* $Jo < Jn$*, where* Jn *is the value of* $Fe : (K, C, Clock) \rightarrow J$ *in the new environment.*

Proposition 4.3.1 *For any* (K, C)*, its* Jo/Jn *before/after the environmental change satisfies one of the three relations* $Jo > Jn$*,* $Jo = Jn$*, and* $Jo < Jn$*.*

Proof. Obvious. ■

Theorem 4.3.1 *TAMPOPO can adapt to environmental changes.*

Proof. Suppose that the environment changes at $Clock = t$; then an old experience during $Clock < t$ can be shown to be replaced by a new experience at some $Clock > t$ by $rewrite/5$.
(Case1) An old set of data (Ko, Co, Jo) in the $Memory$ is above the new environment. In this case, there exists a $SuperiorSet$ of (Ko, Co, Jo) defined below during $Clock > t$. Any $(Kn, Cn, Jn) \in SuperiorSet$ can rewrite the old data (Ko, Co, Jo) in accordance with a line of reasoning similar to that of Proposition 4.2.5.

$$\begin{array}{l} set\_of((Kn, Cn, Jn), \\ \quad \forall Colck > t.evaluate\_one(Kn, Cn, Clock, Lipsitz, Jn) \wedge \\ \quad\quad (Jn < Jo - Lipsitz * \|(Kn, Cn) - (Ko, Cn)\|), \\ \quad SuperiorSet). \end{array}$$

(Case2) An old set of data (Ko, Co, Jo) in the $Memory$ is below the new environment. In this case, there exists a $SuperiorSet$ of (Ko, Co, Jo) defined below during $Clock > t$. Any $(Kn, Cn, Jn) \in SuperiorSet$ can rewrite the old data (Ko, Co, Jo) in accordance with a discussion similar to that of Proposition 4.2.5. If $(Kn, Cn, Jn) \in MSLFeK$, then the fixed point is reached. Otherwise, since $(Kn, Cn, Jn) \notin MSLFeK$, it is rewritten toward the new $MSLFeK$, as shown by Theorem 4.2.2.

$$\begin{array}{l} set\_of((Kn, Cn, Jn), \\ \quad \forall Colck > t.evaluate\_one(Kn, Cn, Clock, Lipsitz, Jn) \wedge \\ \quad\quad (Jn > Jo + Lipsitz * \|(Kn, Cn) - (Ko, Co)\|), \\ \quad SuperiorSet). \end{array}$$

■

Corollary 4.3.1 *TAMPOPO can escape from a fixed point that it acquired in an old environment.*

Proof. From Theorem 4.3.1. ■

Theorem 4.3.2 *TAMPOPO gives a solution of Problem 2.2.1.*

Proof.
(1) Suppose that $improved(Messages, Lipsitz)$ does not hold (Null hypothesis).
(2) $dominated\_by\_someone((K, C, J, in), Mtail, Lipsitz)$ is $false$ for some sublist $[(K, C, J, in)|Mtail] \in Messages$ ((1), Definition 2.2.4).
(3) There exists a set of experience data (K, C, J, in) that is not rewritten ((2)).
(4) Contradiction (Theorem 4.2.2, 4.3.1). ■

4.4 Discussions

Discussion 4.4.1 TAMPOPO plays games with the environment *The unknown function* $Fe : (K, C, Clock) \rightarrow J$ *can be seen as a payoff or a Hamiltonian of the game played by TAMPOPO with the environment* E*.* E *tells TAMPOPO* K*, and TAMPOPO answers* C*. There are many choices of* C *for a given* K*. The problem is how to select the most effective* C *for any* K*. This can be solved when TAMPOPO fully detects* $MSLFeK$*. The detection should be done in real time in a time-varying environment by using only experience.* $Messages$ *is the log of the game and* $Memory$ *is TAMPOPO's private note for memorizing useful moves.*

Discussion 4.4.2 TAMPOPO uses dynamical equilibrium *TAMPOPO is an open system. Its* $Memory$ *is perpetually rewritten. New experiences flow in, and old ones flow out. In this incessant flow, the approximation of* $MSLFeK$ *is formed in* $Memory$ *as a dynamical equilibrium. This is not a stable equilibrium, but a quasi-stable one that allows flexible adaptation to environmental changes.*

Discussion 4.4.3 TAMPOPO has primitive consciousness *A learning machine can be seen as a minimum point detector of some Hamiltonian. Machines lacking global knowledge of the environment can only resort to a local gradient search. Once trapped in a minimum, it is difficult for them to escape so long as a local minimum remains. In contrast, TAMPOPO uses a set of environmental knowledge—Lipsitz—that characterizes the curvature of the Hamiltonian.* $abnormally\_superior/3$ *used the knowledge to detect and delete obsolete experiences, however effective these experiences were formerly.* This primitive consciousness *allows the machine to exit from old* $MSLFek$*.*

5 Conclusions

5.1 Summary

(1) The learning problem was shown to be formulatable as a minimum skyline detection problem for an unknown, time-varying nonlinear function.
(2) A formulation of the minimum skyline detection problem in Concurrent Prolog was given.
(3) A formal specification of a learning machine, TAMPOPO, was given as a solution to the problem.
(4) Behavioral analyses of TAMPOPO were given along the lines of fixed point theory.

5.2 Further research

(1) Enhancement of learning speed: The learning speed of TAMPOPO can be enhanced by several methods, including provision of built-in a *priori* rules in $Memory$, enhancement of the predicate $modify/5$, and provision of application-specific human teaching. These topics require further research.
(2) Applications: The application of TAMPOPO to various real-world problems is another task that needs to be studied further.

Acknowledgments.

I would like to thank Prof. M. Iri of the University of Tokyo for his continuing advice on algorithm design. I also thank the editor and the anonymous referees of Computer Software, who gave useful comments on the initial version of this article.

References

[1] Aha, D.W., Kibler, D., and Albert, M.K.: Instance-based Learning Algorithms, *Machine Learning*, Vol. 6, No. 1 (1991), pp. 37–66.

[2] Amari, S.: A Theory of Adaptive Pattern Classifiers, *IEEE Trans. on Electronic Computers*, Vol. EC–16, No. 3 (1967), pp. 299–307.

[3] Chang, C.L. and Lee, R.C.T.: *Symbolic Logic and Mechanical Theorem Proving*, Academic Press, New York, 1973.

[4] Farmer, J.D., Packard, N.H., and Perelson, A.S.: The Immune System, Adaptation, and Machine Learning. In D. Farmer, A. Lapedes, N. Packard, and B. Wendroff, (eds.), *Evolution, Games and Learning*, North-Holland, Amsterdam, 1986, pp. 187–204.

[5] Fukushima, K.: Cognitron: a Self-organizing Multilayered Neural Network, *Biol. Cybernetics*, Vol. 20, No. 3/4 (1975), pp. 121–136.

[6] Grossgerg, S.: On the Development of Detectors in the Visual Cortex with Applications to Learning and Reaction-Diffusion Systems, *Biol. Cybernetics*, Vol. 21, No. 3 (1976), pp. 145–159.

[7] Hebb, D.O.: *The Organization of Behavior*, John Wiley & Sons, New York, 1952.

[8] Holland, J.H.: A Mathematical Framework for Studying Learning in Classifier Systems. In D. Farmer, A. Lapedes, N. Packard, and B. Wendroff, (eds.), *Evolution, Games and Learning*, North-Holland, Amsterdam, 1986, pp. 307–317.

[9] Hopfield, J.J.: Neural Networks and Physical Systems with Emergent Collective Computational Abilities, *Proc. Natl. Acad. Sci. USA*, Vol. 79, No. 8 (1982), pp. 2554–2558.

[10] Kampfner, R. and Conrad, M.: Computational Modelling of Evolutionary Learning Processes in the Brain, *Bull. Math. Biol.*, Vol. 45, No. 6 (1983), pp. 931–968.

[11] Kauffman, S.A. and Smith, R.G.: Adaptive Automata Based on Darwinian Selection. In D. Farmer, A. Lapedes, N. Packard, and B. Wendroff, (eds.), *Evolution, Games and Learning*, North-Holland, Amsterdam,1986, pp. 68–82.

[12] Kirby, K.G. and Conrad, M.: Intraneuronal Dynamics as a Substrate for Evolutionary Learning. In D. Farmer, A. Lapedes, N. Packard, and B. Wendroff, (eds.), *Evolution, Games and Learning*, North-Holland, Amsterdam,1986, pp. 205–215.

[13] KoHonen, T.: Correlation matrix memories, *IEEE Trans. on Computers*, Vol. C–21, No.4 (1972), pp. 353–359.

[14] Kowalski, R.A.: *Logic for Problem Solving*, North-Holland, NewYork, 1979.

[15] Lloyd, J.W.: *Foundations of Logic Programming*, Springer-Verlag, Berlin, 1984.

[16] Malsburg, C.: Self-Organization of Orientation Sensitive Cells in the Striate Cortex, *Kybernetik*, Vol. 14 (1973), pp. 85–100.

[17] MuCulloch, W.S. and Pitts, W.H.: A Logical Calculus of the Ideas Immanent in Neural Nets, *Bull. Math. Biophys*, Vol. 5 (1943), pp. 115–133.

[18] Nakano, K.: Associatron—A Model of Associative Memory, *IEEE Trans. Syst. Man Cybern.*, Vol. SMC–16, No. 3 (1972), pp. 381–388.

[19] Robinson, J.A.: *LOGIC: Form and Function*, Edinburgh University Press, Edinburgh, 1979.

[20] Rosenblatt, F.: *Principles of Neurodynamics*, Spartan Books, Washington D.C., 1962.

[21] Shapiro, E. (ed.): *Concurrent Prolog: Collected Papers*, Vols. 1 and 2, MIT Press, Cambridge, Massachusetts, 1987.

[22] Sutton, R.: Learning to Predict by the Method of Temporal Difference, *Machine Learning*, Vol. 3, No. 1 (1988), pp. 9–44.

[23] Takeuchi, K. and Amari, S.: Foundations of Topographic Maps and Columnar Microstructure, *Biol. Cybernetics*, Vol. 35, No. 2 (1979), pp. 63–72.

[24] Watanabe, T.: Design of a Knowledge–Based Heuristic Optimizer that Evolves: An Open System Approach, *Trans. Inf. Proc. Soc. Japan*, Vol. 24, No. 1 (1983), pp. 113–124 (in Japanese).

[25] Watanabe, T., Sasaki, K., and Ihara, K.: DANDELION: Duplication and Deletion Strategy that Realizes an Autonomous Learner, *Trans. Inf. Proc. Soc. Japan*, Vol. 24, No. 6 (1983), pp. 847–856 (in Japanese).

[26] Watanabe, T.: Design of an Autonomous Resource Manager by Using an Adaptive Knowledge Base TAMPOPO, *Operating System*, Vol. 34, No. 4 (1987), pp. 1–8. (in Japanese).

[27] Widrow, B.: Generalization and Information Storage in Networks of Adaline Neurons. In M.C. Yovits et al., (eds.), *Self-Organizing Systems*, Spartan, Washington D.C., 1962, pp. 435–461.

Initially published in "Computer Software", Vol. 9, No. 4, in Japanese.

Toshinori Watanabe
Department of Information Systems Design
Graduate School of Information Systems
University of Electro-Communications
1–5–1 Chofugaoka, Chofu-shi, Tokyo
182 Japan

Implementation of Augmented Logic Language (ALL)

Fumio Motoyoshi Taisuke Sato

Summary. It is proven in this paper that when a formula and a set P* of predicate definitions constructed by a generalized completion method are given, the formula can be transformed to an asymptotic normal form with respect to P* using Clark's equational theory E(Σ), which is an axiomization of the Herbran universe. An augmented logic language, named ALL, is proposed here as a new logic programming language having remarkable descriptive power. The ALL interpreter is also presented and can efficiently compute partial solutions of an asymptotic nomal form for a given goal under E(Σ) and P*, although some limitations exist with respect to the class of the goal and predicate definitions. ALL is supported by three-valued logic such that when its execution terminates, the result is a logical consequence of a given goal and definitions. ALL can be viewed as an extension of Prolog, since it has the ability to treat universal quantifiers in a goal clause and to obtain values for variables in negative literals.

1 Introduction

The logic programming language Prolog, which efficiently executes programs written in predicate logics, restricts the class of programs to those consisting of Horn clauses for efficiency. Although attempts were made to extend the executable class, extra-logical mechanisms (i.e., "negation as failure" [4] and "bagof" [2]) were incorporated to maintain syntactical coherence of Horn clauses.

In addition, logical treatment of formulae via inclusion of negations or implications was incorporated [3], yet values for variables in negative literals could not be obtained.

Theoretical studies conducted on equational theory and systems of predicate definitions have revealed the properties concerning decision procedures for transformating formulae, and, consequently, the formulae termed *disjunctive normal forms* are known to exist.

The development of an augmented logic language (ALL) interpreter, described here, has made it possible to efficiently obtain the disjunctive normal forms for a goal by limiting the class of definitions and goals. Though Prolog may be considered an interpreter of this kind, it cannot execute formulae of the form $\forall x : (p(x,y) \rightarrow q(x,z))$, nor can it obtain values for free variables in the antecedent part of an implication (as a special case, this formula would be simply a negation if the consequent part were false), both of which are possible with ALL.

ISBN 0-12-037105-7

In ALL, predicate definitions are typically made as follows (logical symbols are represented by using the JIS-X0208 character set):

```
even(x) ⇔ x = 0 ∨ ∃y:( x = s(y) ∧ ¬ even(y) ).
```

If the next formula is typed to get the answers

```
the x:¬even(x),
```

the first answer will be

```
s(0),
```

and if further computation is necessary, the subsequent answer will be

```
s(s(s(0))).
```

In this example, the syntax `the x:` is used to indicate the free variables for which the user want values to satisfy the part of the formula following : . If the form $\exists x$: is used instead of `the x:`, the answer will be `T` or `F`, representing a truth value.

Section 2 describes the symbol notation and terminology used in this paper, while Section 3 discusses the relationship between the ALL interpreter and the theoretical backgound for the equational theory $E(\Sigma)$. Since the ALL interpreter is implemented as an efficient rewriting system, the interpreter is described by using a set of transformation rules presented in Section 4, and techniques for efficiently executing the interpreter are also included. In Section 6, the limitations of the ALL interpreter are described, and Section 7 gives some examples.

The rewriting system of the ALL interpreter consists of an unfolding operation of user predicates and equivalence-preserving transformations in three-valued logic, and the obtained result is a partial solution of the disjunctive normal form of Chapter 3, supported by this logic. The partial solution may be considered as corresponding to the answer set of Prolog; however, the interpreter will stop execution without obtaining the answer if the program exceeds the permitted class, since the rules are limited for efficiency. The interpreter may also fall into an infinite loop and not terminate, though it is the programmar's responsibility to prevent this, just as in Prolog.

2 Notation and Terminology

The following symbols are used as specified: x, y, z for logical variables; a, b, e for terms; f, g for function symbols; p, q, r for logical formulae; and i, j, k, l, m, n for integer indexes. Furthermore, when suffixed, these symbols have the same meaning as when unsuffixed. The symbol Σ indicates the set of function symbols under consideration, and constants are considered as function applications of null arguments. Free variables in a formula e are represented by $\mathbf{V}_f(e)$, and a substitution is written as $p\{x : e\}$, which is the formula e substituted for x in p. In the substitution, the free variables $\mathbf{V}_f(e)$ should not be bound in p (renaming should be done if names conflict).

The following notation is used to show the variable dependencies:

$$\begin{array}{rll} e[x_1, \ldots, x_n] & \text{means} & \{x_1, \ldots, x_n\} \equiv \mathbf{V}_f(e[x_1, \ldots, x_n]), \\ e[x, \ldots] & \text{means} & x \not\equiv e[x, \ldots] \text{ and } x \in \mathbf{V}_f(e[x, \ldots]), \\ e[\hat{x}] & \text{means} & x \notin \mathbf{V}_f(e[\hat{x}]), \\ e[\hat{x}, y_1, \ldots, y_n] & \text{means} & x \notin \mathbf{V}_f(e[\hat{x}, y_1, \ldots, y_n]) \end{array}$$

and $\{y_1, \ldots, y_n\} \equiv \mathbf{V}_f(e[\hat{x}, y_1, \ldots, y_n])$.

The primitive predicate = plays an important role in ALL. It is used as an infix operator and satisfies the equational theory E(Σ) [4], which is described in Section 3.

A user predicate in ALL is defined by an equivalence relation $\Leftrightarrow$ in three-valued logic and may be considered as an extension of the completion of Horn clauses [11]. By means of this completion, the ALL interpreter can use the predicates to unfold a goal through the equivalence relations. The connective $\Leftrightarrow$ has the value true if and only if both its sides have the same truth value. Truth values are represented by $\top$, $\perp$, and $\sqcup$, meaning true, false, and unknown, respectively. Here the generalized completion is simply called completion, and it explicitly indicates the closed world assumption when negations exist in definitions or goals.

To rewrite predicates written in Prolog by completion, clauses with the same head predicate are connected into a definition whose body is a disjunction of the goal parts of the clauses, with the attached unification operations to be matched with the arguments [11]. For example,

```
add(0,z,z),
add(s(u),y,s(v)) :- add(u , y , v).
```

are translated as

```
add(x,y,z) ⇔
  (x=0 ∧ y=z) ∨ ∃u,v:(x=s(u) ∧ z = s(v) ∧ add(u,y,v)).
```

Variables in the LHS of a definition are called parameters.

3 Logical Background and the ALL Interpreter

The following equational theory E(Σ) was proven to be complete [8], meaning that for any formula without free variables, either it or its negation can be derived from E(Σ), where Σ is a set of function symbols.

$$\begin{aligned} E(\Sigma) \stackrel{\text{def}}{=} \{ \; & f(x_1, \ldots, x_m) = f(y_1, \ldots, y_m) \rightarrow \; x_1 = y_1 \wedge \cdots \wedge x_m = y_m \, , \\ & \neg f(x_1, \ldots, x_m) = g(y_1, \ldots, y_n) \, , \\ & \neg x = e[x, \ldots] \\ & \quad \mid f, g \in \Sigma \, , \; f \not\equiv g \; , \; x \not\equiv e[x, \ldots] \}. \end{aligned}$$

It was additionally shown that any formula consisting of the predicate = and symbols in Σ can be transformed into an equivalent disjunctive normal form by quantifier elimination methods [6, 9]. Since the disjunctive normal form is used to represent answers generated by ALL, it is described as follows:

Let the formula

$$\exists y_1, \ldots, y_l : (x_1 = e_1 \wedge \cdots \wedge x_n = e_n)$$

be called a basic formula with respect to $x_1, \ldots, x_n$. If $\alpha, \beta_1, \ldots, \beta_h$ are basic formulae with respect to $x_1, \ldots, x_n$, let

$$\Psi \;\equiv\; \alpha \wedge \neg\beta_1 \wedge \cdots \wedge \neg\beta_h$$

be called a disjunctive form with respect to $x_1, \ldots, x_n$ ($h \geq 0$). (In a special case, when $n = 0$, the disjunctive form is either true or false, indicating that E(Σ) is complete.) Then, if $|\Sigma| \equiv \infty$, any formula consisting of symbols in Σ and a predicate $=$ with free variables $x_1, \ldots, x_n$ can be transformed into $\Psi_1 \vee \cdots \vee \Psi_m$ $(m \geq 0)$ under $\mathrm{E}(\Sigma)$, where Ψ_i is a disjunctive form with respect to $x_1, \ldots, x_n$. If $|\Sigma| < \infty$, the above transformation is possible under $\mathrm{E}(\Sigma) \cup \mathrm{DCA}$ instead of $\mathrm{E}(\Sigma)$ [12], where

$$\mathrm{DCA} \equiv \{\vee_{f \in \Sigma} \exists y_1, \ldots, y_m : x = f(y_1, \ldots, y_m)\}.$$

The following property was shown to be true with respect to $\mathrm{E}(\Sigma) \cup \mathrm{P}^*$ in three-valued logic(meaning that user predicates may have an unknown truth value in addition to true and false [8, 10], where P^* is a set of user predicate definitions as described in the previous section). The next two statements are equivalent [10]:

1. A formula p is derived from $\mathrm{E}(\Sigma) \cup \mathrm{P}^*$.
2. A formula that is obtained from p by unfolding its contained user predicates a particular number of times and then replacing all newly appeared predicate calls with unknowns is derived from $\mathrm{E}(\Sigma)$.

In other words,

$$\exists n.\mathrm{E}(\Sigma), \mathrm{P}^* \models_3 \mathrm{G} \Leftrightarrow \mathrm{E}(\Sigma) \models_3 \mathrm{G}^{(n)}[\sqcup; \sqcup], \qquad (A)$$

where $A \models_3 B$ means that B is true for any model of B in three-valued logic, and with $\mathrm{G}^{(n)}$ being defined as

$$\mathrm{G}^{(0)} \stackrel{\mathrm{def}}{=} \mathrm{G},$$

$$\mathrm{G}^{(n+1)} \stackrel{\mathrm{def}}{=} \text{just once unfolded } \mathrm{G}^{(n)} \text{ for all predicates except } =,$$

and $\mathrm{G}^{(n)}[e_+; e_-]$ being the formula obtained from $\mathrm{G}^{(n)}$ in which its positive user predicates are replaced by e^+ and its negative ones by e^-.

The RHS of (A) means that $\mathrm{G}^{(n)}[\sqcup; \sqcup]$ is true for any model of $\mathrm{E}(\Sigma)$. On the other hand, it has been shown [18] that the RHS of (A) is equivalent to

$$\mathrm{E}(\Sigma) \models_2 \mathrm{G}^{(n)}[\bot; \top],$$

where $A \models_2 B$ means that B is true for any two-valued model of A. Therefore, the LHS of (A) is reduced to a two-valued logic problem, which is decidable according to the completeness of $\mathrm{E}(\Sigma)$ if n is fixed. Furthermore, when the predicate definition P^* is "strict" with respect to a ground literal L, then

$$\mathrm{E}(\Sigma) \cup \mathrm{P}^* \models_3 \mathrm{L} \Leftrightarrow \mathrm{E}(\Sigma) \cup \mathrm{P}^* \models_2 \mathrm{L},$$

where "P^* is strict with respect to L" means that no predicates in L depend both positively and negatively on the same predicate in P^* [10].

The above properties indicate that whether or not a ground literal L is true can be semi-decidable under $\mathrm{E}(\Sigma)$ and strict definitions P^*, and that a complete theorem–proving system exists in the sense that L is proved only when $\mathrm{E}(\Sigma), \mathrm{P}^* \models_2$ L for a strict definition P^*.

Let us consider $G(x)$ in $\mathrm{E}(\Sigma) \cup \mathrm{P}^*$, where $G(x)$ is a formula made from the free variable x and predicates in P^*. Then, for any constant a,

$$\mathrm{E}(\Sigma) \cup \mathrm{P}^* \models_3 G(a)$$

and

$$\exists n : (\mathrm{E}(\Sigma) \models_2 G(a)^{(n)}[\bot; \top])$$

are equivalent, from the above discussions. Therefore, if G_n is defined as

$$G_n(x) \stackrel{\mathrm{def}}{=} G(x)^{(n)}[\bot; \top],$$

it is true that

$$\mathrm{E}(\Sigma) \cup \mathrm{P}^* \models_3 G(a) \quad \text{iff} \quad \exists n : (\mathrm{E}(\Sigma) \models_2 G_n(a)), \qquad (B)$$

whereas (B) is not generally true if $\models_3$ is replaced by $\models_2$. A sufficient condition for such a case to hold is that P* should be strict with respect to $G(x)$.

Since $G_n(x)$ is a formula consisting only of the predicate =, (B) can be transformed into a disjunctive normal form. In addition, from the monotonity of three-valued logic and Proposition 3.1 of Sato [18], there exists $R_n(x)$ such that

$$G_{n+1}(x) \;\Leftrightarrow\; G_n(x) \vee R_n(x).$$

At least $R_n(x)(\equiv G_{n+1}(x))$ satisfies the above relation. The disjunctive normal form derived from $G_n(x)$ is an increasing disjunction for n, and hence we may call the disjunctive normal form of $G_n(x)$ the (n-th order) asymptotic normal form of $G(x)$.

The operation for obtaining the asymptotic normal form may be considerd a "complete" interpreter for first-order programs in three-valued logic. The reason is that for any set P* of predicate definitions and goal $G(x)$, we can obtain a solution with a desired similarity to the whole solution $\vee_{n=0}^{\mathrm{inf}} G_n(x)$. Three-valued logic is essential, since in two-valued logic, predicate definitions may include a contradiction such as $p(x) \Leftrightarrow \neg p(x)$; thus any formula would be a solution. Contrastingly, in three-valued logic, all predicate definitions are consistent. It should be noted that even if the definitions are consistent, a procedure for obtaining such a solution is not known for general first-order programs. Moreover, the above $G_n(x)$ does not generally converge to a solution in two-valued logic.

Thus far, the predicates in $G^{(n)}(x)$ have been uniformly unfolded. However, even if the unfolding operation is not uniform, the following statement is true. Let $G'(x)$ be a non-uniformly unfolded formula of $G(x)$, and let the maximum and minimum numbers of unfolding operations for the all predicates in $G'(x)$ be m and n; then

$$G^{(m)}(x)[\bot;\top] \;\rightarrow\; G'(x)[\bot;\top] \;\rightarrow\; G^{(n)}(x)[\bot;\top]. \qquad (C)$$

On the other hand, $G'(x)$ can be transformed into the form of $H(x) \vee R(x)$ (where $H(x)$ consists of only = and Σ) and $G'(x)[\bot;\top] \;\Leftrightarrow\; H(x) \vee R(x)[\bot;\top]$; therefore, $H(x) \;\rightarrow\; G^{(n)}(x)[\bot;\top]$ is true, and $H(x)$ may be called a nth-order partial solution.

The ALL interpreter efficiently obtains $H(x)$ by using unfolding operations and equivalence-preserving transformations. This $H(x)$ can be considered a partial solution of the given goal, supported by (B) and (C). However, since the minimum number of unfolding operations is not guaranteed to increase, the interpreter is incomplete in the sense of (B); that is, not all solutions are necessarily acquired. Furthermore, since the transformation rules are restricted in order to obtain efficient execution, solutions may not be obtained for particular set of definitions and goal because of the lack of applicable rules. The class of program that ALL can execute without stopping is essentially the same as for a first-order compiler [17]; yet when the problem lies on a path that the interpreter does not actually reach, the program can be run on the interpreter, but not compiled. Moreover, the termination problem is more complex than that for Horn clauses.

The limitations of ALL are similar to those of Prolog when the program class is restricted to Horn clauses for efficiency. Nonetheless, the restriction on ALL is looser than that on Prolog, and, as a result, the syntax $\forall x : (p(x, y) \rightarrow q(x, z))$ is permitted, as described in Section 7. In addition, the obtained answer is a partial set of solutions that is logically supported by three-valued logic.

Trials were carried out to extend Prolog logically [3], where goals with implication were permitted. The resultant extensions, however, cannot handle formulae with universal quantifiers, nor can they obtain answers for variables in negative literals. ALL possesses inherent advantages, since it can handle both situations and has computing complexity of the same order as that of Prolog when "occur checks" are performed.

4 Transformation Rules

When given a goal, the ALL interpreter computes a partial solution (Section 3) by unfolding operations for given definitions and equivalence-preserving transformations under $E(\Sigma)$ in three-valued logic. The rules for the unfolding operations are given in Section 4.1, and those for the transformations under $E(\Sigma)$ are given in Section 4.2 for usual logic and in Section 4.3 for the predicate $=$.

The ALL interpreter has two top-level forms, with its intermediate formula always being in one of the following forms:

$$\exists v : (\forall u : p \wedge q \wedge a) \ \vee \ r, \tag{T1}$$

$$\exists v : (\forall u : (p \rightarrow s) \wedge q \wedge a) \ \vee \ r. \tag{T2}$$

Rules (1)–(29) in the following sections are formulated so that expressions of the form $x = e[\hat{x}]$ are accumulated into a.

Given a goal $p[x_1, \cdots, x_n]$, ALL begins computing with the initial top-level form

$$\exists.(\forall.p[x_1, \cdots, x_n] \wedge \top \wedge \top) \ \vee \ \bot, \tag{T3}$$

and transforms this formula by applying the rules until the top-level form becomes

$$\exists u.(\forall.\top \wedge \top \wedge x = e[u]) \ \vee \ r. \tag{P1}$$

When the intermediate formula is in the form (P1), ALL simplifies the formula $x = e[u]$ with its constraints attached, and outputs the result as a solution. It then resumes the computation if the user requires other solutions.

4.1 Unfolding operations

If the predicate in p is a user-defined one, it is unfolded as

$$\exists v : (\forall u : p \wedge q \wedge a) \ \vee \ r$$
$$\Rightarrow \exists v : (\forall u : unfold(p) \wedge q \wedge a) \ \vee \ r, \tag{1}$$

$$\exists v : (\forall u : (p \rightarrow s) \wedge q \wedge a) \ \vee \ r$$
$$\Rightarrow \exists v : (\forall u : (unfold(p) \rightarrow s) \wedge q \wedge a). \tag{2}$$

4.2 Rules for usual logic

First, if the top-level form is in the form $(T1)$ and p is an atomic formula, one of the following rules is applied:

$$\exists v : (\forall : (p_1 \vee p_2) \wedge q \wedge a) \ \vee \ r$$
$$\Rightarrow \exists v : (\forall : p_1 \wedge q \wedge a) \vee (\exists v : (p_2 \wedge q \wedge a) \vee r), \tag{3}$$

$$\exists v : (\forall u : (p_1 \wedge p_2) \wedge q \wedge a) \ \vee \ r$$

$$\Rightarrow \exists v : (\forall u : p_1 \wedge (\forall u : p_2 \wedge q) \wedge a) \ \vee \ r, \tag{4}$$

$$\exists v : (\forall : \exists x : p \wedge q \wedge a) \ \vee \ r$$
$$\Rightarrow \exists x_\top, v : (\forall : p\{x : x_\top\} \wedge q \wedge a) \ \vee \ r, \tag{5}$$

$$\exists v : (\forall u : (\forall x : p) \wedge q \wedge a) \ \vee \ r$$
$$\Rightarrow \exists v : (\forall x_\top, u : p\{x : x_\top\} \wedge q \wedge a) \ \vee \ r, \tag{6}$$

$$\exists v : (\forall u : \bot \wedge q_1 \wedge a_1) \vee (\exists v' : (r_1 \wedge q_2 \wedge a_2) \vee r_2)$$
$$\Rightarrow \exists v_2 : (\forall : r_1 \wedge q_2 \wedge a_2) \ \vee \ r_2, \tag{7}$$

$$\exists v : (\forall u_1 : \top \wedge (\forall u_2 : q_1 \wedge q_2) \wedge a) \ \vee \ r$$
$$\Rightarrow \exists v : (\forall u_2 : q_1 \wedge q_2 \wedge a) \ \vee \ r, \tag{8}$$

$$\exists v : (\forall u : \neg p \wedge q \wedge a) \ \vee \ r$$
$$\Rightarrow \exists v : (\forall u : (p \rightarrow \bot) \wedge q \wedge a) \ \vee \ r. \tag{9}$$

The following rules are used if the top-level form is in the form $(T2)$ and p is not an atomic formula:

$$\exists v : (\forall u : ((p_1 \vee p_2) \rightarrow s) \wedge q \wedge a) \ \vee \ r$$
$$\Rightarrow \exists v : (\forall u : ((p_1 \rightarrow s) \wedge (p_2 \rightarrow s)) \wedge q \wedge a) \ \vee \ r, \tag{10}$$

$$\exists v : (\forall u : ((p_1 \wedge p_2) \rightarrow s) \wedge q \wedge a) \ \vee \ r$$
$$\Rightarrow \exists v : (\forall u : (p_1 \rightarrow (p_2 \rightarrow s)) \wedge q \wedge a) \ \vee \ r, \tag{11}$$

$$\exists v : (\forall u : (\exists x : p \rightarrow s) \wedge q \wedge a) \ \vee \ r$$
$$\Rightarrow \exists v : (\forall x_\top, u : (p\{x : x_\top\} \rightarrow s) \wedge q \wedge a) \ \vee \ r, \tag{12}$$

$$\exists v : (\forall : (\forall x : p \rightarrow s) \wedge q \wedge a) \ \vee \ r$$
$$\Rightarrow \exists x_\top, v : (\forall : (p\{x : x_\top\} \rightarrow s) \wedge q \wedge a) \ \vee \ r, \tag{13}$$

$$\exists v : (\forall u : (\top \rightarrow s) \wedge q \wedge a) \ \vee \ r$$
$$\Rightarrow \exists v : (\forall u : s \wedge q \wedge a) \ \vee \ r, \tag{14}$$

$$\exists v : (\forall u : (\bot \rightarrow s) \wedge q \wedge a) \ \vee \ r$$
$$\Rightarrow \exists v : (\forall u : \top \wedge q \wedge a) \ \vee \ r, \tag{15}$$

$$\exists v : (\forall u : (\neg p \rightarrow s) \wedge q \wedge a) \ \vee \ r$$
$$\Rightarrow \exists v : (\forall u : (p \vee s) \wedge q \wedge a) \ \vee \ r, \tag{16}$$

$$\exists v : (\forall u : ((p_1 \rightarrow p_2) \rightarrow s) \wedge q \wedge a) \ \vee \ r$$
$$\Rightarrow \exists v : (\forall u : (p_1 \wedge (p_2 \rightarrow s) \vee s) \wedge q \wedge a) \ \vee \ r. \tag{17}$$

4.3 Rules for =

If the top-level form is in the form $(T1)$ and the predicate of p is $=$, the applied rules are as follows:

$$\exists v : (\forall u : x = x \wedge q \wedge a) \ \vee \ r$$
$$\Rightarrow \exists v : (\forall u : \top \wedge q \wedge a) \ \vee \ r, \tag{18}$$

$$\exists v : (\forall u : x = e[x, \ldots] \wedge q \wedge a) \ \vee \ r$$
$$\Rightarrow \exists v : (\forall u : \bot \wedge q \wedge a) \ \vee \ r, \tag{19}$$

$$\exists v : (\forall u : f(a_1, \ldots, a_m) = f(b_1, \ldots, b_m) \wedge q \wedge a) \ \vee \ r$$

$$\Rightarrow \exists v : (\forall u : (a_1 = b_1 \wedge \cdots \wedge a_m = b_m) \wedge q \wedge a) \ \vee \ r, \tag{20}$$

$$\exists v : (\forall u : f(a_1, \ldots, a_m) = g(b_1, \ldots, b_n) \wedge q \wedge a) \ \vee \ r$$
$$\Rightarrow \exists v : (\forall u : \bot \wedge q \wedge a) \ \vee \ r \quad (\text{when} \ \ f \not\equiv g), \tag{21}$$

$$\exists v : (\forall u : x_c = e[\hat{x_c}] \wedge q \wedge a) \ \vee \ r$$
$$\Rightarrow \exists v : (\forall : c\{x_c : e[\hat{x_c}]\} \wedge q\{x_c : e[\hat{x_c}]\} \wedge (x_c = e[\hat{x_c}] \wedge a\{x_c : e[\hat{x_c}]\}))$$
$$\vee \ r$$
$$(\text{when} \ \ \mathbf{V}_f(x_c = e[\hat{x_c}]) \text{ and } u \text{ have no common elements}), \tag{22}$$

$$\exists v : (\forall u : x_\top = e[\hat{x_\top}] \wedge q \wedge a) \ \vee \ r$$
$$\Rightarrow \exists v : (\forall : \bot \wedge q \wedge a) \ \vee \ r$$
$$(\text{when} \ \ \mathbf{V}_f(x_\top = e[\hat{x_\top}]) \text{ and } u \text{ have common elements}). \tag{23}$$

If the top-level form is $(T2)$ and the predicate of p is $=$, the rules are

$$\exists v : (\forall u : (x = x \to s) \wedge q \wedge a) \ \vee \ r$$
$$\Rightarrow \exists v : (\forall u : s \wedge q \wedge a) \ \vee \ r, \tag{24}$$

$$\exists v : (\forall u : (x = e[x, \ldots] \to s) \wedge q \wedge a) \ \vee \ r$$
$$\Rightarrow \exists v : (\forall u : \top \wedge q \wedge a) \ \vee \ r, \tag{25}$$

$$\exists v : (\forall u : (f(a_1, \ldots, a_m) = f(b_1, \ldots, b_m) \to s) \wedge q \wedge a) \ \vee \ r$$
$$\Rightarrow \exists v : (\forall u : (a_1 = b_1 \wedge \cdots \wedge a_m = b_m \to s) \wedge q \wedge a) \ \vee \ r, \tag{26}$$

$$\exists v : (\forall u : (f(a_1, \ldots, a_m) = g(b_1, \ldots, b_n) \to s) \wedge q \wedge a) \ \vee \ r$$
$$\Rightarrow \exists v : (\forall u : \top \wedge q \wedge a) \vee r \quad (\text{when} \ \ f \not\equiv g), \tag{27}$$

$$\exists v : (\forall x_\top, u : (x_\top = e[\hat{x_\top}] \to s) \wedge q \wedge a) \ \vee \ r$$
$$\Rightarrow \exists v : (\forall u : s\{x_\top : e[\hat{x_\top}]\} \wedge q \wedge a) \vee r, \tag{28}$$

$$\exists v : (\forall u[\hat{x_c}] : (x_c = e[\hat{x_c}] \to s) \wedge q \wedge a) \ \vee \ r$$
$$\Rightarrow \exists \mathbf{V}_f(e[\hat{x_c}]), v :$$
$$(\forall u[\hat{x_c}] - \mathbf{V}_f(e[\hat{x_c}]) :$$
$$s\{x_c : e[\hat{x_c}]\} \ \wedge \ (c\{x_c : e[\hat{x_c}]\} \wedge q\{x_c : e[\hat{x_c}]\})$$
$$\wedge (x_c = e[\hat{x_c}] \wedge a\{x_c : e[\hat{x_c}]\}))$$
$$\vee \ (\exists x_{newc}, v - x_c : (q\{x_c : x_{newc}\} \wedge a\{x_c : x_{newc}\}) \ \vee \ r)$$
$$(\text{where} \ \ newc \equiv \forall u : \neg x_c = e[\hat{x_c}] \wedge c). \tag{29}$$

Rules (28) and (29) play important roles in ALL and enable it to handle universal quantifiers and negations. They are derived from the following relations, which are specialized forms of those used in a first-order compiler [17]:

$$\forall y_1, \ldots, y_n : (x = e[\hat{x}] \to q)$$
$$\Leftrightarrow \ (\exists y_1, \ldots, y_n : (x = e[\hat{x}] \wedge q)) \ \vee \ (\forall y_1, \ldots, y_n : \neg x = e[\hat{x}])$$
$$(\text{when} \ \ \{y_1, \ldots, y_n\} \subset \mathbf{V}_f(e)),$$
$$\forall x : (x = e[\hat{x}] \to q) \ \Leftrightarrow \exists x : (x = e[\hat{x}] \wedge q).$$

The proof of the first formula is provided in the appendix, since the equivalence of both sides is not obvious. The second formula can be similarly proven.

The last part of Rule (29) adds a constraint to x_c. Note that the constraints attached to variables are processed just after a value is assigned, as specified in (22) and (29).

4.4 Simplification of the answer

The followings rules simplify the disjunctions of variables included in answer a:

$$\exists x : p[\hat{x}] \Rightarrow p[\hat{x}], \tag{30}$$

$$\exists x : (x = e[\hat{x}] \wedge q[\hat{x}]) \Rightarrow q[\hat{x}], \tag{31}$$

$$\forall x : p[\hat{x}] \Rightarrow p[\hat{x}]. \tag{32}$$

5 Implementation Techniques

During transformations, it is inefficient to rewrite a formula literally according to Rules (1)–(32), especially since efficiency is significantly affected by the unfolding of user predicates and substitution of values for variables, which correspond to the expressions unfold(p) and $p\{x : e\}$, respectively. Techniques for efficiently executing programs by ALL interpreter are described in this section.

5.1 Representation by environment and body

An expression object in ALL is represented by a pair— namely, an expression body and an environment that is a list of bindings. A binding is also a pair—namely, a parameter name and a value. Therefore, both the body and the environment are necessary to refer to the actual expression. This method is similar to that used in Lisp interpreters [1]. However, the actual arguments passed to the predicates are also ALL expression objects, whereas in Lisp, arguments are the bodies evaluated in the environments. ALL does not "evaluate" —or substitute in the environment— the arguments, and therefore it can manipulate universally quantified variables, as will be described.

In ALL, parameters are different from logical variables; in other words, objects for variables are created when ALL encounters quantifiers. This method is different from that of conventional Prolog implementations in which the variables are represented by environments, and in which there is therefore no difference between variables and parameters. In fact, Prolog does not use this concept of parameters. ALL is different because it treats variables and parameters as different objects in order to manipulate both existential and universal quantifiers and in order to efficiently unfold predicates.

Since the environments for formulae p, s, q, and r in top-level forms (T1) and (T2) are generally different, each formula in ALL is separately represented as a body and environment pair. Although pairs for s, q, and r are actually created, the pair p is more efficiently represented by using two system variables instead of creating a data object. Actual pairs are created if parts of p are to be attached to s, q, or r.

5.2 Variable object substitution

In Rules (5), (6), (12), and (13), where the scopes of quantifiers are extended, a renaming operation is necessary in order to avoid name conflicts. ALL creates a variable object for representing a logical variable when these rules are applied, and ALL then extends the environments by adding a binding that is a pair consisting of the variable name and a newly created variable object. Data structures are different for existential and universal variables, since they are treated differently.

On the other hand, when Rules (22), (28), and (29) are applied, substitutions to the variables in the expressions occur; for example, the expression $q\{x : e\}$ represents the expression q in which e is substituted for x. ALL uses a variable object as an indirect pointer within the expression when a variable substitution occurs; consequently, only the value slot of the variable is changed to point to the substituted value, instead of the value being actually substituting wherever the variable occurs. In addition, the substituted value is actually constructed by using the body and the environment in (29), which was produced by the preceding application of a rule. This construction is necessary in order to manipulate the universal variables, for a reason given later. Although efficiency is lost by using this construction operation, the computing complexity for constructing a value is of the same order as for checking the cyclicity in (19) and (25), which correspond to the occur checks in Prolog.

This indirect pointer creates a problem. Existentially quantified variables are distributed over disjunctions in (3), whereas they should be treated as different objects after the distribution. Closer observation of applications of the rules reveals that the RHS of $\vee$ in the rules is processed when either the LHS becomes false ($\perp$) or the user wants other solutions. In both cases, the LHS of $\vee$ has never been referenced in processing the RHS. ALL can thus cancel the substitutions for variables after the distribution, then continue with the calculation. This technique corresponds to backtracking in Prolog.

The process for manipulating universally quantified variables is more difficult than that for existentially quantified variables, because the former variables are distributed over conjunctions $\wedge$ by (4), where the variable objects for the LHS may be used in the RHS; in fact, when (29) is applied, the universally quantified variables are replaced by existentially quantified variables, and the scope is extended to the entire conjunction. As a result, ALL cannot share the variable objects in the left and right parts of a conjunction. Hence, when ALL applies Rule (29), a new existentially quantified variable is created, and the value part of the variable binding is changed to point to the new variable. Universally quantified variables are made to point to their bindings so that the above operation is possible. When the manipulation of the LHS of $\wedge$ is finished, ALL recovers the binding of the old universal variable and treats it as if it were the variable at the time of the distribution, which is possible since the values assigned to variables are in expanded forms without the environment. Accordingly, the newly created variables are never referenced through the environment by the RHS of $\wedge$. If the newly created variable is distributed by (3), the variable may be referenced through the environment, and the binding at distribution time should therefore be stored and recovered when the

RHS of $\vee$ is processed.

6 Limitations of ALL

When ALL runs for any given predicate definitions and a goal, three cases can occur: (1) a partial solution or $\perp$ may be obtained, (2) the program may fall into a loop, or (3) no rules may be applied. The second case may also occur in Prolog, while the third is due to ALL's limitation of restricting the rules in order to execute the interpreter efficiently.

It is a difficult problem to specify the exact class for which ALL obtains a partial solution even if the termination problem is solved. Actually, it is not easy to give a sufficient condition for termination that is practical. Two sufficient conditions for obtaining a solution are given here.

One sufficient condition is for programs to consist entirely of Horn clauses, which can be rewritten into Prolog programs. In this case, if the program terminates, the answer is either a partial solution or $\perp$.

Another condition is for the negative literals of Horn clauses to be replaced by

$$\forall x : (p(x, y, w) \rightarrow q(x, z, w)), \qquad \text{(G)}$$

with the condition that if $p(x, y, z)$ is executed as a goal, it needs only Horn clause predicates, with the result obtained as a disjunctive normal form consisting of only basic formulae with respect to x. If $q(x, z, w)$ is executed as a goal with w being a constant, the solutions are obtained. In other words, in the antecedent part, all the partial solutions for a universally quantified variable x can be computed from y and w, and in the consequent part, a partial solution for z can be computed from x and w. The condition also holds if x, y, z, or w is either empty or a set of variables. When the condition is satisfied, since a disjunction of basic formulae

$$\alpha_1 \vee \cdots \vee \alpha_n$$

is obtained by $p(x, y, z)$, the original goal G is equivalent to

$$\forall x : ((\alpha_1 \vee \cdots \vee \alpha_n) \rightarrow q(x, z, w)).$$

Therefore, if Rules (10)–(13), (28), and (29) are applied to this formula, the result is equivalent to that obtained by executing $q(x, z, w)$ while assuming x to be an existentially quantified variable. Although the condition does not explicitly specify the class of executable programs, it may be considered as a sufficiently practical one, as shown in the following examples.

7 Execution Examples

Examples of execution by ALL are shown in Figures 1 – 3. As may be seen, ALL accepts both ASCII characters and JIS (especially symbol) characters. Characters after "%" are comments.

Figure 1 is an example in which `even` is defined and `¬even(x)` is executed. In the definition, `even` refers to the negation of `even` itself and is therefore not "strict" with respect to the goal. In spite of this non-strictness, ALL obtains the solution.

Let the execution be traced briefly here. The first top level form is

$$\exists : \forall : (\neg even(x)) \wedge \top \wedge \top \vee \perp.$$

ALL applies Rules (1) and (9) to obtain

$$\exists : \forall : ((x = 0 \quad \vee \exists y : (x = s(y) \wedge \neg even(y))) \rightarrow \bot) \wedge \top \wedge \top \vee \bot.$$

In this way, the execution proceeds, and the next formula appears:

$$\exists : \forall y : (x_{\neg x=0} = s(y) \rightarrow (\neg even(y) \rightarrow \bot)) \wedge \top \wedge \top \vee \bot,$$

to which formula Rule (29) is applied:

$$\exists y : \forall : (\neg even(y) \rightarrow \bot) \wedge \neg s(y) = 0 \wedge x = s(y) \vee \exists (x_{\neg x=0}) : \top.$$

In the right disjunct, the free variable x is shown in parentheses and indicates the constraint for x. By further execution,

$$\exists y : \forall : (y = 0 \vee \cdots) \wedge \neg s(y) = 0 \wedge x = s(y) \vee ...$$

is obtained, and this becomes

$$\exists y : \forall : \top \wedge \top \wedge (y = 0 \wedge x = s(0)) \vee \cdots,$$

which yields a partial solution,

$$x = s(0).$$

Figure 2 is a program for computing prime numbers. The definition is a direct translation of the mathematical one: a prime number is an integer p greater than one whose divisor is one or p itself. Under the definition, when `prime(x)` is input, prime numbers are successively obtained. This program needs to be modified to be compiled by a first-order compiler, since in `div`, `d` is not always computed from `e` (precisely, when `e` $= 0$), and this disables the compilation. In ALL, `div` is called with `d` in the form `s(s(x))`, which allows execution. The execution time is almost the same as for the compiled modified code executed by the Prolog interpreter.

Figure 3 is an example in which the answer has a constraint. This program fails in Prolog, whereas ALL can execute it. The constraint is a conjunction of negations of = predicates.

8 Summary

The augmented logic language (ALL) was developed and implemented as a transformation system and has a descriptive power stronger than that of Prolog. In addition, since ALL's supporting theory is logically formulated, the results obtained by the ALL interpreter comprise a logical consequence.

The ALL interpreter is implemented as a process for deriving partial solutions from any predicate definitions and a goal in which the only primitive predicate is =, with efficiency being obtained by restricting the class of the definitions. Unlike

```
> even(x) ⇔                                % even(x) iff x is 0
>  x=0 ∨ ∃ y:(x=s(y) ∧¬ even(y));          % or ¬ even(x-1)
even > the x: ¬ even(x);                   % solve x s.t. ¬ even(x)
s(0) ;                                     % 1 satisfies
s(s(s(0))) ;                               % 3 too
s(s(s(s(s(0)))))                           % 5 too
T
```

Fig. 1 Example 1 of the execution by the ALL interpreter

```
> add(x,y,z) ⇔                                  % x+y=z iff
>   x=0 ∧ y=z ∨                                 % x=0 ∧ y=z or
>   ∃ p,q:(x=s(p) ∧ z=s(q) ∧ add(p,y,q));        % (x-1)+y=z-1
add
> div(d,e) ⇔                                    % d divides e iff
>   ∃ x:d=s(x) ∧                                % d>=1 and
>   ( e=0 ∨ ∃ u:(add(d,u,e) ∧ div(d,u)));       % e=0 or d divides e-d
div
> prime(a) ⇔                                    % a is a prime iff
>   ∃ x:a=s(s(x)) ∧                             % a>=2 and
>   ∀ d:(div(d,a) → (d=s(0) ∨ d=a));            % divisor=1 or itself
prime
> the x:prime(x);                               % obtain prime x
s(s(0)) ;                                       % 2 is a prime
s(s(s(0))) ;                                    % 3 too
s(s(s(s(s(0))))) ;                              % 5 too
s(s(s(s(s(s(s(0))))))) ;                        % 7 too
s(s(s(s(s(s(s(s(s(s(s(0)))))))))))             % 11 too
T
```

Fig. 2 Example 2 of the execution by the ALL interpreter

```
> pp(x) ⇔ x=s(0) ∨ ∀ y: ¬ x=s(y);
pp
> the x: ¬ pp(x);
s(y_5)
 where neq(y_5,0)                       % constrained answer
T
```

Fig. 3 Example 3 of the execution by the ALL interpreter

a first-order compiler, predicate definitions are easily added incrementally to a program, thereby enabling these definitions to be used as a library, since a predicate definition does not affect other definitions.

Arithmetic operations can be embedded in ALL by adding primitive predicates, such as $add(x, y, z)$ and then building transformation rules for those predicates. Moreover, it may be possible to construct a compiler for ALL by partially evaluating the ALL interpreter with a given program where incremental compiling is possible, in contrast to the situation with a first-order compiler. Such enhancements allow ALL to be implemented as a practical programming language.

Acknowledgements. Sincere gratitude is extended to Dr. S. Tomura, a member of the Computer Language Section at the Electrotechnical Laboratory, for his instructive discussions.

References

[1] Abelson, A., Sussman, G. J., and Sussman, J.: *Structure and Interpretation of Computer Programs*, MIT Press, Cambridge, 1985.
[2] Bowen, D. L., Byrd, L., Pereira, L. M., Pereira, F. C. N., and Warren, D. H. D.: *Prolog on the DECSYSTEM-10 User's Manual*, Univ. of Edinburgh, 1981.
[3] Bowen, K. A.: Programming with full first-order logic, *Machine Intelligence*, Vol. 10 (1982), pp. 421–440.
[4] Clark, K. L.: Negation as Failure, *Logic and Database*, Plenum Press, New York, 1978, pp. 293–322.
[5] Colmerauer A.: Equations and Inequations on Finite and Infinite trees, *Proc. of FGCS '84* (1984), pp. 85–99.
[6] Comon, H. and Lescanne, P.: Equational Problems and Disunification, *J. Symbolic Computation*, Vol.7 (1989), pp. 371–425.
[7] Kowalski, R.: *Logic for Problem Solving*, North-Holland, New York, 1979.
[8] Kunen, K.: Negation in Logic Programming, *J. Logic Programming*, Vol. 4 (1987), pp. 289–308.
[9] Kunen, K.: Answer Sets and Negation as Failure, *Proc. 4th Int. Conf. on Logic Programming*, Melbourne, 1987, pp. 219–228.
[10] Kunen, K.: Signed Data Dependencies in Logic Programs, *Computer Science Technocal Report 719*, Univ. of Wisconsin-Madison, 1987.
[11] Lloyd, J. L.: *Foundations of Logic Programming*, Symbolic Computation Series, Springer-Verlag, 1984.
[12] Maher, M. J.: Complete Axiomatizations of the Algebras of Finite, Rational, and Infinite Trees, *Proc. of 3rd Annual Symposium on Logic in Computer Science*, Edinburgh, 1988, pp. 348–357.
[13] Motoyoshi F.: Constrained variables and function evaluation, *First Conference Proceedings*, Japan Society for Software Science and Technology, Tokyo, 1984, pp. 315–318 (in Japanese).
[14] Motoyoshi, F. and Sato, T.: An algorithm for a First-order Interpreter, *Computer Algebra and Its Application to Mathematics Education*, Lecture Note 646, Research Institute for Mathematical Science in Kyoto University, 1988 (in Japanese).
[15] Reiter, R.: Equality and Domain Closure in First Order Databases, *J. ACM*, Vol. 27 (1980), pp. 235–249.
[16] Sato, T.: On the Consistency of First-Order Logic Programs, *ETL Technical Report TR-87-12*, Tsukuba, 1987.
[17] Sato, T. and Tamaki, H.: First-Order Compiler: A Deterministic Logic Program Synthesis Algorithm, *J. Symbolic Computation*, Vol 7, Nos. 3 & 4 (1989), pp. 605–627.
[18] Sato, T.: A First-Order Unfold/Fold System, *ETL Technical Reprt TR-90-17*, Tsukuba, 1990.

Appendix

Proof of

$$\begin{aligned} &\forall y_1, \ldots, y_n : (x = e[\hat{x}] \rightarrow q) \\ &\Leftrightarrow\ (\exists y_1, \ldots, y_n : (x = e[\hat{x}] \wedge q)) \vee (\forall y_1, \ldots, y_n : \neg x = e[\hat{x}]), \\ &\qquad (\{y_1, y2, \ldots, y_n\} \subset \mathbf{V}_f(e[\hat{x}])). \end{aligned}$$

The next two cases are sufficient, since two-valued logic is employed for =.

(1) When $\neg\exists y_1, \ldots, y_n : x = e[\hat{x}]$

As is commonly known,

$$\neg\exists y_1, \ldots, y_n : x = e[\hat{x}] \ \Leftrightarrow\ \forall y_1, \ldots, y_n : \neg x = e[\hat{x}],$$

and if $\forall y_1, \ldots, y_n : p \Leftrightarrow \top$, then generally $\forall y_1, \ldots, y_n : (p \vee q) \Leftrightarrow \top$ for any q. Then

$$\begin{aligned} \text{LHS} &\equiv \forall y_1, \ldots, y_n : (\neg x = e[\hat{x}] \vee q) \\ &\Leftrightarrow \top. \end{aligned}$$

The second disjunct of the RHS is true. Therefore

$$\top \Leftrightarrow \text{LHS} \Leftrightarrow \text{RHS}.$$

(2) When $\exists y_1, \ldots, y_n : x = e[\hat{x}]$

Let $e[\hat{x}]\{y_i : z_i\}$ indicate the substitution z_i for y_i in $e[\hat{x}]$. Then

$$\begin{aligned} \text{LHS} \Leftrightarrow\ & \exists y_1, \ldots, y_n : x = e[\hat{x}] \\ & \quad \wedge \forall y_1, \ldots, y_n : (\neg x = e[\hat{x}] \vee q), \\ \Leftrightarrow\ & \exists z_1, \ldots, z_n : x = e[\hat{x}]\{y_i : z_i\} \\ & \quad \wedge \forall y_1, \ldots, y_n : (\neg x = e[\hat{x}] \vee q), \\ \Leftrightarrow\ & \exists z_1, \ldots, z_n : (x = e[\hat{x}]\{y_i : z_i\} \\ & \quad \wedge \forall y_1, \ldots, y_n : (\neg e[\hat{x}]\{y_i : z_i\} = e[\hat{x}] \\ & \qquad \vee q\{x : e[\hat{x}]\{y_i : z_i\}\})). \end{aligned} \tag{R1}$$

On the other hand, from E(Σ) and the condition that $\{y_1, \ldots, y_n\} \subset \mathbf{V}_f(e[\hat{x}])$, we obtain

$$\begin{aligned} (R1) \Leftrightarrow\ & \exists z_1, \ldots, z_n : (x = e[\hat{x}]\{y_i : z_i\} \\ & \quad \wedge \forall y_1, \ldots, y_n : \\ & \qquad (\neg(y_1 = z_1 \wedge \cdots \wedge y_n = z_n) \\ & \qquad \vee q\{x : e[\hat{x}]\{y_i : z_i\}\})), \\ \Leftrightarrow\ & \exists z_1, \ldots, z_n : (x = e[\hat{x}]\{y_i : z_i\} \\ & \quad \wedge \forall y_1, \ldots, y_n : \\ & \qquad (\neg y_1 = z_1 \vee \cdots \vee \neg y_n = z_n \vee q\{x : e[\hat{x}]\{y_i : z_i\}\}). \end{aligned} \tag{R2}$$

And since $\forall y_i : \neg y_i = z_i \Leftrightarrow \bot$, $(1 \leq i \leq n)$, if $\forall y_1, \ldots, y_n : p \Leftrightarrow \bot$, then $\forall y_1, \ldots, y_n : (p \vee q) \Leftrightarrow \forall y_1, \ldots, y_n : q$,

$$\begin{aligned} (\text{R2}) \Leftrightarrow\ & \exists z_1, \ldots, z_n : (x = e[\hat{x}]\{y_i : z_i\} \wedge \forall y_1, \ldots, y_n : (q\{x : e[\hat{x}]\{y_i : z_i\}\}), \\ \Leftrightarrow\ & \exists z_1, \ldots, z_n : (x = e[\hat{x}]\{y_i : z_i\} \wedge q\{x : e[\hat{x}]\{y_i : z_i\}\}). \end{aligned} \tag{R3}$$

At the same time,

$$\begin{aligned} & \text{first disjunct of RHS} \\ & \Leftrightarrow \exists z_1, \ldots z_n : x = e[\hat{x}]\{y_i : z_i\} \wedge (\exists y_1, \ldots, y_n : (x = e[\hat{x}] \wedge q)), \\ & \Leftrightarrow \exists z_1, \ldots z_n : (x = e[\hat{x}]\{y_i : z_i\} \\ & \qquad \wedge \exists y_1, \ldots, y_n : (e[\hat{x}]\{y_i : z_i\} = e[\hat{x}] \wedge q\{x : e[\hat{x}]\{y_i : z_i\}\})), \\ & \Leftrightarrow \exists z_1, \ldots z_n : (x = e[\hat{x}]\{y_i : z_i\} \\ & \qquad \wedge \exists y_1, \ldots, y_n : (y_1 = z_1 \wedge \cdots \wedge y_n = z_n \wedge q\{x : e[\hat{x}]\{y_i : z_i\}\})), \\ & \Leftrightarrow \exists z_1, \ldots z_n : (x = e[\hat{x}]\{y_i : z_i\} \wedge \exists y_1, \ldots, y_n : q\{x : e[\hat{x}]\{y_i : z_i\}\}), \\ & \Leftrightarrow \exists z_1, \ldots z_n : (x = e[\hat{x}]\{y_i : z_i\} \wedge q\{x : e[\hat{x}]\{y_i : z_i\}\}), \end{aligned} \tag{R4}$$

and

second disjunct of RHS

$\equiv\ \forall y_1, \ldots, y_n : \neg x = e[\hat{x}],$

$\Leftrightarrow\ \neg\exists y_1, \ldots, y_n : x = e[\hat{x}],$

$\Leftrightarrow\ \bot.$ $(R5)$

By applying (R3), (R4), and (R5),

LHS $\Leftrightarrow$ RHS.

In the above two cases, LHS $\Leftrightarrow$ RHS always holds. ■

Initially published in "Computer Software", Vol. 8, No. 5, in Japanese.

Fumio Motoyoshi
Natural Language Section,
Machine Understanding Division,
Electrotechnical Laboratory,
1–1–4 Umezono, Tsukuba-shi, Ibaraki
305 Japan

Taisuke Sato
Machine Inference Section,
Machine Understanding Division,
Electrotechnical Laboratory,
1–1–4 Umezono, Tsukuba-shi, Ibaraki
305 Japan

The Determinacy of a Prolog Predicate Call

Hajime Sawamura

Summary. We first argue that the determinacy of a Prolog predicate call plays very important roles in the transformation and compilation of Prolog programs and in the development of reliable Prolog programs. We then propose a concept of determinacy suitable for these purposes and introduce two decidable classes of predicates and predicate calls—a-determinacy and r-determinacy—and examine their properties. Furthermore, we describe equivalent but alternative definitions of them, as well as their extensions.

A considerable number of predicates and predicate calls can be demonstrated to be deterministic by means of a-determinacy and r-determinacy, since these concepts are defined in a natural and syntactic way, reflecting Prolog programmers' intuition about the determinacy of predicates and predicate calls.

1 Introduction

The terms "determinacy" and "nondeterminacy" often appear in diverse branches of computer science such as automata and formal language theory, computation theory, programming languages, and their semantics and verification, as well as in other fields of science. Although their definitions differ according to the field, very few problems have required the determinacy itself to be decided. In this paper, we discuss problems where detecting the determinacy of a predicate call becomes crucial in Prolog, which is a nondeterministic programming language [1]. We then propose a definition of determinacy suitable for those problems, introduce two concepts of determinacy, and describe their properties.

Several authors have studied nondeterministic programming languages that make it possible to express procedures of an essentially nondeterministic nature. According to *Kowalski* [5], programs written in these languages are nondeterministic in the two main senses: don't care (DC) and don't know (DK). Prolog realizes the "don't know" characteristic of nondeterminacy by backtracking, and it is not only important but also inevitable that such nondeterminacy of a predicate call should be detected in optimizing the transformation of Prolog programs and in the development of reliable Prolog programs.

However, we have shown that the decision problems of both DC nondeterminacy and DK nondeterminacy are unsolvable [8]. Therefore, our next goal is to define a class of predicates and predicate calls as widely decidable as possible. In Section 2, we describe the significance of detecting the determinacy of a predicate call from two viewpoints. In Section 3, we introduce two decidable classes of predicates and

ISBN 0-12-037105-7

predicate calls, called a-determinacy and r-determinacy, respectively, and examine their properties. Furthermore, we present equivalent but alternative definitions of them as well as their extensions.

2 Determinacy Detection and Its Applications

In this section, we describe the significance and use of determinacy detection.

2.1 Source-to-source optimization of Prolog programs

We have shown [8, 9] that the determinacy information of a predicate call plays an important role in the optimization of Prolog programs, since it makes it possible to remove useless backtracking and reduce the overhead of the predicate call mechanism. In fact, for inline expansion, automatic insertion of cuts, and some local transformations, the determinacy information of a predicate call is a key condition for such optimizing transformations to become applicable to Prolog programs.

On the basis of the above techniques, a practical Prolog optimizer, which is not for pure Prolog but for the full set of Prolog, has been implemented [9, 10]. Performance evaluation experiments showed that the Prolog optimizer attained about 20% time efficiency for ordinary Prolog programs and 40 $\sim$ 60% time efficiency for obviously redundant programs [11].

It is most likely that in general, inline expansion forces a program text to expand too much, particularly for Prolog programs whose program constructs are only predicate calls (procedures) and their conjunctions. However, it was found that our determinacy conditions for predicates and predicate calls prevent inline expansion from being applied to a program text excessively and having a bad effect on the space efficiency. As a result, these conditions function as a criterion for inline expansion.

2.2 Prolog programming methodology

In practical Prolog programming, programs are often written in a deterministic way or are meant to be deterministic. Prolog programmers often make a point of ensuring the determinacy of a predicate call for the sake of easy program debugging and highly reliable program development [3]. This is because in programming with nondeterministic programming languages, such as Prolog, it is easy to lose track of a complicated control and/or data flow unless constant attention is paid to the determinacy or nondeterminacy of a predicate call. Thus a close relationship can be seen between the determinacy of a predicate call and the reliability of Prolog programs. For Prolog programmers, the determinacy of a predicate call is considered a valuable factor in raising program reliability.

For sequential programs, there has been great concern about program properties such as correctness, termination, and equivalence. For parallel programs, in addition to these properties, eventuality and invariance have been matters of major concern. In nondeterministic programs, the determinacy of a predicate call is considered one of the most important clues for ascertaining program reliability as cross-references among predicate calls become more complicated.

The two classes of determinacy given in the following section could be used as key information for highly reliable program development and program debugging.

3 The Determinacy of a Predicate Call

In this section, taking account of the significance and utilization of the determinacy of a predicate call, which we discussed above, we introduce two decidable classes of predicates and predicate calls, respectively called a-determinacy and r-determinacy, and examine their properties.

3.1 Notational conventions

We assume that readers are familiar with the syntax and the semantics of Prolog [1]. A Prolog program is a finite list of ordered clauses of the form

$$H \ :- B1, \ldots, Bn. \ (n \geq 0),$$

where H is called a head, each Bi is called a predicate call or goal, and $B1, \ldots, Bn$ is called the body of the clause. Given a goal, a list of clauses whose heads have the same name and arity as the goal is called the defining clauses or predicate definition for the goal.

We will use the following, distinct symbols as syntactical variables ranging over the syntactic domains of Prolog.

[Symbols]

(1) The letters P, G, and H (with or without subscripts) represent goals (predicate calls) or heads of clauses, which take the form of predicate names followed by some arguments.The letters p, q, and r represent predicate names or propositions.

(2) The letters Γ and Δ (with or without subscripts) represent (possibly empty) sequences of goals delimited by commas. If Γ is an empty sequence, it denotes a "true" predicate. The letter A (with or without subscripts) represents a nonempty sequence of terms in Prolog. The letter X represents a sequence of distinct variables.

3.2 Definition of determinacy

Definition 1 (Determinacy of a predicate call goal) *The determinacy of a predicate call goal is defined as follows: A predicate call goal is deterministic if it succeeds through at most one clause of its defining clauses when it calls them and if it never succeeds again when it is backtracked.*

Note that this definition implies that the following goals are deterministic:

(i) A predicate call that does not terminate at the first execution.

(ii) A predicate call that succeeds at the first execution, but does not terminate on backtracking.

Let us illustrate this definition in a box model of control flow [2]. In the model, the nondeterministic computation of a goal is captured by representing the control flow for the goal in a box with four arms, as shown in Figure 1.

A Prolog query and a sequence of goals in a body can also be viewed as an AND sequence of boxes with four arms, as seen in Figure 2.

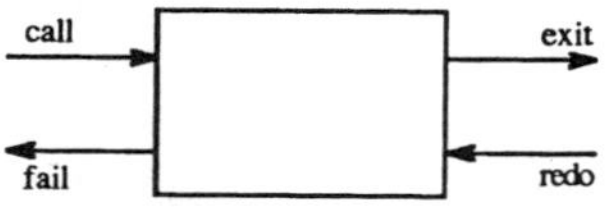

Fig. 1 A box model of control

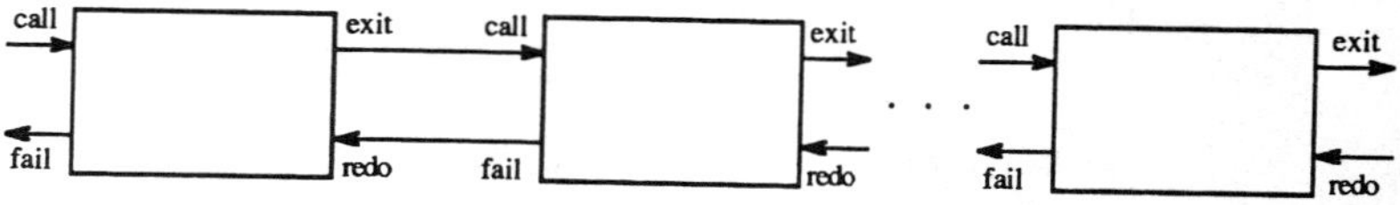

Fig. 2 A conjunction of goals

Then, with several defining clauses, a possible control flow for a deterministic goal can be illustrated, as in Figure 3. This shows that the defining clauses are exclusively connected because of the determinacy of the goal; that is, a node $\oplus$ directs control to the left when it is backtracked and downward when it fails. Of course, this is meant to be a recursive flow diagram.

Substantially the same definition of determinacy as ours is found in [6, 13]. Our definition can be widely accepted as showing the meaning of determinacy and nondeterminacy in Prolog. Furthermore, it is more general than Kowalski's definition [5], which states that a predicate relation is deterministic if it is functional (in the sense that our definition is never concerned with —i.e., which arguments of a predicate are inputs and which are outputs). Our definition depends only on the success or failure of a predicate call. On the other hand, *Debray and Warren* [4] consider the functionality of a predicate relative to a mode, where a predicate is termed functional if all alternatives may produce the same result. This definition subsumes our definition if the mode information of a predicate is not taken into account, and it goes well with the purposes described in Section 2. However, it seems rather difficult to detect determinacy by this method , because the definition is too general. Therefore, our definition is preferable for establishing determinacy in Prolog. In a practical sense, our definition is sufficient, because a predicate is often defined so as to be deterministic rather than functional.

In any definition, however, it is impossible to determine whether a Prolog predicate is deterministic as well as functional. The proofs are given in a previous paper [8]. Below, we define mutually related decidable classes of predicates and predicate calls, called a-determinacy and r-determinacy, and examine their properties. After that, we describe equivalent but alternative definitions of them, as well as their extensions.

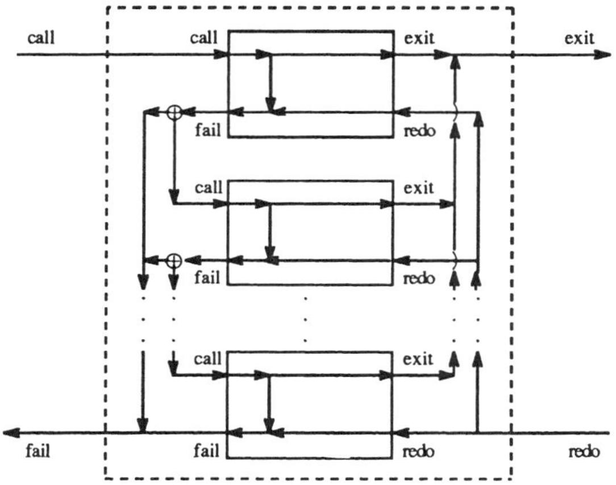

Fig. 3 A control flow of deterministic goals

3.3 a-determinacy and r-determinacy

In general, the success or failure of a predicate call depends on the contents of its arguments—in other words, on the states of variables. The r-determinacy defined below captures such an argument dependency of a deterministic predicate call. On the other hand, a-determinacy means determinacy that does not depend on predicate arguments at all.

Definition 2 (a-determinacy and r-determinacy) *In the following definition, we assume that the constructs dynamically modifying a program, such as "assert" and "retract," do not appear in defining clauses. In other words, predicate definitions are supposed to be completely specified prior to their execution.*

A predicate call $p(A)$ is termed a-deterministic or r-deterministic if it satisfies the following mutually recursive conditions:

(i) If p is a built-in (evaluable) predicate of Prolog and $p(A)$ is deterministic, then $p(A)$ is a-deterministic and r-deterministic.

(ii) Let a predicate definition of the predicate p be

H_1 :- $[\Gamma_1, !,]\Delta_1$,

$\vdots$

H_i :- $[\Gamma_i, !,]\Delta_i$,

$\vdots$

H_n :- $[\Gamma_n, !,]\Delta_n$,

where the cut symbol ! is the rightmost occurrence in the body if more than one cut occurs, and Γ_i does not occur in the body otherwise. Then for each $H_i (1 \leq i \leq n)$, if either (1) or (2) of the following conditions holds, then $p(A)$ is a-deterministic, *and for each H_i that is unifiable with $p(A)$, if (1), (2), or (3) holds, then $p(A)$ is r-deterministic.*

(1) There are cut symbols in the body of the i-th clause, and every goal of Δ_i is a-deterministic or r-deterministic.

(2) There is no cut symbol in the body of the i-th clause; it is the last clause in the predicate definition, and every goal of Δ_i is a-deterministic or r-deterministic.

(3) There is no cut symbol in the body of the i-th clause; it is not the last clause in the predicate definition, $p(A)$ is not unifiable with any $H_j (i+1 \leq j \leq n)$, and every goal of Δ_i is a-deterministic or r-deterministic.

Remarks:

(a) A predicate call can sometimes be shown to be deterministic even if its predicate definition is given in a mutually recursive manner. For example, in the following mutually recursive predicate definitions,

q :- Γ, !, r,

r :- Σ, q, Δ, !,

the predicate calls q and r are both a-deterministic and r-deterministic by the above definition. More generally, the principle can be stated as follows. As above, let the predicate definition of a predicate p be

H_1 :- $[\Gamma_1, !,]\Delta_1$,

$\vdots$

H_i :- $[\Gamma_i, !,]\Delta_i$,

$\vdots$

H_n :- $[\Gamma_n, !,]\Delta_n$.

Then for each i $(1 \leq i \leq n)$, we call the part Δ_i the critical part of the predicate definition with respect to the predicate p. For determinacy to be decidable, it is necessary that no cycle should appear in cross-references among predicate calls that are included in the critical parts of the predicate definitions in a Prolog program. A cross-reference, in general, forms a directed graph. In the above example, there are obviously no mutual calls in the cross-references among critical parts.

(b) Given a program (a set of predicate definitions), we can extract a-deterministic predicates by using the above definition, and this extraction is uniquely determined. Whether they are a-deterministic does not depend on the order in which predicates are to be tested. This is due to the uniqueness of the cross–references among critical parts.

(c) When composite goals such as $(G1; G2)$, $(P \rightarrow G1; G2)$ are included in the critical parts, for simplicity they are treated as nondeterministic goals. For a goal $(G1; G2)$ to be deterministic, it is necessary that both $G1$ and $G2$ are deterministic and that their success is exclusive.

The correctness of our definition is guaranteed by the following corollary.

Corollary 1 *If a goal $p(A)$ is a-deterministic or r-deterministic, then it is deterministic.*

Proof. By induction on the structure of the definition. The case of condition (i) is obvious. For the case of (ii), it is sufficient to examine the three conditions of (ii), but this is straightforward from Prolog's execution semantics [1] and the inductive hypotheses. ■

The definitions of a-determinacy and r-determinacy are based on three concepts: the cut's behavior, deterministic built-in predicates, and unifiability statically determined. In other words, the definitions never refer to what types of arguments a predicate takes when it is called. They are determined without any commitment to the semantics of a predicate. Here, by the semantics of a predicate, we mean the domain of terms in which the predicate succeeds.

From the definition, if a goal is a-deterministic, it is always deterministic irrespective of its argument form. In other words, an a-deterministic goal is absolutely deterministic in the sense that it does not depend on its argument form in the goal. Therefore, when a goal $p(A)$ is found to be a-deterministic, we sometimes call the predicate p a-deterministic or, simply, deterministic. In contrast to the absolute determinacy of a-determinacy, an r-deterministic goal is relatively deterministic, since its predicate depends on how it is called. Hence, the predicate itself of an r-deterministic goal is sometimes called r-deterministic.

From these observations, we have

Corollary 2 *If a goal is a-deterministic, it is also r-deterministic.* ■

Furthermore, from our definition, we have

Corollary 3 *A deterministic predicate call, except for built-in predicates, is determined not to be a-deterministic if it has at least two defining clauses and if they include no cut symbols.* ■

Of course, as is easily seen from the following program, the conditions in this corollary seem to be too strong:

H :- Γ, fail,
H :- Δ,

where no cut symbols occur in Γ and Δ, and every predicate call in Δ is a-deterministic or r-deterministic. Such a syntactical extension could be incorporated into our definition without difficulty, but we prefer to give as general a definition of determinacy as possible.

Corollary 4 *At the propositional level—that is, when the predicate to be examined is a proposition—a-determinacy coincides with r-determinacy.* ■

Corollary 5 *For every argument A of a predicate p, $p(A)$ is r-deterministic if a predicate p is a-deterministic.*

Proof. ($\Rightarrow$) From the arbitrariness of the argument A, consider a goal $p(X)$, where X denotes a sequence of distinct variables. It cannot be r-deterministic with Condition (3), from the definition of r-determinacy. Therefore, if $p(A)$ is r-deterministic for every argument A, it must be r-deterministic with Condition (1) or (2), from the definition of r-determinacy. Hence it is a-deterministic.
($\Leftarrow$) By Corollary 2. ■

Corollary 6 *For every argument A of a predicate p, a goal $p(A)$ is r-deterministic if a goal $p(X)$ is r-deterministic.*

Proof. ($\Rightarrow$) Obvious. ($\Leftarrow$) Similar to the proof of Corollary 5. ∎

Corollary 7 *A goal $p(X)$ is r-deterministic if a predicate p is a-deterministic.*

Proof. From Corollaries 5 and 6. ∎

3.4 Alternative definitions of a-determinacy and r-determinacy

Corollaries 5 and 7 suggest an equivalent alternative definition of determinacy. That is, r-determinacy can be defined first, and then a-determinacy can be defined in terms of Corollary 5 or Corollary 7. Formally, we define r-determinacy and a-determinacy as follows. As before, we assume that the constructs dynamically modifying a program, such as "assert" and "retract," do not appear in defining clauses.

Definition 3 (r-determinacy) *A predicate call $p(A)$ is termed r-deterministic if it satisfies the following conditions:*

(i) *If p is a built-in (evaluable) predicate of Prolog and $p(A)$ is deterministic, then $p(A)$ is r-deterministic.*

(ii) *Let a predicate definition of the predicate p be*

$$H_1 \text{ :- } [\Gamma_1, !,]\Delta_1,$$
$$\vdots$$
$$H_i \text{ :- } [\Gamma_i, !,]\Delta_i,$$
$$\vdots$$
$$H_n \text{ :- } [\Gamma_n, !,]\Delta_n,$$

where the cut symbol ! is the rightmost occurrence in the body if more than one cut occurs, and Γ_i does not occur in the body otherwise. Then, for each $H_i (1 \leq i \leq n)$ that is unifiable with $p(A)$, if (1), (2), or (3) holds, $p(A)$ is r-deterministic:

(1) *There are cut symbols in the body of the i-th clause, and every goal of Δ_i is r- deterministic.*

(2) *There is no cut symbol in the body of the i-th clause; it is the last clause in the predicate definition, and every goal of Δ_i is r-deterministic.*

(3) *There is no cut symbol in the body of the i-th clause; it is not the last clause in the predicate definition, $p(A)$ is not unifiable with any $H_j (i+1 \leq j \leq n)$, and every goal of Δ_i is r-deterministic.*

Definition 4 (a-determinacy$_1$) *A predicate p is termed a-deterministic if for every argument A, a goal $p(A)$ is r-deterministic.*

Alternatively, we can express this simply as follows:

Definition 5 (a-determinacy$_2$) *A predicate p is termed a-deterministic if a goal $p(X)$ is r-deterministic, where X denotes a sequence of distinct variables.*

These definitions of a-determinacy seem to be simpler than the initial one, but it should be noted that a-determinacy$_1$ is not effective. Therefore, an algorithm for detecting the determinacy of a predicate call will be founded on the former definition of a- and r-determinacy or on the latter definition of r-determinacy and a-determinacy$_2$. In the Prolog optimizer [9, 11], the determinacy detection algorithm was implemented in accordance with the former definition of a- and r-determinacy.

Smolka [12] proposes SProlog (Self-Documented Prolog) with language constructs that allow us to make the control structure of Prolog explicit, doing away with the need for the naïve backtracking mechanism and cuts of Prolog. As to determinacy, he proposes methods for declaring a procedure a functional procedure and for asserting a procedure call as a function call. For example, a functional procedure $fact$ that computes the factorial of a natural number is declared as

$$fproc\ fact : \downarrow integer \times \uparrow integer.$$

When a predicate call p should be called as a function call, it is explicitly written as $fc\ p$. In this paper, we have proposed a method for extracting determinacy information directly from a program text without requiring programmers to declare and assert it. Conceptually, detecting a-determinacy amounts to declaring that a procedure is a functional one, and detecting r-determinacy amounts to asserting that a procedure call is a function call.

3.5 Examples

Let us take three examples to illustrate a- and r-determinacy and their relations.

Example 1. *The predicate p is a-deterministic.*
$p(a)$:-$write(a1)$, nl, !, $write(a2)$,
$p(b)$:-$write(b)$. *Put differently, a goal $p(X)$ is r-deterministic, since it succeeds with the first clause, but will immediately fail on backtracking because of the determinacy of the built-in predicate write and the cut.*

Example 2. *The goal q([a,b]) is r-deterministic, but the goal q(X) is not.*
$q([c])$:-$write(c)$, $p(b)$,
$q([a|X])$:-$write(a)$, $p(X)$,
where the predicate calls $p(X)$ and $p(b)$ call their defining clauses above. The goal $q([a,b])$ succeeds only with the second clause, and fails when backtracked because of the determinacy of the predicates write and p.

Example 3. *The following predicate transform is a-deterministic, whatever the predicate fold is.*
$transform('end\_of\_file')$:-!,
$transform(T)$:-$fold(T,R), write(R), write('.'), nl,!, fail.$

So far, we have described various concepts of the determinacy of a predicate call and their definitions. Some might say that a- and r-determinacy are possibly too weak to cover a significant class of deterministic predicates and predicate calls. In fact, however, they have made it possible to detect a number of deterministic predicates and predicate calls appearing in practical programs [9, 10]. This is because the concepts of a- and r-determinacy are defined in a way that reflects the intuition that Prolog programmers usually have about the determinacy of predicates and predicate calls.

3.6 Extensions

a- and r-determinacy have been specified syntactically. Here, we touch on some methods that extend the class of our determinacy by means of other language constructs and semantic considerations.

(1) *Mellish* [6] proposes that for efficient compilation of Prolog programs, the mode information of a predicate should be exploited to detect determinacy. Below, we show how the mode information of a predicate can be used to detect the determinacy of a predicate call. We consider the following program:

```
:- mode programming_language(+,−),
computer_language(P) :- programming_language(P, Inventor), human(Inventor),
programming_language(lisp, mcCarthy),
programming_language(prolog, colmerauer),
programming_language(pascal, wirth),
human(mcCarthy),
human(colmerauer),
human(wirth).
```

The predicate call programming_language(P, Inventor) can be seen to be r-deterministic with the help of its mode declaration, since none of its defining clauses is compatible with another, given the first argument of the predicate. In this way, the mode declaration of a predicate provides powerful information for detecting determinacy.

(2) In Condition (3) of the definition of r-determinacy, when a goal is unifiable with the head of the defining clauses, we propagate the unification (substitution) information to the body as well, in order to elaborate the detection of the determinacy of the goals in the body. That is, in the defining clauses

H_1 :- $[\Gamma_1, !,]\Delta_1$,

$\vdots$

H_i :- $[\Gamma_i, !,]\Delta_i$,

$\vdots$

H_n :- $[\Gamma_n, !,]\Delta_n$,

when a goal $p(A)$ is unifiable with the head H_i of the defining clauses, we use the unification (substitution) information to detect the determinacy of the body Δ_i.

(3) More generally, the unifiability of a goal with its defining clauses should be analyzed in more detail, using the types of predicate arguments inferred by type-inference (e.g., *Mishra* [7]). This would be helpful for expanding the class of r-deterministic goals. Extensions (2) and (3) can be called, in a word, semantic ones in which data and control flow analyses among Prolog predicates are intended. Extension (2) is simple, but theoretical considerations and implementation problems

related to (3) remain subjects for future research.

4 Concluding Remarks

We have shown that the determinacy of a Prolog predicate call plays a very important role in the transformation and compilation of Prolog programs and in the development of reliable Prolog programs. We proposed a concept of determinacy suitable for these purposes and introduced two decidable classes of predicates and predicate calls—a-determinacy and r-determinacy—and investigated their properties. Furthermore, we presented equivalent but alternative definitions of them as well as their extensions. The refinement of determinacy in Prolog, such as a- and r-determinacy, has not been done so far in the other papers [4, 6]. *Debray* [4] dealt only with the functionality of a predicate, and *Mellish* [6] discussed only the determinacy that corresponds to a-determinacy.

Our concepts naturally and syntactically capture the ordinary and intuitive sense of the determinacy of predicates and predicate calls that Prolog programmers encounter in programming practices, and hence they allow us to show an extensive class of predicates and predicate calls to be deterministic. On the other hand, if we consider the determinacy definitions in order to determine how to use cuts in Prolog programs, we can see that they involve very moderate and orderly uses of cuts.

Acknowledgments. I would like to express my gratitude to Dr. Tosio Kitagawa, the president of IIAS, and Dr. Hajime Enomoto, the director of IIAS, for their continuing guidance and encouragement. I also thank Mr. T. Takeshima, Dr. T. Yokomori, and Mr. T. Minami for lively discussions on determinacy.

References

[1] Bowen, D. L.: *DEC System-10 Prolog User's Manual*, Version 3.43, Dept. of Artificial Intelligence, Univ. of Edinburgh, 1983.

[2] Byrd, L.: *Understanding the Control Flow of Prolog Programs*, Research Paper 151, Dept. of Artificial Intelligence, Univ. of Edinburgh, 1980.

[3] Chikayama, T.: *Prolog Programming Style*, unpublished memo, 1983.

[4] Debray, S. K. and Warren, D. S.: Detection and Optimization of Functional Computations in Prolog, *LNCS 225*, 1986, pp. 490–504.

[5] Kowalski, R.: *Logic for Problem Solving*, North Holland, 1979.

[6] Mellish, C. S.: Some Global Optimizations for a Prolog Compiler, *J. of Logic Programming*, Vol. 2, No. 1 (1985), pp. 43–66.

[7] Mishra, P.: Towards a Theory of Types in Prolog, *Proc. of the 1984 Int. Symp. on Logic Programming*, IEEE Computer Society, 1984, pp. 289–298.

[8] Sawamura, H. and Takeshima, T.: Recursive Unsolvability of Determinacy, Solvable Cases of Determinacy and Their Applications to Prolog Optimization, *Proc of the 1985 Symposium on Logic Programming*, IEEE Computer Society, 1985, pp. 200–207.

[9] Sawamura, H., Takeshima, T., and Kato, A.: Source-Level Optimization Techniques for Prolog, *IIAS Research Report*, No. 52 (1985), Fujitsu Ltd.; also ICOT-TM-0091.

[10] Sawamura, H.: Source-to-Source Optimization of Prolog Programs, *IIAS Research Report*, No. 19 (1986), Fujitsu Ltd.(in Japanese).

[11] Sawamura, H.: A Source-to-Source Prolog Optimizer and Its Performance Evaluation, *Trans. Inf. Proc. Soc. Japan*, Vol. 28, No. 4 (1986), pp. 339–348(in Japanese).

[12] Smolka, G.: Making Control and Data Flow in Logic Programs Explicit, *Proc. of the 1984 Lisp and Functional Programming Language Conf.*, ACM, 1984, pp. 311–322.

[13] Warren, D. H. D.: Implementing Prolog—Compiling Predicate Logic Programs, *D.A.I. Research Reports*, Nos. 39 and No. 40, Dept. of Artificial Intelligence, Univ. of Edinburgh, 1977.

Initially published in "Computer Software", Vol. 4, No. 4, in Japanese.

Hajime Sawamura
International Institute for Advanced Study of Social Information Science (IIAS)
Fujitsu Laboratories Ltd.
140 Miyamoto, Numazu, Shizuoka
410–03 Japan

Distributed C Language Based on a Higher-Order RPC Technique

Kazuhiko Kato   Atsushi Ohori   Takeo Murakami
Takashi Masuda

Summary. This paper describes the design and implementation of Distributed C, a language based on a higher-order remote procedure call technique that extends the conventional remote procedure call technique for application to a wider range of data types, including higher-order functions and pointers. Distributed C incorporates a transparent distributed communication mechanism and allows any statically typed data of C to be passed to remote procedures.

1 Introduction

Recent widespread use of distributed computing environments is confronting us with the need to increase productivity in the development of distributed applications. One of most significant factors in improving productivity is better language support that allows higher-level description of communicating programs. This paper presents the design and implementation of a distributed programming system that aims at facilitating the development of distributed application programs.

Distributed applications consist of collections of programs that communicate with each other by exchanging messages, using some form of network protocol. An important issue in designing a distributed programming system is therefore how to provide proper support for communications. Three typical approaches that have been adopted in distributed systems are described below.

1. Use of operating system calls or system libraries for communication taken directly from an existing non-distributed programming language, such as C, Pascal, or Lisp.
2. Use of special programming language designed for distributed applications.
3. Use of an existing programming language with a stub generator for remote procedure calls.

The first approach, although broadly used, is rather primitive and provides only very low-level abstraction for communication. An application program must

ISBN 0-12-037105-7

directly invoke low-level operating system calls or system libraries, so it is difficult to port the resulting programs to other operating systems. Another serious problem involved in this approach is that it provides virtually no mechanism for preserving the data types of a programming language during communication. It is the programmer's responsibility to ensure that the data being exchanged is consistently interpreted by each language system involved. This is particularly problematic when the distributed environment is heterogeneous—that is, when it consists of sites that have different hardware architectures. In such a heterogeneous environment, the data representations of the sites differ, and communication must incorporate appropriate data conversion. When the data values are of composite types, such as records, lists, or nested combinations of these, the required data conversion is complicated. Writing such complicated data conversion programs is intolerably cumbersome and error-prone.

With the second approach, the programmer can benefit from programming languages specially designed for distributed environments. As surveyed in [2], distributed languages are designed on the basis of various programming paradigms. Communication is properly abstracted and is an integrated part of the language. This high-level abstraction yields programs of higher portability, although porting of the language processor to other operating systems is still nontrivial. One drawback of this approach is that the programmer must learn an entirely new programming language in order to write distributed applications. Another is the difficulty of reusing existing programs written in conventional languages.

The third approach has been developed to overcome the disadvantages of the first approach without taking the drastic measure of designing an entirely new language. By combining remote procedure calls with automatic stub generation, this approach provides message-passing semantics for the procedure calls found in most programming languages. The stubs perform most of the communication-specific operations at runtime, so communication is largely transparent to the programmer; one can write and use remote procedures in almost the same way that one can write and use local procedures. The handling of hardware heterogeneity can also be incorporated into this approach. The arguments of a remote procedure are encoded into a canonical data representation at marshaling time, and the canonical representation is decoded to obtain the internal representation of the other machine at unmarshaling time. Including these encoding and decoding operations in the stubs of both sites makes it possible to preserve the data types in a heterogeneous environment.

The practical usefulness of this approach has been well recognized, and the approach is used as a basis for many commercial distributed systems [6, 7, 9, 16, 17]. However, there are still restrictions in conventional remote procedure call systems. One is that the application programmer must write an interface description for remote procedures as well as for the procedure itself. Another is that the data types that can be used as arguments of a remote procedure are restricted. For example, pointers or higher–order functions cannot be used directly as arguments of a remote procedure. Although these types of data are frequently used in ordinary applications, remote access to the data requires the programmer to write a certain amount of code to circumvent the type limitation of the remote procedure call mechanism. Elimination of the first restriction would not be so difficult; it should be possible to develop a preprocessor that automatically derives the interface information from procedure definitions. Elimination of the second restriction, however, is far from straightforward. In the approaches to stub generation so far proposed, treatment of data types is rather *ad hoc*, and there seems to be no established method that deals uniformly with the various data types of programming languages, including higher-order functions and pointers.

Two of us [12] recently developed a transparent communication theory that can be used to eliminate the above-mentioned type restriction in communication. The theory establishes a method of translating a statically typed polymorphic higher–order programming language with transparent communication capability into a language that contains only a low-level remote procedure call mechanism. The operational aspect of the theory can be regarded as a systematic generalization of stub generation for remote procedure calls. In addition to data of simple types, it allows type-safe use of values of various data types, including polymorphic higher-order functions and abstract data types, in a heterogeneous distributed environment. Moreover, the required data conversion and communication are completely transparent to the programmer. A monomorphic part of the method, which we call here the *higher-order remote procedure call* (HiRPC) technique, can be used to develop a distributed extension of an existing, statically typed language.

In this paper, we report on the design and implementation of the Distributed C language based on the HiRPC technique. Distributed C allows any statically typed C-language data, excluding dynamically typed features such as type casting and union types, to be passed as arguments to remote procedures. The rationale for selecting C as the base language for application of HiRPC is the popularity of the language. With the Distributed C processor, C programmers can develop distributed applications in a way very similar to that used for developing non–distributed applications, and many existing non-distributed applications written in C can be easily ported to a distributed environment with little modification of source code.

The rest of this paper is organized as follows. Section 2 overviews the HiRPC technique. Sections 3 and 4 describe the design and implementation of Distributed C language, which is based on HiRPC. Section 5 presents experimental results on the implementation of Distributed C. Section 6 describes related work. Section 7 concludes this paper.

2 Higher-Order Remote Procedure Calls

To make the present paper self-contained, we include an overview of those parts of the techniques presented in a previous paper [12] that are relevant to the development of Distributed C. In particular, we describe only the algorithmic aspects of the techniques, and impose the restriction that a type must be monomorphic. The interested reader is referred to the above paper [12] for a full treatment of the polymorphic type system, as well as of the underlying type-theoretic accounts for the translation algorithm described here. In giving this overview, we adopt a slightly more concrete presentation and include a detailed treatment of references (pointers), which comprise a special case of the treatment of the abstract data types presented in the above-mentioned paper [12].

To describe the technique, we first define a simple language $\mathcal{LD}$ with inter-language communication capability as an extension of the simply typed lambda calculus. This language serves as a model of various high-level user languages for distributed systems. We define a core language $\mathcal{LC}$ as a model of implementation languages for user languages modeled by $\mathcal{LD}$. $\mathcal{LC}$ can be readily implemented with a standard remote procedure call mechanism. We then describe a method for translating $\mathcal{LD}$ to $\mathcal{LC}$. One important aspect of this method is that it uses type information in a crucial way. The data being exchanged must be typed to ensure that they are consistently interpreted by the languages involved in communication. This is particularly important in heterogeneous environments. This point has been exploited in [8]. The technique also uses type information to perform the data conversion required for higher types.

2.1 The language $\mathcal{LD}$ as a model of user languages

The set of types of $\mathcal{LD}$ is given by the syntax

$$\tau ::= unit \mid b \mid \tau \times \tau \mid \tau \to \tau \mid ref(\tau) \mid rref(\tau),$$

where *unit* is a trivial type whose only element is *void*, $\times$ is a product type constructor, $\to$ is a function type constructor, b stands for base types, and $ref(\tau)$ is the type of *references* for values of type τ. Reference types of this form are implemented (for example, in Standard ML) and correspond to the pointer types or address types in other programming languages. The term $rref(\tau)$ stands for *remote reference types*—that is, types of references located in a remote site. Remote references are typically implemented as pairs composed of a site identifier and a reference within the site. To emphasize the distinction between these two forms of references, we sometimes call the former *local reference types.*

This distinction requires the programmer to be aware of the "location" of references, because the notion of references is associated with a store (or memory), which is usually local to each site. We could of course treat all references uniformly by regarding them all as remote references. However, such treatment would require dynamic resolution of the location of a reference, even if it is a local reference. The above distinction can be regarded as a compromise between the efficient handling of local references and the convenience of transparent treatment of remote references.

Although we treat only products and references, it is possible to extend $\mathcal{LD}$ to include various other type constructors by defining them through higher-order functions and exporting these functions.

The set of terms of $\mathcal{LD}$ is given by the syntax

$$M ::= c^\tau \mid x \mid \lambda x : \tau.M \mid M(M) \mid \textbf{import}\ x : \tau\ \textbf{in}\ M\ \textbf{end} \mid \textbf{export}\ M\ \textbf{as}\ x : \tau\ \textbf{end},$$

where c^τ stands for typed constants, including the following primitive functions for products and references:

$$\begin{array}{rll} \textbf{pair}_{\tau_1,\tau_2}^{\tau_1\to\tau_2\to\tau_1\times\tau_2} & \textbf{fst}_{\tau_1,\tau_2}^{\tau_1\times\tau_2\to\tau_1} & \textbf{snd}_{\tau_1,\tau_2}^{\tau_1\times\tau_2\to\tau_2} \\ \textbf{mkref}_\tau^{\tau\to ref(\tau)} & \textbf{deref}_\tau^{ref(\tau)\to\tau} & \textbf{assign}_\tau^{(ref(\tau)\times\tau)\to unit} \\ \textbf{rmkref}_\tau^{\tau\to rref(\tau)} & \textbf{rderef}_\tau^{rref(\tau)\to\tau} & \textbf{rassign}_\tau^{(rref(\tau)\times\tau)\to unit}. \end{array}$$

The first three are, respectively, pairing, first projection, and second projection. $\textbf{mkref}_\tau$ takes a value of type τ and returns its new reference. $\textbf{deref}_\tau$ is a dereferencing operation. $\textbf{assign}_\tau$ takes a reference and a value v and changes the value of the reference to v. **rmkref**, **rderef**, and **rassign** are for remote references. As in the above explanation, we usually omit the type tag τ in c^τ if it is determined by the shape of c.

$M(M)$ stands for function application, and $\lambda x : \tau.M$ is lambda abstraction. The construct **export** M **as** $x : \tau$ **end** makes the expression M available to a remote system through the name x. In M, the form **import** $x : \tau$ **in** M **end** binds, the identifier x to the corresponding remote value of type τ, which should have been made available by a remote system's **export** declaration. Note that the type τ in these constructs can be any type of $\mathcal{LD}$, and this allows transparent higher-order inter-language communication.

With appropriate syntax sugar, this language can be used for distributed applications.

2.2 The core language $\mathcal{LC}$

In this section, we define the core language $\mathcal{LC}$ that is to serve as a model of implementation languages for $\mathcal{LD}$. To do this, we must first make an assumption about the types of data that can be directly exchanged by using the underlying operating system support. We call the types of such data *communication types*. Here we assume them to belong to the following set of types:

$$\delta ::= \overline{b} \mid \delta \overline{\times} \delta \mid \overline{ref}(\sigma),$$

where $\overline{b}$ is the type b in canonical representation. The constructors $\overline{\times}$ and $\overline{ref}$ are, respectively, the type constructors for products and for references in canonical representation. A value of type $\overline{ref}(\sigma)$ usually includes the identification of the creating site. The type σ in $\overline{ref}(\sigma)$ means that the value type of a reference type can be an arbitrary type of $\mathcal{LC}$, defined below.

This assumption about the set of communication types is based on our observation that the above set of types can usually be directly supported by a distributed system. This assumption, however, does not imply that all the above types are needed to implement $\mathcal{LD}$. The minimal requirement for the set of communication types to support complete implementation of $\mathcal{LD}$ is that it contains base types and reference type constructors. All the other composite types can be handled by transferring functions to implement these types by the method we will describe below.

The set of types of $\mathcal{LC}$ (ranged over by σ) is given by the syntax

$$\sigma ::= b \mid \bar{b} \mid \sigma \times \sigma \mid \sigma \overline{\times} \sigma \mid ref(\sigma) \mid \overline{ref}(\sigma) \mid rref(\sigma) \mid \sigma \to \sigma \mid \sigma \Rightarrow \sigma.$$

$\sigma_1 \Rightarrow \sigma_2$ stands for types of functions that are converted so that they can be accommodated in the calling convention used in a system's remote procedure call.

The set of terms of $\mathcal{LC}$ (ranged over by M) is given by the following syntax:

$$\begin{aligned} M ::= {} & c^\sigma \mid x \mid \lambda x : \sigma.M \mid M(M) \mid \mathbf{RPC}(M, M) \mid \mathbf{RP}(M) \\ & \mid \mathbf{export*}\ M\ \mathbf{as}\ x : \delta\ \mathbf{end} \mid \mathbf{import*}\ x : \delta\ \mathbf{in}\ M\ \mathbf{end}. \end{aligned}$$

RPC is a primitive for calling a remote function. **RPC** takes a remote reference to a function and an argument of appropriate type and issues a system service that performs a remote procedure call in the predefined communication protocol. This service is a standard one supported in most distributed systems, and typically involves preparation of a message consisting of a remote reference to a function and to an argument, transmission of the message to a remote process, execution of a function application in the context of the remote process, and reception of the result. **RP** converts a function of type $\tau_1 \to \tau_2$ into a function of type $\tau_1 \Rightarrow_2$ so that it can be accommodated in the calling sequence defined in the communication protocol. **import∗** and **export∗** are similar to **import** and **export** in $\mathcal{LD}$, except that the allowable types of values are restricted to the communication types defined above.

The set of constants (denoted by c^σ) includes primitive functions for products and local references:

$$\begin{array}{lll} \mathbf{pair}_{\tau_1,\tau_2}^{\tau_1 \to \tau_2 \to \tau_1 \times \tau_2} & \mathbf{fst}_{\tau_1,\tau_2}^{\tau_1 \times \tau_2 \to \tau_1} & \mathbf{snd}_{\tau_1,\tau_2}^{\tau_1 \times \tau_2 \to \tau_2} \\ \mathbf{mkref}_\tau^{\tau \to ref(\tau)} & \mathbf{deref}_\tau^{ref(\tau) \to \tau} & \mathbf{assign}_\tau^{(ref(\tau) \times \tau) \to unit} \end{array}$$

The set also includes the following set of constants for converting internal values into canonical form, and vice versa:

$$\begin{array}{ll} \mathbf{encode}_b^{b \to \bar{b}} & \mathbf{decode}_b^{\bar{b} \to b} \\ \mathbf{pencode}_{\sigma_1,\sigma_2}^{\sigma_1 \times \sigma_2 \to \sigma_1 \overline{\times} \sigma_2} & \mathbf{pdecode}_{\sigma_1,\sigma_2}^{\sigma_1 \overline{\times} \sigma_2 \to \sigma_1 \times \sigma_2} \\ \mathbf{rencode}_\sigma^{ref(\sigma) \to \overline{ref}(\sigma)} & \mathbf{rdecode}_\sigma^{\overline{ref}(\sigma) \to ref(\sigma)}. \end{array}$$

Note that $\mathcal{LC}$ does not contain any primitive for manipulating remote references. All of the above constants are functions on local values and are easily implemented.

2.3 Translating $\mathcal{LD}$ into $\mathcal{LC}$

We now describe a method for translating the user language $\mathcal{LD}$ into the core language $\mathcal{LC}$. The strategy is to define in $\mathcal{LC}$, for any given type τ of $\mathcal{LD}$, the communication type $(\tau)^o$ and the following functions:

$$\Phi_\tau : \tau \longrightarrow (\tau)^o,$$
$$\Psi_\tau : (\tau)^o \longrightarrow \tau.$$

Φ_τ is a function that takes a value of type τ and transforms it into an appropriate value that can be sent to the remote system. The function Ψ_τ takes the value created by Φ_τ and sent by the remote system, and it "restores" a value of type τ in the local system.

If τ does not contain a function type constructor, then $(\tau)^o$ is simply the communication type corresponding to τ. For general types, an appropriate definition for $(\tau)^o$ is the following:

$$\begin{aligned}
(b)^o &= \overline{b}, \\
(\tau_1 \times \tau_2)^o &= (\tau_1)^o \overline{\times} (\tau_2)^o, \\
(\tau_1 \rightarrow \tau_2)^o &= \overline{ref}((\tau_1)^o \Rightarrow (\tau_2)^o), \\
(ref(\tau))^o &= \overline{ref}(\tau), \\
(rref(\tau))^o &= rref(\tau).
\end{aligned}$$

$rref(\tau)$ is a reference in a canonical form created and sent from a remote site—that is, the type $\overline{ref}(\tau)$ in a remote site. Note that $(\tau)^o$ is always a communication type, even if τ is not.

If τ does not contain function type constructors, Φ_τ and Ψ_τ can be given by simple inductive definitions using the primitives to convert data into canonical form. For function types, obtaining a correct definition is less simple. For a given term having a function type, we need to generate a term that has the same operational behavior as that of the original function term, but that has a communication type. This is achieved by inductively lifting the definitions of Φ and Ψ for communication types to higher-order function types. If we abstract the details of communication protocols, then sending and receiving values can be modeled by a pair of isomorphic domains D and D' connected by bijections $\phi_D : D \rightarrow D'$ and $\psi_D : D' \rightarrow D$. If we have two pairs of domains (D, D') and (E, E') connected by pairs of bijections (ϕ_D, ψ_D) and (ϕ_E, ψ_E), the following function constructors lift these bijections to function spaces:

$$\begin{aligned}
\phi_{D \rightarrow E} &= \lambda f \in D \rightarrow E.\lambda x \in D'.\phi_E(f(\psi_D(x))), \\
\psi_{D \rightarrow E} &= \lambda f' \in D' \rightarrow E'.\lambda x \in D.\psi_E(f'(\phi_D(x))).
\end{aligned}$$

In order to send a function $f : D \rightarrow E$ to the corresponding function space $D' \rightarrow E'$, we apply $\phi_{D \rightarrow E}$ to f to generate a function $f' : D' \rightarrow E'$. When applied to a value in D', this function first gets the corresponding value x' in D by using ψ_D, then applies f to x', yielding a result y in E. Finally, the function sends the result back to E', by using ϕ_E. This mechanism makes it possible to transform any function from D to E into a function from D' to E'. The function $\psi_{D \rightarrow E}$ can be understood similarly. These situations are shown in Figure 1.

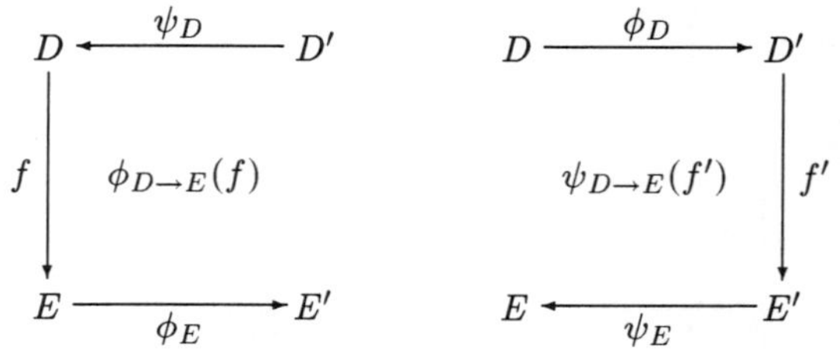

Fig. 1 Lifting communication to function types

By combining the above technique and the inductive application of conversion primitives, we obtain the following definitions for Φ and Ψ:

$$
\begin{aligned}
\Phi_b(M) &= \mathbf{encode}_b(M), \\
\Phi_{\tau_1,\tau_2}(M) &= \mathbf{pencode}_{\tau_1\times\tau_2}\ (\mathbf{pair}_{\tau_1,\tau_2}\ (\Phi_{\tau_1}\ (\mathbf{fst}_{\tau_1,\tau_2}(M)))\ (\Phi_{\tau_2}\ (\mathbf{snd}_{\tau_1,\tau_2}(M)))), \\
\Phi_{\tau_1\to\tau_2}(M) &= \mathbf{rencode}_{\tau_1\to\tau_2}(\mathbf{mkref}_{\tau_1\to\tau_2}\ \mathbf{RP}(\lambda x : (\tau_1)^o.\Phi_{\tau_2}\ (M\ (\Psi_{\tau_1}(x))))), \\
\Phi_{ref(\tau)}(M) &= \mathbf{rencode}_\tau(M), \\
\Phi_{rref(\tau)}(M) &= M;
\end{aligned}
$$

$$
\begin{aligned}
\Psi_b(M) &= \mathbf{decode}_b(M), \\
\Psi_{\tau_1\times\tau_2}(M) &= \mathbf{pair}_{\tau_1,\tau_2}\ (\Psi_{\tau_1}\ (\mathbf{fst}_{\tau_1,\tau_2}\ (\mathbf{pdecode}_{\tau_1,\tau_2}(M))), \\
&\qquad \Psi_{\tau_2}\ (\mathbf{snd}_{\tau_1,\tau_2}\ (\mathbf{pdecode}_{\tau_1,\tau_2}(M)))), \\
\Psi_{\tau_1\to\tau_2}(M) &= \lambda y : \tau_1.\Psi_{\tau_2}(\mathbf{RPC}(M, \Phi_{\tau_1}(y)), \\
\Psi_{ref(\tau)}(M) &= \mathbf{rdecode}_\tau(M), \\
\Psi_{rref(\tau)}(M) &= M.
\end{aligned}
$$

Conversion of values of the type $rref(\tau)$ is not needed, since they are values of remote references and are only used as parameters of functions for manipulating remote references, whose definition is given in the definition of $\mathcal{TR}$.

Since Φ and Ψ can deal with arbitrary types of $\mathcal{LD}$, we are ready to define an algorithm $\mathcal{TR}$ for translating arbitrary (type-correct) terms of $\mathcal{LD}$ into $\mathcal{LC}$. A definition of the algorithm is given in Figure 2.

3 Design of the distributed C language

We designed Distributed C by applying the HiRPC techniques described in the previous section to the C language [10]. To write distributed applications in C, programmers must explicitly use the low-level communication primitives provided by an operating system, since C makes no provision for distributed communication. We could expect that the transparent incorporation into C of distribution, which is the most notable feature of HiRPC, would drastically decrease the cost of describing distributed applications and of porting previously developed, nondistributed C programs to a distributed environment.

$$
\begin{aligned}
\mathcal{TR}(\mathbf{rmkref}_\tau) &= \Psi_{\tau\to ref(\tau)}\ RMKREF^{(\tau\to ref(\tau))^o},\\
\mathcal{TR}(\mathbf{rderef}_\tau) &= \Psi_{ref(\tau)\to\tau}\ RDEREF^{(ref(\tau)\to\tau)^o},\\
\mathcal{TR}(\mathbf{rassign}_\tau) &= \Psi_{(ref(\tau)\times\tau)\to unit}\ RASSIGN^{((ref(\tau)\times\tau)\to unit)^o},\\
\mathcal{TR}(c^\tau) &= c^\tau \ \text{ (except the above three primitives)},\\
\mathcal{TR}(x) &= x,\\
\mathcal{TR}(\lambda x:\tau.M) &= \lambda x:\tau.\mathcal{TR}(M),\\
\mathcal{TR}(M_1\ M_2) &= \mathcal{TR}(M_1)\ \mathcal{TR}(M_2),\\
\mathcal{TR}(\mathbf{import}\ x:\tau\ \mathbf{in}\ M\ \mathbf{end}) &= \mathbf{import*}\ x:(\tau)^o\ \mathbf{in}\ (\lambda x:\tau.\mathcal{TR}(M))\ (\Psi_\tau(x))\ \mathbf{end},\\
\mathcal{TR}(\mathbf{export}\ M\ \mathbf{as}\ x:\tau\ \mathbf{end}) &= \mathbf{export*}\ \Phi_\tau\ \mathcal{TR}(M)\ \mathbf{as}\ x:(\tau)^o\ \mathbf{end},
\end{aligned}
$$

where $RMKREF$, $RDEREF$, and $RASSIGN$ are the following functions in a remote process:

$$
\begin{aligned}
RMKREF^{(\tau\to ref(\tau))^o} &= \Phi_{\tau\to ref(\tau)}\ \mathbf{mkref}_\tau,\\
RDEREF^{(ref(\tau)\to\tau)^o} &= \Phi_{ref(\tau)\to\tau}\ \mathbf{deref}_\tau,\\
RASSIGN^{((ref(\tau)\times\tau)\to unit)^o} &= \Phi_{(ref(\tau)\times\tau)\to unit}\ \mathbf{assign}_\tau.
\end{aligned}
$$

Fig. 2 The translation algorithm

The HiRPC technique can be applied only to a programming language that has a statically determined type system—that is, one in which the values of variables are determined at compile time. When the type system of a programming language includes dynamically determined data types, the HiRPC technique is applicable only to the statically determined portion of the system. The type system of the C language, which was originally designed for system programming, is mostly statically determined, but includes dynamic typing features such as *union* data types and *cast*. The version of Distributed C that we designed and implemented supports only the statically determined portion of the C language type system.

3.1 Syntax of distributed C

While designing the syntax of Distributed C, we kept the following two goals in mind:

- Provide maximum distributed transparency by making programmers unaware of the existence of the distinct address spaces and the hardware architecture heterogeneity.
- Minimize extensions to the syntax of the C language.

These goals were adopted so that programmers who have already learned the C language can do distributed programming easily and so that existing non-distributed C programs can be ported to distributed environments with little rewriting.

Table 1 Correspondence Between $\mathcal{LD}$ and Distributed C

$\mathcal{LD}$	Distributed C
c^{τ}	Constants of C
x	Variables of C
$\lambda x : \tau.M$	Function definition of C
$M(M)$	Function application of C
$\mathbf{pair}^{\tau_1,\tau_2}, \mathbf{fst}^{\tau_1,\tau_2}, \mathbf{snd}^{\tau_1,\tau_2}$	Both *struct* and arguments specification in function definition and application in C. A n-ary tuple ($n > 2$) is represented by a cascade of multiple pairs.
$\mathbf{mkref}^{\tau}, \mathbf{deref}^{\tau}, \mathbf{assign}^{\tau}$	Pointers and basic operators `\&`, `*`, `=` in C

We now describe the syntax of Distributed C. The following part of the syntax of the model language $\mathcal{LD}$,

$$c^{\tau} \mid x \mid \lambda x : \tau.M \mid M(M),$$

and the primitive functions **pair**, **fst**, **snd**, **mkref**, **deref**, and **assign** correspond straightforwardly to the concrete syntax of the C language (Table 1). We introduced the following new syntax:

1. Declaration of remote functions,
2. Declaration of remote pointers,
3. Declaration of copy-on-reference and copy-on-call argument-passing methods,
4. Declaration of array data-passing methods.

The remaining subsections of Section 3 describe the introduced syntax in detail.

3.1.1 Declaration of remote functions

When a programmer of a callee program wants a function to be called from programs in remote address spaces, he must explicitly state this intention. (This corresponds to **exports** in $\mathcal{LD}$.) The caller program of the remote function must explicitly declare that the function is remote. (This corresponds to **import** in $\mathcal{LD}$.) By the following syntax, the callee program can declare that the function can be called from remote address spaces.

```
export <type specifier> <function name>(<arguments>)
       [@ <callerID variable>]
{ <function body> }
```

The square brackets `[...]` denote optional items. When `@ <callerID variable>` is specified, the program ID (usually a site address and a process identifier) of the caller is substituted for `<callerID variable>` at runtime, and `<function body>` can use this variable. The following is an example of remote function definition:

Example 1 (Definition of a remote function)

```
struct complex {
  double real;
  double imag;
} ;

/* export the function body as add : complex × complex → complex end   */
export struct complex
add(struct complex x, struct complex y) @ caller_var
{
  struct complex r;

  r.real = x.real + y.real;
  r.imag = x.imag + y.imag;
  return r;
}
```

A caller program declares the remote function name and its type in the header part of the program as

```
import <type spec> <function name>(<arguments>) [@ <calleeID variable>];
```

This declares that `<function name>` is a remote function. When the optional `<calleeID variable>` is specified, the remote function is in the remote process specified by the variable (more precisely, the call entry, or address, of the remote process). After the `import` declaration, the caller program can call the remote function as

```
<function name>(<arguments>) [@ <calleeID variable>]
```

The optional `calleeID variable` must be specified either in the `import` declaration or at the time of the remote call. If it is specified in both, the specification at remote call time has priority. If it is specified in neither, a compile time error is generated. Note that since `<calleeID variable>` can be specified by the value of a variable, a process at a remote site that includes a remote procedure cannot be fixed at compile time.

Examples 2 and 3 illustrate the use of remote function definitions and remote function calls.

Example 2 (Declaration of Remote Function Use)

```
/* import add : complex × complex → complex
   in (the rest of the declaration) end   */
import complex add(complex, complex) @ callee_id;
```

Example 3 (Remote Function Call)

```
/* import add : complex × complex → complex in  z = add(x, y) end  */
z = add(x, y) @ callee_id;
```

3.1.2 Declaration of remote pointer

As explained in Section 2.1, remote pointer types and local pointer types must be distinctively declared.[1] In Distributed C, the syntax of declaration for the local pointer types is as same as in the C language, while the syntax for the remote pointer types is designated by prefixing a keyword, `remote`, to the pointer type declaration. Example 4 illustrates the declaration of the remote function **add**, which was defined in Example 1, with its input parameters passed by remote pointers.

Example 4 (Declaration of remote-pointer arguments)

```
/* export the function body as
     add : rref(complex) × rref(complex) → complex) end   */
export struct complex add(remote struct complex *x,
                          remote struct complex *y)
{
  struct complex r;

  r.real = x->real + y->real;
  r.imag = x->imag + y->imag;
  return r;
}
```

Example 5 shows the header part of a callee program of the remote function.

[1] As noted in Section 2.1, this is not an indispensable restriction.

Example 5 (Declaration of a remote function)

```
import complex add(remote struct complex *,
                   remote struct complex *) @ callee_id;
```

3.1.3 Declaration of copy-on-reference and copy-on-call argument passing

The HiRPC technique described in Section 2 causes callbacks whenever the value pointed to by a remote pointer is referenced. To reduce the number of callbacks, the memory area pointed to by a remote pointer can be passed to a remote function that takes remote pointer arguments at the time of the remote function call. This mechanism is called *copy-on-call*, while the original remote pointer passing mechanism of HiRPC is called *copy-on-reference.*

The programmer can specify copy-on-reference argument passing by prefixing the keyword **remote** to the argument type declaration in a remote function declaration. When the keyword **remote** is not prefixed, the copy-on-call is used. In the body of the remote function definition, arguments passed by copy-on-reference are treated as remote pointers, while the arguments passed by copy-on-call are treated as local pointers. Mutual substitution of those pointers is not permitted. Examples 6 and 7 illustrate the declarations of a remote function whose arguments are passed by copy-on-reference and copy-on-call.

Example 6 (Declaration of copy-on-reference argument passing)

```
export void func(remote struct list *l)
{
  remote struct list *temp;

  for (temp = l; temp!=NULL; temp=temp->next)
    if (temp->item == ...) ...
}
```

Example 7 (Declaration of copy-on-call argument passing)

```
export void func(struct list *l)
{
  struct list *temp;

  for (temp = l; temp!=NULL; temp=temp->next)
    if (temp->item == ...) ...
}
```

3.1.4 Declaration of array-type argument passing

Since array-type variables are treated as pointers in C, we must deal with the treatment of arrays. An array of type τ is really a pointer to τ; a continuous area of memory is allocated for a specified number of τ–type elements, and the top address of the memory area is initially set as the value of the pointer. Unlike strongly typed procedural languages such as Pascal or Ada, C does not support any linguistic constructs for examining the number of elements in an array variable. When the array variable is passed by copy-on-reference, the size of the array is not needed, because the addresses or offsets from the top of the array are specified in each reference. However, when an array variable (= pointer–type variable) is passed to a remote function by copy-on-call, the size of the array is needed in order to send the memory area to the remote function before the reference in the remote function body. To resolve this problem, we introduced a syntax for declaring the array size of arguments of a remote procedure. The callee function declares the size of an array argument, as shown in Example 8.

Example 8 (Declaration of a copy-on-call array argument—callee side)

```
export void sort([n]int *a) @ caller_var
{ /* function body */ }
```

In the example, an argument `a` is defined as a pointer type for an integer array, and the number of the elements in array `a` must be explicitly specified by the programmer. Example 9 shows a function that remotely calls the function defined in Example 8 by copy-on-call.

Example 9 (Declaration of a copy-on-call array argument—caller side)

```
  ...
import sort(int *);
  ...
int a[100];
  ...
sort([40]data) @ server_id;
  ...
```

Here, the remote function `sort` is called with the integer array argument `data`, which has 40 elements. When the declaration illustrated in Example 10 is put in the header part of the caller program, the argument of the remote function `sort` is, by default, an integer array of 100 elements.

Example 10 (Declaration of a copy-on-call array argument—caller side)

```
import void sort([100]int *);
```

4 Implementation of Distributed C

This section describes the language processor and the runtime system of Distributed C.

4.1 Distributed C translator

We implemented a language processor of Distributed C as a source-to-source translator into C. The processor takes Distributed C programs and generates the equivalent C programs, including runtime library calls, by using the translation algorithm described in Section 2. The generated programs can be compiled to give executable code by using existing C compilers.

To shorten the time needed for developing the translator, we used the source code of a language processing system for COB, developed at the IBM Tokyo Research Laboratory. COB is an upwardly compatible extension of the C language and has object-oriented features [13]. The COB processing system is a source-to-source translator that generates C code; the system itself is written in COB. We chose the COB processing system as a framework for creating a Distributed C processing system. The source code of the COB processing system consists of 20,000 lines of COB code. To implement Distributed C, we added 5,000 lines of

COB code for the translation algorithm and runtime communication routines. We adopted XDR (External Data Representation [11]) for canonical data representation, as described in Section 2.2 (the types of δ), and we used the XDR library to encode to and decode from the canonical data representation. XDR guarantees the transformation of basic data types such as integers, floating point numbers, strings, and records between CPUs with heterogeneous architectures.

The copy-on-reference argument passing of Distributed C is identical to the treatment of remote pointers discussed in Section 2. On the other hand, copy-on-call argument passing, which is an optimization technique for remote pointers, must be dealt with in a special way. To implement copy-on-call passing, the C code for the following operational semantics is generated:

1. Assume that pointer p is passed to a remote function by the copy-on-call mechanism. We define a *closure* of pointer p as the memory area reached by following all pointers starting from p until (i) a pointer points to a NULL value, (ii) a remote pointer is found, or (iii) a function pointer is found. Make a *closure packet* by scanning and marshaling the closure of pointer p into the packet by using the Φ encoding routines. In the current implementation, depth–first search is used for scanning, and the XDR encoding routines are used as Φ.
2. Transfer the closure packet to the address space in which the remote function is located. That address space is called the *remote address space*.
3. In the remote address space, the closure packet is unmarshaled and expanded by using Ψ decoding functions. As a result, a closure isomorphic to the original closure of p is constructed in the remote address space.
4. Execute the body of the remote function in the remote address space.
5. To reflect the side effects due to the execution of the body of the remote function, the expanded closure is marshaled, transferred, unmarshaled, and expanded in the original address space, just as above. This time, the returned closure is created in a new memory area of the original address space, and the value of the pointer p is set to the top address of the new area. (If the original closure is not referenced by others, it is collected as garbage.)

As a result of this closure transfer, the memory area pointed to by a remote pointer is moved to the memory area on the remote address space, and the body of the remote function can access the area as if it were local. Therefore the remote function does not require callback in order to access the transferred closure. Since the transferred closure is accessed exactly like the local closure, the transformation does not conflict with the type system described in Section 2.

4.2 Runtime system

We used the well-known method for remote procedure call implementation described in [3] to implement the **RPC** and **RP** of $\mathcal{LC}$. An overview of the runtime

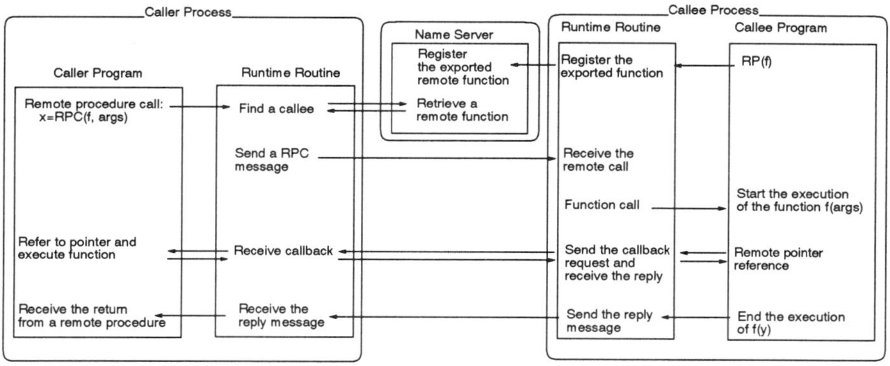

Fig. 3 Overview of the runtime mechanisms of Distributed C

mechanism of our implementation of Distributed C is shown in Figure 3. The Distributed C translator is based on the $\mathcal{TR}$ algorithm described in Section 2 and produces runtime routines for both the callee and the caller programs. As the current execution environment is UNIX on the Sun3 and Sun4 workstations, the runtime routines include communication programs using UNIX sockets. The name server in Figure 3 is a process that stores the mapping from an exported remote function name to the sites where the function is located. The name server can be at any site of the network. (The address of the name server should be known to every site *a priori*.) When the **RP** primitive is executed by a callee process, that process communicates with the name server, and the exported function name and the process identifier (site ID and process ID) of the callee process are registered in the name server. These registered identifiers are used as the `<calleeID>`'s mentioned in Section 3.1.1. A caller program of a remote function communicates with the name server and retrieves the `calleeID` of the exported remote function by specifying the remote function name as a retrieval key.

The runtime mechanism of Distributed C shown in Figure 3 differs from that of the conventional remote procedure call systems described in [3] in that marshaling and unmarshaling of arguments and communication between the caller and the callee are required not only at the time of the remote function call and the return, but also during the execution of the remote function body. In Distributed C, remote function calls to exported functions and callbacks are both treated in the same framework. This originates from the systematic treatment of the higher-order remote procedure calls.

5 Experiments

The language processor and the runtime system described in Section 4 were created on several Sun3 (M68020 CPU) and Sun4 (SPARC CPU) workstations. The language processor takes Distributed C programs and generates the equivalent C programs, including runtime routines that include XDR calls and a facility for communicating through sockets. XDR deals with the conversion of internal data representation between the Sun3 and Sun4, so a function in a Sun4 process can be called from a Sun3 process, and vice versa. The generated C programs are compiled by using existing C compilers; currently the GNU C compiler [15] is used. With this implementation, experiments were made to evaluate the runtime performance of Distributed C. This section describes the results of those experiments.

5.1 Examined programs: remote hash table retrieval

An array representing a hash table was retained in the caller process, and the top address of the array (i.e., a remote pointer to the hash table) was passed to the remote function as an argument through either copy-on-reference or copy-on-call. The key to be retrieved was also passed to the remote function as an argument. With copy-on-reference, a hash function in the callee program indirectly accesses the hash table in the caller through the callback mechanism; with copy-on-call, the entire hash table is transferred from the caller to callee at the time of the remote function call, and the hash table is returned to the caller upon the return from the remote function. Changing the collision ratio of the hash table keys changes the number of callbacks. The difference in performance between the copy-on-reference and copy-on-call argument passing mechanisms can thus be measured.

Figure 4 shows the callee program written in Distributed C. It includes a remote function `search()` that performs hash table retrieval. The exported remote function `search()` takes two arguments: a remote pointer of `struct record` type and a retrieved key of integer type. Each entry of the hash table stored in the caller process has a `record` structure. To resolve key conflicts in retrieving the hash table, *open addressing* with linear scanning is used. The program shown in Figure 4 uses the copy-on-reference argument passing method; that is, only referenced elements of the hash table stored in the caller process are accessed by callback. If the programmer wishes to use copy-on-call argument passing, the argument declaration part of the remote function `search()` in Figure 4 should be changed to the following:

```
/* Exported remote function (callee side) */
export struct item
search([tsize] struct record *table, int key) @ caller_var
{ /* function body */ }
```

The identifier `tsize` is an integer variable, and the programmer should set the number of elements in the hash table to this variable.

Figure 5 shows the caller program that remotely calls the `search()` function. The program uses copy-on-reference argument passing. The variable `table` is a pointer to the top of the hash table. This pointer is passed to the callee program as a remote pointer. If the programmer wishes to use copy-on-call argument passing,

```
struct item {
  int number;
  int name;
  int address;
};

struct record {
  int key;
  struct item value;
};

/* Hash function */
int hash(int key)
{ return key  TABLE_SIZE; }

/* Exported remote function (callee side) */
export struct item search(remote struct record *table, int key)
{
  struct record temp;
  int h;

  h = hash(key);
  temp = table[h];               /* remote reference */
  while (temp.key != key){
    h = (h + 1) % TABLE_SIZE;
    temp = table[h];             /* remote reference */
  }
  return temp.value;
}
```

Fig. 4 The callee program retrieving a hash table

the remote function call in Figure 5 should be changed to the following:

```
  ...
  ret_val = search([TABLE_SIZE] table,
                   key_table[rand() % (TABLE_SIZE/4)]) @ CALLEE_ID;
  ...
```

Here, the number of entries in the hash table is defined as a constant 200; the entire size of the hash table is

$$\texttt{sizeof(struct record)} * 200 = 16 * 200 = 3,200 \text{ (bytes)}.$$

Therefore, for copy-on-call, 3,200 bytes are transferred to the callee process at the time of the remote procedure call, and the same number of bytes are transferred

```
...
#define TABLE_SIZE 200
import struct item search(remote struct record *, int)
struct record table[TABLE_SIZE];
int i,h, key;
int key_table[TABLE_SIZE];
...
caller ()
{
  ...
  /* Remote function call */
  ret_val = search(table, key_table[rand()%(TABLE_SIZE/4)]) @ CALLEE_ID;
  ...
}
```

Fig. 5 The caller program that provides a hash table

back to the caller process upon the return from the remote function.

5.2 Experimental results

In the experiments, various numbers of elements were inserted into the hash table. The average times for retrieving random keys were measured. All the retrieved keys had been previously inserted into the hash table.

The caller programs were executed on a Sun3 workstation (M68020 CPU, 12 MB main memory), and the callee programs were executed on a Sun4 workstation (SPARC CPU, 12 MB main memory). The workstations were connected by a 10 Mbps Ethernet. The network protocol was TCP/IP. The Sun XDR libraries were used as the canonical data representation library.

Figure 6 shows the measurements of the average response time for retrieving a hash table by using a remote function call. The probability of collision was changed by varying the number of the elements inserted into the hash table. The number of collisions affects the performance, because a collision requires a callback when the copy-on-reference mechanism is used.

Figure 7 compares the theoretical and experimental average numbers of collisions (i.e., callbacks). The theoretical value was derived from the evaluation formulas presented in [1, pp. 130–132].

Careful examination of the two graphs reveals the following:

- When copy-on-reference is used, one remote procedure call and one callback take about 19 milliseconds; when copy-on-call is used, one remote procedure

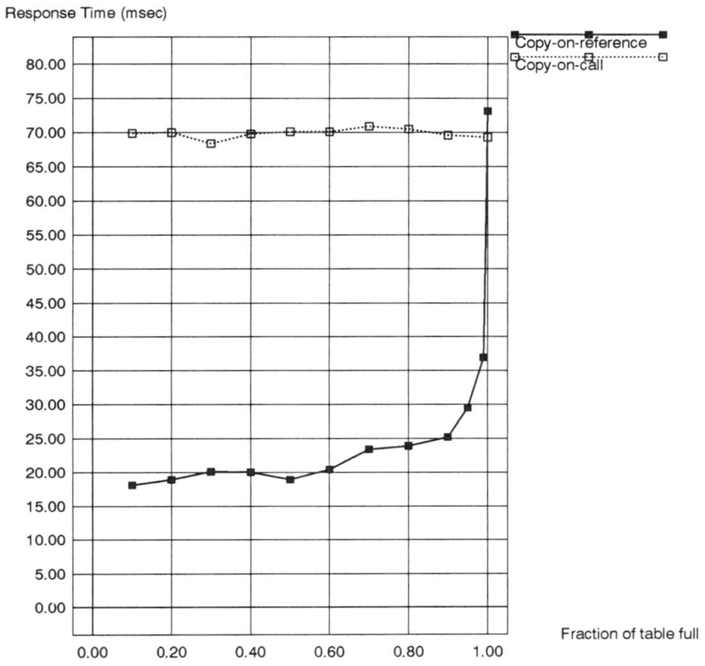

Fig. 6 Average response time for retrieving a hash table by using a remote function call. X-axis: (number of elements inserted into the hash table)/(tonal number of elements in the hash table); Y-axis: average response time for retrieving a key (milliseconds).

call and two memory transfers of 3,200 bytes take 70 milliseconds.

- From the range $0 < X \leq 0.9$ in Figure 6, we can see that, as expected, copy-on-reference is faster than copy-on-call when a relatively small part is accessed.

- Copy-on-reference is advantageous when the insertion ratio is less than 1.0—that is, when the average number of accesses to the hash table is less than 6.5. When the table is accessed more than 6.5 times, copy-on-call is advantageous. This experimental result agrees with the expectation that copy-on-call would be more effective when a large portion of the remote data is accessed. The choice between copy-on-call and copy-on-reference involves a trade-off between the number of remote references; the time taken to process a callback in copy-on-reference, and the amount of data transferred in copy-on-call.

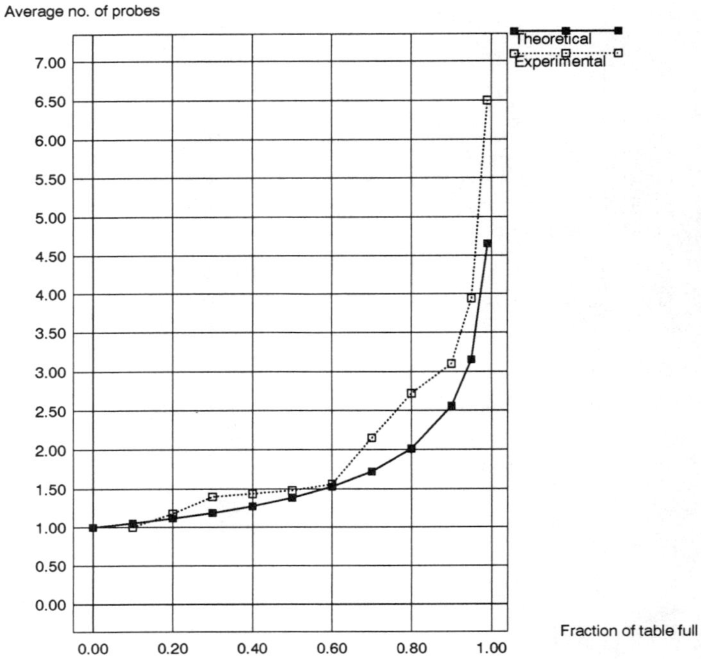

Fig. 7 Theoretical and experimental average numbers of collisions (i.e., callbacks). X-axis: (number of elements inserted into the hash table)/(total number of elements in the hash table); Y-axis: number of accessed elements in the hash table (milliseconds).

6 Related Work

Like Distributed C, some other distributed language systems take the approach of embedding stub generators in their language processors, and they require no special interface description other than ordinary procedure interface declarations. One example is the CLAM distributed programming system [5]. CLAM adopted C++ as its core language. The developers of CLAM extended a C++ language processor to translate procedure calls into remote procedure calls. CLAM facilitates the programmer's work more than conventional RPC systems, but essentially it merely embeds the RPC technique in its language processor. Thus it inherits the restrictions of the previous RPC techniques mentioned in Section 1. Moreover, a systematic justification for introducing distribution into an existing language is not given. For these reasons, programmers must explicitly describe marshaling and unmarshaling routines (which they call bundler and unbundler routines) to pass pointer type arguments to remote procedures. The bundler and unbundler mechanisms in CLAM are similar to the copy-on-call mechanism in Distributed C. However, no mechanism corresponding to the copy-on-reference mechanism is supported.

Some distributed object-oriented systems support *object mobility*, in which passive or active objects are moved between sites. Emerald [4], the name of a new distributed object-oriented language and its distributed execution system, is typical of such systems. In Emerald, programs are described on the basis of a message-passing paradigm suited for distributed environments (the second approach in Section 1). Keeping distributed transparency, Emerald can specify other objects as arguments of method calls with call-by-reference. This feature is similar to the copy-on-reference of Distributed C. Furthermore, Emerald supports mechanisms for moving argument objects between sites, called *copy-on-move* and *copy-on-visit*. In the former, the moved objects remain at the destination site after the called method is processed; in the latter, the moved objects are returned to the source sites. The copy-on-visit mechanism is close to the copy-on-call mechanism of Distributed C. In other words, copy-on-call can be seen as an implementation of copy-on-visit in a non-object-oriented language system where communications are abstracted as procedure calls.

7 Conclusion

We have described the design and implementation of Distributed C, a language based on the higher-order remote procedure call technique that extends the conventional remote procedure call technique for application to a wider range of data types, including higher-order functions and abstract data types. Distributed C incorporates a transparent distributed communication mechanism and allows any statically typed data of C to be passed to remote procedures. Distributed C has two argument passing mechanisms for references: copy-on-reference and copy-on-call. The former mechanism calls back the caller each time a remote reference is de-referenced; the latter sends a closure of a reference at calling time, and the remote reference is replaced by a local reference in the callee. We did experiments on workstations connected by a local area network and described the characteristics of the two argument passing mechanisms.

The theory of transparent communication [12], on which HiRPC is based, guarantees type safety of communicating programs. To preserve this desired property, Distributed C does not support the dynamic typing features of C, such as the union types and type casting. Since the HiRPC technique does not assume any particular language implementation, the development method of Distributed C presented here can also be adopted to develop distributed extensions of other statically typed languages.

As future work, we recommend the development of a toolkit for incorporating the HiRPC technique into various programming languages. Since the required extensions to the programming languages should have a common structure derived from HiRPC technique, a promising way to develop various distributed extensions would be to develop a translator generator. Incorporating the translation scheme of HiRPC into compiler compiler techniques [14] makes it possible to develop a generator that inputs the syntax and the typing rules of a programming language and that generates a mechanism for translating the distributed extension of the language into the original language.

Acknowledgements. We thank Tsutomu Kamimura and Tamiya Onodera of the IBM Tokyo Research Laboratory for permission to use the language processor of COB.

References

[1] Aho, A. V., Hopcroft, J. E., and Ullman, J. D.: *Data Structures and Algorithms*, Addison-Wesley, 1983.

[2] Bal, H. E., Steiner, J. G., and Tanenbaum, A. S.: Programming Languages for Distributed Computing Systems, *Computing Surveys*, Vol. 21, No. 3 (1989), pp. 261–322.

[3] Birrell, A. D and Nelson, B. J.: Implementing Remote Procedure Calls, *ACM Trans. Computer Systems*, Vol. 2, No. 1 (1984), pp. 39–59.

[4] Black, A., Hutchinson, N., Jul, E., Levy, H., and Carter, L.: Distribution and Abstract Types in Emerald, *IEEE Trans. Software Engineering*, Vol. SE-13, No. 1 (1987), pp. 65–76.

[5] Call, L. A., Cohrs, D. L., and Miller, B. P.: CLAM—An Open System for Graphical User Interfaces, *ACM OOPSLA'87*, 1987, pp. 277–286.

[6] Corbin, J. R.: *The Art of Distributed Applications: Programming Techniques for Remote Procedure Calls*, Sun Technical Reference Library, Springer-Verlag, 1990.

[7] Draves, R., Jones, M., and Thompson, M.: MIG—The Mach Interface Generator, Technical report, Carnegie-Mellon University, Feb. 1988.

[8] Hayes, R. L: *UTS: A Type System for Facilitating Data Communication*, PhD Thesis, Univ. of Arizona, 1989.

[9] Kato, K.: Open Operating Systems—Focusing on Remote Procedure Calls, *Winter Tutorial on Distributed Operating Systems*, Japan Society for Software Science and Technology, 1991 (in Japanese).

[10] Kernighan, B. W. and Ritchie, D. M.: *The C Programming Language*, Prentice Hall, Second Edition, 1988.

[11] Sun Microsystems: *XDR: External Data Representation Standard*, RFC 1014, Jun. 1987.

[12] Ohori, A. and Kato, K.: Semantics for Communication Primitives in a Polymorphic Language, *Proc. 20th ACM Symp. on Principles of Programming Languages*, Jan. 1993, pp. 99–112.

[13] Onodera, T. and Kamimura, T.: Object-Oriented Programming in COB, *Computer Today*, Vol. 7, No. 40 (1990), pp. 26–38 (in Japanese).

[14] Sassa, M.: *Programming Language Processing Systems*, Software Science Series, Vol. 5, Iwanami, 1989 (in Japanese).

[15] Stallman, R. M.: *Using and Porting GNU CC*, Free Software Foundation, Inc., 1991.

[16] XEROX Corporation: *Courier: the Remote Procedure Call Protocol*, Dec. 1981, XEROX System Integration Standard XSIS-038112.

[17] Zahn, L., Dineen, T. H., Leach, P. J., Martin, E. A., Mishkin, N. W., Pato, J. N., and Wyant, G. L.: *Network Computing Architecture*, Prentice Hall, 1990.

Initially published in "Computer Software", Vol. 9, No. 3, in Japanese.

Kazuhiko Kato

Department of Information Science
Faculty of Science
University of Tokyo
7–3–1 Hongo, Bunkyo-ku, Tokyo 113, Japan
Current address:
Institute of Information Sciences and Electronics
University of Tsukuba
1–1–1 Tenoudai, Tsukuba, Ibaraki 305, Japan

Atsushi Ohori

Oki Electric Industry
Kansai Laboratory
Crystal Tower, 1–2–27 Shiromi
Chuo-ku, Osaka 540, Japan
Current address:
Research Institute for Mathematical Sciences
Kyoto University
Sakyo-ku, Kyoto 606–01
Japan

Takeo Murakami

Department of Information Science
Faculty of Science
University of Tokyo
7–3–1 Hongo, Bunkyo-ku, tokyo 113, Japan
Current address:
Fujitsu Laboratories LTD.
1015, Kamikodanaka Nakahara-ku, Kawasaki 211

Takashi Masuda

Department of Information Science
Faculty of Science
University of Tokyo
7–3–1 Hongo, Bunkyo-ku, Tokyo 113, Japan

Adding a Multilingual Feature to Smalltalk-80

Toru Aratani Noriyuki Kamibayashi Mineharu Yokoyama
Masatomi Inagaki

Summary. This paper gives guidelines for the implementation of text-processing features in a general programming language and describes an actual realization in Smalltalk-80. Traditionally, the Japanese text-processing feature is implemented with 16 bits per character string. The conventional 8 bits per character string is also supported for efficiency and compatibility with existing programs. But this use of two kinds of strings makes application programs complicated and difficult to build, since no uniform method of processing text exists. It also prevents application programs from being shared among various users' environments supporting different character sets. By taking advantage of the object-oriented features of Smalltalk-80, we established a framework wherein multiple character sets and internal representations of strings are handled efficiently and uniformly. The ability to process a string without any *a priori* knowledge of its internal representation allows truly international application programs to be developed in Smalltalk-80. This multilingual feature is defined, and an implementation that makes full use of the object-oriented features of Smalltalk-80 is described.

1 Introduction

Information can be transmitted in a multitude of ways, the most common being text, image, and sound. With the proliferation of international network systems, there has been an increase in the need for truly international application programs. This, in turn, has led to a rise in the importance of text as a medium and to a need for programs that support multilingual text. The criteria for choosing the internal character representation of a programming language have conventionally been performance and efficient usage of memory space. This makes application programs dependent on the underlying language and the adopted character set, and thwarts attempts to distribute programs internationally.

The goal of the work described in this paper is to unify the description of character processing in application programs for different programming environments and to make possible the international distribution of application programs. To achieve this goal, we must establish a general programming interface for programming languages and promote efficient processing of multiple character sets simultaneously. We name this character processing facility "multilingual," and we propose that

ISBN 0-12-037105-7

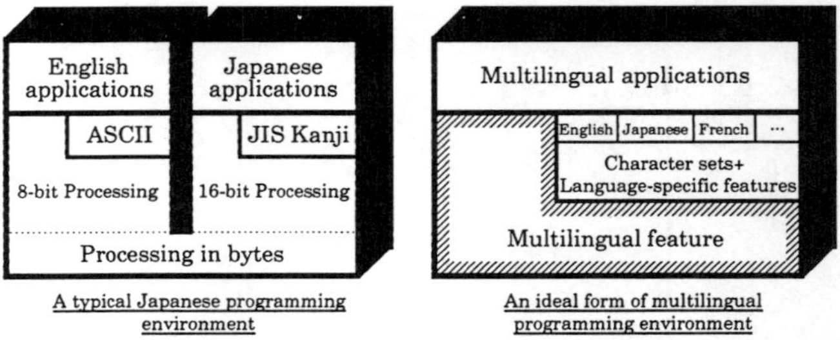

Fig. 1 Comparison of programming environments for existing and multilingual applications

application programs be written in programming languages that support this multilingual feature, rather than in languages that support an additional character set and provide another character processing facility.

Figure 1 illustrates that a programming environment for a specific (natural) language and a multilingual programming environment can be implemented by combining the programming environment with the multilingual feature and a character processing feature specific to the said (natural) language. This allows, for example, a character display function for Japanese character fonts, and it enables kana characters to be converted into kanji characters by using a common interface of the multilingual feature.

The number of characters processed by an application program can be as low as 128 (ASCII) or as high as 8,000 when JIS kanji characters have to be processed. In addition, there are many character encoding schemes for exchanging text data among programs. A truly multilingual facility requires efficient processing of text data for any character set and encoding scheme adopted by the application program. Obviously, text processing should be performed uniformly.

We have built a framework that supports different internal representations of strings in the Smalltalk-80 programming environment [1, 2]. This framework enables us to realize a multilingual feature and uniform handling of different types of character sets. Smalltalk-80 provides an excellent medium for expressing a problem by using objects and a class hierarchy. The multilingual feature implemented in Smalltalk-80 is cleanly represented in the class hierarchy and will support future enhancements. Multilingual Smalltalk-80 is not only a system that incorporates the multilingual feature, but also one in which the notion of the multilingual feature is represented by using object-oriented concepts; it reflects experience gained in Interlisp-D [10], the first general purpose programming language to have incorporated the multilingual feature described in this article. Application programs built in multilingual Smalltalk-80 can be written uniformly for different (natural) languages and can be distributed internationally.

This multilingual feature has been adopted as a standard feature in Smalltalk-80 since Version 2.4, a product developed by ParcPlace Systems Co., Ltd., KV6, and Version 2.4J, the corresponding Japanese version developed by Fuji Xerox Co.,

Ltd. The implementation of this feature does not degrade the performance of the system in any way and allows the development of truly international application programs.

In the next section, we discuss the advantages and disadvantages of current methods for processing the Japanese language and the efforts to incorporate the multilingual feature into various programming languages. In addition, we introduce the requirements for text-processing features (the multilingual feature). Section 3 describes our implementation of the multilingual feature in Smalltalk-80, and Section 4 describes the characteristics of our implementation. Finally, in Section 5, we discuss issues that we would like to address in the future.

2 Text-processing Features (of a General Purpose Programming Language)

In the past, the ability to process Japanese text had to be specifically provided by the application program. Today, a number of general purpose programming languages provide this feature. Efforts to standardize Japanese text-processing features are under way for languages such as FORTRAN, COBOL, C, and Common Lisp [3]. In general, these efforts aim to incorporate the following characteristics:

(1) the ability to handle different character sets,

(2) speed and space efficiency, and

(3) compatibility with the original system.

In addition, we believe that it is imperative to implement a multilingual text-processing feature that allows definitions of text-processing routines in an application program independent of a character set supporting a specific (natural) language. This additional requirement is:

(4) a uniform interface independent of the underlying character set.

In addition to the above-mentioned requirements for text processing, we also believe that

(5) multiple internal representations of text data should be supported by the programming language.

2.1 Current methods for implementing Japanese text-processing features

There are two major methods for implementing Japanese text-processing features in programming languages:

(i) the use of 16 bits per character instead of the usual 8 bits per character, and

(ii) the addition of a new internal representation using 16 bits per character for Japanese characters.

The former method is adopted by Japanese SNOBOL4 [9] and a few implementations of Japanese Common Lisp and other languages. This method provides adequate functionality for the processing of text data as character units. The drawbacks are that it is not compatible with existing programs in which a string is used as an input/output buffer and that it lowers the efficiency of programs; when

Japanese data are not used, it is inefficient, since alphanumeric (English) data take up twice the normal memory space. Because of these problems, this method is not very popular.

Most programming languages adopt the second method. This method allows the introduction of 16-bits-per-character representation for Japanese text data, without affecting existing programs that use text data represented by 8 bits per character. Using two internal representations of text data allows the development of more efficient programs. In programming languages such as FORTRAN and C, each internal representation must be defined as a different data type within the program. Alphanumeric characters and Japanese characters are distinguished as different types of data. However, these programming languages do not support polymorphism, and the same procedure cannot be applied to different data types — the exception being when functions have generic names. Consequently, there is a need within the program to determine whether a character is represented by using 8 bits or 16 bits.

This method of introducing Japanese text-processing features does not satisfy the fourth requirement introduced above. The definition of text data-processing routines is complicated by the use of two different kinds of internal representation. In addition, two programs — one for English, in which a character is represented by 8 bits, and one for Japanese, in which a character is represented by 16 bits — exist for every single text-processing function. This prevents the collection and reuse of software. Text-processing features should be able to handle any text data uniformly, regardless of the internal representation.

2.2 Implementation of the multilingual feature in LISP

LISP is not a typed language, and variables do not have types. Polymorphism is not supported positively, but a polymorphic function can be provided by testing the data type at runtime. Though Interlisp-D [10] and Japanese Common Lisp [4] both provide internal representations with 8 bits and 16 bits per character, their text-processing functions have been extended to handle both internal representations; that is, they support multilingual features. An existing program can, without modification, process Japanese text data represented in 16 bits per character.

Both Interlisp-D and Japanese Common Lisp have two internal representations of text data, one with 16 bits per character and the other with 8 bits per character. The latter is implemented as an optimization of the former and is used exclusively for alphanumeric characters. Interlisp-D hides the existence of the two string-internal representations. They are represented as a single primitive data type. Japanese Common Lisp, on the other hand, represents each internal representation as a different data type, and programmers rely on documented functional specifications for information regarding the proper usage of data types.

2.3 Implementation of the multilingual feature in Smalltalk-80

Smalltalk-80 [1, 2] is a popular, object-oriented programming language [8]. There already exists a version of Smalltalk-80 that supports Japanese text [5]. In this system, however, Japanese character code is divided into two 8-bit bytes. A character is represented by using two of the original 8-bits-per-character string and thus requires special handling.

In Smalltalk-80, a variable is a reference to an object, and, as in Lisp, types are not supported. An object belongs to a data type, or class, as it is called in Smalltalk-80. Classes support polymorphism. A user is free to define classes and categorize them hierarchically, making full use of Smalltalk-80's inheritance mechanism. As in the case of Interlisp-D, the two internal representations of strings can be implemented as a single primitive class of string. However, in an object-oriented programming language, we can express the conceptual relations among different types of data by using the class hierarchy. This makes it easy for programmers to use internal representations properly and to handle strings as sequences of characters, regardless of their internal representations.

We impose the following six requirements for incorporating the multilingual feature in Smalltalk-80:

(1) Support for multiple character sets

The original Smalltalk-80, because of the limitation on the internal representations of characters and strings, can only handle 256 characters — that is, character codes between 0 and 255. Our goal is to be able to support 65,536 characters (character codes between 0 and 65,535 — that is, all 16-bit character codes), like JStar [7] and Interlisp-D [10] — systems that support multilingual features. Note that 16-bit character codes allow the handling of characters in Latin languages (dozens or hundreds of characters) and Japanese characters (about 8,000 characters) simultaneously.

(2) Maintenance of processing speed and space efficiency

Processing speed and space efficiency should be maintained for alphanumeric characters. The processing performance for other characters should be as close as possible to that of alphanumeric characters.

(3) Maintenance of compatibility with the original system

When a feature of an existing programming language is extended or modified, compatibility should be maintained with programs already written in the language. If we introduce a new protocol (set of routines) for multilingual text processing, we lose the compatibility of the system with existing programs, and we impose a burden on programmers by forcing them to learn to use the new protocol. The multilingual feature should be compatible with alphanumeric text-processing styles and should provide efficient text processing for programs written in these styles. The 8-bit character representation should be provided for compatibility with programs that assume the use of 8-bit characters. In addition, it should be possible to program without differentiating between different internal representations of strings.

(4) Support for a uniform text-processing interface independent of the underlying character set

To allow uniform treatment of all characters, we build an abstract interface for their internal representation — described in requirement (5) — thereby providing a means for handling different character sets without differentiating between their different internal representations.

(5) Support for multiple internal representations of strings

We introduce a 16-bit-character internal representation in addition to the original 8-bit character representation.

In the future, it may be necessary to support Chinese kanji characters and other characters, which will require 24-bit or 32-bit character codes. A programming environment will also need to support various character-encoding schemes. Special assumptions about the values of character codes (for example, that the MSB of each byte is one) should therefore not be made. Furthermore, it should be easy to add and modify internal representations of strings.

(6) Provision of certain text-processing utilities

Smalltalk-80 is not only a programming language, but also a programming environment. Thus it is necessary to provide functions such as the input and output of Japanese characters to and from files and the display of characters on a bitmapped screen. These functions are normally provided by the underlying operating system.

3 Adding a multilingual feature to Smalltalk-80

In this section, we show how it is possible to extend character objects, string objects, symbols, and the compiler and thereby to support different character sets in the Smalltalk-80 programming environment.

In Smalltalk-80, objects are managed in a manner similar to that in LISP. Objects are dynamically placed in a heap area and are identified by object pointers that refer to the location of objects. The system's memory management mechanism handles the allocation and de-allocation of objects, allowing the programmer to program in relative freedom.

3.1 Character object

Each character object is an instance of the class `Character` and has the value of its character code as its attribute. In the original Smalltalk-80, a character object is allocated a location in the heap area. Character codes (0–255) of character objects are stored in their instance variables. To prevent the multiple existence of character objects with the same character codes, these objects are registered in a table called `CharacterTable`.

As explained in the next section, multilingual Smalltalk-80 has two classes of strings for representations with 8 bits per character and 16 bits per character. However, this does not require the definition of a new class of characters for each string class. If two types of characters are provided, one would have to determine whether or not corresponding characters in the different character sets should be handled as identical [3]. Therefore we provide only one class, `Character`, which is an extension of the usual `Character`, to ensure the unique correspondence between characters and character objects. Two internal representations of `Character` are possible and are described below:

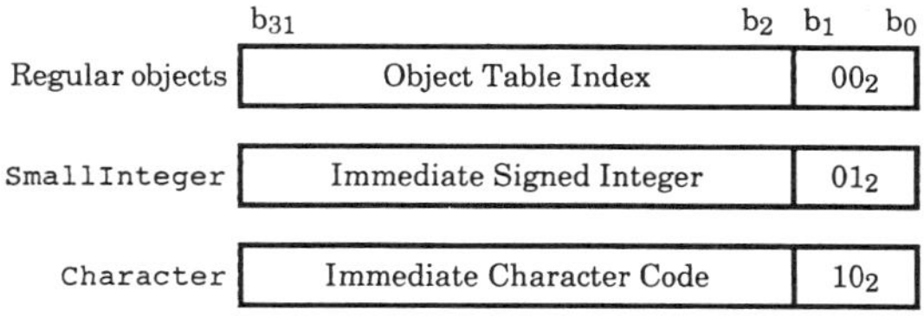

A tag (b_0–b_1) in an object pointer indicates whether an object is a regular object or an immediate object identified only by its object pointer. The conversion between a character object and its character code (`SmallInteger`) is performed by bitwise operation on the object pointer.

Fig. 2 An example of an object pointer's format

(1) Representing characters with regular objects

The original character object can hold a character code of any value. Thus, if the size of `CharacterTable` is expanded, the system can support 65,536 character objects.

Since over ten bytes are necessary for each of the 65,536 characters in the `CharacterTable`, this method requires a large area of memory space and is not desirable.

(2) Representing characters with immediate object pointers

The correspondence between characters and character codes is one-to-one and does not change dynamically. Thus we can represent characters with the immediate value of an object pointer. This method assumes that we provide a means of mutual conversion (Figure 2).

This method does not require a `CharacterTable` and space for character objects. It enables character objects to be converted into character codes, and vice versa, very quickly. However, the change in the format of the object pointer requires modification of the Smalltalk-80 virtual machine.

Though we adopted this method for speed, the difference between the two methods lies in the implementation of the mutual conversion between character objects and character codes. The choice between the two methods is an internal problem for character objects.

3.2 String objects

The role of string objects, instances of class `String`, is to represent sequences of character objects. For space efficiency, the original Smalltalk-80 adopts an internal representation that uses 8-bit codes for characters, rather than one that uses 32-bit object pointers for character objects. If we access an element of a string object, the system automatically converts from character codes to character objects and vice versa.

3.2.1 Internal representation of string objects

To cope with the range of character codes (0–65,535), we examined the following internal representations of string objects:

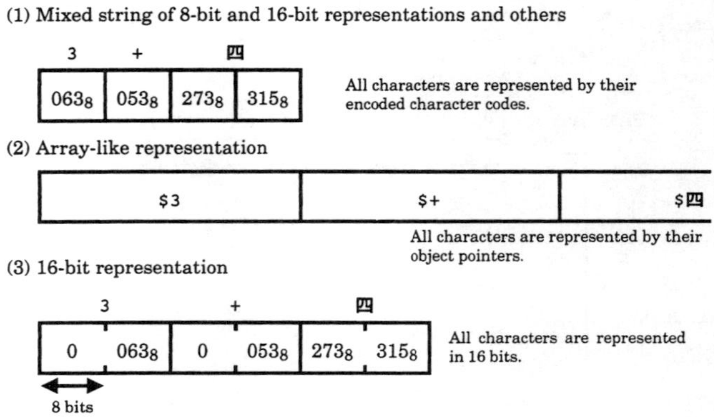

Fig. 3 Representation methods for string objects

(1) Sequences of bytes (mixed strings of 8 bits and 16 bits or other representations of character codes)

A character object is represented internally by a sequence of bytes encoded from its character code. A character whose character code can be represented by using 8 bits is represented as a byte, while a character that cannot be represented by using 8 bits is represented as a sequence of bytes, as illustrated in Figure 3-(1).

Even though this method provides what may be the most compact representation of strings, it does not perform satisfactorily in terms of processing speed. An additional drawback is that it is difficult to access strings randomly. Since text-processing features are built by using the character encoding scheme adopted by the underlying environment, it is hard to maintain a generic system that supports various external string representations that may be adopted by the operating system and other external environmental factors.

(2) Sequences of object pointers of character objects

A character is represented by its object pointer rather than by its character code value (this representation is the same as an `Array`, shown in Figure 3-(2)). There is no need to convert between character codes and object pointers when an element of a string is accessed. Thus this method is simple and fast, but it is very inefficient in its use of space. In our version of Smalltalk-80, each character needs 32 bits. If character codes can be represented by using 16 bits, the following method is better.

(3) Sequences of character code values represented in 16 bits

This method expands the character code width from 8 bits to 16 bits. A character is represented by a 16-bit character code value in a string, as illustrated in Figure 3-(3). This method provides easy access and has sufficient processing speed, but it requires twice the memory space when only alphanumeric characters (code values less than 256) are processed. Thus it is not satisfactory as a text-processing feature

Table 1 A Comparison of Internal Representations of String Objects

	Kinds of character	① Mixed string	② Array	③ 16-bit representation	④ Both 8- and 16-bit representation
Access speed	any	× Random access is impossible.	O+ Random access is possible. Conversion to character code is not required.	O Random access is possible.	O Random access is possible.
Space efficiency	alphanumeric	O 8 bits per character	× 32 bits per character	△ 16 bits per character	O 8 bits per character
	other	O 16 bits per character	× 32 bits per character	O 16 bits per character	O 16 bits per character

of a general purpose programming language, because Japanese characters are not always used.

(4) Combined use of two internal representations of 8 bits and 16 bits

This method resolves the 16-bit representation's space inefficiency and allows the use of both 8-bit and 16-bit representations. A string is represented by using 8 bits when all the characters in the string have code values less than 255 and is represented with the 16 bits whenever the string contains a character with a code value greater than 255.

After comparing these methods, we adopted the fourth method, which is superior in both access speed and space efficiency (see Table 1).

3.2.2 The structure of string objects

Most functions of a string object operate characters within the string that are independent of the internal representation. Only the read and write functions that access elements within a string depend on the internal representation. In Smalltalk-80, the structure of string objects and/or their class(es) should reflect this relationship between functions that depend on the internal representation and generic functions that are independent of it. Below, we examine two methods that describe possible implementations:

(1) Representation using string objects (instances)

The two internal representations are represented by two classes, `ByteString` and `TwoByteString`, and are encapsulated by instances of the class `String` (see Figure 4). Each instance of `String` holds a buffer of 8 bits or 16 bits, and common functions for strings of both internal representations are defined as methods of the class `String`. Functions dependent on the internal representation are defined as methods of `ByteString` or `TwoByteString` and can be called from methods of the

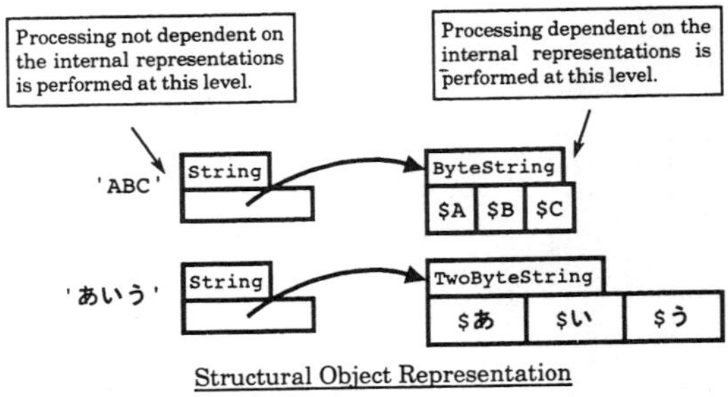

Fig. 4 A structure for string objects (1)

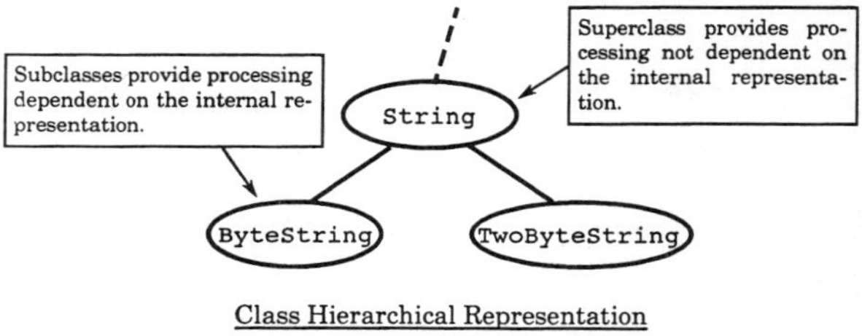

Fig. 5 A structure for string objects (2)

class `String`.

(2) Representation using string classes

An abstract class `String` for all strings is provided. Each internal representation and methods dependent on this representation are defined by subclasses, `ByteString` and `TwoByteString` (see Figure 5). Common methods for all string objects are defined in the class `String` and inherited by `ByteString` and `TwoByteString`.

These two methods are compared in Table 2. We adopt the second method for its space efficiency and simplicity of objects (instances).

3.2.3 Abstraction of internal representations

To abstract string objects from the two kinds of internal representation, one needs to define a common message protocol for the internal representations. Methods that depend on the internal representation are `at:`, `at:put:`, and `size` (methods that respectively read, write a character, and give the size of the receiver) and are defined in both `ByteString` and `TwoByteString`. Polymorphism allows the use of the same message. Other methods for string objects are defined by using these methods and are independent of the internal representation. All these methods are defined in `String` and are inherited by `ByteString` and `TwoByteString`.

Below, we describe methods that hide the ability of each string representation and allow any kind of character or string to be processed.

Table 2 Comparison of Abstraction Methods That Hide the Internal Representations of Strings

	(1) Structural Object Representation	(2) Class Hierarchical Representation
Processing speed	× Slow for each access to the internal buffer.	○ No change.
Space efficiency	× A string is represented by two objects.	○ No change.
Impact on programming	△ The structure of strings is complex. ○ Compatible for existing programs independent of internal representations.	○ The structure of strings is simple. △ Programs that depend on the class hierarchy of strings become ineffective.
Misc.	Switching of internal representations does not need `become:` (an operation swaps two objects).	Switching of internal representation needs `become:`.

- **Comparison of string objects**

In the original Smalltalk-80, methods of comparing string objects, such as `=`, `<=`, `>=`, do not compare the memory patterns of objects. These methods are defined on the results of comparison of each corresponding character element, and the internal representation does therefore not affect the result of a string comparison.

- **Dynamic switching of internal representation**

Applications can freely change a character element of a string after the string has been created. Thus a program needs to examine the internal representation of a string object when writing to a string, and it needs to determine whether a specific character object can be stored in the string object. Programs become less portable as they become more dependent on the kinds of character that they support.

If a character whose code value is greater than 255 is stored in a string with 8-bit characters, the internal representation of the string must be changed to the 16-bit representation (see Figure 6). With this mechanism, an 8-bit representation has virtually the same features as the 16-bit representation. On the other hand, when all the characters in a string have character code values of less than 256, the internal representation of the string is not switched to the 8-bit representation, as this would require that all character codes in the string be scanned whenever an element of the string is rewritten.

- **Creation of string objects**

An instance of a class is created by sending either of the messages `new` or `new:` to the class in Smalltalk-80. To fully hide the existence of two internal representations of strings and to make string objects look like the same kinds of object, instances of classes that represent all the different types of string objects must be created by only one class. In multilingual Smalltalk-80, the class `String` creates instances of one internal representation or the other when it is sent one of the messages `new` or

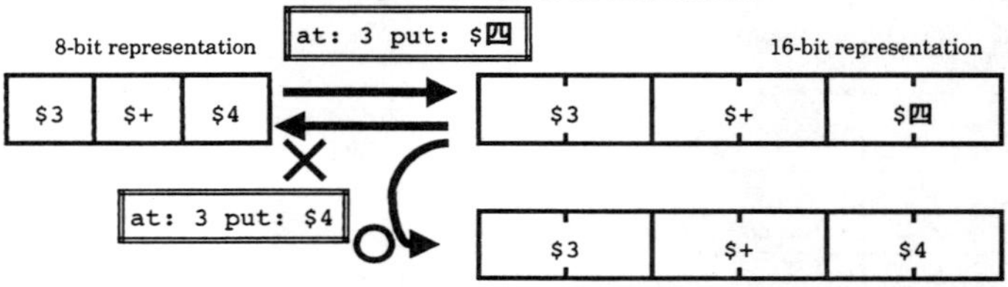

Storing the character $四 to an 8-bit representation string '3+4' requires that the string become:s 16-bit representation. Conversely, when the character $4 is stored to a 16-bit string '3+四', the string does not return to an 8-bit representation.

Fig. 6 Dynamic switching of the internal representations of strings

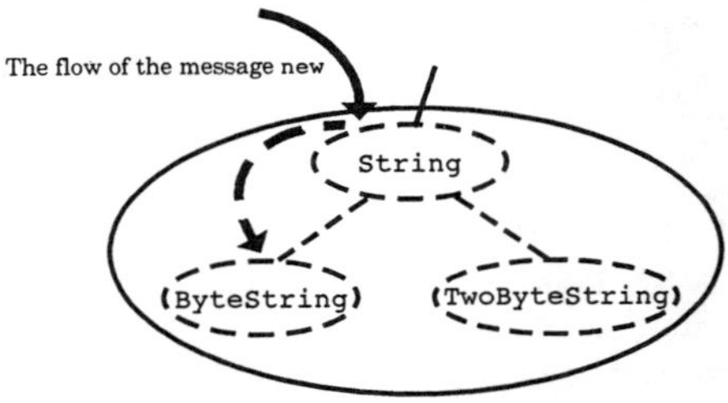

Since `String` is an abstract class it forwards the messages new and `new:` to `ByteString` or `TwoByteString`. A string object is created by using appropriate representation for most processing purposes. It is enough to know of the existence of `String`; `ByteString` and `TwoByteString` can be treated similarly.

Fig. 7 Creation of a string object

`new:` (see Figure 7).

3.2.4 Improving efficiency of text processing

The internal representation and text-processing algorithm for strings with 8-bit representations are the same as for strings of the original Smalltalk-80 and are equal in space efficiency and processing speed. The same processing speed for 16-bit strings as for 8-bit strings was achieved by building primitive methods for 16-bit representation. Figures 8 and 9 show the access time for an element of a string and the time taken to copy strings, for each representation. They also show the differences between the original Smalltalk-80 and our multilingual Smalltalk-80. All measurements were performed on a Sun3/160 workstation. The time taken to copy 8-bit representation strings was the same in the original Smalltalk-80. The copying time for 16-bit strings is twice as long as that for 8-bit strings. The speed per byte at which strings are processed is the same in both methods.

The dynamic switching capability ensures that no error is triggered, no matter which representation is used. However, there is a sharp drop in speed when strings of different representations are processed (the dotted line in Figure 9). The dynamic

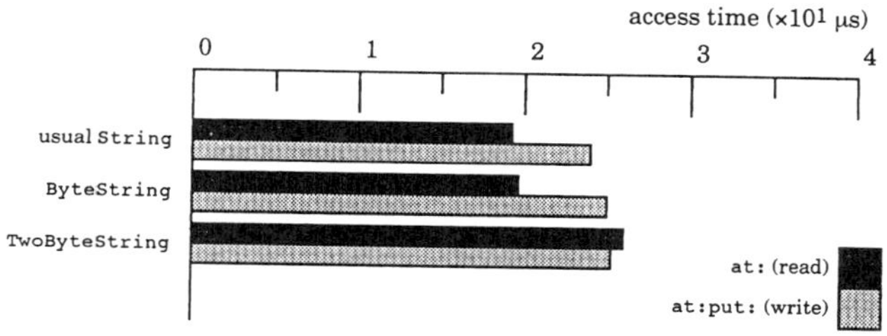

Fig. 8 Access time for a character element

switching of strings consumes more time — 1 ms, for example, for a ByteString 500 bytes long. Therefore we should not mix the different representations of strings. But if we insist on a specific representation of a string, a program becomes dependent on the kind of character that it uses, and it becomes less portable and less reusable. When a string is created, the application should not require a specific internal representation of a string. The system or the environment in which the application runs should choose the representation automatically.

In multilingual Smalltalk-80, the initial representation of a string, which is created when the message new is sent to the class String, is selected as either 8 bits or 16 bits. In an environment in which only alphanumeric characters are used, the 8-bit representation is selected, and when Japanese characters are used, the 16-bit representation is selected. When a string object is created from an existing string, the new string inherits the old string's representation. These mechanisms check the switching of string representation and the occurrence of copying between strings of different representations. Typically this behavior occurs a few times during text editing and at compilation. Its impact on the overall text processing speed can be ignored.

3.3 Other extended functions

To use 65,536 characters freely in Smalltalk-80, the functions of symbols and the compiler must also be extended.

- **Symbols**

Symbols (instances of the class Symbol) are named objects. The system guarantees the uniqueness of each symbol. Symbols use the same structure as strings to represent their names and do not use string objects. For symbols, we adopt the same method as that used to extend string objects.

- **The compiler**

The compiler uses a table to keep the lexical meaning of each character that appears in the source code. The size of the original table is 256, and one would have to increase this size to 65,536 to allow the compilation of source code written with many different types of character set. As can be imagined, this table would be sparse. To save memory space, we adopted a method that uses a table for character

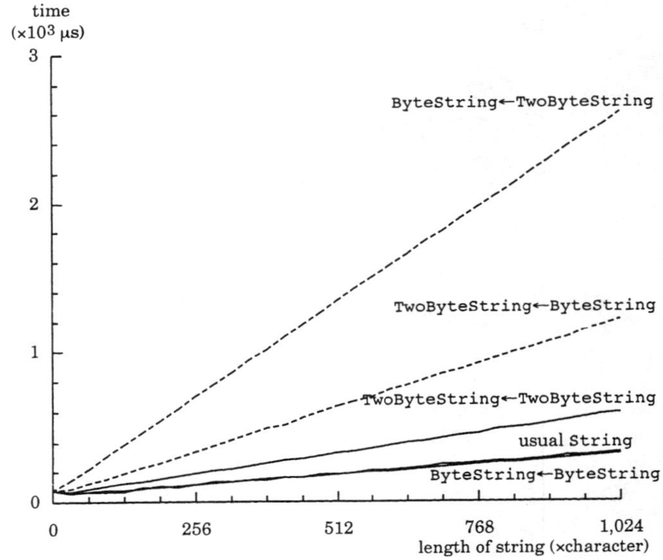

Fig. 9 Comparison of string copying times for primitive methods

code values from 0 to 255; for code values greater than 256 that are not used often, a method calculates the lexical meaning from the code value. As long as there is no use of a particular internal character code system in which the meaning of a character cannot be described by using a simple expression, this method can support representations with 24 bits and 32 bits per character.

4 Summary and Discussion

4.1 Abstraction of text processing and improvement of its efficiency

It is critically important in a general purpose language such as Smalltalk-80 that the multilingual feature be implemented in a manner that maintains speed and space efficiency when only English or Japanese text-processing features are required. However, for reasons of portability and reusability, application programs should not be made less generic by specifying specific internal representation of strings within the programs.

In multilingual Smalltalk-80, there are two internal representation of strings. One uses 8 bits to represent a character, and the other uses 16 bits. Proper use of the two representations will allow optimization of the processing speed and space efficiency. Message protocols of strings in both representations are unified through polymorphism. The initial representation of a string can be chosen as a parameter of the programming environment. Thus the same efficient text processing can be achieved without sacrificing the level of abstraction of application programs.

4.2 Compatibility with existing text-processing features

When a programming language or a programming environment is extended, it is critical that care should be taken to maintain support for existing programs and applications. In Smalltalk-80, objects are modular. Existing programs do not depend upon low-level aspects and the internal representation of characters and strings. Programmers can regard the relation between character objects and string objects as

a string = a sequence of characters.

The multilingual feature successfully supports this property and maintains compatibility with existing programs. Most existing tools on Smalltalk-80 can be used on multilingual Smalltalk-80 without any modifications. For example, the text editor available in Smalltalk-80 is capable of handling multilingual text in multilingual Smalltalk-80 without any modification.

In multilingual Smalltalk-80, the class of strings is divided into two classes. The message `isMemberOf: String` (a method that determines whether the receiver is an instance of the class `String`) does not say whether the receiver is a string object. This testing method explicitly uses information regarding the class hierarchy and should not be used for the purpose of determining whether the receiver is a string [6]. Instead, the message `isString` should be sent to an object. In reply to this message, the object itself should answer whether it is a string. In multilingual Smalltalk-80, string objects can be distinguished by using this method.

4.3 Adaptation for specific (natural) languages

Support for various kinds of character in the programming environment of Smalltalk–80 requires not only those features mentioned in Section 3, but also the input/output from and to the operating system, peripheral devices, and so on — features provided as library functions in other programming languages. For example, to use Japanese characters freely requires appropriate fonts, display functions, functions for code conversion (between the different internal representations), and file I/O functions.

By combining the multilingual feature, each character set of a language, and the text-processing feature specific to that language, we can easily create a programming environment for that language. Figure 10 shows an example of how an environment can be "Japanized" by incorporating a kana-to-kanji converter, display functions for Japanese characters, and input/output functions with schemes for encoding ISO, JIS, and EUC (extended UNIX code) characters into multilingual Smalltalk-80. Multilingual Smalltalk-80 has common application programs and is also a common base that can be used to obtain a system for each language.

4.4 Extendibility of text processing

The class hierarchy of string objects shown in Section 3.2.2 can be extended naturally to support a 24-bit character code in the future or to introduce special internal representations that increase processing efficiency. By introducing new string classes as subclasses of the class `String`, we can extend strings and maintain a coherent hierarchy of string classes. This approach has the added advantage that

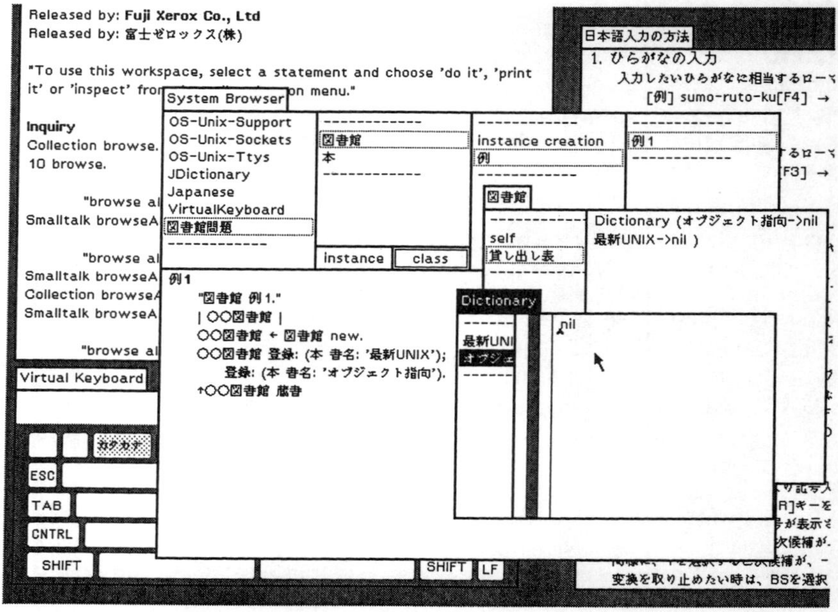

Fig. 10 "Japanized" Smalltalk-80 supports both a multilingual feature and Japanese text processing

we do not have to change the code that supports existing strings. Figure 11 illustrates how a `ThreeByteString` that represents a string of 24-bit code characters can be implemented in the system.

4.5 Extendibility of Smalltalk-80 itself

The handling of 8-bit and 16-bit strings in multilingual Smalltalk-80 was achieved by an approach similar to that adopted in adding Japanese capabilities to Interlisp-D and Common Lisp. A characteristic of multilingual Smalltalk-80 is that the multilingual feature was implemented by taking advantage of features inherent to Smalltalk-80. Although character and string data exist as primitive data types in ordinary programming languages, they are merely kinds (classes) of object. Without altering the general features of objects and the memory format of objects in Smalltalk-80, we have modified the functions of character objects and string objects. Since most text-processing functions are dependent on the functions of character objects and string objects, multilingualization of string data is accompanied by the multilingualization of the compiler.

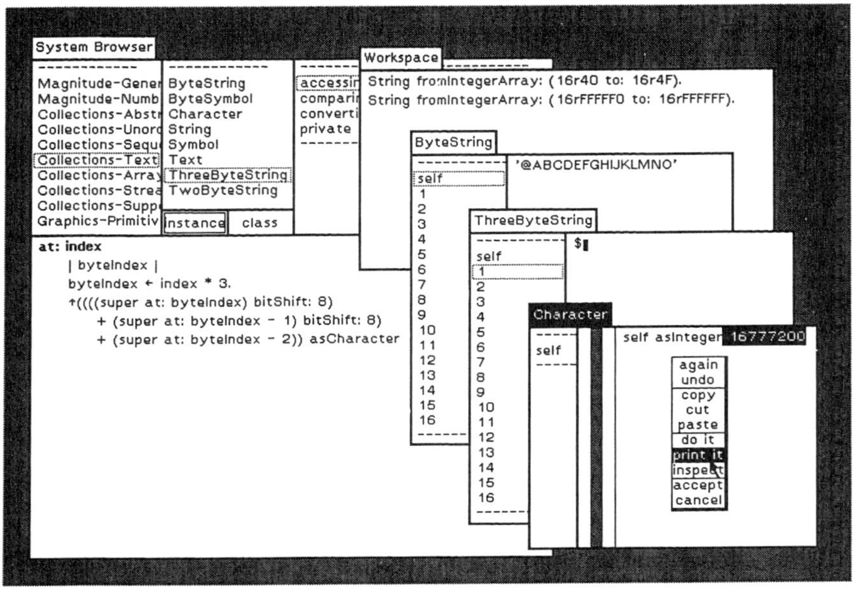

Fig. 11 A 24-bit character code implementation

5 Future Work

• A unified framework to provide language-specific processing

Though multilingual Smalltalk-80 makes it possible to process text without determining its class and internal representation, it does not provide processing specific to a language. Only a few simple processing capabilities, such as testing of character types, are supported. For example, in Japanese there is no distinction of uppercase and lowercase characters, as there is in Roman alphabets. Programs that require this distinction are of no use with Japanese characters. If an application program is to be broadly shared, it should not include descriptions that are dependent on a specific language and its associated characters and processing methods, such as "kinsoku-shori" (a line-breaking operation specific to Japanese text). Instead, such descriptions should be provided by the programming environment. For these purposes, application programs should describe character processing at as abstract a level as possible. Processing specific to the language needs should be provided by the underlying environment.

• Input/output features

With conventional encoding schemes for external files, it is hard to access a random character efficiently within text data. Existing programs that are designed for alphanumeric characters often perform random access by the byte instead of by the character. To allow such programs to be used for processing other characters, the input/output features of characters should be designed so as to inhibit programs that assume "1 byte = 1 character." When large amounts of data are stored in a file, both processing speed and space efficiency are required, making it hard to ensure uniform treatment of external files containing only alphanumeric characters and those containing many kind of characters.

6 Conclusion

We have given guidelines that enable common application programs to be used for different languages by establishing text-processing features that are independent of the kinds of character and the combinations (e.g., alphanumeric characters only, Japanese characters only, and both alphanumeric and Japanese characters) in which they are used. We have shown that conventional methods for Japanization, in which a string of 16 bits per character is introduced, are not good enough; a multilingual feature is needed, in which both 8-bit and 16-bit strings can be processed uniformly. We also describe an implementation of such a multilingual feature in Smalltalk-80, which fully utilizes the object-oriented framework.

Acknowledgments. We would like to thank the following people: the referees for their valuable comments; Kazuo Obuchi and Moriyuki Kato for giving us the opportunity to perform this research; Takemi Yamazaki for his help in research and development; Kaoru Ueda, Nobuo Otsuka, and Yasuo Soda for taking part in this research and providing valuable insights; and Dr. L. Peter Deutsch for his valuable comments on multilingual Smalltalk-80.

References

[1] Goldberg, A.: *Smalltalk-80: The Interactive Programming Environment*, Addison-Wesley, 1984.

[2] Goldberg, A. and Robson, D.: *Smalltalk-80: The Language and Its Implementation*, Addison-Wesley, 1984.

[3] *Report on the Standardization of Japanese Text Processing in Information Technology*, Inf. Proc. Soc. Japan, 1988 (in Japanese).

[4] *Report on Micro Computers [II] — Lisp*, Japan Electronic Industry Development Association, 1987 (in Japanese).

[5] Ozaki, M., Matsunaga, Y., and Kamibayashi, N.: Prototype of Smalltalk-80J, *Proc. 32th Annual Convention IPS Japan*, 1986, pp. 425–426 (in Japanese).

[6] Snyder, A.: Encapsulation and Inheritance in Object-Oriented Languages, *OOPSLA '87 Proceedings*, 1987.

[7] Uetani, A. (ed.): *JStar Workstation*, Maruzen, 1986 (in Japanese).

[8] Yonezawa, A.: On Object-Oriented Programming, *Comput. Softw.*, Vol. 1, No. 1 (1984), pp. 29–41 (in Japanese).

[9] Yoshida, K. and Ushijima, K.: Implementation of SNOBOL4 with Japanese Text Processing Facility, *Comput. Softw.*, Vol. 2, No. 3 (1985), pp. 36–46 (in Japanese).

[10] *Interlisp-D Reference Manual*, Xerox Corp., 1985.

Initially published in "Computer Software", Vol. 7, No. 3, in Japanese.

Toru Aratani
Systems and Communications Lab.
Fuji Xerox Co., Ltd.
Yokohama, Kanagawa, 240 Japan

Noriyuki Kamibayashi
Systems and Communications Lab.
Fuji Xerox Co., Ltd.
Yokohama, Kanagawa, 240 Japan

Mineharu Yokoyama
Systems and Communications Lab.
Fuji Xerox Co., Ltd.
Kawasaki, Kanagawa, 213 Japan

Masatomi Inagaki
Document Systems Development Center
Fuji Xerox Co., Ltd.
Kawasaki, Kanagawa, 213 Japan

Japanese Character Set Handling in Kyoto Common Lisp

Taichi Yasumoto Taiichi Yuasa

Summary. We investigate the feasibility and effectiveness of supporting Japanese Character Set Handling (JCSH for short) in Common Lisp without changing its language specification. For program portability and straightforward coding, uniform handling of all characters, including double-byte characters and single-byte characters, is highly desirable. However, such character handling seems to decrease efficiency in both time and space, of programs. In fact, some Common Lisp systems in Japan require the programmer to explicitly distinguish double-byte characters and single-byte characters. To see the time and space overhead of uniform JCSH, we have actually extended Kyoto Common Lisp (KCL for short) and compared the performance with the original KCL. We will present our implementation technique for reducing memory and runtime overhead, and report performance measurements.

1 Introduction

In European and American countries, most people use a relatively small number of written characters in daily life. Accordingly, the number of characters used for computer systems in those countries is also relatively small. Since the number is less than 256 ($=2^8$), these characters can be represented with 8-bit (or single–byte) code. However, this is not always sufficient. In Japan, people use more than 6000 characters, and therefore their computer systems required double-byte representation. To save memory space, Japanese computer systems use more than one coded character set. A typical example is the use in many computer systems of both the ASCII coded character set and the Japan Industrial Standard (JIS) X0208 coded character set, along with some conventions for distinguishing characters from the two sets.

Efforts have been made to handle double-byte characters in various programming languages, including Common Lisp. Common Lisp is a programming language designed as a proposed Lisp language standard [1]. It is widely used in Japan, where several Common Lisp systems have been developed. There have been many heated discussions about the language specification for handling double-byte characters [2]. The main issue is whether the language specification of Common Lisp should be changed.

The language specification of Common Lisp does not depend on any particular coded character set. Therefore it is possible for an implementation to handle double-byte characters without any change in the language specification. In fact,

ISBN 0-12-037105-7

such implementations have already been developed, and some are actually in use. It is a real advantage to be able to use double-byte characters without changing the language specification, since most Common Lisp programs, which were developed on top of a system that supports only single-byte characters, can handle double-byte characters without any change. In addition, programmers can efficiently develop programs that handle double-byte characters, because they do not need to worry about the difference between single-byte characters and double-byte characters.

On the other hand, uniform handling of double-byte characters and single-byte characters may reduce memory efficiency and runtime efficiency. A naïve implementation is to represent every character with double bytes. By expanding single-byte characters into double-byte encoding and using some mechanism to distinguish the two kinds of characters, we can input and output any character on those operating systems that allow the mixed use of two coded character sets. This simple solution, however, reduces memory efficiency. For instance, even if a string contains only single-byte characters, it occupies twice as much memory space as in those Lisp systems that support only single-byte characters. Since most system–supplied strings are made up of only single-byte characters, the size of the system will become significantly larger [2, 3]. When the system works on a virtual-memory operating system, the increased size of the system will cause more page faults and reduce the runtime efficiency.

A more realistic implementation is to have two kinds of internal representation: *single-byte strings*, consisting of only single-byte characters, and *double-byte strings*, containing double-byte characters. When a character in a single-byte string is replaced with a double-byte character, the string is automatically converted into a double-byte string. In this way, the user does not have to be aware that there are two kinds of internal representation. Although this implementation saves memory space, it causes a runtime overhead on character and string operations (including input and output).

Because of such drawbacks in efficiency, proposals have been made to modify the Common Lisp language specification to force the programmer to distinguish single–byte characters (or single-byte strings) and double-byte characters (or double-byte strings) [4, 5]. However, explicit discrimination between the two kinds of character (or strings) will decrease the portability of existing programs and increase the cost of developing new programs.

It is inevitable that a Common Lisp system with Japanese Character Set Handling will be less efficient than a Common Lisp system without JCSH. If the difference in efficiency is small enough, there is no need to change the language specification; otherwise, it must be changed to some extent. Therefore the decision as to whether to change the language specification for JCSH depends on the degree of the loss of efficiency. Unfortunately, there have been no reports on this topic as far as we know.

We added the ability of JCSH to an existing Common Lisp system, and, by comparing the system with the original, we actually measured the loss of efficiency. For this experiment, we chose Kyoto Common Lisp (KCL for short) [6, 7]. The original KCL was designed without any consideration of the need for handling the Japanese character set, and it is supposed that a character is represented with a single byte. Thus, for example, we could not use double-byte characters as character objects. Although double-byte characters can be included in strings, they cannot be handled in the same way as single-byte characters. These are problems common to all Common Lisp systems that were designed without any consideration of JCSH.

When we implemented JCSH in KCL, we paid particular attention to the following considerations:

- Retaining the source codes of the original KCL as much as possible. This reduces the cost of modifying the system to support JCSH. In addition, this is necessary to correctly measure the loss of efficiency.
- Maintaining the high portability of KCL. This makes it possible to compare the loss of efficiency on various machines.
- Modifying KCL so that it behaves in the same way as the original KCL for those applications that do not use double-byte characters. There are cases in which the extended KCL executes application programs that do not use double-byte characters. In such cases, the system algorithms must be the same in order to measure the performance difference correctly.

With these considerations, we believe that we can provide valuable information about JCSH in Common Lisp systems, and we will report the details in this paper.

In Section 2, we will present our principles for making JCSH useful and feasible, and we will clarify the meaning of JCSH. In Section 3, we will list those problems associated with JCSH. We will also report certain details of our implementation of JCSH on KCL. Finally, in Section 4, we will evaluate the extended KCL by comparing it with the original KCL.

2 Principles of JCSH

In this section, we will clarify what we mean by JCSH. Our goal is to investigate the feasibility and effectiveness of Common Lisp systems that can handle Japanese characters appropriately without any change in the language specification. We adapted the following principles for JCSH:

1. Double-byte characters and single-byte characters are handled uniformly.

   As we mentioned before, the system-supported characters are not restricted to single-byte characters in the language specification of Common Lisp. Therefore the system should handle double-byte characters in exactly the same way as single-byte characters. We must be able to use double-byte characters wherever we can use single-byte characters and to handle each double-byte character as a first-class object. Rather than introducing new built-in functions that handle double-byte characters, we extend existing built-in functions so that they can handle double-byte characters.

   Figure 1 shows a sample interaction between a user and a system that follows this principle. In the figure, ">" in the first column is a prompt from the system, followed by an S-expression input by the user. The result of evaluation is output in the next line. This example shows some details of "uniform JCSH", which are summarized as follows:

```
>(setq a "日本語ok")
"日本語ok"

>(char a 2)
#\語

>(length a)
5

>(setq a "abcde")
"abcde"

>(setf (char a 2) #\う)
#\う

>a
"abうde"

>(length a)
5

>(defun 改行まで読みとばす (stream char)
   (declare (ignore char))
   (do () ((char= (read-char stream nil #\Newline t) #\Newline)))
   (values))
改行まで読みとばす

>(set-macro-character #\注 #'改行まで読みとばす)
T

>注　この日本語KCLは、日本語が使えます。
注　上記のように、注の構文情報を定義すると、注から改行までは
注　コメントになります。
(+ 1  2)
3

>
```

Fig. 1 Sample of Japanese character set handling in Common Lisp

(a) A string can contain double-byte characters as well as single-byte characters.

(b) The Nth element in a string is the character object that corresponds to the Nth character in the string.

(c) Double-byte characters and single-byte characters are input and output in exactly the same format (that is, prefixed with a sharp sign and a backslash).

(d) The *length* of a string is the number of characters in the string.

(e) A single-byte character in a string can be replaced with any double–byte character. Conversely, a double-byte character in a string can be replaced with any single-byte character.

(f) Double-byte characters can be used in a function name.

(g) Readtables can store syntactic attributes of characters for double-byte characters as well as for single-byte characters (In this example, the syntactic attribute for the double-byte character "注" is defined so that the character starts a comment in the input line.).

This example shows that it is quite natural to handle double-byte characters in the same way as single-byte characters. Although it may seem unnecessary to be able to define syntactic attributes for double-byte characters, it is actually useful, since some double-byte characters look like single-byte characters (for example, double-byte "；" and single-byte ";").

2. The implementation is independent of the coding system.

   One of several coding systems for Japanese characters (including JIS, Shift JIS, and EUC) is used, depending on the situation. Since it seems too early to assume any particular coding system, we made the following assumptions about the character set:

   (a) Characters are supplied from outside of the Lisp system by, say, a Japanese front-end processor offered by the operating system. The Lisp system is not concerned with how Japanese characters are input.

   (b) The system supports only single-byte characters and double-byte characters. As in the original KCL, we use the ASCII coded character set for single-byte characters. Thus the most significant bit of a single-byte characters is always 0. Double-byte characters are represented with double-byte codes whose most significant bits are 1. This representation is essentially the same as the Extended UNIX Code (EUC) coding system. For formatted output, double-byte characters are assumed to occupy twice as much space as single-byte characters on the output device (such as a display or a printer).

   (c) The difference between the coding system of the underlying operating system and the above representation is solved by adding a character code converter to the basic I/O routines of KCL.

3. Double-byte characters are not equivalent to single-byte characters.

   Some double-byte characters, such as double-byte alphanumerics, have single–byte counterparts. It is sometimes convenient if the system regards these characters as equivalent to the corresponding single-byte characters. For instance, the user may want to use double-byte characters to specify built–in function names that consist of single-byte characters. However, there are still debates about such equivalence relations. Therefore, we decided not to introduce any equivalence relations for our experiment. In addition, we decided to treat all double-byte characters as constituent characters by default. A constituent character is a character that is not a white space, an escape character, or a macro character. If the user wants to use a double-byte character as a non-constituent character, he can easily specify it by modifying the readtable.

3 Implementation of JCSH on KCL

In order to add the ability of JCSH to KCL, we modified the data representations of data objects such as characters and strings, and we modified the routines on

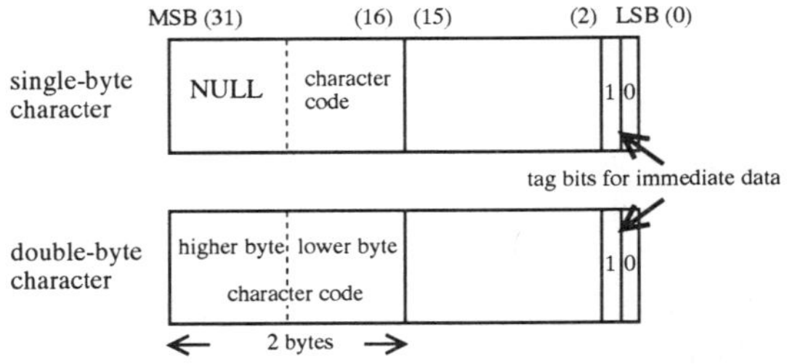

Fig. 2 Representation of character objects

these data objects. Because of the large number of built-in functions in Common Lisp, a lot of modifications had to be made. Rather than describe all the details, we overview our implementation of JCSH on KCL by indicating the problems and our solutions for uniform JCSH.

3.1 Character objects

In the extended KCL, character objects are represented as immediate data that can hold double bytes [8]. An immediate datum means that the object representation is encoded directly in a pointer. In general, objects represented as immediate data need not be garbage collected and can be handled efficiently. In addition, we have the following reason for implementing character objects as immediate data.

The original KCL has a character table, in which all the characters that the system supports are registered. A character object is represented as a pointer to an entry of this table. Since the original KCL does not support double-byte characters, it is made to handle at most 256 characters. Therefore, the character table needs to have only 256 entries. In order to support double-byte characters, however, the character table must have more than 6000 entries. It is unrealistic to have such a large table in the system. Since a pointer to an object occupies four bytes, there is enough space to represent double-byte characters as immediate data, even if we reserve some tag bits to distinguish pointers from immediate data. Thus immediate data can be implemented without memory overhead.

As shown in Figure 2, the character code is stored in the higher half-word of a character object. For single-byte characters, the actual character code is stored in the lower byte and the NULL code (single byte 0) is stored in the higher byte. For double-byte characters, the higher byte of the character code is stored in the higher byte, and the lower byte of the character code is stored in the lower byte. By accessing the higher word of a character object, we can quickly retrieve the character code both for single-byte characters and double-byte characters. This implies that character operations such as equality and comparison operations are performed without overhead, even when we support two kinds of character.

3.2 String objects

In this section, we will describe how the data representation of strings and string operations are modified to cope with the new representation.

3.2.1 Data representation of strings

Strings may contain only single-byte characters, only double-byte characters, or both kinds of character. The packed representation is the most space-efficient, but it is not desirable because strings, as kinds of array, must access their elements quickly through indexing (with the packed representation, the system has to parse the string from the beginning to find the Nth element).

The most simple solution that allows fast element access is to represent all characters in a string with double bytes (see Figure 3). Single-byte characters can be padded with the NULL code, which is not used as the first byte of any double-byte character. With this representation, even if the application program does not use double-byte characters at all, each single-byte character in a string occupies two bytes, and thus the size of the string becomes twice as large as before—see Figure 3 (a). Since many user-supplied strings contain only single-byte characters and since the KCL system itself has a lot of strings with only single-byte characters (such as system messages and on-line documents), the total loss of memory space is too large for this representation to be acceptable.

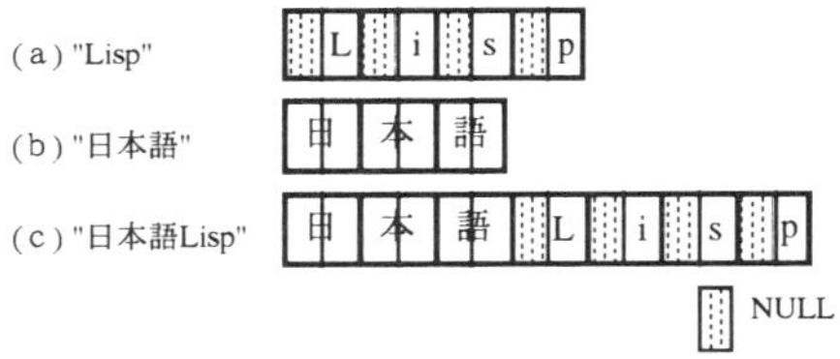

Fig. 3 Strings using two bytes for each character

Our solution is to use two internal representations for strings: single-byte strings and double-byte strings (see Figure 4). In single-byte strings, every character occupies a single byte, whereas in double-byte strings, every character occupies two bytes. These two representations are handled as follows:

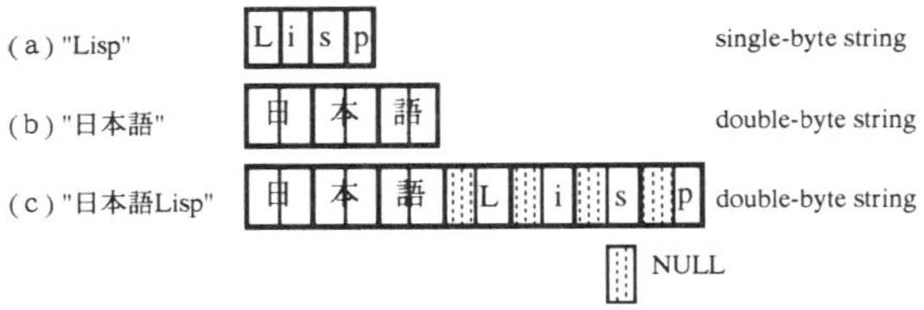

Fig. 4 Single-byte strings and double-byte strings

- When a new string is created, if it contains at least one double-byte character, then it is represented as a double-byte string. If not, it is represented as a single-byte string.
- When a character in a single-byte string is replaced with a double-byte character, the system first converts the string into a double-byte string. The NULL code is added in front of each single-byte character. Common Lisp supports *adjustable strings*, whose sizes may vary after their creation. When a double–byte character is added to an adjustable single-byte string (by means of the built-in function `vector-push`), the string is also automatically converted into a double-byte string.
- Double-byte strings are not automatically converted into single-byte strings, even if all the elements become single-byte characters after some operations.

Figure 5 illustrates how strings are converted by string operations. With this implementation, strings with only single-byte characters occupy the same space as before. Double-byte strings with some single-byte characters occupy more space than with the packed representation. In particular, double-byte strings with only single-byte characters occupy twice as much space. Although the system could compactify such strings into single-byte strings on certain occasions (during garbage collection, for example), we doubt that if such automatic compaction is useful, since, once converted into a double-byte string, a single-byte string tends to contain double-byte characters again. Note that in this implementation, automatic conversion takes place at most once for each single-byte string. Thus the conversion may not occur frequently.

We need some mechanism for distinguishing the two kinds of string representation. Each string object of KCL consists of a *header* and a *body*. The header has a type tag indicating that it is a string object. This tag is referenced in many routines, including the garbage collector and some built-in functions. It is not wise to use different type tags for the two kinds of strings, because it would require many changes to the system. Rather, we add another field to the header to indicate the kind of the string. For this purpose, we need only one extra bit for each string header.

String conversions are performed as illustrated in Figure 6. The string header contains a bit field to indicate the kind of the string, the pointer to the body, and some other information, such as the length of the string. Pointers to a string object always point to the header, but not directly to the body. The conversion steps include rewriting the string kind, copying the string body while allocating two bytes to each character, and replacing the pointer to the old body with the pointer to the copied body. The area occupied by the old body is recycled by the garbage collector. In this way, the string is converted without changing the address of the header, and there is no need to replace pointers to the string object.

The header contains the byte length instead of the number of characters. This simplifies the garbage collection, as we will describe later.

3.2.2 Modifications to string operations

String operations consist of three basic parts:

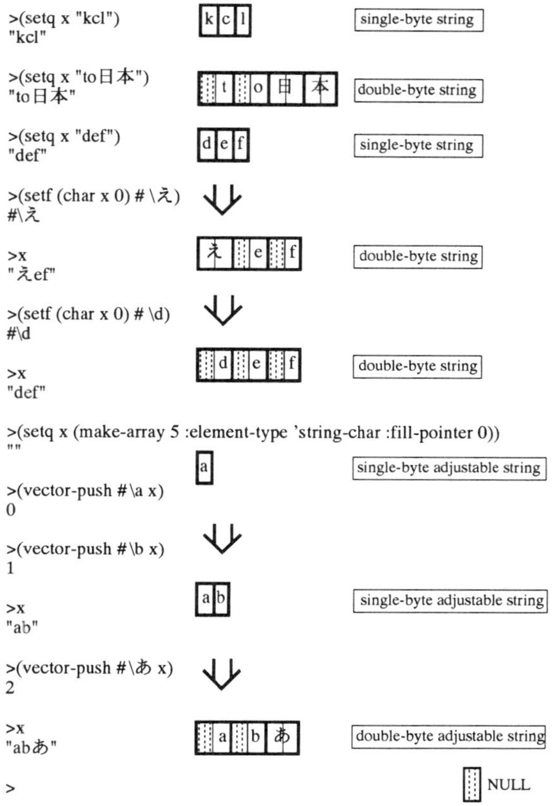

Fig. 5 Examples of automatic string conversion

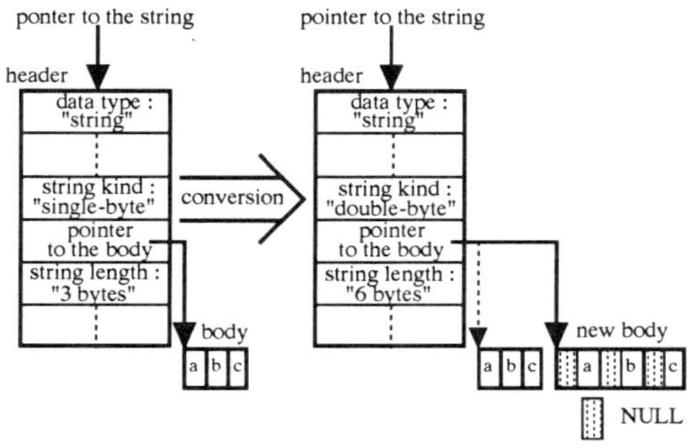

Fig. 6 String conversion

- Obtaining the length of a string,
- Retrieving elements of a string,
- Replacing elements of a string.

KCL has three routines, one for each of these basic operations, and the built-in functions on strings invoke these routines. These routines are modified to cope with the new string representations:

- The routine for obtaining the length of a string.

  This routine refers to the kind and the byte length of the string. It returns the byte length of the string body if the string is a single-byte string, and returns half of the byte length if the string is a double-byte string.

- The routine for retrieving elements of a string.

  This routine first checks the kind of the string by looking up the string header. For a single-byte string, it takes out the character code at the byte address of the given index. For a double-byte string, it takes out the character code at the half-word address of the given index.

- The routine for replacing elements of a string.

  This routine first checks the kind of the string. If the string is a single-byte string and the new element is a single-byte character, it simply replaces the character code. If the new element is a double-byte character, it converts the string into a double-byte string and then replaces the character code. If the string is a double-byte string, it simply replaces the character code regardless of the kind of the new character.

3.2.3 Displaced strings

Some strings in Common Lisp do not have their own elements, but are used to refer to other strings. These strings are called *displaced strings*, and those strings referenced through them are called *displaced-to strings*.

In KCL, a displaced string and the corresponding displaced-to string share the body; that is, the header of the displaced string points to the body of the displaced-to string. When one of the strings is converted into a double-byte string, the header of the other string must be modified accordingly. Thus the automatic conversion of displaced strings and displaced-to strings needs special handling, as explained below.

1. When a displaced string is created, its string kind is the same as that of the displaced-to string.
2. When a displaced-to string is converted into a double-byte string, the headers of all the displaced strings are modified accordingly. The header of the displaced-to string contains the list of the displaced strings.
3. When a displaced string is converted, the corresponding displaced-to string is converted first, and the headers of all the displaced strings are modified as in Case 2.

3.3 Symbol name strings

Since symbol name strings are never modified by user programs, it is possible to use the packed representation for name strings. However, it is convenient to use the same representation as for ordinary strings, since some built-in functions accept both symbols and strings. In fact, this is necessary, so that the system can handle name strings and ordinary strings uniformly. Thus we use two kinds of symbol name strings, as we do for ordinary strings. Special attention has to be paid to maintaining the uniqueness of symbols.

- If the name string contains only single-byte characters, it must always be a single-byte string.
- The name string is a double-byte string only if it contains at least one double-byte character.

For instance, when `intern` receives a double-byte string that contains only single-byte characters, it always returns a symbol whose name string is a single-byte string. If such a symbol exists already, then `intern` returns the symbol, but does not create a new symbol (`intern` is a built-in function, which looks for a symbol whose name string is the same as the given string).

With this implementation, we can determine the kind of the name string by looking at the first byte. If it is NULL or its most significant bit is 1, then the name string is double-byte; otherwise, it is single-byte. Thus no extra space is necessary for distinguishing the two kinds of name string. Note that this implementation does not allow symbols whose name strings begin with NULL, but this will cause no problems in practical applications.

3.4 Readtables

Readtables are data objects in which syntactic attributes of characters, used by the reader, are registered. In the original KCL, a readtable is represented as a table that has an entry for each character. When the system supports only single-byte characters, a readtable has at most 256 entries. It is, however, unrealistic to have entries for all double-byte characters.

Application programs do not always use all double-byte characters, and most double-byte characters are used as constituent characters. We need entries for double-byte characters in readtables only when they are defined as non-constituent characters.

Figure 7 illustrates the structure of a readtable in the extended KCL. Entries for double-byte characters are registered in a hash table. We use a hashing function based on the lower bits of the character code, so that characters with close codes are distributed around the hash table. The hash table is created only when necessary.

With this extended readtable, syntactic attributes of single-byte characters are retrieved in the same way as in the original KCL. The syntactic attribute of a double-byte character C is retrieved as follows:

1. If the "pointer to hash table" is NULL, then C is constituent. In this case, the hash table has not been created yet. This means that no double-byte character has been defined as non-constituent.

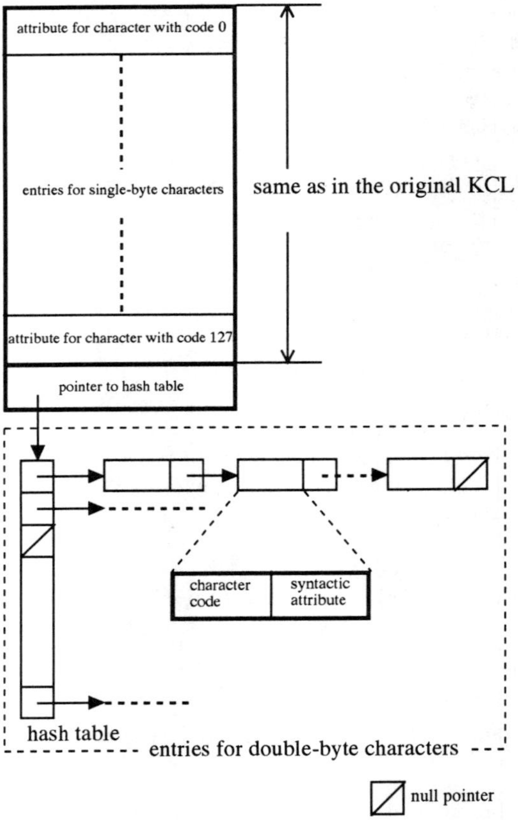

Fig. 7 Extended structure of readtables

2. Otherwise, the appropriate entry of the hash table is selected, and the list in the entry is searched. Each element of the list consists of a pair of a character code and the syntactic attribute. If there is no element that has the character code of C, then C is constituent. We maintain the list so that all elements correspond to non-constituent double-byte characters. An element is added only when a double-byte character is defined as non-constituent, and it is deleted when the character is defined back as constituent. Thus the lists in the hash table are kept as short as possible.

In this way, the retrieval of the syntactic attribute for a double-byte character is slower than for a single-byte character. However, for a single-byte character, the retrieval is as fast as in the original KCL.

KCL also has a table called *dispatch table* similar to readtables for handling dispatching macro characters. By extending the structure of dispatching tables in the same way as readtables, we can allow double-byte characters to be used to follow dispatching macro characters.

3.5 The garbage collector

The garbage collector of KCL is essentially a mark-and-sweep collector. It first marks all cells in use (the mark phase) and then collects all unused cells by sweeping the heap (the sweep phase). Bodies of data objects such as strings are relocated during the sweep phase to make a contiguous reusable space.

Since we extended the structure of readtables, we had to modify the garbage collector routine for readtables. On the other hand, the garbage collector routines for strings and symbols need no modifications, since the headers of these objects contain the byte size of the body, rather than the number of characters.

3.6 I/O functions

The following modifications had to be made for I/O functions:

- Modifications to the pretty printer and the formatted output.

  These functions have to count on the width of characters to work properly as intended. Since double-byte characters occupy two columns on the display, we had to modify these functions.

- File Pointers.

  A file pointer is the current position within a file. In most Common Lisp implementations, including KCL, a file pointer is represented by the number of bytes that have been read from or written to the file so far. If the system supports only single-byte characters, the file pointer is simply incremented by one each time a character is read or written. To support double-byte characters, the incrementing routine has to be modified to count the number of bytes actually input or output.

4 Performance Evaluation

In this section, we evaluate the performance of the extended KCL by comparing it with the the original KCL. For this experiment, we used the SUN3 workstation, on which the first version of the extended KCL was implemented.

4.1 Memory overhead

To measure the memory overhead, we compared the sizes of the executable files of the two systems. The size of the original KCL was 2,099,963 bytes, whereas the size of the extended KCL was 2,145,658 bytes. Note that the extended KCL initially contains no double-byte characters at all, and that it works in exactly the same way as the original KCL. The extended KCL is 1.02 times larger than the original KCL, and we can thus say that the sizes are almost the same. The main reasons for the increased size are the extensions of string objects and the additional code for handling double-byte characters.

```
(dotimes (j 1000)
  (reverse "abcd...wxyzあいうえ...しすせそ"))
```

(a) for the extended KCL

```
(defun str-rev (a)
  (do ((b (reverse a))
       (max (length a))
       (i 0 (1+ i)))
      ((>= i max) b)
    (when (logbitp 7 (char-code (char b i)))
      (rotatef (char b (1+ i)) (char b i))
      (incf i))))
(dotimes (j 1000)
  (str-rev "abcd...wxyzあいうえ...しすせそ"))
```

(b) for the original KCL

Fig. 8 Programs for reversing a string with double-byte characters

4.2 Runtime efficiency in handling double-byte characters

To compare the readability and execution speed of programs that operate on double-byte characters, we wrote two equivalent programs, one for the extended KCL and the other for the original KCL. These programs reverse a string that contains double-byte characters. The source code for the extended KCL in Figure 8 (a) simply uses the built-in function **reverse**, whereas the program for the original KCL in Figure 8 (b) requires an auxiliary function **str-rev** to correctly reverse the string. The built-in function **reverse** in the original KCL is used also in the function **str-rev**, but it reverses the byte sequence. Therefore, **str-rev** has to swap the first byte and the second byte of each double-byte character. To do this, **str-rev** scans the entire string obtained by **reverse** and finds those bytes that are the second bytes of double-byte characters (that is, those bytes whose most significant bits are 1).

Needless to say, we can write programs much more easily in the extended KCL. This indicates the significance of handling double-byte characters and single-byte characters uniformly. To compare the execution times, we measured the time taken to execute the compiled programs 1000 times. The program for the extended KCL took 1.566 seconds, and the program for the original KCL took 6.138 seconds. Obviously, the extended KCL can execute the program much faster than the original KCL. Although uniform handling of characters causes some overhead, programs are executed much more efficiently in the extended KCL if they need to handle double-byte characters.

4.3 Runtime efficiency in handling single-byte characters only

To evaluate the efficiency loss caused by JCSH, we replaced the string to be reversed with one made up entirely of single-byte characters (see Figure 9). It took 3.333 seconds on the original KCL and 3.492 seconds on the extended KCL. The runtime

```
(defun str-rev (a)
  (do ((b (reverse a))
       (max (length a))
       (i 0 (1+ i)))
      ((>= i max) b)
    (when (logbitp 7 (char-code (char b i)))
      (rotatef (char b (1+ i)) (char b i))
      (incf i))))
(dotimes (j 1000)
  (str-rev "abcdefghijklmnopqrstuvwxyz"))
```

Fig. 9 Program for reversing a string with single-byte characters

overhead is very small.

To see the performance of I/O functions, we loaded the file `setdoc.lsp`, which contains all the on-line documents of KCL in English and whose size is 173,036 bytes. It took 22.317 seconds to load the file on the extended KCL, whereas it took 21.809 seconds on the original KCL. Again, the overhead is very small.

The extended KCL checks whether it should use a single-byte operation or a double-byte operation each time a function for operating on characters and strings is invoked. Single-byte operations work in exactly the same way as in the original KCL, because data representations for strings, symbols, and readtables are the same as in the original KCL. Therefore the runtime overhead is caused only by the checks to determine whether to use a single-byte operation or a double-byte operation and by the other operations that are not found in the original KCL. All new operations in the extended KCL are simple ones, such as the operation for initializing the string kind (single-byte string or double-byte string) in the string header when a new string is created. These new operations do not cause serious runtime overhead. Since we did not make any modifications to the control flow mechanism of KCL, there can be no overhead in the control flow mechanism.

4.4 Runtime overhead on garbage collection

To see the runtime overhead on garbage collection, we forced the system to start garbage collection immediately after the system started up. The garbage collection took 0.884 seconds on the original KCL and 0.892 seconds on the extended KCL. The difference is negligible. Since the garbage collectors of the two systems are almost the same, the major reason for the difference seems to be the difference in the sizes of the two systems.

5 Conclusions

We have investigated the feasibility and effectiveness of supporting Japanese Character Set Handling on Common Lisp without changing its language specification.

We succeeded in preserving the runtime and space efficiency by using appropriate data representations based on insights into the actual use of double-byte characters. Although it may be possible to create a more efficient implementation by modifying the language specification (for example, by allowing the user to declare that a certain string contains only single-byte characters), we cannot expect a great performance gain, judging from the results of our experiment. The performance gain would not be large enough to offset the disadvantages of modifying the language specification, which makes it difficult to write and read programs.

It is possible to write programs that handle Japanese characters on systems that do not support JCSH. However, such programs usually depend on the system and the character coding system, and they thus tend to have low portability. In addition, such programs tend to be so complicated that the programmer has to expend much effort on unimportant parts of the program.

Our extensions to KCL to support uniform JCSH are designed to preserve the high portability of the original KCL. Indeed, the extended KCL has been ported to various machines without any modification of the extensions. The only exception is the character code converter, which depends on the coding system of the operating system. We prepared one converter for each of the three major coding systems (JIS, Shift JIS, and EUC). These three coding systems cover almost all machines in Japan, and thus we need only to select one of the three converters when porting the extended KCL.

References

[1] Steele, G. L.: *Common Lisp: the Language*, Digital Press, 1984.

[2] Kurokawa, T., Yuasa, T., Hashimoto, Y., and Ito, T.: *Technical Issues on International Character Set Handling in LISP*, ISO/IEC JTC1/SC22/WG16 LISP, N33, 1988.

[3] Ohta, K., Yamamura, Y., and Morisawa, Y.: Using Japanese Characters in Common Lisp—An Implementation on the Lisp Machine Explorer, *Preprints Work. Gr. for Symbolic Processing, IPSJ*, 87-SYM-42, 1987, pp. 1–8 (in Japanese).

[4] Motoyoshi, F.: Japanese Character Set Handling in Common Lisp, *Preprints Work. Gr. for Programming Language, IPSJ*, 88-PL-16, 1988, pp. 65–68 (in Japanese).

[5] Motoyoshi, F.: A Proposal for Embedding Japanese Characters in Common Lisp, *Preprints Work. Gr. for Symbolic Processing, IPSJ*, 87-SYM-40, 1987, pp. 1–8 (in Japanese).

[6] Yuasa, T. and Hagiya, M.: *Kyoto Common Lisp Report*, Teikoku Insatsu Publishing, 1985.

[7] Yuasa, T.: Design and Implementation of Kyoto Common Lisp, *J. Inf. Process.*, Vol. 13, No. 3, 1990, pp. 284–295.

[8] Yuasa, T. and Yasumoto, T.: Implementation of Immediate Data on KCL (Kyoto Common Lisp) and Its Evaluation, *Proceedings of Papers Annual Meet. on Information and Systems of the Inst. Electronics, Inf. & Comm. Eng. Japan*, D-357, 1989, pp. 77 (in Japanese).

Initially published in "Computer Software", Vol. 9, No. 5, in Japanese.

Taichi Yasumoto
Faculty of Integrated Arts and Science
Aichi University of Education
Kariya, Aichi
448 Japan
yasu@auems.aichi-edu.ac.jp

Taiichi Yuasa
Department of Information and Computer Science
Toyohashi University of Technology
Toyohashi, Aichi
441 Japan
yuasa@tutics.tut.ac.jp

Drill Text Understanding with Integrated Natural Language and Picture Processing

Tsutomu Endo Hidehiro Ohki Kazuhiro Takaoka

Summary. Generally, a text contains both natural language expressions and pictorial expressions. In particular, a drill text is written with the intention of handling pictures corresponding to a question and of solving the problem. Understanding the mutual relation between both expressions, making each less ambiguous by referring to the other, and transforming one expression into another are necessary to understand the text. Therefore a drill text understanding system has to be built in an integrated environment of natural language and picture processing. This paper presents a method for cooperative understanding of a drill text for first grade mathematics. The system consists of a number of interpreting modules corresponding to components of the text. These modules try to interpret the component by using a variety of knowledge modules based on the structural and semantic features of that component. Modules communicate with each other if necessary.

1 Introduction

Understanding text is essential for the automatic building of a large-scale knowledge base. Generally a text contains not only sentences of natural language but also picture patterns and tables. In explanatory texts such as encyclopedias or handbooks, linguistic and pictorial expressions could be analyzed independently after partitioning both expressions from the text. However, in a drill text written with the intention of handling picture expressions corresponding to a question and/or solving the problem, it is necessary to understand the mutual relation between both expressions, make each less ambiguous by referring to the other, and transform one expression into another. Therefore a drill text understanding system has to be built in an integrated environment of natural language and picture processing.

It is difficult to control the understanding process by straightforward or sequential methods, because a drill text has a variety of structures. In such a situation, cooperative distributed processing is desired, in which autonomous modules perform sophisticated problem solving and cooperatively interact with other modules to solve a single problem [5, 8, 9, 13]. *Maruichi et al.* [14] proposed an organizational model of computation for representing a system such as a school of fish, a team sport, or a company. In this model, each agent has its own message-interpreter for realizing autonomy, and the notion of an environment is defined as a place

ISBN 0-12-037105-7

where agents exist. However, the application of this model to natural language and picture understanding represent future work.

This paper intends to define a mechanism of cooperative understanding of both language and pictures by building a problem-solving system for a drill text for first grade mathematics, in which natural language and picture patterns are complementary to each other. Our system consists of a number of interpreting modules that try to interpret components of the text. These modules use a variety of knowledge modules according to the structural and semantic features of the components concerned, and they communicate with each other if necessary.

Kirsch is one of the pioneers in the research area of manipulating natural language and picture patterns in a comprehensive and unified way [11]. *Okada and Takagi* proposed systems for understanding moving picture patterns, using verb-centered concepts [15, 10]. *Nishida et al.* [16] proposed a computer program that takes natural language sentences and produces a model of an objective world with three dimensions. Neither of these teams' systems, however, has dealt with actual texts. Also, their arguments focused on either type of information and did not take co-reference into consideration. *Novak et al.* [6] proposed a program that would understand textbook physics problems specified by a combination of English text and diagrams. However, diagrams were entered by means of a user interface. *Abe et al.* [3, 4] proposed a system that would understand the plot of a story by reference to both image and linguistic information. The image recognition part of their system tries to identify only objects that are mentioned directly in narratives or are inferred indirectly. Unlike their system, our system is required to recognize every object in the text, regardless of linguistic information. Our system has another advantage. It is quite easy to change, modify, or expand, because the modules for the control structure and those for understanding the text are made independently.

2 Overview of Understanding System

2.1 Input text

Figure 1 shows examples from first-grade mathematical drill texts [1, 2]. Generally, a text consists of text components, such as a problem number, problem sentence, sub-problem number, problem picture, answer field, or formula. This has following features:

(1) A text is written from left to right.

(2) The type, form, and configuration of text components vary from text to text.

(3) The characters used in the text are *Hiragana*, numerals, and symbols, and they are normalized in font and size.

(4) The text written in *Hiragana* is spacially segmented, phrase by phrase.

(5) Almost all picture patterns in the text are drawn free-hand, except for such patterns as rectangles, circles, or tables, and their size, shape, and direction are slightly different from each other.

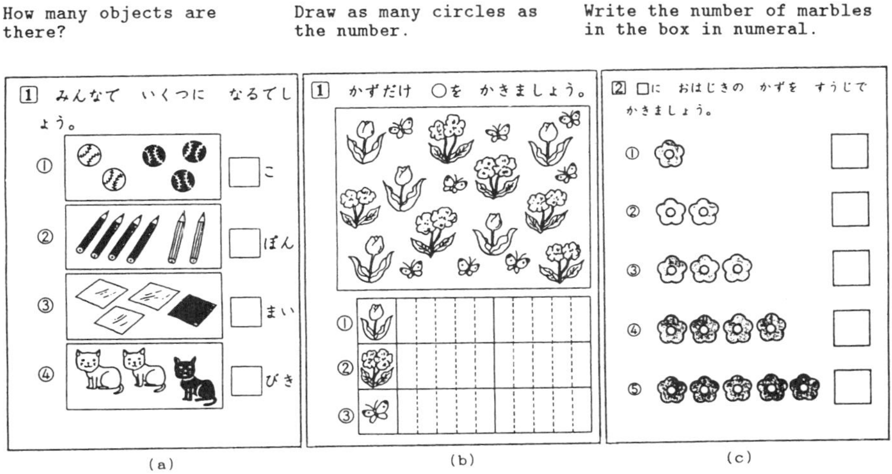

Fig. 1 Example of mathematical drill text

2.2 Modules and atoms

Since the drill text has the variety of structures mentioned above, it is difficult to adopt a top-down control structure based on predefined text models [12]. Also, the way to manipulate pictures and to answer questions varies from text to text. Therefore, a flexible control structure that can change the analyzing method according to the input text is desired.

We propose an understanding system that is comprised of multiple modules acting concurrently and asynchronously [7]. In communication with other modules, each module tries to interpret a part of the text. Figure 2 shows the architecture of the system. The interpreting module (IM), segmenting module (SM), and image data logically form a processing unit that is called an *atom*. Two modules in an atom act synchronously and try to interpret the image data cooperatively. The interpreting module manipulates only symbolic data and requests the segmenting module to manipulate image data. However, the interpreting module does not understand natural language or recognize a picture pattern by itself. It requests various kinds of knowledge modules to do so, according to the features of the image data concerned. A group of modules on the left side in Figure 2 comprises the knowledge module, and it will be described in detail in Section 3 and Section 4. The main function of the interpreting module is the creation, activation, or deactivation of a module, and the sending, receiving, or storing of a message.

Given input image data, an atom is created and tries to interpret the data. If it is difficult, the segmenting module partitions the data, copies the original image data into partitioned subimage data, and repeats the same processing. Figure 2 shows the process of segmenting from input text to both problem sentence and problem picture, from sentence to characters, and from picture to primitive picture.

Any atom asynchronously communicates only with the atoms or knowledge

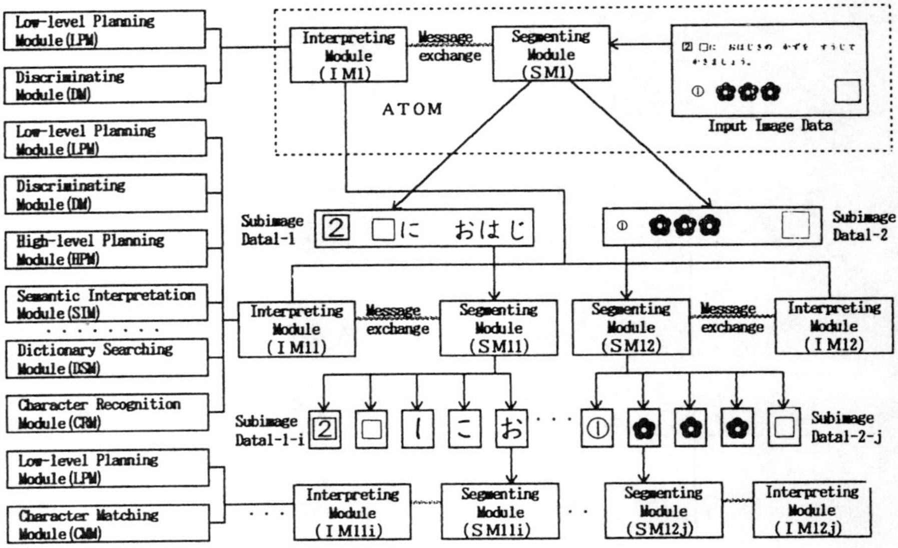

Fig. 2 Architecture of the text understanding system

modules that it created directly and with the atom that created it. A knowledge module also communicates only with the atom that created it. This restriction makes it easy to control communication among many modules. However, all atoms from a hierarchical structure corresponding to the inclusion of text components. Therefore, an atom can send a message to any atom by repeating the above communication to the root module. This means that a module can use the data of other modules, which is important for the cooperative understanding of natural language and picture patterns. The final state of generated atoms represents both the structure and interpretation of the input text. Our system has another notable feature: the segmenting module can repartition image data without influencing the upper modules, because each atom keeps copied image data.

2.3 Segmenting module

A segmenting module is activated by the interpreting module in the atom and manipulates image data directly. If it receives an order from the interpreting module, it obeys the order. Otherwise, it partitions image data into subimages in the following way.

First, it thresholds image data by using some threshold value, and it examines the projections of the binary image in the x and y directions. (Figure 3 shows an example of these projections of a drill text.) Then, the segmenting module partitions the image vertically or horizontally at the locations where the values of the projections point to zero. Since the text is written from left to right, the first partition of the input text is done horizontally. The segmenting module in one

How many objects are there?

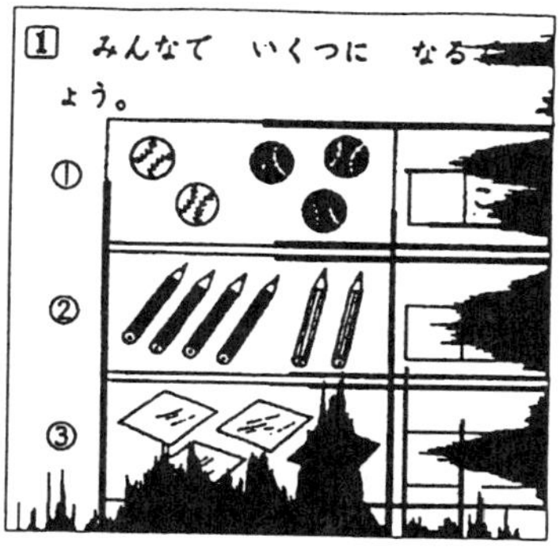

Fig. 3 Projections of text onto x and y axes

atom partitions the image data only in one direction. When further partition by the projection data is difficult, the segmenting module extracts connected components from the binary image data and makes a circumscribing rectangle of their subimage data.

The segmenting module keeps as attribute data the x and y coordinates of the upper left corner of the segmented image and the size (that is, the length and width) of the image. It sends the attribute data if the interpreting modules requests it.

3 Knowledge Module

A knowledge module is activated by the interpreting module and consists of declarative data and procedures. It requests necessary data from the parent module and receives it as a message. It also sends the result of processing on request. The function of the main knowledge modules are described in this section.

3.1 Discriminating module

A discriminating module (DM) determines the type of subimage data that the segmenting module generated from the image data concerned. The type is the name of the text components, such as text, problem sentence, problem picture, character, primitive picture, answer field, table, and so on. For example, the type of input image data is text. The input data of DM is both the type of image data and the attributes of the subimage data. DM uses the text model, as shown in Figure 4. The model does not represent a detailed description of the features of every text component and of the spatial relationships among components, but represents a description of typical features and local relationships of text components that appear together in drill texts. The slot "`size`" in Figure 4 represents the length and width of the text component in terms of the number of pixels. For example, the component "`problem_sentence1`" is 15-25 pixels wide and 400-500 pixels long. The text model is also used by modules for language understanding and picture recognition, as described in Section 4.

```
object([name,text],[component,problem_sentence,picture_pattern],
        [struct,[above,problem_sentence,picture_pattern]])
object([name,problem_sentence],[component,problem_sentence1])
object([name,problem_sentence],
        [component,problem_sentence1,problem_sentence2],
        [struct,[above,problem_sentence1,problem_sentence2]])
object([name,problem_sentence1],[component,problem_number,character,
         character,...],[struct,[left_of,problem_number,character],
        [left_of,character,character],...],[size,[400,500],[15,25]])
object([name,picture_pattern],[component,problem_picture,answer_field],
        [struct,[above,problem_picture,answer_field]])
object([name,picture_pattern],[component,subproblem_picture(1),
         subproblem_picture(2),...],[struct,[above,subproblem_picture(1),
         subproblem_picture(2)],...])
object([name,subproblem_picture],[component,subproblem_number,
         problem_picture,answer_field],[struct,[left_of,subproblem_number,
         problem_picture],[left_of,problem_picture,answer_field]])
object([name,problem_picture],[component,primitive_picture,...])
object([name,problem_picture],[component,rectangle,primitive_picture,...],
        [struct,[inside,primitive_picture,rectangle],...])
object([name,answer_field],[component,rectangle])
object([name,answer_field],[component,rectangle,aux_numeral],
        [struct,[left_of,rectangle,aux_numeral]])
```

Fig. 4 Example of text model

3.2 Planning module

A planning module decides what module should be activated next. It is divided into the low-level planning module (LPM) and the high-level planning module (HPM). The former decides the module name from the type of image data, and the latter determines the module from both the interpretation type and the data type of the image. The interpretation type is the name of the output of modules for language understanding and picture recognition, such as character component symbol, character code, word sequence, phrase sequence, parsing tree, case structure, command sequence, picture primitive name, picture descriptive expression, and so on. LPM and HPM decide the module name by using the rules shown in Table 1 and Table 2. The descriptions within parentheses in Table 1 are the parameters for partition and show the direction of the projection. If the segmenting module cannot partition the image in the direction designated by the parameter, it tries to extract connected components from the image and make them subimages.

3.3 Character processing module

This module identifies characters in the text and is divided into the character matching module (CMM) and the character recognition module (CRM). CMM detects the character components by matching the image data to a template with a given shape. CRM decides the character code from the combination of character components. Character recognition is performed in two stages because one character is sometimes partitioned into connected strokes by the segmenting module.

Table 1 Low-level Planning Rule

Data type	Module name
Text	Segmenting Module (Horizontal)
Problem Sentence	Segmenting Module (Vertical)
Problem Picture	Segmenting Module (Counter-direction)
Primitive Picture	Picture Recognition Module
Character	Character Matching Module
Unknown	Segmenting Module (Counter-direction)

Table 2 High-level Planning Rule

Data type	Interpretation type	Module name
Character	Character Component Symbol	Interpreting
Sentence	Character Component Symbol	Character Recognition
Sentence	Character Code	Dictionary Search
Sentence	Word Sequence	Morphological Analysis
Sentence	Phrase Sequence	Syntax Analysis
Sentence	Parsing Tree	Semantic Analysis
Sentence	Case Structure	Semantic Interpretation
Sentence	Command Sequence	Interpreting
Text	Command Sequence	Problem Solving

If the interpreting module directs the segmenting module to partition the image data according to the width of one character when the data is interpreted as a problem sentence, CRM is unnecessary. However, a character may be used not only in a sentence, but also in a picture. For example, an auxiliary numeral is often expressed in one character. Therefore the character is recognized by using two kinds of modules.

3.4 Language processing module

Knowledge modules for language processing are categorized into five classes dictionary searching (DSM), morphological analysis (PAM), syntax analysis (GAM), semantic analysis (SAM), and semantic interpretation (SIM). DSM transforms a character sequence that is given by the character recognition module into a word sequence by selecting the longest match in the word dictionary. In order to make the matching process less ambiguous, DSM can use a space as a delimiter. The location of the space is given by examining the coordinates of the character data. DSM is also used to recognize the meaning of characters in a picture pattern.

PAM produces a phrase sequence from the word category sequence. Here a phrase is the character sequence that is segmented with one or more spaces in

Table 3 Classification of Phrases

Symbol	Phrase	Example
ngni	Noun phrase with postposition "ni"	nakani (inside)
ngno	Noun phrase with postposition "no"	sikakuno (of square)
ngwo	Noun phrase with postposition "wo"	kazuwo (the number : object)
ngde	Noun phrase with postposition "de"	suujide (in numerals)
ngwa	Noun phrase with postposition "wa"	chigaiwa (the difference : subject)
ng	Noun phrase without postposition	ikutu (how many)
vgd	Verb phrase for problem definition	imasu (exist)
vgq	Verb phrase for question	arudeshou (Is there .... ?)
vgn	Verb phrase for noun modifier	onaji (same)
vgv	Verb phrase for verb modifier	awaseruto (in addition to)

a text. The phrases are classified according to their syntactic function. This is summarized in Table 3.

GAM produces a parsing tree from a phrase sequence. The structure of a problem sentence is simple and is described by a context-free grammar. The following is a part of the rewriting rules of the grammar:

```
sentence -> (modvg),np,(np),(np),vp,
sentence -> sentence,conj,sentence,
np -> ng|ngwa|ngga|ngwo|ngni|ngde|modng,np,
modng -> ngno|(np),(np),vgn,
vp -> vgq|vgd    modvg -> (np),vgv.
```

GAM uses a top-down parsing method for this grammar.

SAM produces the case structure from the parsing tree. In contrast, SIM generates from the case structure a command sequence that solves the problem given in a picture expression. Table 4 shows an example of commands extracted from a detailed analysis of the drill texts. However, the command sequence is not necessarily determined from the case structure of the problem sentence alone. The picture expression may also be needed, and this will be discussed in detail in Section 4.3.

3.5 Picture recognition module

A variety of modules, such as preprocessing, feature extraction, pattern matching and models, are used for picture recognition. These modules are called subroutines and form a picture recognition module with the control routine. Multiple picture recognition modules for every component of the text act concurrently and asynchronously. The following are important procedures used in the picture recognition module:

(1) Rectangle recognition.
Various kinds of rectangles appear in the drill text. This procedure identifies

Table 4 Examples of Commands

Function	Command name	Content
Picture Recognition	identify(a)	Identification of object a in the picture
	recognize(?X)	Recognition of unknown object in the picture
Problem Solving	count(a,?X)	Counting the number of object a in the picture
	matching	Matching two objects in the picture
	comparel	Comparing the length of two objects in the picture
	differl	Selection of the different kind of object
	orderl(a,n)	Selection of the n-th object from the left of object a
	add(a1,a2)	Addition of the number of object a1 and object a2
	sub(a1,a2)	Subtraction of the number of object a2 and object a1
Answer Generation	writen(a,l)	Writing the number of object a at the location l
	paint(a)	Painting object a
	line(a,b)	Linking object a to object b with a line
	encircle(a)	Enclosing object a with a circle

a rectangle or square in the image data and extracts the coordinates of its four vertices.

(2) Normalization.
This procedure achieves normalization with respect to geometrical operations, such as translation, rotation, and magnification, by using affine transformation.

(3) Feature extraction.
This consists of thresholding, computation of gray-level histograms, edge detection, thinning, segmentation, property measurement, finding straight lines by Hough transform, and so on.

(4) Matching.
The following are matching procedures:

- **Template matching.**
  This is a simple matching of a template representing a known object with two-dimensional image data.
- **Contour p matching.**
  This is a matching based on the properties and relational structures of branch points or high-curvature points in the contour of an object
- **Polygonal-matching.**
  This is a shape matching by polygonal approximation of the contour of an object.
- **Feature-matching.**
  This is a matching based on the shape properties of an object's region,

such as its area, perimeter, center, elongatedness, width, or dispersedness.

- **Skeleton-matching.**
  This is a matching based on the skeleton of an object region.

3.6 Other modules

There are modules for executing commands for solving problems and generating answers. The important task of these modules is to communicate with other modules.

4 Cooperative Understanding of Language and Picture

The interpreting modules try to understand a drill text by interpreting individual text components and integrating the component interpretations into an overall interpretation. A module often cannot completely interpret a component without the assistance of other modules. Therefore modules cooperate by generating tentative and partial results and exchanging them with each other. This section describes the basic operation of the interpreting module and examples of cooperative understanding.

4.1 Interpreting module

An interpreting module controls the interpretation process through such operations as determining the data type with the discrimination module, deciding which module should be activated next by the planning module, activating or deactivating other modules, exchanging message with the parent or child module, and saving messages and results.

A message that modules exchange is classified in the following way:

(1) Image data attribute ;

(2) Image data type ;

(3) Interpretation type and result ;

(4) Module name, instruction, and parameters ;

(5) Sending request and message type (1)–(4) .

Though a module sends a message only when it receives a sending request from the destination module, it can send a sending request to the destination module at any time. For example, when module A needs some information from module B, module A receives the information after sending the request message to module B. Since the message passing is done in accordance with the destination module's request, each interpreting module must maintain all information. Therefore an interpreting module has the following data buffers:

(1) Attribute and type of image data concerned ;

(2) Pairs of interpretation type and result of image data concerned ;

(3) Attribute, data type, interpretation type, and result of subimages ;

(4) Message logging buffer ;

(5) Unprocessed message queue .

When a new atom is created, the interpreting module operates with the following steps:

1) Receive the type of image data by sending a request message to the parent module ; store it in the buffer.

2) Activate the segmenting module (SM).

3) Activate the low-level planning module (LPM), send the data type to it, and receive the parameters and name of the module to be activated next.

4) If the received name is "*segmenting* (SM)," execute the following procedure otherwise, go to Step 5:

    4-1) Send the parameter to SM after confirming the request message from SM.

    4-2) Receive the name and attribute of the subimage data by sending a request message to SM ; store the information in the buffers.

    4-3) Activate the discriminating module (DM) for all subimage data ; send the data attributes to it.

    4-4) Receive data types from DMs ; store the types in the buffers.

    4-5) Activate the child interpreting module (IM) for every subimage by giving the data name as the parameter.

    4-6) Send the data type of the subimage after confirming the request message from the child IM ; go to Step 6.

5) Activate the knowledge module whose name is given by the LPM ; send the necessary data to the module after confirming its request message.

6) Send a request message for the interpretation result to the parent IM, child IMs, and knowledge modules.

7) Take one message out of the unprocessed message queue. If the message queue is empty, wait for a message to be received.

8) Depending on the message type, execute one of the following procedures:

    8-1) If the message is an interpretation type and result,

        8-1-1) store the interpretation type and result in the buffer;

        8-1-2) activate the high-level planning module (HPM);

        8-1-3) send the image data type and the interpretation type to HPM after confirming the request message from HPM;

        8-1-4) send the request for the module name to HPM;

        8-1-5) if the sender of the interpretation is a knowledge module, send the stop message to the module after confirming its request message; go to Step 7.

8-2) If the message is a module name,

8-2-1) if the name is "*interpreting* (IM)," go to Step 8-2-3;

8-2-2) activate the module with that name;

8-2-3) send the stop message to HPM after confirming the request message from HPM and go to Step 6.

8-3) If the message is a sending request, according to the message type, take the corresponding information out of the buffer; send it to the appropriate module; go to Step 7.

In the above procedure, "confirming the request message" means retrieving the message queue. If the request does not exist in the queue, the interpreting module waits for an appropriate message to be received. All messages that are sent or are received are stored in the logging buffer.

4.2 Picture recognition

Leaf atoms and non-leaf atoms of the hierarchical structure in Figure 2 use a different recognition method. A picture recognition module of the leaf atom requests clues from the parent module to help in recognizing a picture. These clues are the results of the interpretations of other modules. Then it carries out the following processing according to the given clue:

Command sequence of the problem sentence

For example, given the text in Figure 1(c), picture recognition modules of leaf atoms receive commands such as "*identify*(*marbles*)" and "*identify*(*rectangle*)" from the semantic interpretation module of the problem sentence. The words "*marbles*" and "*rectangle*," which are the parameter of the commands, become the key for retrieval of the picture knowledge base, as shown in Figure 5. The recognition module picks out the necessary model and attempts to recognize the picture in the top-down manner. In Figure 5, the *c-unit* slot is the auxiliary numeral of that object. The *pre-process* slot represents the preprocessing method of image data. If the slot value is null, a procedure sequence (that is, edge detection, computation of a gray-level histogram, thresholding, and thinning) is used as a default value. The slot *type*, *filename*, and *procedure* represent the image type after preprocessing, the file name of the model data to be stored, and the matching method, respectively. The *sub-class* slot is used in order to retrieve subordinate concepts when a clue is given for such an abstract concept as "*Omochani irowo nurimashou* (Paint the toy)."

Auxiliary numeral in the picture

For example, the problem sentence of the text in Figure 1 (a) has no information for picture recognition. However, there are such auxiliary numerals as "*ko*," "*pon*," "*mai*," and "*biki*" at the right of the answer field. These words are available for restricting the search space of the knowledge base. If the text contains more than one auxiliary numeral, the module gives priority to the word that exists in the same sub-problem region as the image data concerned.

```
object([name,toy],[super-class,[]],[sub-class,marbles])
object([name,marbles],[super-class,toy],
       [sub-class,marbles-1],[c-unit,ko])
object([name,marbles-1],[super-class,marbles],[sub-class,[]],
       [model,marbles-model-1])
model([name,marbles-model-1],[pre-process,[]],
      [type,two-dimensional-vector-picture],
      [filename,marbles1.mod],[procedure,contour-p-matching])
```

Fig. 5 Example of picture knowledge

If no clue is provided by other interpreting modules, the recognition module exhaustively applies the procedures described in (4) of Section 3.5 and attempts to recognize image data in the bottom-up manner. For example, because there is no apparent information to recognize of the text, as there was in Figure 1(b), the module attempts to identify all image data by matching all the objects in the knowledge base, such as "*butterfly*," "*tulip*," or "*table*."

On the other hand, a picture recognition module of the non-leaf atom uses a syntactic method based on the text model, as in Figure 4. Input data results both from all-child interpretation modules and interrelationships among child-image data. The recognition module selects the model whose components and structure correspond to input data and makes the object name the interpretation. The result is presented in the same format as text models.

4.3 Understanding the problem sentence

In a text such as that in Figure 1(c), the command sequence is generated solely from the problem sentence, without reference to a picture expression. However, understanding of most of the problem sentences requires coreference between language and picture expressions. The following are examples of cooperative understanding:

Reducing ambiguity at the word level

For example, the word "*kazu* (number)" in a sentence "*Kazudake maruwo kakimashou* (draw as many circles as the number)" has two senses. One is the number of objects as in Figure 1(b). Another is the numeral, as in "3" or "*san* (three)." The semantic interpretation module resolves this ambiguity with picture information. If there exist some numerals in a text, the module picks the numeral sense. In Figure 1, the numeral enclosed with a circle is supposed to represent the sub-problem number.

Command generation

The basic command structure of a problem sentence is composed of three processes. First is the recognition of picture components: e.g., "*identify*" and "*recognize*." Second is the problem solving: e.g., "*count*" and "*compare*." Third is the answer generation: e.g., "*write*" and "*paint*." This structure is available for default information. Each command has essential parameters. When the semantic interpretation module cannot generate the command structure using only the case structure of the problem sentence, it attempts to use both picture information and default information. For example, the command, "*count(?X)*" is generated from the problem sentence in Figure 1(a), but the object to be counted and the answer generation method are unknown. In this case, the interpretation module corresponding to the picture component produces the following result:

```
object([name,sub-problem-picture(1)],
  [component, [object([name,[sub-problem-number,1]]),
               object([name,problem-picture],
     [component,object([name,rectangle],
        [inside,object([name,[ball,
                              [coordinates-of-centroid]]]),.....],
        [coordinate-sequence-of-four-vertices])]),
               object([name,answer-field],
     [component,object([name,square],[inside,[]],
        [coordinate-sequence-of-four-vertices]),
                object([name,[auxiliary-numeral,ko]])])]).
```

From this representation and the default command structure, the interpreting module generates the command sequence: "*command*([*recognize*(*ball*), *count*(*ball*), *recognize*(*square*), *writen*(*ball, square*)])."

In the text of Figure 1(b), the command sequence can be generated in a way similar to that in Figure 1(a). In addition, the module utilizes the following information: (i) there are three kinds of objects in the problem picture, (ii) counting should be performed on a single object, (iii) there is a table, (iv) the row and column of a table have a great significance, (v) there are three sub-problem numbers at the left of the table, (vi) the left-most field of each row contains the same picture object as the problem picture, and (vii) the table has a number of null fields. Based on this information, the module generates the command sequence "*Recognize objects in the problem picture and draw as many of them as there are of them in the corresponding null fields of the table.*"

5 Experiments

The system is being implemented on UNIX workstations distributed on a local area network. Each module is implemented as a process of UNIX and image data, as a file on the disk. The operating system routines "*fork*" and "*exec*" are used to create new processes and to activate them. The pipe and socket routine are also used for communication between modules. Most of the programs are written in C, but the system is free from programming language restraints because of the independence of each module. An original text is converted by optical scanner into a digitized image with $1,024 \times 1,024$ pixels and a dynamic range of 256 gray levels.

We carried out a few experiments by using modules that have already been completed. Figure 6 shows an example of the text segmentation of Figure 1(b) by atoms only. Some subimages are omitted due to lack of space. Each atom generates child atoms until its image data cannot be partitioned by data projections in the vertical and horizontal directions or by the connectedness of the components. In

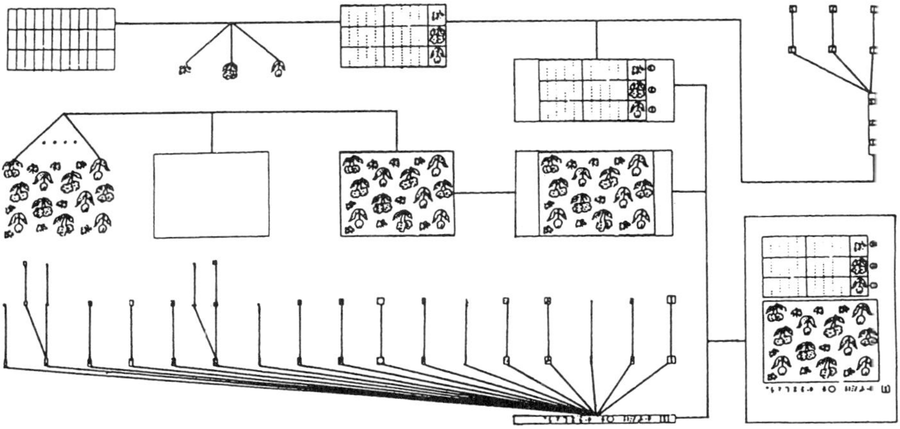

Fig. 6 Result of segmentation of text

Figure 6, primitive pictures are extracted from the picture field, as are connected strokes from the text field. The dotted lines in the original data's table are replaced by solid lines in order to prevent excessive generation of meaningless connected components. The segmenting module elongates each line segment a little so as to connect them to each other.

It was also confirmed experimentally that the programs for sentence understanding, character recognition, and picture recognition worked independently. We are now modifying them so that they can be invoked by the interpreting module. Figure 7 shows a process in which the command sequence is generated from the input problem sentence.

Let us consider the system performance on the basis of experimental results. The concurrent processing by multiple atoms could partition about twenty input texts into their components, though, in part, because it used the elongating technique of line segments. The largest problem in the partitioning process is that too many atoms are generated, because the segmenting module of one atom partitions image data in one direction only. By adding knowledge modules to atoms, the number of generated processes increases. We must carry out further examination of this problem, as well as an evaluation of the performance of the workstation.

A hand simulation shows that language understanding will put too heavy a load on the atom that manipulates sentence data. This results from the fact that the data of an atom is an image. It would be necessary to introduce an atom whose data is a symbol.

```
Problem sentence:
   sikakuni ohajikino kazuwo suujide kakimashou.
   (Write the number of marbles inside the square in numerals.)
Morphological analysis:
   [ngni(sikaku,figure),ngno(ohajiki,phys_obj),ngwo(kazu,number),
    ngde(suuji,numeral),vgq(kaku,write)]
Syntax analysis:
   sentence([np([ngni(square)]),np([modng([ngno(marbles)]),
            np([ngwo(number)])]),np([ngde(Numeral)]),
            vp([vgq(write)])])
Semantic analysis:
   meaning([[q,[[pred,write],[obj,number_of(marbles)],
                 [loc,square],[form,numeral]]]])
Semantic interpretation:
   command([identify(marbles),count(marbles),
           identify(square),writen(marbles,square)])
```

Fig. 7 Process of sentence understanding

6 Conclusions

We have presented a method of cooperative understanding of a drill text by using a number of processing modules in a network environment with multiple UNIX workstations. The results of our study may be summarized as follows:

(1) Multiple modules acting concurrently and asynchronously were very effective for partitioning a variety styles of drill texts into their components. These modules did not necessarily need a detailed text model. This shows that our method is applicable to texts other than drill texts.

(2) It was found that information from the language of a drill text for first-grade mathematics is effective for selecting or deciding a model in picture recognition, and that information from the picture expression is indispensable for the reduction of ambiguity at the word level and for semantic interpretation—that is, for the generation of a command sequence.

(3) Existing programs of linguistic and pictorial processing are easily reusable because knowledge modules for understanding text are defined according to a limited function, and both algorithm and data structure are independent of each other.

The above results give us research prospects for achieving a wide range of processing (from raw data processing at the pixel level to such symbolic computation as recognition, understanding, or problem solving) under an integrated environment, and for engineering the cooperative understanding of natural languages and picture patterns.

We are now attempting to solve the problems mentioned in Section 5, to develop the knowledge representation and algorithms of incomplete modules, and to examine experimentally the communication protocol between modules. The verification of whether or not the system is working and the introduction of modules for solving problems and generating answers are the subjects for future study.

References

[1] Shougaku 1 nen sansuujuku, Kyouiku Shoseki Co., 1989 (in Japanese).

[2] Shou 1 sansuu 5 hunkan training, Kyougaku Kenkyuusha Co., 1990 (in Japanese).

[3] Abe, N., Soga, I., and Tsuji, S.: Interpretation of Act using both Language and image Data - Identification Objects Through Utterance, *Trans. Inf. Proc. Soc. Japan*, Vol. 23, No. 2 (1982), pp. 124–132 (in Japanese).

[4] Abe, N., Soga, I., and Tsuji, S.: Interpretation of Act Using both Language and Image Data - Extraction of a Plot and Its Question Answering, *Trans. Inf. Proc. Soc. Japan*, Vol. 23, No. 2 (1982), pp. 133–141 (in Japanese).

[5] Anzai, Y.: A Model of Integrated Information Processing Mechanisms for Human and Computer Based on Cooperative Functional Modules, *Trans. Inst. Electronics, Inf. & Comm. Eng. Japan, Part D*, Vol. J70-D, No. 11 (1987), pp. 2026–2037 (in Japanese).

[6] Bulko, W. and Novak, G.: Understanding Text with an Accompanying Diagram, *Tech. Rep. AI Lab. The University of Texas at Austin*, AI88-69, 1988.

[7] Endo, T. and Takaoka, K.: Drill Text Understanding in Cooperation with Picture Processing, *Proc. 42th Annual Convention IPS Japan*, No. 2Q-2, 1991 (in Japanese).

[8] Gasser, L.: Conceptual Modeling in Distributed Artificial Intelligence, *J. Japan Soc. Artif. Intell.*, Vol. 5, No. 4 (1990), pp. 401–410.

[9] Ishida, T.: Technologies and Applications of Distributed Artificial Intelligence, *J. Japan Soc. Artif. Intell.*, Vol. 5, No. 4 (1990), pp. 441–448 (in Japanese).

[10] Ito, Y., Takagi, A., Rokusawa, K., Simizu, M., Kitaoka, K., and Ohara, H.: The Tally Process of Japanese Sentences with Visual Information in the World of Two-Dimensional Figures, *Trans. Inst. Electronics & Comm. Eng. Japan, Part D*, Vol. J69-D, No. 7 (1986), pp. 1083–1094 (in Japanese).

[11] Kirsch, R. A.: Computer Interpretation of English Text and Picture Patterns, *IEEE Trans. Electronic Comput.*, Vol. EC-13 (1964), pp. 363–376.

[12] Kise, K., Sugiyama, J., Babaguchi, N., and Tezuka, Y.: Layout Model Based Analysis of Document Structure, *Trans. Inst. Electronics, Inf. & Comm. Eng. Japan, Part D-II*, Vol. J72-D-II, No. 7 (1989), pp. 1029–1039 (in Japanese).

[13] Lesser, V. R.: An Overview of DAI : Viewing Distributed AI as Distributed Search, *J. Japan Soc. Artif. Intell.*, Vol. 5, No. 4 (1990), pp. 392–400.

[14] Maruichi, T., Ichikawa, M., and Tokoro, M.: An Organization Model of Computation and Its Application, *Trans. Inf. Proc. Soc. Japan*, Vol. 31, No. 12 (1990), pp. 1768–1779 (in Japanese).

[15] Okada, N.: Towards a Unified Understanding of Natural Language and Picture Patterns, In: Nagao, M.(ed), *Language and Artificial intelligence*, North-Holland (1987), pp. 171–193.

[16] Yamada, A., Nishida, T., and Doshita, S.: Reasoning about Relative Location with Potential Model on Two-dimensional Space, *Trans Inf. Proc. Soc. Japan*, Vol. 29, No. 9 (1988), pp. 824–834 (in Japanese).

Initially published in "Computer Software", Vol. 8, No. 6, in Japanese.

Tsutomu Endo
Department of Computer Science and Intelligent Systems
Faculty of Engineering
Oita University
700 Dannoharu, Oita
870–11 Japan

Hidehiro Ohki
Department of Computer Science and Intelligent Systems
Faculty of Engineering
Oita University
700 Dannoharu, Oita
870–11 Japan

Kazuhiro Takaoka
Department of Computer Science and Intelligent Systems
Faculty of Engineering
Oita University
700 Dannoharu, Oita
870–11 Japan

Naming of Objects in Large-Scale Distributed Systems

Nobuhisa Fujinami Yasuhiko Yokote

Summary. Naming is one of the most convenient ways of sharing objects in computer systems. This paper proposes the Hierarchy-Relative Naming Scheme, which is a way of naming and addressing suitable for large-scale distributed systems. We assume that such systems have locality and logically hierarchical structures. We separate IDs from addresses. Addresses represent objects' location, while IDs are location-independent. IDs and addresses have relative representations, which are translated if they are transmitted among naming contexts. This ensures uniqueness of IDs while efficiency and availability are preserved. Then, we introduce the methods which make our scheme suitable for mobile naming contexts and dynamic reconfiguration of networks and systems. Implementation problems of our scheme and their solutions are also presented.

1 Introduction

Naming is one of the most convenient ways of sharing objects in computer systems — that is, of referring to a single entity from different places. In object-oriented systems, object identifiers (IDs for short) that are unique within systems are commonly used for the purpose of sharing. Distributed systems generally provide IDs that include the addresses of the hosts (where the objects are instantiated) and that have assured uniqueness within the systems. However, recent distributed systems have become much larger in scale, and giving unique host IDs within systems necessitates international organizations that assign IDs. Furthermore, quite a large bit size is required for unique IDs. For instance, the Amoeba distributed system [5] uses 72 bits of its 128-bit capabilities to specify objects. Moreover, the possibility of running short of IDs still remains, considering the rapid evolution of computer systems. For example, if each of the 10^{10} people on the Earth had one hundred computers, including desktop, portable, and built-in computers, and if each computer had 10^9 objects, there would be $10^{21} \approx 2^{73}$ objects on the Earth.

Existing large-scale distributed systems also have problems of mobile hosts, object migration for load balancing and for communication efficiency, and reconfiguration of networks. An IP address, for example, changes if the host moves to another network, and the user must be aware of the host's location. It is preferable that the current locations of objects or hosts have nothing to do with their names; that is, migration should be transparent.

ISBN 0-12-037105-7

The Hierarchy-Relative Naming Scheme proposed in this paper gives short representations for IDs of logically near objects and has no possibility of running short of IDs, even if the system evolves. This feature is realized by translating object IDs and addresses each time they are transferred among tree-structured naming contexts. Our scheme also allows object/host migration transparency.

The rest of the paper is organized as follows: Section 2 gives our assumptions for large-scale distributed systems and the goals of this paper. Section 3 briefly describes our naming scheme. Section 4 explains the method for constructing object IDs. Section 5 discusses object migration transparency, and Section 6 discusses host migration and network reconfiguration transparency. Section 7 describes a method of connecting systems for expansion. Implementation problems and their solutions are discussed in Section 8. Section 9 overviews related research, and Section 10 concludes the paper.

2 Assumptions and Goals

We assume that the each of distributed systems discussed in this paper has the following properties:

Very large-scale: The system consists of so many various kinds of computers that broadcast is impossible. It is hard to assign unique, fixed-size IDs to each host.

Migration: Objects and hosts migrate independently of each other.

Locality: Communication and migration are much more rarely directed toward distant objects or hosts, such as those in different local networks, than toward nearby ones.

Hierarchy: The system has local naming contexts with hierarchical structure.

The last assumption is not a restriction, since most practical systems are hierarchically managed. For example, wide area networks, local area networks, hosts, operating systems, and processes can be used as the hierarchy of local naming contexts. The hierarchy does not have to be related to the physical structure[1] or the social structure.[2] Representing the hierarchy as a tree structure, we assume that every two objects connected by parent-child branches can directly communicate with each other. The system may have other connections, as most networks do. Such connections can be made by a human or are automatically made when two naming contexts communicate with each other frequently — when, for example, hosts on different levels of the hierarchy share a local network.

For distributed systems, we design global IDs (names) with the following features that match the above assumptions:

Uniqueness: Each object has just one ID, and each ID denotes just one object. The ID never changes until the object is deleted.

---

[1] For instance, all hosts in one local network may share the same naming context. In this case, uniqueness is ensured by the inclusion of host IDs in object IDs.

[2] E.g., companies and countries.

Migration Transparency: An ID is independent of object/host migration and network/system reconfiguration. The location of an object is represented by a different method.

Scalability: The naming scheme makes it easy to add hosts and to reconfigure the system.

Efficiency: The overhead of using global IDs is small.

Availability and Fault Tolerance: Distant faults have little influence on the availability of operations on IDs.

3 Overview and Notation

This section presents an overview of the Hierarchy-Relative Naming Scheme with its notation.

Each naming context gives a local ID (or *LID*) to an object instantiated in it and a local address (or *LAD*) to an object currently in it. LIDs and LADs are unique within the naming context. At instantiation time, the LID and the LAD of an object are equal. Since the manager of a naming context is also an object, it has an LID and an LAD that are unique within its parent naming context, if any. There is only one *root naming context*, which has no parent naming context, in a system. The root can change as the system expands.

Each object in the system has an *original naming context*, in which the object was instantiated, and a *current naming context*, in which the object currently exists. In our scheme, the object ID (or *OID*) of an object represents its original naming context and its LID in that context, and its object address (or *OAD*) represents its current naming context and its LAD in that context. OIDs and OADs have relative representations seen from the object that memorizes them. If a message or an object is transmitted, the OIDs and OADs in them are translated. The *interpretations* of OIDs and OADs are their meanings that are unique within the system in the conventional sense. The interpretation of the OID of one object never changes until it is deleted. The translation of OIDs and OADs preserves their interpretations.

The unit of communication is a message. The receiver of a message is specified by its OID. The managers of naming contexts handle the relationship between the OID and the OAD. Users have no knowledge of OADs.

Each object remembers its OID. It is "0:", meaning "myself," at instantiation time, and it varies as the object migrates. The naming context manager, which is also an object, has the following additional information:

- *Reverse OID*: the virtual OID of the manager seen from the original place, which is "0:" if it never migrates;
- All pairs of LIDs and OADs of objects instantiated in it; and
- All pairs of OIDs and LADs of objects currently in it.

The manager may further cache the pairs of OIDs and OADs of the senders of the messages going through the naming context. If the naming context has connections other than parent-child ones, the destination OID seen from the source and the source OID seen from the destination are needed.

The storage size required by the naming context manager is proportional to the sum of the numbers of objects instantiated in it, objects currently in it, and objects referred to from it (cache size). If, for example, a host corresponds to one naming context, the storage size depends on the performance of the host, not the size of the system.

4 Object IDs and Their Interpretations

An OID identifies an object. The format of an OID is

$$m : l_1.l_2.\cdots.l_n,$$

where m and n are non-negative integers, and each l_i is an LID.[3] The interpretation of an OID is defined as follows:

Definition 1. Interpretation of OID. *The interpretation of OID $m : l_1.l_2.\cdots.l_n$ in naming context S is*

$$L_1.L_2.\cdots.L_{N-m}.l_1.l_2.\cdots.l_n,$$

where $L_1.L_2.\cdots.L_N$ is the sequence of LIDs from the current root naming context to S.

Examples: Seen from a naming context manager, an OID that denotes the object instantiated in it is $0 : l$, where l is the LID of the object. Without object migration, the OID seen from an object denoting the object in the same naming context with LID$=l$ is $1 : l$, and the OID of the object itself is 0:. Notice that the OID seen from a naming context manager and the OID seen from an object in it are different.

Figure 1 shows an example of local naming contexts with hierarchical structure. For simplicity, the LIDs are all different from each other, but may be the same if their naming contexts are different. Connections other than tree branches are omitted. The OID of object B seen from A is 1 : 32, and that of D is 3 : 2.21.52. The OIDs of B and D seen from C are 2 : 11.32 and 3 : 2.21.52, respectively. The interpretation of B's OID is 1.11.32 when seen from both A and C, and that of D's OID is 2.21.52.

When OIDs such as those of the sender, the receiver, and the arguments of a message are transmitted to another naming context, they are translated in order to keep their interpretations invariant. If, in Figure 1, a message is sent from object C to D, the receiver's OID of 3 : 2.21.52 is translated into 2 : 2.21.52 when the naming context manager with LID=12 receives the message. The translation follows as 1 : 2.21.52, 0 : 2.21.52, 0 : 21.52, 0 : 52, and 0:, and the message arrives at D. At this moment, the receiver's OID represents object D itself. On the other hand, the sender's OID 0: is translated into 3 : 1.12.41 when it arrives at D. The following is the rule for the translation of OIDs:

Rule 1. OID translation. *Let the transmitted OID be $m : l_1.l_2.\cdots.l_n$.*

[3] This is similar to a relative pathname, except that the number before ":" is the number of "../"s.

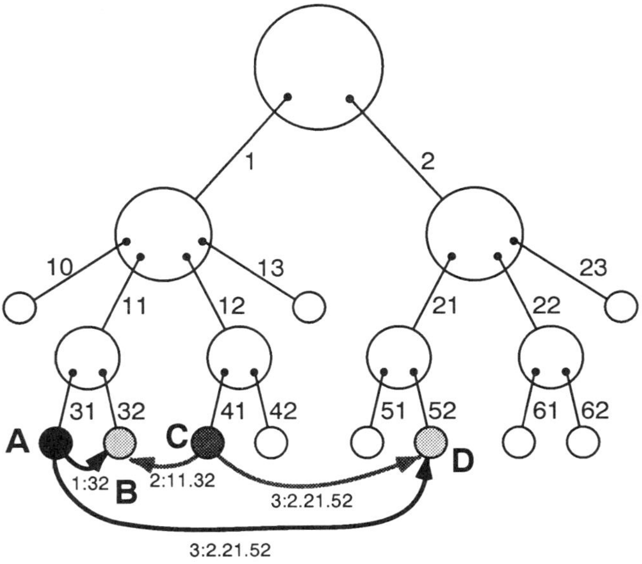

Fig. 1 Hierarchical naming contexts. (Circles represent objects or naming contexts. Numbers represent LIDs.)

If transmitted to parent naming context: *If m is positive, decrease m by one. If m is zero, insert the LID of the naming context manager or the object after ":".*[4]

If transmitted to child naming context or child object with LID=l: *If m is positive, increase m by one. If m is zero, compare l with l_1. If they are equal, delete l_1. Otherwise, increase m by one.*

If transmitted to a naming context that is not listed above: *Perform the above translations one by one, going through the parent-child connections until the destination naming context is reached. The collected expression is as follows: Let the OID of the destination naming context manager be $M : L_1.L_2.\cdots.L_N$, and let the OID of the source naming context seen from the destination be $N : L'_1.L'_2.\cdots.L'_M$.*

If $m > M$, *replace m with $m - M + N$.*

If $m < M$, *replace m with N and insert $L'_1.L'_2.\cdots.L'_{M-m}$. after ":".*

If $m = M$, *let k be the maximum number that satisfies $l_1 = L_1, \cdots, l_k = L_k$. If $l_1 \neq L_1$, let k be zero. Delete k LIDs after ":," and replace m with $N - k$.*

---

[4] This translation is performed in the parent naming context. Memorizing the LID of the object itself is unnecessary.

This rule does not require the naming context managers to use the interpretations of OIDs. In particular, if the communication is done only through parent-child connections, naming context managers have only to know the children's LIDs, not global information such as the LIDs of other naming context managers. To determine whether two OIDs in different naming contexts represent an identical object, one can transmit them to the same naming context using Rule 1 and compare them. It is not necessary to use their interpretations.

5 Object Addresses and Object Migration

An OAD gives a hint as to the current location of an object. (The optimum path to the indicated location is the routing problem, which is not discussed in this paper. At worst, one can choose parent-child connections only.) An OAD consists of three parts: a body, a timestamp, and an uncertainty value. The timestamp indicates the time when the location is correct. The uncertainty value is used in Rule 3 in Section 6. When the OAD of an object is inferred from its ancestor's OAD by appending the sequence of LIDs from the ancestor to the object as LADs, the uncertainty value denotes the number of appended LADs. The value is a non-negative integer or ∞. The body of an OAD has the same format as an OID, except that the LIDs are replaced by the LADs. The interpretation of an OAD is defined in the same way as that of an OID. The translation rule for transmission is also the same. Without migration, the OID and the body of the OAD have the same value.

A message includes the sender's OID and OAD. The timestamp of the OAD is the time of message construction, and its uncertainty value is 0. A message also includes the receiver's OID and OAD. If the current location is not known, the body of the OAD is the same as the corresponding OID, and its uncertainty value is ∞.

The procedure for object migration is as follows:

Procedure 1. Object Migration.

Begin migration: *The migrating object sends a disconnection message to its original naming context manager. The managers through which the message passes invalidate pairs LID-OAD, OID-LAD, or OID-OAD of the object.*

Do migration: *The object moves. The OIDs belonging to the object, including its own OID, are translated.*

End migration: *The manager of the new current naming context assigns an LAD to the object. The manager keeps the pair of the object's OID and the new LAD. The object then sends the OID and the new OAD to the manager of the object's original naming context.*[5] *The manager updates the OAD and sends back an acknowledgment.*

The assigned LAD is the same as the LID of the object, if the new current naming context is the original naming context. Otherwise, the LAD must be different from the LIDs of all objects instantiated in the new naming context, since, even if the object has migrated, returning will cause a problem.

[5] In an implementation, the manager of the current naming context may sends the message.

If the object does not receive the acknowledgment, it repeatedly sends the OID and the new OAD at a certain interval. This is for network partitioning that disjoins the original naming context.

Examples: In Figure 2, object B has migrated and received LAD 53 from the naming context manager with LID=LAD=21. B's OID, memorized by B, has been translated from 0: into 3 : 1.11.32. B sends its OID 3 : 1.11.32 and OAD 0: to the manager of its original naming context (3 : 1.11). This information is cached by the naming contexts with "*" marks. The managers of the current and original naming contexts, indicated by "◯" marks, always keep this information. As the OID and the OAD are translated by Rule 1, the pair in, for example, the original naming context is the pair of 0 : 32 and 2 : 2.21.53.

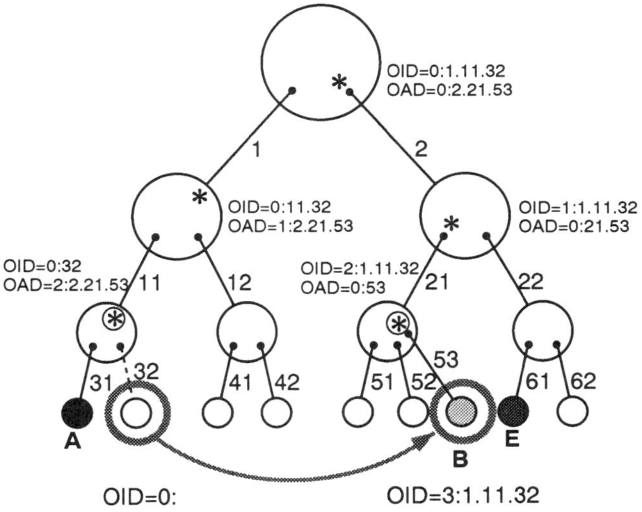

Fig. 2 Object migration. (Circles represent objects or naming context. Numbers represent LADs.)

In each naming context, the receiver's OAD of a message is rewritten according to its OID. This is done when the OID and the OAD are in the form of the naming context — that is, after the translation of Rule 1 in Section 4, if the object receives the message from its child, and otherwise before the translation.

Rule 2. Rewriting the OAD of Object A in Naming Context S.

If A is in S or instantiated in S, *replace the OAD with the correct OAD, which S knows.*

If A is not in S while OAD indicates that A is in S, *return an error.*[6] *If*

[6] There is an alternative way, which is to rewrite the body of the OAD so that it has the same value as the OID. We adopt the way of returning an error because this also eliminates messages to nonexistent objects.

the pair of the OID and the OAD is cached by the naming context that the error message goes through, the pair is invalidated.

If S caches the pair of A's OID and OAD, and the timestamp of the cache's OAD is newer, *replace the OAD with the cache's OAD.*

Otherwise, *do nothing.*

After the OAD has been rewritten, the message is transmitted according to the address information. If a message is sent from object A to B in Figure 2, B's OID and OAD are both 1 : 32 at message construction time. The current naming context manager rewrites the OAD 0 : 32 as 2 : 2.21.53. If a message is sent from object E to B, the receiver's OAD is 3 : 1.11.32 at message construction time. The naming context manager with LID=LAD=2 rewrites the OAD 1 : 1.11.32 as 0 : 21.53 according to the cached information, and the message arrives at object B without going through the original naming context.

6 Migration of Naming Context and Dynamic Reconfiguration of Networks

This section discusses the cases of the logical migration of naming contexts and physical migration of hosts or local networks. We assume that each host or local network corresponds to one naming context. The objects in the naming context migrate together. If this assumption does not hold — for example, if a host has only a part of a naming context — host migration is treated as migration of all objects in the host.

It is not efficient to translate all the OIDs and OADs in all the objects in the migrating naming context. We do not touch OIDs other than that of the naming context manager. The manager translates the OIDs and OADs of the messages to and from inside and outside of the naming context. The manager's OID is translated according to Rule 1, in the same way as Rule 2 in Section 5. Migration of a naming context is performed according to the following procedure, instead of Procedure 1:

Procedure 2. Migration of Naming Context S.

Begin migration: *The manager of S sends a disconnection message to its original naming context manager. The managers through which the message passes invalidate all the pairs LID-OAD, OID-LAD, and OID-OAD of S and its descendants.*

Do migration: *S moves. The OIDs belonging to the manager of S are translated, including the manager's own OID.*

End migration 1: *The manager of the new current naming context assigns an LAD to S. The manager keeps the pair of the object's OID and the LAD. Then S sends the OID, the new OAD, and a virtual OID "0:" to the manager of the original naming context. The manager updates the OAD and returns acknowledgment. It includes the current value of the virtual OID "0:", called the reverse OID. It must be quoted so that it is not translated.*

End migration 2: *The manager of S sends a prompt message to its descendent objects from outside of S to send their OIDs and the OADs to the managers of their original naming contexts.*

The last operation is for those objects that moved with S but whose OIDs are not S's descendants. Rule 3 cannot infer the addresses of such objects. The operation can be implemented as remembering all the OIDs of the objects migrating from outside S, or as sending prompt messages to the child naming contexts and the objects that came from outside, recursively. Since migration of a large naming context is rare, the cost of prompt messages is low.

Rule 2 in Section 5 is updated as follows:

Rule 3. Rewriting OAD of object A in naming context S.

If A is an object in S or its descendant *(that is, if A's OID is $m : l_1.l_2.\cdots.l_n$, and there exists $1 \le k \le n$ such that object B with OID=$m : l_1.l_2.\cdots.l_k$ is in S), then replace A's OAD with $0 : L.l_{k+1}.\cdots.l_n$, where B's LAD is L. Let the timestamp be the current time, and let the uncertainty value be $n-k$.*

If A is an object instantiated in S or its descendant *(that is, if A's OID is $0 : l_1.l_2.\cdots.l_n$, and the object B with LID=l_1 is instantiated in S), then replace A's OAD with $M : L_1.L_2.\cdots.L_N.l_2.\cdots.l_n$, where B's OAD is $M : L_1.L_2.\cdots.L_N$. Let the timestamp be that of B's OAD, and let the uncertainty value be $n-1$.*

If neither A nor one of its ancestors is in S while OAD indicates it is *(that is, if A's OAD is $0 : L_1.L_2.\cdots.L_N$, and there is no object with LAD=L_1 in S), then return an error.*

If A is an object or its descendant whose OID and OAD are cached by S, and if the uncertainty value derived from the cache's OAD is smaller or the timestamp of the cache's OAD is newer *(that is, if A's OID is $m : l_1.l_2.\cdots.l_n$, and there exists $1 \le k \le n$ such that the pair of the OID $m : l_1.l_2.\cdots.l_k$ and the OAD $M : L_1.L_2.\cdots.L_N$ of object B is cached [if there are multiple ks, the largest one is used], and if $n-k$ is smaller than the uncertainty value of A's OAD, or if it is equal and the timestamp of B's OAD is newer than that of A's OAD), then replace A's OAD with $M : L_1.L_2.\cdots.L_N.l_{k+1}.\cdots.l_n$. Let the timestamp be that of B's OAD and let the uncertainty value be $n-k$.*

Otherwise, *do nothing.*

Further, the following translation of OIDs and OADs is performed in the moved naming context to maintain the consistency between the inside and outside of the naming context.

Rule 4. Translation of OIDs and OADs in naming context S. *Let S's OID be $M : L_1.L_2.\cdots.L_N$, and let the reverse OID be $N-1 : L'_1.L'_2.\cdots.L'_M$.*

If they are transmitted to the parent naming context, *after rewriting the OAD according to Rule 3, undertake the following:*

Translation of OID: *Let the OID be $m : l_1.l_2.\cdots.l_n$.*

If $m > N$, *replace m with $m - N + M$.*

If $m < N$, *replace m with M, and insert $L_1.L_2.\cdots.L_{M-m}$. after ":".*

If $m = N$, *let k be the maximum number that satisfies $l_1 = L'_1, \cdots, l_k = L'_k$. If $l_1 \ne L'_1$, let k be zero. Delete k LIDs after ":", and replace m with $M-k$.*

Translation of OAD: *Translate the OAD in the same way as the OID only if the OAD is not a descendant of S.*

When the OID and the OAD have been transmitted to the parent naming context, they are translated according to Rule 1 in Section 4.

If they are transmitted from the parent naming context, *undertake the following:*

Translation of OID: *Let the OID be* $m : l_1.l_2.\cdots.l_n$.

If $m > M$, *replace* m *with* $m - M + N$.

If $m < M$, *replace* m *with* N, *and insert* $L'_1.L'_2.\cdots.L'_{M-m}.$ *after ":".*

If $m = M$, *let* k *be the maximum number that satisfies* $l_1 = L_1, \cdots, l_k = L_k$. *If* $l_1 \neq L_1$, *let* k *be zero. Delete* k *LIDs after ":," and replace* m *with* $N - k$.

Translation of OAD: *Translate the OAD in the same way as the OID only if the OAD is not a descendant of S.*

After this translation, rewrite OADs according to Rule 3.

Examples: In Figure 3, the naming context S with LID=LAD=12 has migrated and received 23 as its LAD. The OID and the OAD of S are cached ("∗" and "○" marks indicate this) in the same way as in Section 5. S's own OID is 2 : 1.12, and the reverse OID is 1 : 2.23. If a message is sent from object A to F, the receiver's OID and OAD are both 2 : 12.42 in the first place. The naming context manager with LID=LAD=1 then rewrites the OAD 0 : 12.42 as 1 : 2.23.42. When the message arrives at S, the OID is 2 : 1.12.42, and the OAD is 0 : 42. The OID is translated into 0 : 42, which is the internal representation in S. According to Rule 4, the OAD is not translated, because it is a descendant of S, and the message is transmitted to F. If a message is sent from object C to B, the receiver's OID is 2 : 11.32, since B's OID seen from C is independent of the migration of S. S translates the internal representation of OID 1 : 11.32 into the external representation 2 : 1.11.32 according to Rule 4.

In the case of physical migration, there is a problem constructing the OID of the migrating naming context. The OID is also necessary for generating the OID of the parent naming context manager, to which the new OAD is sent at the time of connection. In the case of logical object migration, the OID of the object is translated as the object moves. Physical migration does not allow this procedure. The destination cannot usually be determined at disconnection time.

As regards the format of OIDs, it is enough to construct an OID if the number of steps to the common ancestor and the sequence of LIDs to the original location are known. Thus the host that begins to migrate gets some candidates for OIDs from the ancestors at disconnection time. They are used to notify the OID and the new OAD. To ensure that the acknowledgment of the notification is from the manager of the instantiated naming context, an appropriate authentication method, such as public key authentication, is used. If it succeeds, the OID is determined. Authentication by keys is similar to the use of global unique IDs; however, situations that require authentication are limited in our scheme, and one can use keys

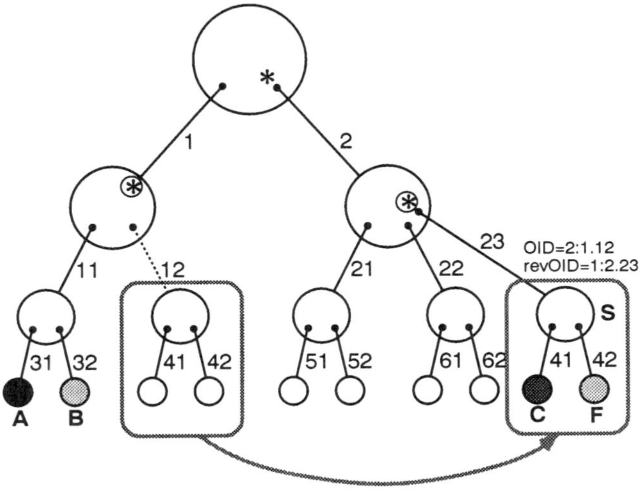

Fig. 3 Migration of naming context. (Circles represent objects or naming contexts. Numbers represent LADs.)

long enough to ignore the chance of incorrect construction of the OID. The chance is essentially small, since authentication is used with candidates for OIDs.

7 Connecting Two Systems

This section describes a method for connecting two systems that adopt the Hierarchy–Relative Naming Scheme. If the tree structure is preserved, connection causes no problems. Two types of connection methods are allowed: letting the root of one system be a child of the naming context of the other system, and making a new root naming context, which becomes the parent of the two old roots. At connection time, the interpretations of OIDs and OADs may be changed simultaneously. Since these correctly represent the original locations and the hints of the current locations, it is not necessary to translate existing OIDs and OADs. Thus the connection operation is local.

If the systems are large enough, it is possible to attempt connection of the same pair of systems at different places. For example, while someone is connecting two systems in Figure 4 by means of Link i, someone else may be trying to connect them by means of Link ii. If both of the connections are allowed, there can be more than two OIDs representing the same object. This may happen if the connection is made by the first method — letting the root of one system (say, A) be a child of the naming context of the other system (say, B). Assuming an appropriate authentication method, the following procedure is used:

Procedure 3. Connection Protocol.

Confirming the Root: *Get the authentication of B's root, and compare it with*

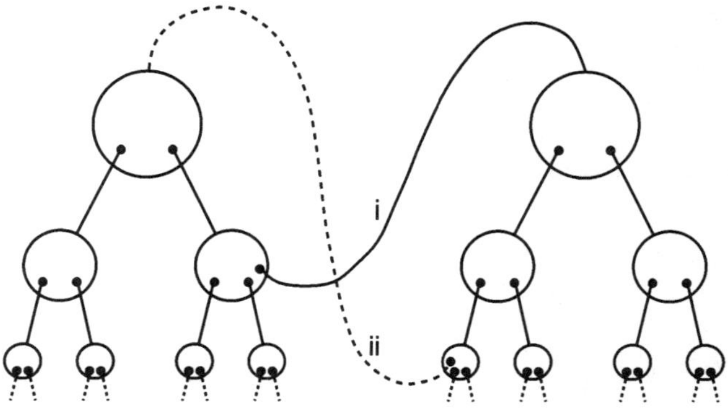

Fig. 4 This case causes a problem. (Circles represent objects or naming contexts.)

that of A's root. If it is different, go to the next step. If it is equal, A and B must already be connected with each other. Send a message to B's root, and confirm that A's root receives it.

Lock: *Lock A's root, and confirm that B's root is not locked. If it is locked, unlock it to avoid deadlocks, wait for the lock of B's root to be released, and try the protocol again.*

Connect: *Assign A's LID in the naming context of B, and connect A's root to B.*

Unlock: *Release the lock of A's root.*

If another connection in which A is allowed to be a child of B's naming context is being tried, locking A's root fails. If another connection is made when A's root is locked, or if another connection in which B is allowed to be a child of A's naming context is being tried, B's root is already locked. In this way, the protocol avoids duplicate connection, like that shown in Figure 4.

To make a connection other than a parent-child one — for example, to make a second connection of two systems — the connected naming contexts have to know each other's OID. In a large-scale distributed system, it is not rare for the OID to be unknown. Even in this case, it can be determined by getting the authentication of ancestors "1:", "2:", "3:", ⋯ and finding a common ancestor.

8 Implementation Problems

The implementation of the Hierarchy-Relative Naming Scheme has problems of variable length OIDs and OADs and translating OIDs and OADs when they are transmitted between naming contexts. This may lead to inefficient implementation, because the naming context manager has to seek messages for all the OIDs and the OADs and has to translate them into new ones that may have different lengths. For assigning host IDs, it is not appropriate to use fixed-size names all over the world, as in the current method of IP addresses. A suitable method for implementing the Hierarchy-Relative Naming Scheme is needed. This section discusses these problems.

Variable-Length OIDs and OADs. OIDs and OADs are used in implementation only when referring to objects between different address spaces. For referring to objects in a program, short and fixed-length IDs (SIDs) are used. An SID is unique within the address space of the program. When an object is instantiated in the address space, only an SID is assigned. If it is known by the objects outside the address space — for instance, as a result of sending its OID as a message argument — an LID is also assigned, and the OID is constructed. If the program refers to an object outside the address space, an SID is assigned to refer to it within the program. The SID of an object is reused if there are no references to it in the address space and the LID is not assigned to it. The size of SIDs is sufficient if different SIDs can be assigned to the objects referred to in one address space.

An SID is implemented as an index of an object table. The table has the addresses of the objects if they are in the same address space. For external objects or objects with external references, the table has their OIDs. Each table entry of an SID has at least one of these and indicates the access method of the object. For communication, a program executes a "send" system call, using SIDs as destinations and arguments. In the system call, the SIDs are translated into OIDs and sent to the receiver's kernel. The kernel translates the OIDs into SIDs for the receiver's address space. If the sender and the receiver are in the same address space, the translation is omitted. If they are in the same host, a more efficient method of translation can be used.

Translation of OIDs and OADs. Except for the OIDs of the sender and the receiver, OIDs in a message are not used on the way to the receiver. Performance can be improved by translating the OIDs in message arguments at the receiver side, not at each naming context the message goes through. The path of the message is recorded for this translation, and the OIDs are translated as described in the third case of Rule 1 in Section 4. This technique also solves the problem of encrypted messages, because the arguments can be decrypted and translated on the receiver side.

Assigning Host IDs. We assume that each host corresponds to one naming context. The method of assigning an OID (that is, a host ID) to each naming context is ideally as follows. The host gets its LAD from the first local network that the host is connected to. The LAD is used as an address in the network. Each packet has LADs as its sender and receiver fields. The OIDs of the sender and the receiver are treated as packet data. If a local network is connected to another (larger) network through a gateway, the local network corresponds to one naming context and gets its LAD from the other network. The LAD is used as an address of the gateway in this (larger) network. It is assumed that the address of the gateway in a local network is known by all the hosts in it. Connections other than parent-child ones are made if necessary. By repeating this procedure, host IDs can be assigned without the need for a single organization in the world assigning IDs. There is no chance of running short of IDs.

However, adaptability to the existing network system of IP connection cannot be neglected. IP addresses are, at this moment, host addresses that are uniquely defined within the world. It is possible to implement the scheme by using IP addresses as LADs. Using the implementation of Virtual Internet Protocol [8] for network communication improves the efficiency.

9 Related Work

The addressing method of the Hierarchy-Relative Naming Scheme is an extension of the Propagating Cache Method in the Virtual Network [8]. The Virtual Network considers migration-transparent communication between mobile hosts. It assumes that a host ID (Virtual Network Address, or VN-Address) is unique within the network. Each host has its own original local network (native network), which is determined by the host ID. The location of a host is indicated by a host address (Physical Network address, or PN-address) with a timestamp, which determines the network address of the current local network. The gateways of native and current networks memorize the relation between the host ID and the host address. Other gateways may cache the relations of host IDs and addresses of the senders of network packets. The interpretations of OIDs and OADs correspond to host IDs and addresses in the Hierarchy-Relative Naming Scheme. Since the rewriting rule is extended by using the hierarchical structure of OIDs and OADs, migration of naming contexts is allowed, corresponding to migration of gateways.

There is another method of giving global names without global management: the Domain Port Model (DPM) [2]. This method does not assume hierarchical structure. It gives global names by specifying the sequences of ports to the next domain. Thus the structure of naming contexts (domains) is flexible. To ensure uniqueness, the path between each pair of domains must be uniquely decided independently of the actual path of message passing. This is realized by the translation rules kept in each domain. The rules can be incomplete, and uniqueness is not always ensured. Though our method assumes a hierarchical structure for the naming contexts, it does not restrict the physical structure. Since most practical systems are hierarchically managed, the advantage of having unique IDs in our method outweighs the restriction that results from this assumption.

Other ways of hierarchical naming are illustrated by GALAXY [6, 7], the DEC global name service [3], and the Stanford design [1]. GALAXY adopts hierarchical symbolic names, using distributed directory management and IDs for identifying objects. The ID consists of the host ID and the local ID, each 64 bits long. The host IDs are assumed to be unique in the world. This is not suitable for our purposes. The DEC global name service adopts absolute paths. Each naming context is called a directory and has a unique directory identifier (DI). Directory translation entries (translation rules) are added for changing the root directory. Since DIs are assumed and changing the root causes global addition of translation rules, this too is unsuitable for our purposes. In the Stanford design, the structure of naming has nothing to do with the location of objects. The name is directly bound to the object. The existence of the name "A/B/C" does not imply the existence of a directory "A/B". Objects have managers, which are addressed by caching. These methods of using multicast or broadcast for cache misses and assuming one root for one system do not suit our purposes.

10 Conclusion

This paper has proposed the Hierarchy-Relative Naming Scheme, which is a way of naming and addressing objects that is suitable for large-scale distributed systems. The scheme has the following characteristics:

- It gives a unique ID to each object.
- Short IDs are used for nearby objects.
- It allows implementation of scalable systems.
- Communication uses only local information.
- It allows object migration.
- It allows mobile hosts and dynamic reconfiguration of networks.

Our scheme separates the representation and the interpretation of object IDs (OIDs) and object addresses (OADs). Relative expressions are used for representations. Using different representations of OIDs and OADs in different naming contexts improves *efficiency*. Local communication can be performed without translation rules, just like communication in conventional naming schemes. The implementation technique can make the cost of variable-length IDs less than expected. This interpretation relates the OIDs and OADs to conventional ones and ensures the *uniqueness* of OIDs. The interpretation is a virtual concept. The global information used for interpretation is never used for implementation. Even in connecting systems, the interpretations of OIDs and OADs are changed simultaneously, while their representations remain unchanged. The connecting operation is local. This leads to *scalability* and is suitable for large-scale and evolving systems. The locality of the operations on OIDs and OADs leads to high *availability* and *fault tolerance*. The hierarchical application of the Propagating Cache Method archives *migration transparency* with respect to object/host migration and network reconfiguration.

Our scheme requires an appropriate method of authentication for reliable communication with mobile hosts and connected subsystems. Since security and authentication are indispensable to practical distributed systems, this requirement is not a restriction. Our scheme allows us to apply large-scale authentication [4] and to determine formally who is relied on in the operation of the systems. We are investigating the problem of security and authentication using this approach. This research is based on the hierarchical naming of objects in the Apertos operating system[7] [9], and the scheme has been implemented in that system. We are going to evaluate it and make a practical implementation.

Acknowledgments. We would like to express our gratitude to Dr. Mario Tokoro (Keio University and Sony CSL) for supervising our research. We would also like to thank Dr. Atsushi Mitsuzawa (NTT) and the other members of Sony CSL for their valuable advice.

[7] It was originally called the Muse Operating System.

References

[1] Cheriton, D. R. and Mann, P.: Decentralizing a Global Naming Service for Efficient Fault-tolerant Access, *ACM Transactions on Computer Systems*, Vol. 7, No. 2 (1989), pp. 147–183.

[2] Harada, Y. and Miyamoto, E.: An Open Distributed Language Kamui-C — Introduced Open Systems Naming Model, *Proceedings of 8th Conference of Japan Society for Software Science and Technology*, September 1991 (in Japanese).

[3] Lampson, B.: Designing a Global Name Service, *Proceedings of 5th ACM Symposium on Principles of Distributed Computing*, August 1986, pp. 1–10.

[4] Lampson, B., Abadi, M., Burrows, M., and Wobber, E.: Authentication in Distributed Systems: Theory and Practice, *Proceedings of the 13th ACM Symposium on Operating System Principles*, October 1991.

[5] Mullender, S. J., van Rossum, G., Tanenbaum, A. S., van Renesse, R., and van Staveren, H.: Amoeba, A Distributed Operating System for the 1990s, *IEEE Computer*, Vol. 23, No. 5 (1990), pp. 44–53.

[6] Sinha, P. K., Maekawa, M., Shimizu, K., Jia, X., Ashihara, H., Utsunomiya, N., Park, K. S., and Nakano, H.: The Galaxy Distributed Operating System, *IEEE Computer*, Vol. 24, No. 8 (1991), pp. 34–41.

[7] Sinha, P. K., Shimizu, K., Utsunomiya, N., Nakano, H., and Maekawa, M.: Network-Transparent Object Naming and Locating in Distributed Operating Systems, *Technical Report 89-033*, Department of Information Science Faculty of Science, University of Tokyo, November 1989.

[8] Teraoka, F., Yokote, Y., and Tokoro, M.: A Network Architecture Providing Host Migration Transparency, *Proceedings of ACM SIGCOMM'91*, September 1991.

[9] Yokote, Y., Mitsuzawa, A., Teraoka, F., Fujinami, N., and Tokoro, M.: Continuous-Grained Objects in the Muse Operating System, *Technical Report SCSL-TM-91-008*, Sony Computer Science Laboratory Inc., February 1991.

Initially published in "Computer Software", Vol. 10, No. 3, in Japanese.

Nobuhisa Fujinami
Sony Computer Science Laboratory Inc.
Takanawa Muse Building, 3–14–13 Higashi-gotanda
Shinagawa-ku, Tokyo, 141 Japan

Yasuhiko Yokote
Sony Computer Science Laboratory Inc.
Takanawa Muse Building, 3–14–13 Higashi-gotanda
Shinagawa-ku, Tokyo, 141 Japan

WINCS: A Programming Supporting System for Developing Window Control Programs

Takeshi Imanaka Norio Fujimoto Kuniaki Uehara
Jun'ichi Toyoda

Summary. WINCS(WINdow Class Synthesizer) synthesizes programs for window manipulation in the object-oriented language ESP (Extended Self-contained Prolog), selecting and organizing built-in classes to meet users' requirements. Built-in classes are provided to control the windows in ESP, which runs on a Prolog machine, MELCOM PSI. Although ESP has rich and useful built-in classes, many constraints must be considered while consulting the manual in making use of these classes. To solve this problem, WINCS not only retrieves classes that meet a user's requirements but also attempts whenever possible to modify incorrect or incomplete parts of the user's requirements automatically. If this is not possible, WINCS advises and helps the user to correct or complete the requirement. These facilities of WINCS are realized by employing a truth maintenance system (TMS) proposed by Doyle.

1 Introduction

In current programming environments, various library modules and subroutine programs are provided for users' convenience and can be used freely. Particularly as a result of the spread of workstations with bitmap displays, the importance of window systems is being gradually recognized, and many library modules for controlling window interfaces have been developed as parts of programming environments [12]. These library modules control input/output data, define the shape of windows, and so on. Since window control and the object-oriented paradigm are well matched, many window systems offer library modules as classes in terms of the object-oriented paradigm and make it possible to use them by inheritance. Hereafter, we call these library modules simply window classes. For example, X-Toolkit in the X-window system, a window system in ESP (Extended Self-contained Prolog), and a window system in the Lisp-based language Flavor all adopt the object-oriented paradigm and offer many window classes [2, 6, 13].

We can classify these systems into two groups according to the concept of inheritance. The first group includes systems employing the single-inheritance paradigm, such as X-Toolkit. The second includes systems employing the multiple-inheritance paradigm, such as ESP and Flavor. Window systems that employ the single-inheritance paradigm have some advantages and some drawbacks in using

ISBN 0-12-037105-7

the inheritance facility. One of the most notable advantages is that it is very simple to handle superclasses in designing a new class. However, this simplicity has the disadvantage that if a user wants to build a class X that inherits from classes A and B, he must define two hierarchical inheritance relations. For example, X can inherit from both A and B if A is established as a superclass of B and B as a superclass of X. To make matters worse, if the user wants to build a new class that inherits from B and not from A, another class that has the features of B and inherits nothing from A must be newly defined. In X-Toolkit, completely organized classes are only provided for users in order to avoid the problems discussed above. Therefore, what users can customize is limited to a small part of window classes, and their various requirements may often be rejected in X-Toolkit.

Window systems that employ the multiple-inheritance paradigm also have some advantages and disadvantages. One of the most important advantages is the flexibility of inheritance. In general, the user's requirement includes many window attributes (e.g., graphic, output, and label). In ESP, for example, users can make a window control class by inheriting from different window classes, each of which has its corresponding required attribute. The window control classes are defined by a user in order to control (e.g., move, resize, or delete) window interfaces. In ESP, the user's application program can move windows simply by sending a message requesting movement to the window control class. Unfortunately, window systems that employ the multiple-inheritance paradigm have the following disadvantages:

1. There are so many available window classes that users may be confused about how to select the appropriate one.
2. Users have to pay attention to a lot of constraints on inheriting from two or more window classes.

We are sure that window systems employing the multiple-inheritance paradigm will be much more useful if these problems are solved. To this end, we have developed WINCS (WINdow Class Synthesizer), which helps users to build window control classes in ESP. WINCS is now running on a MELCOM PSI II under the SIMPOS operating system.

To operate WINCS, a user first selects appropriate items on a menu provided by WINCS. For example, if the user wants to control a sashed and labeled window, he should select items for these attributes. When the attributes are selected, WINCS retrieves appropriate window classes corresponding to the attributes and synthesizes a new class that inherits from these classes. If the user's requirements do not conform to the constraints on the window system in ESP, WINCS tries to modify the inappropriate part of the requirement or advises the user to do so by using a truth maintenance system (TMS). A TMS is a system for maintaining truth in a knowledge base of artificial intelligence (AI) systems.

2 Synthesis of Window Control Classes in ESP

2.1 Programming environment in ESP

First, let us consider an example of a simple window control class:

```
class my_window has
     nature
                    as_output,
                    as_graphics,
                    inferior_window;
end.
```

The class "my_window" has three superclasses that are described under the label "nature." The superclasses "as_output," "as_graphics," and "inferior_window" are designed to output data, draw graphics, and control inferior windows, respectively. If a message for drawing a circle,

:draw_circle(♯my_window, X1, Y1, R, 1, solid, set),

is sent to the class "my_window," a circle specified by the arguments will be drawn on the window because the class "my_window" inherits from the class "as_graphics." In ESP, since there are about forty available window classes, users can build many kinds of window control class by combining these window classes.

2.2 Problems in making window control classes in ESP

To build window control classes efficiently, programmers should use window classes. Furthermore, they should know which window class is appropriate and how it can be used. In other words, programmers must make a great effort to acquire knowledge for specifying appropriate window classes, since there are so many window classes that a general programmer cannot learn all of them. To make matters worse, window classes must be identified not by function, but by name in programming. As a result, users must select appropriate window classes by consulting a large number of manuals and finding the class names.

Although combinations of many window classes enable users to build various window control classes, users have to pay attention to constraints on these combinations. The constraints are classified into two groups, called incompleteness and conflict. Incompleteness means that some classes must be inherited with other specified classes. Conflict means that some classes cannot be inherited with other specified classes. In this paper, if features of a class A (e.g., methods, and class variables) are inherited by another class B, we simply say that A is inherited by B. One example of a constraint is that the window class "as_menu" for the menu attribute must be inherited with the window class "as_mouse_input" for the mouse-inputting attribute. This constraint is classified as belonging to the category of incompleteness. On the other hand, "as_menu" cannot be inherited with the window class "as_graphics" for the graphic attribute. This constraint is classified as belonging to the category of conflict. Furthermore, though "as_menu" must be inherited with "as_mouse_input," "as_mouse_input" does not need to be inherited with "as_menu." As these examples show, constraints are so complicated that general users find it very troublesome to build a correct and complete window control class.

There is another kind of constraint on the order of inherited superclasses For example, the window class "with_label," which puts a label on a window, must be inherited before the window class "inferior_window" for handling inferior windows. This means that when a user defines a sequence of superclasses for building a window control class, "inferior_window" must be preceded by "with_label." As these examples show, the user must make a great effort to take account of all the constraints on window classes.

3 Outline of WINCS

Synthesis of window control classes is carried out in three phases in WINCS (see Figure 1) [3, 4]. The first phase is called the input phase. In this phase, a user inputs a requirement by selecting items on menu windows provided by WINCS. Each item corresponds to a window attribute, such as graphic, labeled, or sashed. When the user has input his requirement, WINCS will retrieve appropriate window classes for the required attributes. To do this, we have stored Prolog facts that map window attributes to their corresponding window classes in WINCS [9].

The second phase consists of two processes. The first is to detect incompleteness or conflict in the set of retrieved classes. The second is to revise the user's requirement if it includes incompleteness or conflict. If the requirement is incomplete, and if a way of supplementing it is identified by TMS, WINCS supplies the missing window classes. If a way of supplementing it cannot be identified, or if the user's requirement includes conflict, WINCS starts to revise the requirement by interacting with the user. To allow this, we have extracted all the constraints from the ESP manual and stored them in WINCS as TMS nodes.

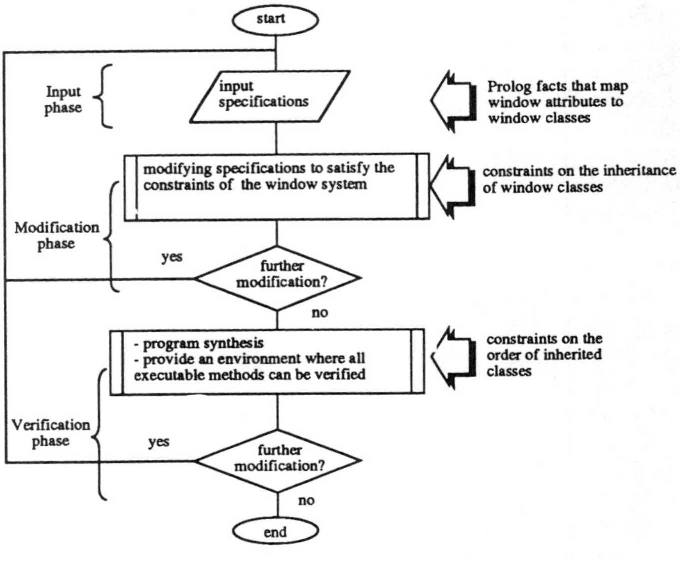

Fig. 1 Flowchart of the execution of WINCS

In the third phase, WINCS puts the retrieved classes in order by considering the constraints and synthesizes the window control classes. This phase also enables the user to activate all available methods for verifying the synthesized window control class. That is, the user can verify whether or not the synthesized window control class works correctly. To allow this, we have stored Prolog facts that map each window class to its available methods.

As shown in Figure 1, the user can go back to the first phase (input phase) at the end of either the second phase (modification phase) or the third phase (verification phase). Through these phases, all that the user needs to do is to select items on menu windows provided by WINCS. As a result, users need not consult manuals anymore, thanks to WINCS. WINCS is especially useful for novice users, but even expert users can make use of it, because they cannot usually keep in mind the contents of the entire manual.

4 Implementation

We will here discuss three kinds of TMS nodes that play an important role in WINCS from the beginning to the end of each phase. The three kinds are preconditions, hypotheses, and contradictions. In WINCS, preconditions, which are always true in a TMS, are employed to represent the constraints on the window system. Hypotheses, which are interchangable between true and false in a TMS, are employed to represent the selection of the window classes to be inherited. Contradictions, which a TMS tries to keep permanently false, are employed to represent constraints on window classes. By using a TMS, WINCS can both discover incompatibility with the constraints in users' requirements and advise users to modify their requirements. The facility for finding contradictions in a TMS is applied to discover incompatibility in the user's requirement. The facility for detecting culprits in a TMS is applied to advise the user to modify the requirement. The advice that WINCS can give consists of showing both alternatives and their explanations. Furthermore, since a hypothetical node can be added to a TMS at any time, WINCS can communicate with the user to revise the requirement step by step.

In WINCS, TMS nodes are represented in terms of Prolog facts as follows:

node_tbl(id, name, supporting_list, in_or_out).

The argument "id" identifies the node. The argument "name" represents the name of this node. Each TMS node has its own state, which is either "in" or "out." The state "in" means that the node is now regarded as true. On the other hand, the state "out" means that the node is not regarded as true. The third argument, "supporting_list," represents all the conditions for determining whether or not the node is to be true. A node whose supporting list is "sl(`In_list`, `Out_list`)" comes to be regarded as true if and only if all the nodes in `In_list` are regarded as true and all the nodes in `Out_list` are not regarded as true [1]. Hereafter, when a node A has the state "in" (or "out"), we simply state that the node A is "in" (or "out").

4.1 How users' requirements are acquired

In the input phase of WINCS, a user can input a requirement by individually selecting items corresponding to window attributes on the menu windows. Since

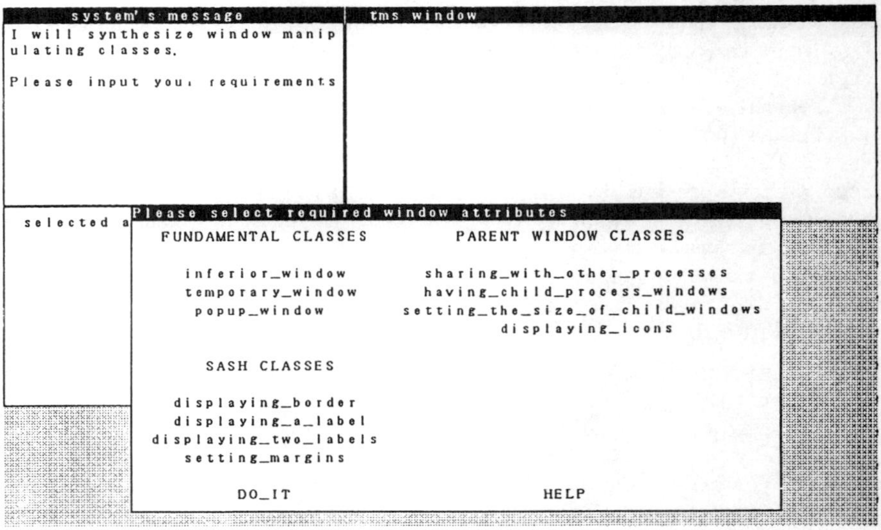

Fig. 2 Menu window for the input phase of WINCS

there are so many window attributes in ESP, we have classified the attributes into four groups and put them into each menu window. Four menu windows are thus provided for input of the user's requirement. Figure 2 shows an example of a menu window; this window is intended to make it easy for a user to input a requirement. Furthermore, WINCS provides a help utility that enables the user to receive explanations about items on the menu window. For example, the user can receive an explanation about "inferior_window" by selecting both "inferior_window" and "help" (see Figure 3).

Once the user has selected all window attributes, WINCS retrieves the window classes corresponding to the selected attributes. To retrieve appropriate window classes, WINCS makes use of Prolog facts that map window attributes to their corresponding window classes. An example of a Prolog fact is as follows:

class_attribute('having_child_process_windows', as_superior).

By using the above Prolog fact, if a user selects an item for having child process windows, WINCS can retrieve the appropriate window class "as_superior." After retrieving the appropriate window class, WINCS generates the following two TMS nodes:

node_tbl($s1$, select(as_superior), [sl([],[$s2$])], in),
node_tbl($s2$, not_select(as_superior), [], out).

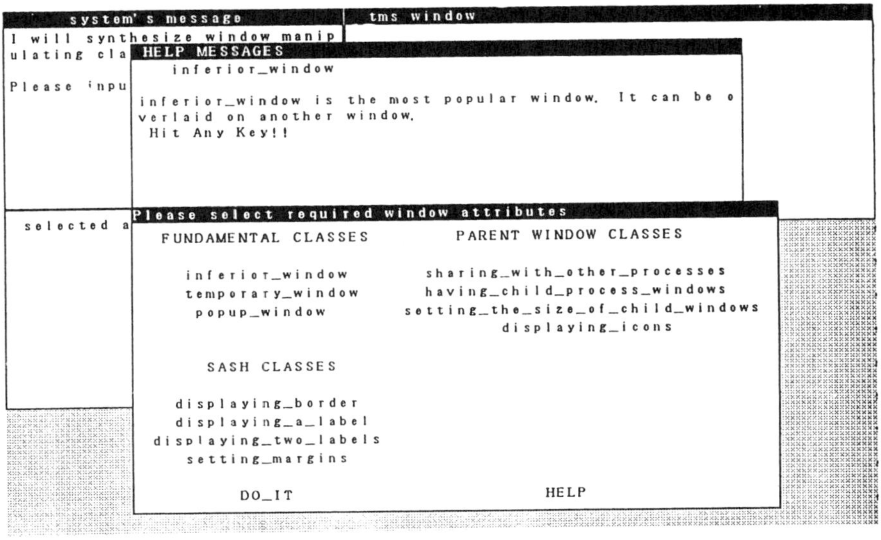

Fig. 3 Example of an explanation of a window attribute

The node $s1$ represents that the window class "as_superior" should be inherited as a superclass to meet the requirement. The node $s2$ represents that the window class "as_superior" should not be inherited. At this time, since the node $s1$ is "in," "as_superior" is regarded as an appropriate class to be inherited. The node $s2$ is "out," because the node with no support must be "out" in a TMS. On the other hand, the node $s1$ is "in," because the node $s2$ in `Out_list` is "out."

As was mentioned above, when a user selects a certain item on the menu, WINCS will first generate two TMS nodes. One is a node denoting that the window class for the selected item is expected to be inherited. The other is a node denoting that the window class for the selected item is not expected to be inherited. Next, WINCS adds a supporting list "[]" to the latter node, and makes it "out." Finally, it adds a supporting list that includes the latter node in `Out_list` to the former node and makes it "in." As a result, the following two TMS nodes "A" and "B" are generated for each of the user's selected items:

node_tbl(A, select(a window class for the selected item), [sl([], [B])], in),
node_tbl(B, not_select(a window class for the selected item), [], out).

Furthermore, the following pair of TMS nodes is generated for each unselected item:

node_tbl(A, select(a window class for the selected item), [], out),
node_tbl(B, not_select(a window class for the selected item), [sl([], [A])]], in).

For example, if a user selects an item for menu windows and does not select an item for mouse input, WINCS generates the following set of TMS nodes:

node_tbl($s1$, select(as_menu), [sl([], [$s2$])], in),
node_tbl($s2$, not_select(as_menu), [], out),
node_tbl($s3$, select(as_mouse_input), [], out),
node_tbl($s4$, not_select(as_mouse_input), [sl([], [$s3$])], in).

In WINCS, there are defaults for window attributes. For example, if the user does not specify the divisible window attribute, WINCS selects an indivisible window attribute by default. A set of TMS nodes for the defaults has been stored in WINCS in advance. The above default is described as follows:

node_tbl($t1$, construct(one_window), [sl([$t4$], [])], in),
node_tbl($t2$, construct(shared_window), [sl([], [$t1$])], out),
node_tbl($t3$, select(as_superior), [], out),
node_tbl($t4$, not_select(as_superior), [sl([], [$t3$])], in).

The node $t1$ denotes that WINCS plans to build a window class for indivisible windows. The node $t2$ represents that WINCS plans to retrieve a window class for divisible windows. Since these nodes are stored in WINCS, a window class for indivisible windows will be inherited if the user does not specify the item for divisible windows. As a result, these nodes work as a default.

WINCS currently stores only this type of default. Although new defaults can easily be added simply by adding TMS nodes, overly complicated defaults confuse a user inputting a requirement. Therefore, the addition of complicated defaults requires great attention.

4.2 Modification of users' requirements by using a TMS

Since the modification of a certain part of a user's requirement may make another part incompatible with the constraints, the modification phase of WINCS must take account of the whole requirement and all the constraints. WINCS employs a TMS because of its ability to manage all the TMS nodes.

In WINCS the selection of window classes is represented as hypotheses. All constraints are represented as preconditions. Thanks to the representation, WINCS can advise the user to modify the requirement by activating the TMS, which tries to maintain the truth of all hypotheses and preconditions.

4.2.1 Basic ideas

When the user's requirement does not conform to the constraint, WINCS will try to modify the requirement. For example, suppose that a certain requirement does not include a mouse input attribute, but includes a menu window attribute. This requirement does not conform to the constraint that a window class for a menu attribute must be inherited with a window class for a mouse input attribute. In this case, WINCS adds a window class for mouse input, because this addition does not influence either the user's selection or the defaults of WINCS.

However, there are some cases in which WINCS cannot identify a window class to be added. For example, suppose that any window class belonging to a group called "fundamental classes" is not selected in a certain requirement. The requirement does not conform to the constraint that one of the fundamental classes "inferior_window," "popup_window," and "temporary_window" must be inherited. However, WINCS cannot identify which window class should be inherited. In this case, WINCS asks the user to select one of these classes.

On the other hand, it may happen that rejection of the user's selection or cancellation of the default is required. In this case, WINCS proposes all alternative modifications and demonstrates their results. For example, suppose that the two window classes "as_output" and "as_menu" are selected in a user's requirement. This requirement does not conform to the constraint that these two classes cannot be inherited together. WINCS proposes three ways of modifying the requirement. The first is that the user should reject a window attribute for "as_output." The second is that the user should reject a window attribute for "as_menu." The third is that the user should select a new window attribute for a divisible window and embody "as_menu" and "as_output" in different areas of the same single window.

After constructing these alternatives, WINCS demonstrates their results. Suppose that the user's requirement also includes a window attribute for a window class "as_single_select" that must be inherited with "as_menu." In this case, WINCS advises the user that he must also reject the window attribute for "as_single_select" if he tries to reject the window attribute for "as_menu."

4.2.2 Representation of constraints in a TMS

Constraints on the window system in ESP are represented as contradiction nodes in a TMS. These constraints are classified into two groups. One involves constraints for adding appropriate window classes to the user's requirement. The other involves constraints for discarding some attributes from the user's selection. Constraints for adding appropriate window classes are represented by contradiction nodes that come to be true when the requirement is incomplete. When a contradiction node comes to be true, the TMS tries to detect all causes and to keep the contradiction node "out." By making use of this facility, WINCS can determine in what respect the requirement is insufficient and add appropriate window classes.

For example, two constraints for adding appropriate window classes are described by nodes $n11$ and $n12$ below:

```
node_tbl(s1, select(inferior_window, [sl(In_list,Out_list)], Status),
node_tbl(s2, not_select(inferior_window, [sl(In_list,Out_list)], Status),
node_tbl(s3, select(popup_window, [sl(In_list, Out_list)], Status),
node_tbl(s4, not_select(popup_window, [sl(In_list, Out_list)], Status),
node_tbl(s5, select(temporary_window, [sl(In_list, Out_list)], Status),
node_tbl(s6, not_select(temporary_window, [sl(In_list, Out_list)], Status),
node_tbl(s7, select(as_mouse_input, [sl(In_list, Out_list)], Status),
node_tbl(s8, not_select(as_mouse_input, [sl(In_list, Out_list)], Status),
node_tbl(s9, select(as_menu, [sl(In_list, Out_list)], Status),
node_tbl(s10, not_select(as_menu, [sl(In_list, Out_list)], Status),
node_tbl(n11, contradiction, [sl([s2, s4, s6], [])], Status),
```

node_tbl($n12$, contradiction, [sl([$s8$, $s9$], [])], Status).

The constraint $n11$ says that one of the fundamental classes must be inherited. The constraint $n12$ says that "as_menu" must be inherited with "as_mouse_input." The TMS nodes $s1$–$s10$ describe the selection of window classes in the user's requirement.

The node $n11$ comes to be "in" when all the nodes in `In_list` "[$s2$, $s4$, $s6$]" are "in." In other words, the node $n11$ comes to be "in" when no fundamental class is selected to satisfy the user's requirement. WINCS can determine in what respect the requirement is incomplete by checking whether the contradiction node is "in" or "out." The node $n12$ describes the more complicated constraint that "as_menu" must be inherited with "as_mouse_input," but "as_mouse_input" need not be inherited with "as_menu." This node thus comes to be "in" only when "as_menu" is selected and "as_mouse_input" is not selected.

The following TMS nodes show an example of a constraint for discarding some attributes in a user's requirement. This constraint says that "as_menu" cannot be inherited with "as_output." The node $n5$ comes to be "in" when all nodes in the `In_list` "[$s1$,$s3$]" are "in." Thus WINCS can determine the conflict by checking whether $n5$ is "in" or "out."

node_tbl($s1$,select(as_menu),[sl(`In_list`, `Out_list`)],Status),
node_tbl($s2$,not_select(as_menu),[sl(`In_list`, `Out_list`)],Status),
node_tbl($s3$,select(as_output),[sl(`In_list`, `Out_list`)],Status),
node_tbl($s4$,not_select(as_output),[sl(`In_list`, `Out_list`)],Status),
node_tbl($n5$,contradiction,[sl([$s1$,$s3$],[])],Status).

4.2.3 How to modify a user's requirements so that they conform to all constraints

To clarify the discussion, suppose that a certain user selected window attributes for "as_output," "as_menu," and "as_single_select" and did not select window attributes for "as_superior" and "as_mouse_input." In this case, the following TMS nodes would be generated in WINCS:[1]

(Example 1)
node_tbl($t1$, construct(one_window), [sl([$t4$],[])],in),
node_tbl($t2$, construct(shared_window), [sl([],[$t1$])],out),
node_tbl($t3$, select(as_superior), [],out),
node_tbl($t4$, not_select(as_superior), [sl([],[$t3$]],in),
node_tbl($s1$, select(as_output), [sl([],[$s2$])],in),
node_tbl($s2$, not_select(as_output), [],out),
node_tbl($s3$, select(as_menu), [sl([],[$s4$])],in),
node_tbl($s4$, not_select(as_menu), [],out),
node_tbl($s5$, select(as_mouse_input), [],out),
node_tbl($s6$, not_select(as_mouse_input), [sl(sl([],[$s5$])],in),
node_tbl($s7$, select(as_single_select), [sl([],[$s8$])],in),
node_tbl($s8$, not_select(as_single_select), [],out),

[1] For clarity, some minor nodes are omitted from this example.

node_tbl($n9$, contradiction, [sl([$s3$,$s6$],[])],in),
node_tbl($n10$, contradiction, [sl([$t1$,$s1$,$s3$],[])],in),
node_tbl($n11$, contradiction, [sl([$s4$,$s7$],[])],out).

The nodes $s1$, $s3$, $s5$, and $s7$ denote that the window classes "as_output," "as_menu," "as_mouse_input," and "as_single_select" (a window class for controlling a menu window in which only one item can be selected) should be inherited to meet the user's requirement. On the other hand, the nodes $s2$, $s4$, $s6$, and $s8$ denote that the window classes for those window attributes that should not be inherited.

In Example 1, the contradiction node $n9$ comes to be "in" because both the nodes in `In_list`, $s3$ and $s6$, are "in." To change this contradiction to "out," the TMS searches for the nodes that support the contradiction and whose `Out_lists` are not "[]" (we call them culprit nodes).[2] In the example above, the TMS can discover two culprit nodes, $s3$ and $s6$. It then plans to change one of these two nodes to "out." In this case, if WINCS changes $s3$ to "out," WINCS must reject the user's selection. On the other hand, if WINCS changes $s6$ to "out," it does not need to reject the user's selection. Consequently, WINCS chooses the latter course.

In the TMS, changing $s6$ to "out" requires the following procedure.[3] First, $s5$ in the `Out_list` of $s6$ is selected. Next, the supporting list of $s5$ is updated by inserting the other culprit, $s3$, as follows:

node_tbl($s5$, select(as_mouse_input), [sl([$s3$],[])], in).

This update changes both the node $s6$ and $n9$ to "out." Inserting $s3$ into the supporting list of $s5$ involves changing $s5$ because $s3$ is kept. In other words, the selection of "as_menu" causes the selection of "as_mouse_input". As a result, if the selection of "as_menu" is rejected later (i.e., if node $s3$ is changed to "out"), selection of "as_mouse_input" will also be rejected automatically.

Furthermore, the contradiction node $n10$ also becomes "in" in the example above. This contradiction is caused by the fact that "as_output" and "as_menu" are selected and "as_superior" is not. Similarly, the TMS searches for culprit nodes and finds three nodes, $t4$, $s1$, and $s3$. Unfortunately, any change of one of these nodes to "out" causes rejection of the user's selection or cancellation of the defaults. In this case, WINCS cannot identify a single solution for changing $n10$ to "out." Therefore it provides the user with all the alternatives and demonstrates what will happen if the user adopts them, as follows:

□If node $t4$ is changed to "out"
-nodes changed from "out" to "in" → $t2$, $t3$
-nodes changed from "in" to "out" → $t1$, $t4$, $n10$
-explanation →
a window attribute "menu" and a window attribute "output" are embodied separately on one divisible window.

[2] In WINCS, the contradiction nodes are changed to "out" by selecting or rejecting window classes. Therefore, the culprit nodes are restricted to nodes whose names start with "select" or "not_select."

[3] In the running system, more complicated nodes named "nogood" would be generated. However, these nodes are omitted here for clarity.

-rejection of the user's selection → no
-activated contradiction →
the window attributes "menu" and "output" cannot be embodied in one indivisible window.($n10$)

□If node $s1$ is changed to "out"
-nodes changed from "out" to "in" → $s2$
-nodes changed from "in" to "out" → $s1$, $n10$
-explanation → reject the window attribute "output"
-rejection of the user's selection →
reject the selection of the window attribute "output"
-activated contradiction →
the window attributes "menu" and "output" cannot be embodied in one indivisible window($n10$)

□If node $s3$ is changed to "out"
-nodes changed from "out" to "in" → $s4$, $n11$
-nodes changed from "in" to "out" → $s3$, $n10$
-explanation → reject the window attribute "menu"
-rejection of the user's selection →
reject the selection of the window attribute "menu"
-activated contradiction →
the window attributes "menu" and "output" cannot be embodied in one indivisible window($n10$)
◇Furthermore, the contradiction node $n11$ becomes "in," and node $s7$ must be changed to "out"
-nodes changed from "out" to "in" → $s8$
-nodes changed from "in" to "out" → $s7$, n11
-explanation → reject the window attribute "single select"
-rejection of the user's selection →
reject the selection of the window attribute "single select"
-activated contradiction →
the window attribute "single select" must be selected with the window attribute "menu."

In this case, changing one of the three nodes to "out" is the solution. As shown above, thanks to inheriting divisible windows (i.e., cancelling the default), the user's requirement can be modified without any rejection if the first alternative is adopted. If the second is adopted, the user's selection of the window attribute "output" will be rejected. If the third alternative is adopted, not only the selection of the window attribute "menu," but also the selection of "single select," will be rejected. All the above alternatives are demonstrated by WINCS, shown in Figure 4. The demonstration includes information about the rejection of the window attributes, the constraint that causes this modification, the effects of the modification, and so on. A scrollbar is available to help users to consult the system about details of the alternatives.

4.3 Synthesis of window control classes and providing an environment for verification

Synthesis of window control classes must take account of constraints on the order of inherited window classes. In order to provide an environment where all executable methods can be verified, we have stored information on mapping from inherited

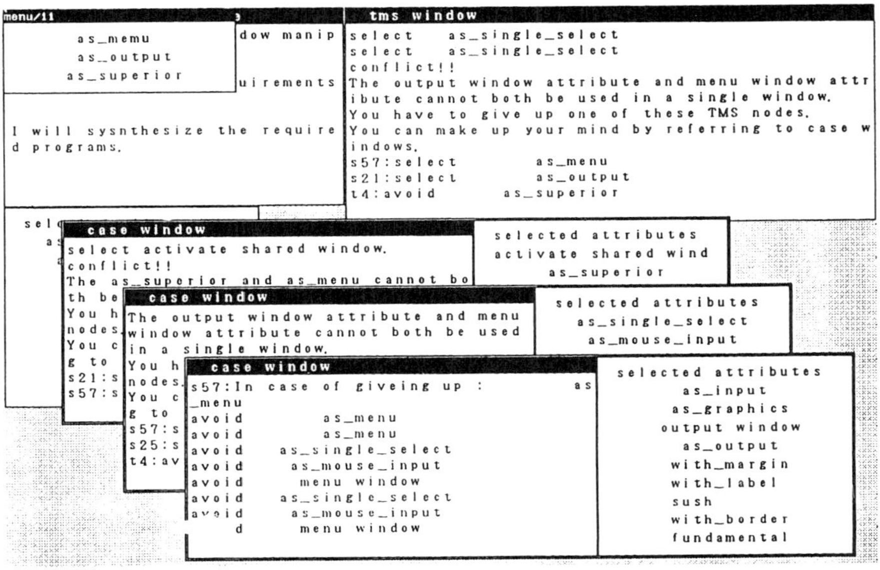

Fig. 4 Demonstration of alternative modification

classes to executable methods in WINCS.

We extracted all the constraints on the order of inherited window classes from the ESP manual [6] and stored them in WINCS as a set of Prolog facts. The format of the Prolog facts requires that the window class in the first argument be inherited before any window class in the second argument and be inherited after any window class in the third argument. For example, the constraint on "as_output" is as follows:

```
order(as_output, [with_label, ...], [inferior_window, ...]).
```

By consulting Prolog facts, WINCS can order window classes. In the case of inheriting from "as_output," "inferior_window," and "with_label," WINCS can easily determine that these classes must be combined with "with_label," "as_output," and "inferior_window," in this order. Figure 5 shows the case in which the user adopts the first alternative modification of Example 1 in Section 4.2.3 and adds some window attributes (e.g., "label"). Thanks to the multiple-inheritance facility in ESP, the source code of the window control class seems to be simple. The program shown in Figure 5 contains three classes, because it uses "as_superior" to divide one window into two sub-windows. Therefore three classes are needed: one for a parent process window and two for child process windows.

When the window control classes have been synthesized, WINCS retrieves all executable methods for the inherited window classes and presents them to users.

```
%%psi000::>sys>user>wincs>wincs_eng>finished.esp.45

class my_window1 has
nature
        with_margin,
        with_label,
        with_border,
        as_superior,
        as_input_buffer,
        inferior_window;
end.

class my_window2 has
nature
        with_margin,
        with_label,
        with_border,
        as_scroll,
        as_output,
        as_graphics,
        as_markers,
        as_input,
        as_mouse_input,
        inferior_window;
end.

class my_window3 has
nature
        with_margin,
        with_label,
        with_border,
        as_menu,
        as_single_select,
        as_mouse_input,
        inferior_window;
end.
```

Fig. 5 Synthesized window control class

To retrieve executable methods, WINCS make use of Prolog facts. The format of Prolog facts is as follows: the first argument is a window class, the second argument is the name of a method, and the third argument is a way of activating the method. For example, one of the Prolog facts for " as_graphics" is

class_method(as_graphics, draw_line, [5, object, x1, y1, x2, y2]).

The Prolog fact says that the method "draw_line" is executable when "as_graphics" is inherited. The third argument means that the method can be activated when "as_graphics" receives the following message:

":draw_line(object name, x coordinate of starting point, y coordinate of starting point, x coordinate of ending point, y coordinate of ending point)."

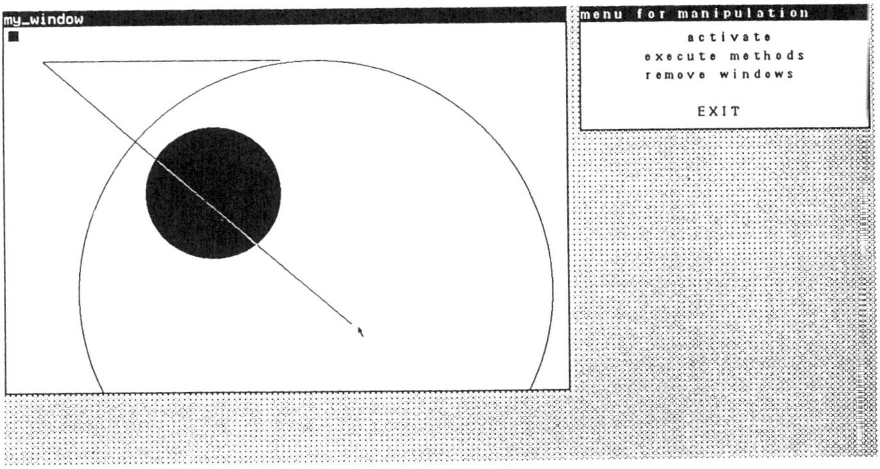

Fig. 6 Example of an execution

After retrieving all executable methods, WINCS presents them in a menu window. If the user selects one of the methods on the menu, WINCS will try to activate the selected method. Figure 6 shows the result after selection of the two methods "draw_line" and "draw_circle."

5 Discussion

As we have shown, WINCS can be regarded as a computer-aided programming supporting system. To evaluate the usefulness of WINCS quantitatively, its programming efficiency should be compared with that of conventional programming. However, conventional programming requires programs to be typed, programming manuals to be consulted, and so on. Therefore it is too obvious to require discussion here that WINCS provides a higher degree of efficiency in programming window control classes than does conventional programming. Instead, we will compare WINCS with related systems to evaluate it qualitatively and discuss its completeness.

5.1 Comparison with related systems

User Interface Management Systems (UIMS) were developed to achieve a goal similar to that of WINCS. Examples include the system developed at Mitsubishi Electric Co. [11]; Canae, which was developed at Nihon Electric Co. [10]; MU, developed at Hitachi [14]; Concord, developed at Canon [7], and so on. The first system introduced a knowledge base and the concept of analogy in order to provide users with easy operations. Canae utilizes a script library that includes characteristic operations for each window to help users. MU provides users with graphic editors for handling windows with infixed format. Concord provides users with a new language called Caisl for specifying interfaces declaratively. As was mentioned above, these systems all have different advantages.

However, they are all based on the assumption that users can build a satisfactory interface by combining usable components that have already been provided in the system. For this reason, they work very effectively in situations with the following features:

1. The kinds of usable interface can be specified explicitly in advance.
2. Users' requirements are not greatly varied, so sufficient components can be stored.

In MU, for example, graphic interface components that have the shape of a thermometer, an ammeter, or the like are provided as useful components in advance.

In comparison with these systems, WINCS seems to have window classes with more micro-level attributes. The number of combinations of window classes in ESP is much larger than that of components of the UIMS. As a result, it is difficult to provide macro components in WINCS. Therefore, WINCS users have to specify the details of window attributes and define a graphic interface by themselves. In other words, WINCS users can specify all the types of window attributes provided by window systems in ESP. Consequently, they can design windows more freely than UIMS users. This feature of WINCS is very important, for the following reasons:

1. General users cannot easily remember or grasp what can be done and what cannot be done in a window system.
2. Users often tend to change their original requirements because of the constraints of the window system.
3. Users sometimes discover fascinating window attributes that were not originally contained in their requirements.

Moreover, users sometimes repeat the process of modification and verification until they are satisfied with the synthesized window control classes. To support this process, WINCS provides a facility for saving TMS nodes in a file. By loading TMS nodes from this file, users can reuse previous designs. Thanks to the TMS, a previously modified requirement may be recovered if a subsequent modification removes the cause of the previous modification in WINCS.

Furthermore, since WINCS does not spoil any advantages of the window system and since it removes difficulty in handling constraints, it keeps all the advantages of the object-oriented paradigm—for example,

1. Application programs can drive window control classes simply by sending messages to them.
2. The program size of synthesized classes is very small.

The first advantage enables users to understand how to use the synthesized class easily. The second advantage enables them to add some methods to the synthesized class without any difficulty. In addition, WINCS can be used to define components of a UIMS, because users can define detailed specifications of the interface components.

5.2 Completeness of WINCS

In this paper, we have defined the completeness of WINCS as "all necessary window classes are definitely retrieved as superclasses." There are two types of requirements that users may input to window class synthesizers. One is window attribute (e.g., "menu," and "graphic") and the other is method (e.g., "write circle," and "output string"). Since WINCS can handle only the former type of requirement, the completeness should be discussed in a situation where a user specifies window attributes. We will discuss the latter type of requirement in a future publication.

The menu items provided by WINCS correspond to all the window attributes that can be handled in ESP. Furthermore, the necessary window class for each attribute is easily identified by consulting the ESP manual. We have extracted all information that maps every window attribute to the appropriate window class, and stored this information by using the Prolog facts named "class_attribute" (see Section 4.1). As a result, WINCS can easily identify the window class for a specified item. Consequently, the completeness of WINCS is guaranteed, given the following three conditions:

1. The ESP manual is valid and complete.
2. Information extracted from the manual is complete and correct.
3. The TMS is implemented completely.

We must also discuss the following points:

1. The completeness is not violated if WINCS adds window classes automatically.
2. The completeness is not violated if WINCS guides users to modify their requirements because of the constraints.
3. The completeness is not violated by the defaults of WINCS.

(1) Addition of window classes

As was discussed in Section 2.2, some window classes must be inherited with other window classes. We definitely extracted all the constraints on window classes from the ESP manual and stored them by using contradiction nodes. Therefore the executability of our synthesized window control class is guaranteed, given the condition that the inherited classes are identified and all the contradiction nodes are changed to "out" by the TMS. Furthermore, the user's selection is never rejected in this case. As a result, the completeness is not violated if some window classes are added by WINCS.

(2) Modification guided by TMS

WINCS can demonstrate all solutions when the user's requirement does not satisfy a constraint. Therefore, if a certain window attribute must be rejected because of the constraint, WINCS definitely warns the user that he must change his requirement. As a result, the completeness of WINCS cannot be violated by a modification guided by the TMS if the following conditions are satisfied:

1. We really extracted all the constraints from the ESP manual and stored them in WINCS.
2. The TMS was completely implemented.

3. A user's selection is made without any careless mistakes (e.g., typing errors and wrong operations).

(3) Making use of defaults

WINCS can demonstrate all information about alternative ways of modifying the requirement to satisfy the constraints. In this demonstration, it can also show rejection of the defaults as one of the alternatives, if this is possible. Therefore users are not constrained by defaults. As a result, the completeness of WINCS cannot be violated by defaults.

6 Future Work

We have discussed both the facilities and implementation of WINCS. WINCS is now running on the MELCOM PSI II developed by Mitsubishi Electric Co., Ltd., and its program size is 3000 lines in ESP. We will now discuss the applicability of WINCS.

6.1 Fields to which WINCS's method can be applied

WINCS can also handle other languages with the multiple-inheritance mechanism. In the general multiple-inheritance paradigm, the problem of inheritance has been widely discussed [5, 8, 15]. When two methods included in different superclasses have the same name, an executable method cannot be identified. In this case, users sometimes face the problem that the expected method cannot be executed. To avoid this problem, many languages based on the multiple-inheritance paradigm introduce constraints on built-in classes (e.g., constraints on the order and constraints on the combination). For example, in Flavor, users can combine built-in "mixin" classes as superclasses, but some combinations are prohibited [13]. Therefore users of these languages must understand all the constraints by consulting the manual when they make use of built-in classes.

6.2 Other solutions of the constraint problem

There are two other solutions to the constraint problem:

1. Storing all combinations that satisfy the constraints.
2. Making all items that cannot be used with the selected items invisible to users.

General window systems based on object-oriented languages with multiple-inheritance use the first method. Unfortunately, only typical combinations of attributes are provided, because there are too many kinds of combinations. As a result, a user must retrieve the combination that is most similar to his requirement if the exact one is not provided. Furthermore, he must add or delete some window classes by himself. This addition or deletion causes the constraint problem again. As a result, the user must take account of constraints by consulting the manual. Even if all combinations of window attributes could be stored, users would have to select an appropriate one from a large set of combinations. This selection would create another serious problem for users. Consequently, in the field of window systems that contain a large set of window attributes, WINCS is more useful than the other systems that adopt the first solution described above.

If they use the second solution above, users need not face any constraint problem, because they can see and select only items that are usable with the previously selected items. However, this solution contains the following problems:

1. Previous input is regarded as more important than subsequent input.
2. Users cannot understand which items are invisible and why the invisible items are omitted from the menu.

As a result, users are forced to input precise requirements successively. WINCS is much more effective, because users can input their requirements without considering the constraints. Furthermore, even if a requirement does not satisfy the constraints, the user can get window control classes simply by modifying the incorrect part of the requirement with the help of WINCS. Incidentally, an ATMS (Assumption-based Truth Maintenance System) that can also maintain the truth of an AI system was recently proposed. Nevertheless, we did not replace the TMS with an ATMS in WINCS for the following reasons:

1. Constraints and users' requirements cannot be described flexibly by the method described in Section 4.1, because it does not include the concept `Out-list`.
2. The facilities of WINCS cannot be made drastically more sophisticated even if the TMS is replaced with an ATMS.

Introducing an ATMS will be a future task, because ATMSs have their own fascinating features (e.g., an efficient computation mechanism).

6.3 Limitation on WINCS's method and future work

WINCS can determine invalidity from the selected window attributes, and propose possible alternatives for modifying the user's requirement. In WINCS, the final decision must be made by the user. However, WINCS can provide users with useful information to help them make up their minds. For example, users can get information about the results of alternative modifications, explanations about executable methods for the synthesized window control classes, and so on.

WINCS cannot do the following:

1. Inspire users with new ideas.
2. Point out simple errors (e.g., typing mistakes).

These facilities are very important from the viewpoint of a programming support system, although they are very difficult to embody. This remains a future task.

Furthermore, when users try to make very complicated facilities, such as combinations of methods for drawing lines, changing fonts, and so on, WINCS cannot support them fully, because this kind of design requires a facility for retrieving window classes by the name of the method. Actually, a user's requirement is not always defined by window attributes such as "menu" and "graphic," but sometimes by methods such as "draw_circle" and "draw_line." For this reason, the facility is so important that we plan to embody it in WINCS. However, to embody this facility, we have to solve the difficult problem of selecting window classes by the method's names, because there are two or more methods that have the same name. Therefore, when we try to retrieve appropriate window classes by the name of methods, we get two or more window classes and have to select one of them. To solve this problem, we have to define methods not only by name, but also by function. Furthermore, the definition must be easy enough for users to write down.

Acknowledgments. We would like to thank Mr. Yuichi Nagasawa of Computer and Information Systems Laboratories, Mitsubishi Electric Co., Ltd., for his helpful assistance in programming WINCS.

References

[1] Doyle, J. : A Truth Maintenance System, *Artif. Intell.*, Vol. 12, No. 3 (1979), pp. 231–272.

[2] Endoh, T. : Uindou Shisutemu Ni Tsuite (On Window Systems), *UNIX Magazine*, Vol. 3, No. 10 (1988), pp. 96–105 (in Japanese).

[3] Fujimoto, N., Nagasawa, Y., Imanaka, T., Uehara, K. and Toyoda, J. : Window Class Synthesizer WINCS, Preprints Work. Gr. for AI, *IPSJ*, Vol. 89, No. 2 (1989), 62-9 (in Japanese).

[4] Fujimoto, N., Imanaka, T., Uehara, K. and Toyoda, J. : Window Class Synthesizer WINCS, *Proc. 37th Annual Convention IPS Japan* (1988), pp. 906–907 (in Japanese).

[5] Fukunaga, K. and Numao, M. : Object-oriented Language Programming Environment, *J. Inf. Proc. Soc. Japan*, Vol. 29, No. 4 (1988), pp. 334–343 (in Japanese).

[6] Institute for New Generation Computer Technology : *PSI/SIMPOS Programming* (SIMPOS ver. 6.0) (1991).

[7] Matsuyama, Y., Naito, H., Mamiya, S. and Asano, T. : Object-Oriented UIMS CONCORD (2) : Specification Language CAISL, *Proc. 38th Annual Convention IPS Japan* (1989), pp. 1275–1276 (in Japanese).

[8] Nado, R. and Fikes, R. : Semantically Sound Inheritance for a Formally Defined Frame Language with Defaults, *Proc. of AAAI-87* (1987), pp. 443–448.

[9] Nagasawa, Y., Fujimoto, N., Imanaka, T., Uehara, K., Ezawa, N., Kuboi, F. and Toyoda, J. : Subsystem for Knowledge Acquisition of WINCS, *Proc. 38th Annual Convention IPS Japan* (1989), p. 515 (in Japanese).

[10] Rekimoto, J., Tarumi, H., Sugai, M., Yamazaki, G., Igari, K., Mori, T., Sugiyama, T., Uchiyama, A. and Akiguchi, C. : Canae : High-Level Software Platform for User-Interface Development Using Editor Parts, *J. Inf. Proc. Soc. Japan*, Vol. 31, No. 5 (1990), pp. 602–611 (in Japanese).

[11] Sakashita, Y., Fukuoka, H., Miyazaki, K. and Tsuji, J. : User Interface System : Overview of the Structure, *Proc. 35th Annual Convention IPS Japan* (1987), pp. 937–938 (in Japanese).

[12] Sun Microsystems : *Sun View Programmer's Guide* (1986).

[13] Symbolics : *Programming the User Interface : Dictionary*, Cambridge, Massachusetts (1988).

[14] Tanikoshi, K., Arai, T. and Tani, M. : A System for Developing User Interface : User Interface with Figure, *Proc. 38th Annual Convention IPS Japan* (1989), pp. 1269–1270 (in Japanese).

[15] Umemura, K. and Osato, N. : Object Oriented Programming in Lisp, *J. Inf. Proc. Soc. Japan*, Vol. 29, No. 4 (1990), pp. 303–317 (in Japanese).

Initially published in "Computer Software", Vol. 8, No. 1, in Japanese.

Takeshi Imanaka
Central Research Laboratories
Matsushita Electric Industrial Co., Ltd.
3–1–1 Yagumo-nakamachi, Moriguchi, Osaka, 570 Japan

Norio Fujimoto
The Sumitomo Marine and Fire Insurance Co., Ltd.
1–41–1 Koyasu-cho, Hachiouji, Tokyo, 192 Japan

Kuniaki Uehara
Department of Computer and Systems Engineering
Faculty of Engineering
Kobe University
1–1 Rokkodai-cho, Nada, Kobe, 657 Japan

Jun'ichi Toyoda
The Institute of Scientific and Industrial Research
Osaka University
8–1 Mihogaoka, Ibaraki, Osaka, 567 Japan

CSCW Platform System Teidan and Its Concurrency Control Algorithm

Jun Rekimoto

Summary. This paper proposes a new computer-supported cooperative work (CSCW) platform architecture called the *distributed model view controller (MVC) paradigm*, and describes the CSCW platform system *Teidan* based on this architecture. Teidan is a synchronous-type CSCW platform system that allows multiple users to share several types of document models over both local and wide area networks. The types of supported documents include text, diagrams, and graphs. The system has been implemented as an extension to an existing user interface management system (UIMS) called *Canae*, which was also developed by the author's group. The concurrency control algorithm used in the system ensures consistency of models without explicit locks.

We have evaluated the performance of Teidan in both local area and wide area networks. The results show that (1) the number of users does not affect the performance, and (2) the distance between users and the Teidan server does affect the performance. We discuss how to avoid the second problem by introducing a virtual time algorithm into our architecture.

1 Introduction

With the increasing popularity of network facilities and the widespread use of Graphical User Interfaces (GUIs), computer-supported cooperative work (CSCW) has become one of the hottest topics in the areas of user interface research and distributed system technology. Many groupware systems have been developed, but almost all of them have been developed as closed systems or provide a shared window only for single-user-oriented applications. Few systems have been designed as platforms for constructing CSCW tools.

CSCW platforms can be divided into two categories. One type aims to make an existing single-user-oriented system shared among a group of users (possibly) without modification. This category includes MMConf [2], XTV [1], and Timbuktu [15] Systems in the other category aim to support development of full multi-user applications from scratch. This type includes LIZA [4], DistEdit [8], and our system, *Teidan*, which is described in this paper.

LIZA provides ready-made collaborative gadgets for CSCW tool developers. DistEdit is a toolkit for adding group editor facilities to existing text editors, such as MicroEmacs. However, considerable effort is needed if tool developers using

ISBN 0-12-037105-7

LIZA want to create a new kind of collaboration. The presentation medium in DistEdit is limited to text only.

In contrast, Teidan is based on the *distributed model view controller (MVC) paradigm*, a new groupware architecture proposed by us. Applications developed with Teidan can share various kinds of presentation objects, such as diagrams, texts, and graphs. Teidan is intended to be a general platform for group-oriented tools.

The rest of the paper is organized as follows. In the next section, we discuss the requirements for CSCW platforms. In Section 3, we describe the architecture of Teidan. In Section 4, we describe two CSCW systems based on the Teidan system. Several design issues, including the concurrency control mechanism, are discussed in Section 5. Finally, in Section 6, we discuss the performance of the system and our experiences in using it.

2 Requirements for CSCW platforms

Before commencing a precise discussion of the Teidan architecture, we would like to describe what is needed in CSCW platforms. We consider that a real CSCW platform must satisfy the following requirements, which were also the design goals of the Teidan architecture.

Flexible Concurrency Control Scheme

To keep the states of distributed applications consistent, a CSCW platform must support a floor control (concurrency control) mechanism. Most existing CSCW systems use lock-oriented concurrency control schemes.

For example, MERMAID [16], which is a desktop conferencing system, provides a lock mode for solving concurrency control problems. One of the participants in a MERMAID conference acts as chairperson. The chairperson can name one participant explicitly and give him or her the right to modify data.

However, enforcing an explicit lock disturbs the users' activity, especially in a brainstorming type of meeting. A chairperson must always be aware of who wishes to modify the data and who is actually about to get a lock. The operations needed to pass lock-right tend to interrupt the members' flow of thought.

One way to avoid explicit locking is to abandon the consistency control and rely on the social protocol among participants, but this is not suitable for serious group work. We need a new group-work-oriented consistency control scheme.

Highly Customizable User Interface

Needless to say, CSCW tools support various kinds of user interaction. Their user interface should be as easy and customizable as that of single-user-oriented tools. Aside from this, group-oriented tools must provide much more customizability than single-user tools. There is a wide variety of group tasks, so each group may have a different requirement for the CSCW tools; each member of the same group may even have a different preference about an aspect of the system (such as the key bindings of a text editor). If you do not like one word processor, you can simply abandon it and use another one. However, if your group has selected one CSCW tool, you cannot avoid using it, even if you hate its user interface.

Therefore a CSCW platform should also act as a good user interface management system (UIMS) that provides a highly customizable user interface, or else it should provide a sound interface with an existing UIMS.

Smooth Transition from Personal Space to Shared Space

An actual collaborative task is a combination of personal work and group work. Even in a synchronous meeting, a participant may want to do personal work (such as taking notes) as well as collaborative work. *Ishii* [5] proposed the concept of seamless shared workspace to support total group activity. Its purpose is to eliminate seams between personal workspace and group workspace.

We believe that a true CSCW platform must support both personal work space and shared work space interchangeably. It should be possible to shift smoothly from the personal work mode to the group work mode. It should also be easy to move (or copy) data from personal space to shared space, and vice versa.

Performance

Even in a wide area network environment, a CSCW tool must be responsive to a user's operations. It is also desirable that the number of members in the group not affect the performance.

3 An Overview of the Teidan System Architecture

In this section, we would like to describe briefly the architecture of the Teidan system.

Teidan is based on a distributed MVC paradigm

Teidan uses an extended MVC paradigm for a distributed environment to provide a uniform shared work space among Teidan users. The original MVC paradigm [7], which was developed at Xerox to implement the user interface of Smalltalk-80, is a framework for constructing a visual, interactive application by using a trio of objects: *model*, *view*, and *controller*. A model represents the information contained in an application. A view is responsible for rendering the contents of the model on the screen. A controller handles user operations. When the contents of the model have been modified, the view redisplays the screen. The controller receives input events from the user and dispatches them to the model or the view.

In Teidan architecture, each document is represented in the MVC object trio (Figure 1). Each Teidan client handles its own MVC objects. A group of model objects (each belonging to each client) may be formed into a coherent set. Models in a coherent set are maintained by the clients and the server to keep their contents identical; if some client has modified its local model, the modification is propagated to other models in the coherent set via the server to maintain consistency. This mechanism allows multiple users to share the (virtually) same model across the network. In Figure 1, three clients have two coherent sets (virtually shared models), consisting of three and two models, respectively.

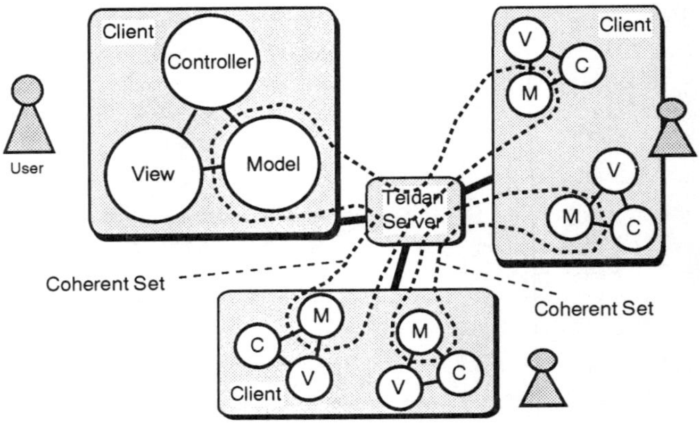

Fig. 1 The architecture of Teidan

Teidan is an extension to the existing UIMS

To provide a CSCW facility as a platform for many applications, we have decided to develop Teidan as an extension to the existing UIMS Canae [11]. Canae, which was also developed by the author's group, is a UIMS on the X-Window system [12]. It supports editing facilities for six kinds of document (text, image, diagram, graph structure, table, and hierarchical structure) as well as normal interactive techniques, such as buttons, menus, or scroll bars. This system has been used for actual application development since 1989. Examples of the applications include various kinds of CASE systems, GUI builders, hypermedia systems, and a GUI front-end for a network management system. At present, more then a hundred applications have been developed by using Canae.

Teidan allows realtime sharing of Canae's media among multiple users. Currently, three media types (text, diagram, and graph) can be shared; work on the rest (image, table, and hierarchical structure) is continuing.

Teidan is based on a server client model

Each user has a corresponding Teidan client process that handles the GUI part. These clients communicate with each other through a server process called the *Teidan server.* The Teidan server acts as a broadcast channel and is also responsible for concurrency control. SunRPC [14] is used as a method for inter-process communication between a client and the server.

4 Sample Applications Developed with the Teidan System

In this section, we describe two examples of CSCW applications that have been developed with Teidan.

The first example is shown in Figure 2. In this example, simple shared diagram editors and shared text editors are used to show various uses of the system. The window at the top left of the screen, entitled "Teidan-Tool," is a control panel

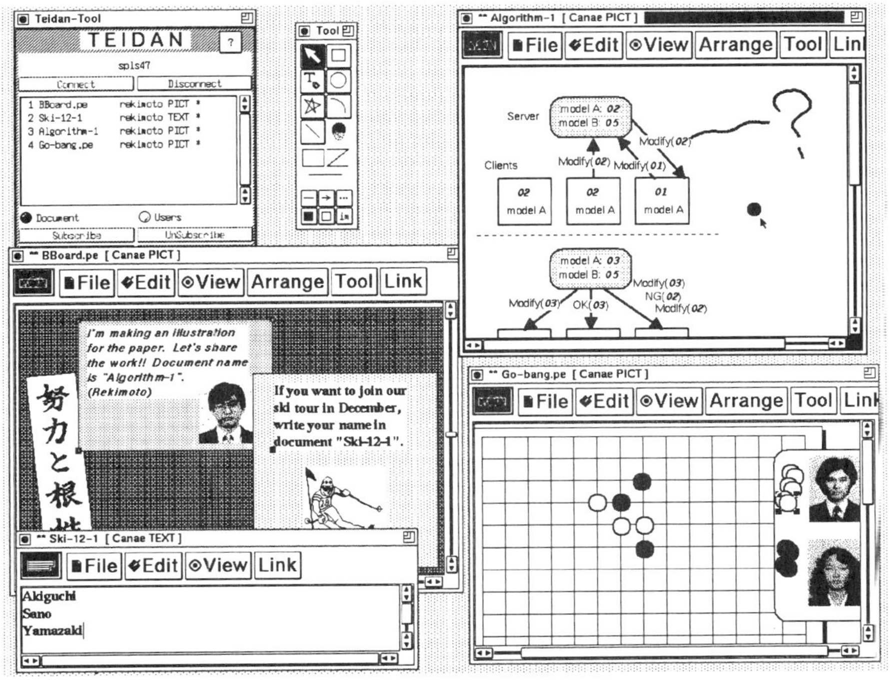

Fig. 2 A screen image of the Teidan system

for the system. This panel shows a list of the models currently being shared by the users. The window below the control panel acts as a shared bulletin board on which users can place their notices. In the example, participants in a ski tour are requested to write their names in a shared text window entitled "Ski-12/1," which is displayed at the bottom of the screen. One of the users is drawing an illustration in a window entitled "Algorithm-1." From a distant location, another coworker is watching this figure and writing a comment about it. In the bottom right window, a distributed *go* game is in progress.

Although this example directly uses shared editors, several mechanisms for customization inherited from Canae are provided to enable domain-specific collaborative tools to be constructed.

Another interesting example is a multi-user dungeon game based on Canae and Teidan (Figure 3). This application, which is called Multi-user NetHack (MNH), is an extended version of NetHack [10]. The original NetHack is a character-display oriented, single-user dungeon adventure game in which a player fights monsters and wins treasure. We have added a GUI to NetHack by using Canae, and have extended it into a multi-user game by using Teidan. In MNH, the data shared among players are the map of a dungeon, monster information, and player information.

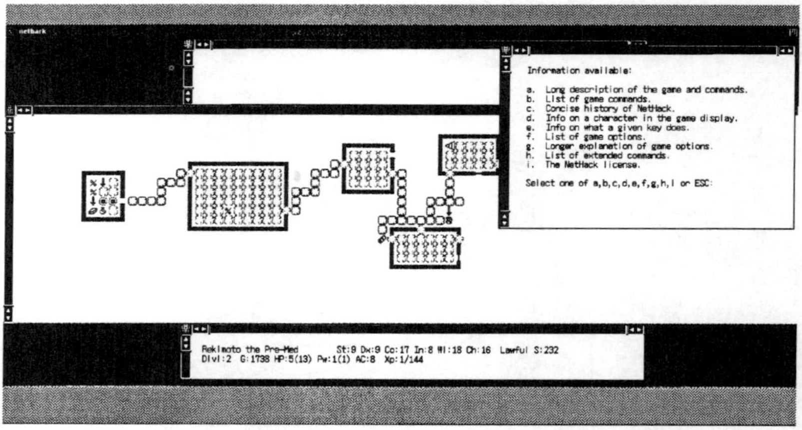

Fig. 3 MNH (multi-user NetHack) is in action

They are represented in several text models of Canae, and these models are shared among the player processes. We would like to mention that it is impossible to construct an application like MNH by using a simple shared screen platform. In MNH, what is shared is internal data (maps, player and monster states), not a screen. Each player's screen is different, depending on the player's game level.

5 Design Issues

5.1 Change propagation

In the Teidan architecture, each client has its own model, and the server maintains consistency among these models. To implement this consistency, we introduce a hook function.

For each media type, Canae provides several editing operations, such as copy, paste, move, and change color. These operations call up some primitive editing methods for the model. The method modifies the contents of the model, and the change in the model is reflected on the screen through the view. For example, a diagram model has 15 primitive methods (insert, delete, change color, group, ungroup, etc.) and a graph structure model has 28 primitive methods.

In Teidan, these methods are protected by hook functions. A hook intercepts an invocation of its associated method and sends out the arguments of the method to the server.

A modification to the model is propagated to other clients as follows (Figure 4):
(1) A user issues an editing command;
(2) A primitive modification method for the model is invoked;
(3) The method triggers a hook and sends the arguments of the modification to the Teidan server by RPC;
(4) The Teidan server broadcasts this modification information to other clients;
(5) On receiving the modification from the server, each client applies it to the

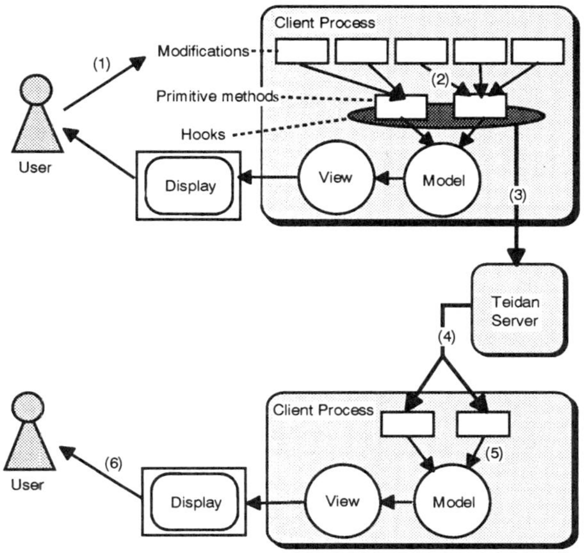

Fig. 4 Change propagation

client's own model;
(6) Each model is modified, and each user's screen is consequently updated.

As described above, the server sends data to the clients as well as receives data from them. Thus if both communications are normal RPCs, there is a possibility of deadlock, because both client and server may block and wait for a reply from each other. To avoid deadlock, messages from the server to a client do not require any reply; the server sends them in an asynchronous mode.

5.2 Concurrency control

If two clients try to modify the same model simultaneously (more precisely, if one client tries to send out a request message *before* receiving a notification message from the server that indicates there has been a modification in another client), then the consistency among the models may be broken. For example, if a client sends a request to change the color of an object (after the server has already received and broadcast a request from another client to delete the same object), the color change request should be aborted by the server (or illegal modification will occur). Therefore concurrency control is needed in such a case.

Teidan provides three concurrency control modes: *lock mode*, *timestamp mode*, and *virtual timestamp mode*. The lock mode is based on a traditional lock management scheme, while the other two modes maintain consistency of objects without explicit locks. These modes can be used interchangeably for application needs. In the (simple and virtual) timestamp mode, a user can freely modify the model without locking it. In a lock mode, if one client obtains a lock, then other clients

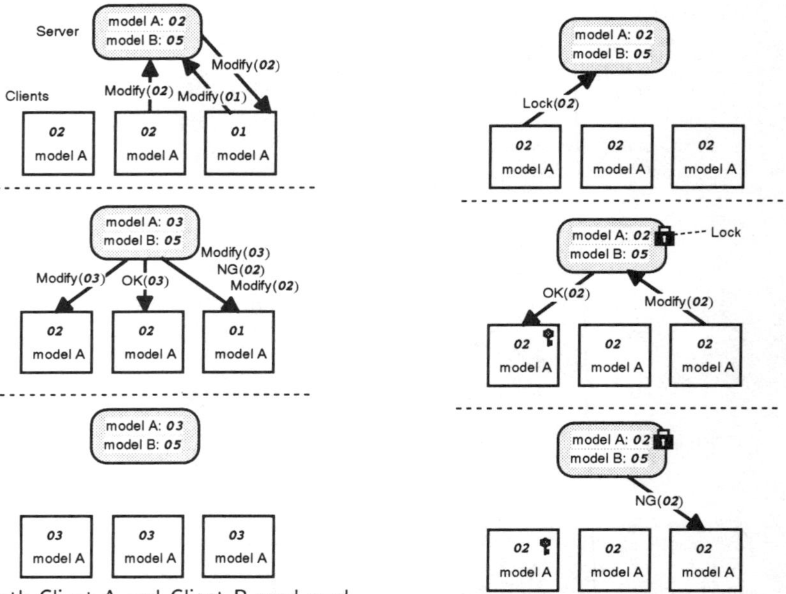

(A) Both Client A and Client B send modification requests simultaneously. The timestamps attached to Client A's request and Client B's request are 02 and 03, respectively. Comparing these timestamps with the server's timestamp, the server replies OK to Client A and NG to Client B. The server's timestamp is incremented to become 03.

(B) All clients' timestamps and the server's are the same. Client A sends a lock request with a local timestamp to the server. This request is accepted, and the model is locked. Once the lock is established, no request from another client (Client A) is accepted, even if the local timestamp is equal to the server's.

Fig. 5 Concurrency control (A: timestamp mode; B: lock mode)

cannot modify the model.

Timestamp Mode

The timestamp mode is the most basic concurrency control mode in the Teidan architecture (Figure 5-A).

Regardless of the mode, the Teidan server maintains a timestamp (called a server timestamp) for each shared model. Each client also has a copy of the timestamp (called a local timestamp). The server timestamp is incremented by one each time a client sends a modification request to the server and the server accepts it. A message from a client always has its local timestamp. Clients and the server handle timestamps as shown in Figures 6 and 7. In these lists, $\Leftrightarrow$, $\Rightarrow$, and $\hookleftarrow$ denote a normal synchronous RPC call, an asynchronous RPC transmission, and an RPC reply, respectively.

This algorithm ensures the consistency of models while permitting clients to

```
ModifyModel(modification)
{
    send out a request (modification and local_timestamp) to the server,
    and wait for a reply from the server.(⇔)
    if (server replies OK) then
        local_timestamp ← server_timestamp
        modify the local model according to the modification.
    else
        do nothing.
}

ReceiveNotificationFromServer(modification, server_timestamp)
{
    local_timestamp ← server_timestamp
    modifies the local model according to the modification.
}
```

Fig. 6 Concurrency control algorithm (client side, timestamp mode)

```
ReceiveModificationRequestFromClient(modification, local_timestamp)
{
    if (local_timestamp ≡ server_timestamp)
        server_timestamp ← server_timestamp + 1
        reply OK to the client. (↩)
        broadcast modification and server_timestamp to other clients. (⇒)
    else
        reply NG to the client.(↩)
}
```

Fig. 7 Concurrency control algorithm (server side, timestamp mode)

modify their models freely. If two or more modifications have been made simultaneously, one of them is accepted by the server and the others are rejected.

Although some user operations might be lost in this algorithm, we regard it as practical for the following reasons:

- In a distributed environment, there are cases in which rejection cannot be avoided anyway (for instance, when the user changes the color of an object that has already been removed by another user).
- In our experience with Teidan, competitive modifications are relatively rare in normal collaborative situations.

Lock Mode

We can introduce a lock mode on top of the simple timestamp mode (Figure 5-B). In a lock mode, the client initially tries to get a lock from the server by sending a request message. The server accepts the message if the local timestamp attached

```
RecevieLockRequestFromClient(local_timestamp)
{
    if (local_timestamp ≡ server_timestamp and no client has a lock of the model) then
        lock the model.
        reply OK to the client. (↩)
    else
        reply NG to the client. (↩)
}

ReceiveModificationRequestFromClient(modification, local_timestamp)
{
    if (local_timestamp ≡ server_timestamp and
        (no client has a lock of the model or
        requesting client has a lock)) then
        server_timestamp ← server_timestamp + 1.
        reply OK to the requesting client.(↩)
        broadcast modification and server_timestamp to other clients. (⇒)
    else
        reply NG to requesting client.(↩)
}
```

Fig. 8 Concurrency control algorithm (server side, lock mode)

to the requesting message is equal to the server's, or the server rejects it if the timestamp is out-of-date. Once the lock is established, a modification request from a client without the lock is always rejected by the server, even if its local timestamp is up-to-date. The algorithm is shown in Figure 8.

Virtual Timestamp Mode

The virtual timestamp mode is based on the (simple) timestamp mode and takes a more radical approach in order to obtain a higher performance. This mode also depends on the assumption of a low probability of collision.

If we can assume that there is no possibility of having concurrent modifications, it is not necessary for a client to wait for the server to acknowledge each modification. On the other hand, in our experience with using the Teidan system and according to reports on other CSCW systems [3], concurrent modification appears to be rare in normal collaborative situations.

Thus, by treating a collision as an exceptional situation, we can improve the algorithm, as illustrated in Figure 9. In this algorithm, modification requests are sent to the server in asynchronous mode (i.e., a client does not wait for the server). Modifications are applied to the model immediately, and are also pushed onto an undo stack for possible future rollback. After some time has elapsed, the server gives the client a reply of either OK or NG (No Good) in asynchronous mode. If OK is received, the client executes the modification (i.e., it deletes the executed operation from the undo stack). If NG is received, the client rolls back the modification by referring to the undo stack. It could be said that we have adapted this idea from

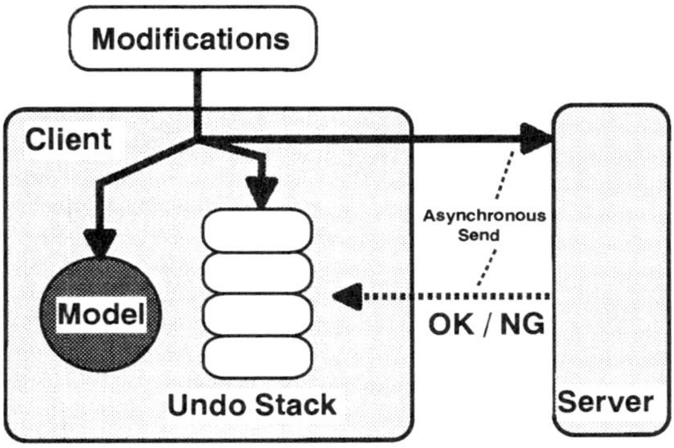

Fig. 9 Improved concurrency control mechanism

the virtual time algorithm, which was invented for distributed simulation [6], and that we have applied it to the group-editor domain.

5.3 Object interchange protocol

In an actual conference, it is not enough to merely prepare and circulate a fixed number of documents at the beginning of the session. Possible situations and requirements that might arise include the following:

- During the meeting, we may want to share new documents dynamically. We cannot predict all the documents that will be needed in the meeting.
- We must be able to make a sub-group. We sometimes want to share a document only with a sub-group, not with all members.
- We must be able to freely join and leave an ongoing meeting.

It is desirable to implement the above requirements by a combination of simple user operations. For this purpose, Teidan introduces a "table-top" metaphor (Figure 10) to make possible a smooth transition between shared and personal work space. Teidan provides a virtual table-top for users. Initially, there are no objects on the table. If a user wishes to make his/her personal object public, he/she puts this object on the table (internally, the ID of the object is registered in the Teidan server). If another user wants to use a document on the table, he/she can pick it up. As a result of this pick up operation, a shared copy of the document is created in the user's space. Thus, a multiple pick-up is also possible. This is one difference between our metaphor and a real table-top.

The Teidan server has a matrix called a *subscription matrix* that keeps a record of who has put documents on the table and who has picked up documents from it. The server uses this matrix to decide which clients should be notified about any modification to an object. A user (client) can check the contents of the matrix by sending a request packet to the server. When a new user joins the meeting during the session, he/she can check the contents of the table and decide which document is to be shared.

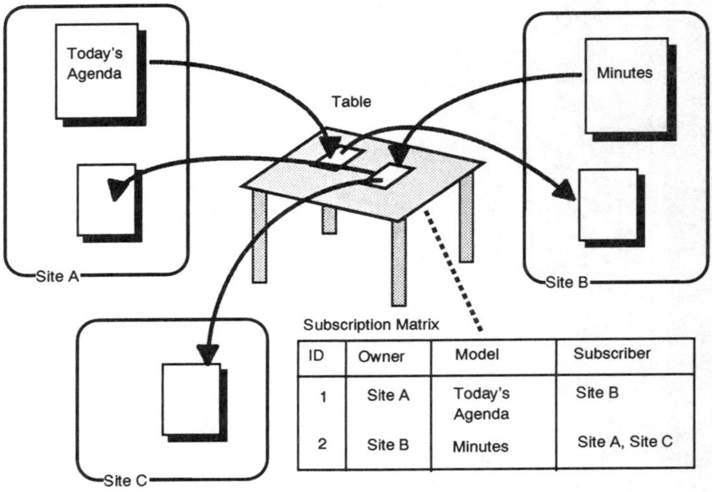

Fig. 10 Document interchange operations based on the table-top metaphor

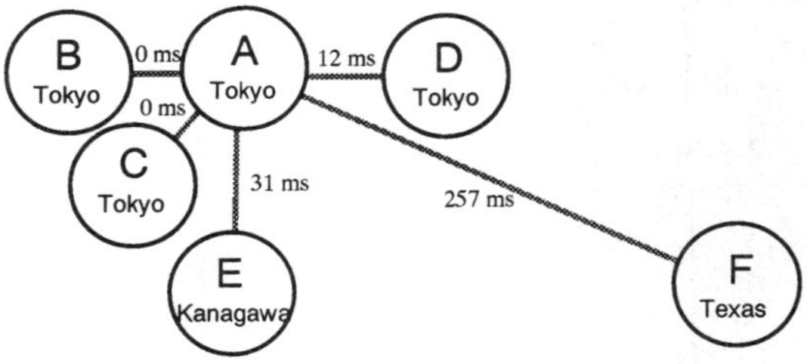

Fig. 11 Round trip times between sites

6 Discussion

6.1 Performance evaluation

In order to evaluate the effectiveness of the algorithm described in Section 5.2, we measured the performance of Teidan in a wide area network. The hosts used in the experiments were A (Tokyo, Japan), B (Tokyo), C (Tokyo), D (Tokyo), E (Kanagawa, Japan), and F (Dallas, Texas, U.S.A.). All the machines were Sun4s except for E, which was a Sun3. A, B, and C were on the same local area network. D, E, and F were connected by gateways. Figure 11 shows the round-trip time for a message between A and the other hosts. The ICMP ECHO protocol was used to measure these values.

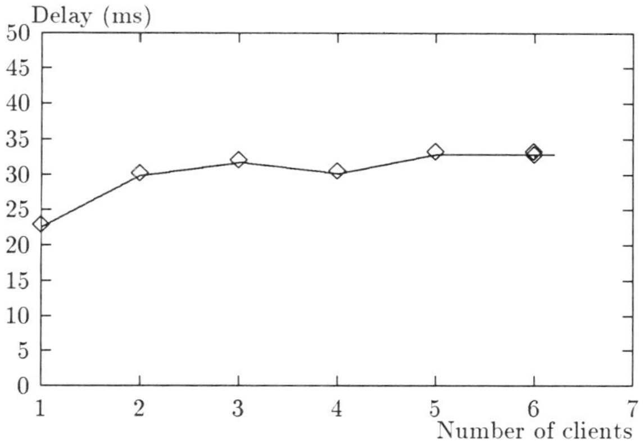

Fig. 12 Delay time vs. number of clients

Experiment 1: Ratio of the local delay time to the number of clients

In this experiment, the server was operating at site A, and clients were at sites B and C. We measured the local delay time (the additional processing time needed by Teidan on top of that needed by a normal Canae editor) by changing the number of clients from one to six.

The result is shown in Figure 12. We do not observe a drastic increase corresponding to the increase in the number of clients, except when the number of clients is changed from one to two.

This is because broadcasts from a server to clients are performed in an asynchronous mode, enabling the server to reply to each client immediately, regardless of the number of other clients.

Experiment 2: Ratio of the delay time to the distance between a client and a server

The client was operating at site A, and the location of the server was changed from C to F. In this experiment, the number of clients was always one. In this situation, we measured the local delay time in the same manner as in Experiment 1, both in the simple timestamp mode and also in the virtual timestamp mode.

In the simple timestamp mode, the result is as shown in Figure 13 as the line labeled "normal." It may be observed that the distance between a client and server and the delay time are closely related. This is because in the simple timestamp mode a client must wait for a reply from the server before modifying its own model. If we were to use Teidan in a wide area network, this delay would be a serious one.

In the virtual timestamp mode, the delay time is depicted by the line labeled "virtual time" in the same graph. Clearly, the performance has improved dramatically, and there is now only a weak relationship between the delay time and the server-client distance.

The virtual timestamp mode assumes that collisions are rare during normal

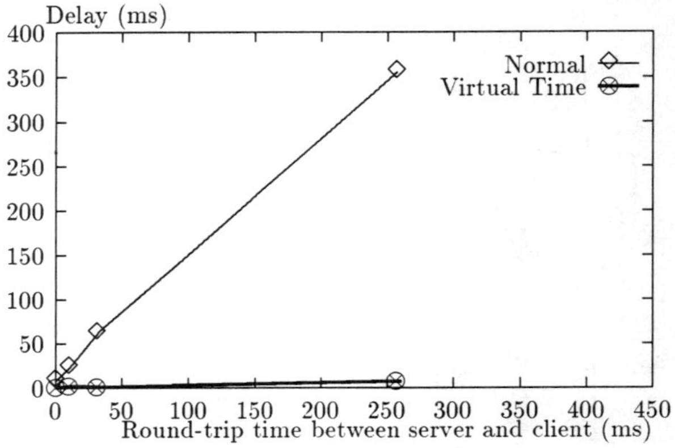

Fig. 13 Delay time vs. distance between server and client

collaborative work. This assumption is supported by our experience and that of other groupware developers and users. However, the probability of collision is not zero, especially in abnormal (competitive) situations. In such cases, the user has to be faced with unwilling rollbacks.

One possible method of avoiding an unwanted rollback is to prepare a *commutable* set of model operations. For example, in a diagram model, two motion operations produce the same result regardless of the order in which they are performed. These operations are called commutable. In a rollback step, a client undoes an uncommitted operation and applies a correct operation that has been passed by the server. However, the client can omit the undo step if these operations are commutable.

Another possibility is to divide one model (document) into several sub-units. Each sub-unit has its own timestamp. If two users operate on the same model but on different units, then a collision will not occur. This type of fine-grain control is also discussed by *Newman-Wolfe and Pelimuhandiram* [9].

6.2 Experience

The application of Teidan described in Section 4 (in the first example) has actually been used by our group to provide non-face-to-face, synchronous meetings since 1991. We would like to discuss here some of the issues arising from our experience.

Needless to say, it was extremely useful to have voice communication when we used the Teidan system. We have been using the multiparty telephone facility of an in-house PBX.

We felt that there was a radical difference between having two participants and having three. When there were two, we were able to use Teidan as an extension of the telephone. However, when the number grew to three or more, we had to make a conscious effort to distinguish the participants. For example, many questions like

"Who moved this circle?" or even "Who is speaking?"[1] were asked.

One possible method of operation is to display the live face of each participant in the same manner as in a desktop TV conferencing system, but we suspect that this would not be a complete solution, because a live face conveys information about who is speaking, but not about who is operating. We are planning to add an animated icon to the system that would represent each participant's integrated state.

Our experience has been that the most obvious advantage of using Teidan over holding a normal face-to-face meeting is the ability to share personal documents without any effort. In a normal meeting, because we cannot always predict which documents will be needed, we almost always feel frustrated by the need for documents that are not being circulated. On the other hand, in a Teidan-enhanced meeting, there is no need to prepare all the documents. When a group finds that some document is necessary, it can be introduced from a participant's personal work space into the public work space with only a few mouse and key operations. This advantage is extremely apparent to us, because our group stores almost all of the documents for our actual work on-line, including diagrams and text files.[2] Actually, besides the actual documents being shared, there is a huge number of other documents with the potential to be shared.

6.3 Shared model vs. shared screen

There are two methods of providing a shared work space: the *shared screen* method and the *shared model* method. A CSCW system based on the shared screen method allows one user to look at another user's screen image. A CSCW system based on the shared model shares the application data, rather than the screen image.

One advantage of the shared screen method is application independence. Screens of existing non-CSCW applications can be shown on the shared screen. However, this scheme has many limitations. For example, one user may want to scroll the contents of the screen, while others may not want to. Therefore forcing users to share exactly the same screen is not the best method.

On the basis of experience with Colab and Cognoter at Xerox, *Stefik* claimed that just looking at other participants' screens (he called this strict WYSIWIS[3]) was not enough to support collaborative work [13].

On the other hand, the shared model is not suitable for sharing existing applications, because this mechanism is strongly related to the data being maintained by the application. However, it does provide a useful platform for constructing new CSCW tools.

Teidan is a system based on the shared model method. In Teidan, what is shared is a model that is maintained by the Canae system. Each user has a client process, which holds a copy of the models (text, diagram, or graph structure). A modification to one model is propagated to the other models, enabling the contents of the models to be kept identical.

---

[1] One reason is that the audio quality of our multiparty telephone is not good.

[2] Diagrams (including illustrations used in this paper) were made by the Canae-based drawing editor called `cxdraw`.

[3] What You See Is What I See

In addition, Teidan is an extension of UIMS Canae. We expect that Teidan can be easily used to modify applications developed with Canae so that they become collaborative tools.

7 Conclusion

In this paper, we have described a CSCW platform system called Teidan and its concurrency control algorithm. Teidan allows multiple users to share several types of document models, including text, diagram, and graph structure, across various networks. The concurrency control algorithm used in the system ensures consistency of models without explicit locks.

We have described the results of measuring the performance of Teidan over a wide area network, and discussed introducing the virtual time algorithm into our algorithm in order to improve the performance.

The application of the algorithm described here is not limited to group editors. For example, a wide-area hypermedia system or a distributed virtual reality system can adopt this technology in order to achieve distributed object coherence with flexibility.

Acknowledgments. The author would like to thank Kazuo Watabe, Hideyuki Fukuoka and other members of the MERMAID project for their contributions to the early discussions about this research. Hiroyuki Tarumi also provided us with valuable comments about the architecture and the system. Much implementation work has been done by Hiroyuki Yagyuu. Finally, Multi-User NetHack (MNH) was developed by Huw Rogers of Manchester University during a summer internship project at NEC.

References

[1] Abdel-Wahab, H.M. and Feit, M.A.: XTV: A Framework for Sharing X Window Clients in Remote Synchronous Collaboration, Documentation in the X-Window system, Version 11, Release 5, 1991.

[2] Crowley, T., Milazzo, P., Baker, E., Forsdick, H., and Tomlinson, R.: MMConf: An Infrastructure for Building Shared Multimedia Applications, *Proc. of the Conf. on Computer-Supported Cooperative Work* (CSCW '90), Los Angeles (1990), pp. 329–342.

[3] Ellis, C.A., Gibbs, S.J., and Rein, G.L.: *Groupware*: Some Issues and Experiences, *Comm. ACM*, Vol. 34, No. 1 (1991), pp. 38–58.

[4] Gibbs, S.J.: LIZA: An Extensible Groupware Toolkit, *ACM CHI '89 Proceedings*(1989), pp. 29–35.

[5] Ishii, H.: TeamWorkStation: Towards a Seamless Shared Workspace, *Proc. of the Conf. on Computer-Supported Cooperative Work* (CSCW '90), Los Angeles (1990), pp. 13–26.

[6] Jefferson, D.R.: Virtual Time, *ACM Trans. Prog. Lang. Syst.*, Vol. 7, No. 3 (1985), pp. 404–425.

[7] Krasner, G.E. and Pops, S.T.: A Cookbook for Using the Model-View-Controller User Interface Paradigm in Smalltalk-80, *Journal of Object-Oriented Programming*, Vol. 1, No. 3 (1988), pp. 26–49.

[8] Knister, M.J. and Prakash, A.: DistEdit: A Distributed Toolkit for Supporting Multiple Group Editors, *Proc. of the Conf. on Computer-Supported Cooperative Work* (CSCW '90), Los Angeles (1990), pp. 343–355.

[9] Newman-Wolfe, R.E. and Pelimuhandiram, H.K.: MACE: A Fine Grained Concurrent Editor, *Conf. on Organizational Computing Systems*, November 1991.

[10] Raymond, E.S. and Threepoint, M.: *A Guide to the Mazes of Menace, unpublished software manual*, May 1990.

[11] Rekimoto, J., Tarumi, H., Sugai, M., Yamazaki, G., Igari, K., Mori, T., Sugiyama, T. Uchiyama, A., and Akiguchi, C.: Canae: A Platform for Constructing Graphical User Interfaces with Editors, *Journal of Information Processing*, Vol. 14, No. 4 (1992), pp. 454–462.

[12] Scheifler, R.W. and Gettys, J.: The X Window System, *ACM Trans. Graph*, Vol. 5, No. 3 (1986), pp. 79–109.

[13] Stefik, M., Bobrow, D.G., Foster, G., Lanning, S., and Tartar, D.: WYSIWIS Revised, *ACM Trans. Office Info. Syst.*, Vol. 5, No. 2 (1987), pp. 147–167.

[14] *Remote Procedure Call Programming Guide*, Sun Microsystems, Inc., February 1986.

[15] *Timbuktu User's Guide*, Farallon Computing Inc., Berkeley, CA., 1988.

[16] Watabe, K., Sakata, S., Maeno, K., Fukuoka, H., and Ohmori, T.: Distributed Multiparty Desktop Conferencing System: MERMAID, *Proc. of the Conf. on Computer-Supported Cooperative Work* (CSCW '90), Los Angeles (1990), pp. 27-38.

Initially published in "Computer Software", Vol. 10, No. 1, in Japanese.

Jun Rekimoto
Software Engineering Laboratory
NEC Corporation
2–11–5 Shibaura
Mintato-ku, Tokyo 108
Japan

ISBN 0-12-037105-7

90040

9 780120 371051